D1084259

CEREMONY & CELEBRATION
INTRODUCTION TO THE HOLIDAYS

מגיד
MAGGID   OUPRESS

Other works by the author

Rabbi Jonathan Sacks

CEREMONY & CELEBRATION
Introduction to the Holidays

The Herman Family Edition

Maggid Books & The Orthodox Union

Ceremony & Celebration
Introduction to the Holidays

First Edition, 2017

Maggid Books
An imprint of Koren Publishers Jerusalem Ltd.

POB 8531, New Milford, CT 06776-8531, USA
& POB 4044, Jerusalem 9104001, Israel
www.maggidbooks.com

© Jonathan Sacks 2017

Cover image: Simchat Torah, Livorno, 1850 (oil on canvas),
Hart, Solomon Alexander (1806–81) / Jewish Museum, New York, USA
Photo © Zev Radovan / Bridgeman Images

The publication of this book was made possible
through the generous support of *Torah Education in Israel.*

All rights reserved. No part of this publication may be reproduced,
stored in a retrieval system or transmitted in any form or by
any means, electronic, mechanical, photocopying or otherwise,
without the prior permission of the publisher, except in the case
of brief quotations embedded in critical articles or reviews.

ISBN 978-1-59264-025-6, *hardcover*

A CIP catalogue record for this title is
available from the British Library

Printed and bound in the United States

In loving memory of

IVOR HERMAN

Yitzchak ben Berol Ha'Cohen ז״ל

who had a deep love of
Judaism, Israel, and the Jewish people

≈

Tammuz 5777 / July 2017

Contents

Rosh HaShana

The Anniversary of Creation

The ten days that begin on Rosh HaShana and culminate in Yom Kippur are the holy of holies of Jewish time. The atmosphere in the synagogue is intense. You can almost touch the Divine Presence. Isaiah said: "Seek God where He is to be found, call on Him when He is close" (Is. 55:6). The rabbis wrestled with this verse. What could it mean? God is the God of everywhere and all time. He is always to be found, always close. The verse seemed to make no sense at all.

This was their reply: "These are the Ten Days of Repentance between Rosh HaShana and Yom Kippur" – meaning, God is always close to us, but we are not always close to Him. He is always to be found, but we do not always seek Him out. To sense the closeness of God needs some special effort on our part. To reach out to the Infinite in finite space, to meet the Eternal in the midst of time, to sense what ultimately lies beyond the senses, requires a focus far beyond the ordinary.

It needs a drama of holiness, enacted in our holiest place, the synagogue, at the holiest of times, *Yamim Nora'im*, the Days of Awe.

To begin, it needs a sound – the shofar – so piercing and strange that it wakes us out of our everyday consciousness into an awareness of being present at something vast and momentous. We need to come close to God for God to feel close to us. That is what happens on the Ten Days of Repentance, and it begins on Rosh HaShana.

It is as if the world has become a courtroom. God Himself is the Judge. The shofar announces that the court is in session, and we are on trial, giving an account of our lives. Properly entered into, this is a potentially life-changing experience. It forces us to ask the most fateful questions we will ever ask: Who am I? Why am I here? How shall I live? How have I lived until now? How have I used God's greatest gift: time? Whom have I wronged, and how can I put it right? Where have I failed, and how shall I overcome my failures? What is broken in my life and needs mending? What chapter will I write in the book of life? The unexamined life, a philosopher said, is not worth living. No one who has genuinely experienced Rosh HaShana and Yom Kippur lives an unexamined life.

These are days of reflection and introspection when we stand in the conscious presence of Infinity, knowing how short and vulnerable life really is, and how little time we have here on earth. This can be, and should be, a life-changing experience. Unfortunately, it not always is. The prayers are long. Some of them, especially the *piyutim*, the liturgical poems with their elaborate acrostics and obscure wordplays, are hard to understand. Others use imagery that can seem remote. The central image of Rosh HaShana is of God as King enthroned in the seat of judgment. That image would once have been self-evident, but there are fewer kings today than there once were, and even in the monarchies that remain, the role of royalty is often more symbolic than judicial. The prayers we say on Rosh HaShana span more than thirty centuries, and some need decoding if they are to speak to us today.

Yet Rosh HaShana and Yom Kippur have retained an undiminished hold on the Jewish imagination. They remain days on which even Jews estranged from Judaism for much of the year come to synagogue, and the world's longest courtroom drama continues: the extended argument between God and His people about the fate of justice and the justice of fate that has been running since the day when Abraham first called God "Judge of all the earth," and that led Albert Einstein to speak about that "almost fanatical love of justice" that made him thank his stars that he was born a Jew.

No people has believed as lucidly and long as have Jews that life has a purpose; that this world is an arena of justice and human dignity; that we are, each of us, free and responsible, capable of shaping our lives in accordance with our highest ideals. We are here for a reason. We were created in love and forgiveness by the God of love and forgiveness who asks us to love and forgive. However many times we may have failed to live up to our aspirations, God always gives us the chance and the power to begin again. On Rosh HaShana and Yom Kippur, the holiest days of a holy people, God summons us to greatness.

I want in this chapter to tell the story of Rosh HaShana and what it might mean for us.

The Mystery

No sooner do we open the Torah, seeking to understand the significance of the day, than we are plunged into mystery. Only twice does the Torah touch on the subject, and in neither case does it provide much information:

> The Lord spoke to Moses, saying: Speak to the Israelite people thus: In the seventh month, on the first day of the month, you shall observe complete rest, a sacred occasion commemorated with loud blasts [*zikhron terua*]. (Lev. 23:23–24)

> On the first day of the seventh month you shall hold a sacred assembly. You shall do no laborious work, and you shall mark a Day of the Blowing of the Shofar [*Yom Terua*]. (Num. 29:1)

Other than details of the sacrifices to be offered, that is all. There is no explanation of what the day represents, or what the sound – *terua* – signifies. Nor does the Torah specify what instrument is to be used. It might be a horn. But equally it might refer to the silver trumpets the Israelites were commanded to make to summon the people (Num. 10:1–10). The central motifs of the other festivals, the unleavened bread and bitter herbs of Pesaḥ, the booth of Sukkot, the affliction (fasting) of Yom Kippur, all have symbolic value. We know what they mean and how they connect with the mood of the day. But the Torah does not tell us what the sound of *terua* symbolizes. Is it the sound of celebration, of warning, of fear or tears? We do not know.[1]

Nor does the Torah use the phrase *Rosh HaShana*, the beginning or "head" of the year, in this context or any other. The only time it appears in Tanakh, the Hebrew Bible as a whole, it refers to Yom Kippur: "In the twenty-fifth year of our exile, at the beginning of the year [*berosh hashana*], *on the tenth of the month*, in the fourteenth year after the fall of the city" (Ezek. 40:1). In fact the Torah seems to make it clear that Rosh HaShana is *not* the beginning of the year. It is the first day, not of the first, but the seventh month. The first month is Nisan.

How then do we arrive at the festival as we know it today?

In the earliest stages of an embryo, when a fetus is still no more than a small bundle of cells, it already contains the genome, the long string of DNA, from which the child and eventually the adult will emerge. The genetic structure that will shape the person it becomes is there from the beginning. So it is with Judaism. "Bible, Mishna, Talmud and Aggada, even what a senior disciple is destined to teach in the presence of his master, was already stated to Moses at Sinai" (Yerushalmi, *Pe'ah* 2:4). The evolution of Rosh HaShana was prefigured at the outset, but to see how it developed we have to decipher the clues.

The Anniversary of Creation

The first thing we notice is that it is "the first day of the seventh month." The number seven, especially when applied to time, always signifies *holiness*. The first thing declared holy in the Torah is the seventh day, Shabbat (Gen. 2:1–3). The seventh or "sabbatical" year is likewise holy. There is to be no work in the fields. The land is to enjoy rest. Debts are released. A similar provision applies to the fiftieth or Jubilee year (at the end of seven seven-year cycles) when, in addition, most ancestral land returned to its original owners. The seventh month fits this pattern. It

---

1. Rabbeinu Baḥya, *Kad HaKemaḥ, Rosh HaShana* (2).

is to the year what Shabbat is to the week, the sabbatical to a cycle of years, and the Jubilee to an era. It is holy time.

What is specific about the holiness of the seventh in a sequence of time is that it is marked by a cessation of work. It marks a period during which we cease creating and remember that we are creations. We stop making and remember that we are made. We, the universe and time itself are the work of a hand greater than merely human, greater in fact than anything we can conceive. On the seventh, be it day, month or year, we focus our attention on God the Creator of all. Rosh HaShana is a festival of creation.

No sooner have we said this than we see that in Judaism there is a dual structure of time, just as there is a unique duality in Judaism as a whole. On the one hand God is the *Creator*, who made heaven and earth and all that lives. But God is also the *Redeemer* who rescued His people from slavery in Egypt and led them through the wilderness to the Promised Land. He is the *Revealer* who appeared to the people at Mount Sinai, made a covenant with them, gave them laws, and from time to time sent them, through the prophets, His word.

God's creation is universal. God's redemption and revelation are particular to the people of Israel who, by their history and way of life, testify to His existence and involvement with the world. The two cycles of time in Judaism represent this duality. One cycle – Pesaḥ, Shavuot and Sukkot – is about redemption and revelation, about the way God acts in history through the shaping events of the Jewish people. The other – the seventh day, seventh month and seventh year – is about creation, God in relation to the cosmos as a whole.

This is the first insight into the meaning of the day. Rosh HaShana is a celebration of the universe as God's work. The sages called it the anniversary of creation. This is the theme of the middle section of the Musaf Amida, *Zikhronot*, "Remembrances." "You remember all of creation, and all things that were formed ... for this day is the opening of all Your works, a remembrance of the very first day." It is echoed in the prayer *HaYom Harat Olam*, "This day is the birth of the world."

Because it is about creation and humanity, the prayers of Rosh HaShana have a universalism not shared by Pesaḥ, Shavuot and Sukkot. The central section of the Amida on those days begins with the words, "You have chosen us from among all peoples," a declaration of Jewish chosenness. By contrast, in the Amida on Rosh HaShana we say, "And so place the fear of You...over all that You have made," an expression of complete universality. Pesaḥ, Shavuot and Sukkot are about what it is to be a Jew. Rosh HaShana is about what it is to be human.

The Kingship of God

The next hint is given in the biblical names for the festival, *Yom Terua* and *Zikhron Terua,* "the day of *terua*" and "a commemoration or remembrance of *terua*." What is *terua*? In all other biblical contexts, it refers to a sound, usually produced by a wind instrument, though sometimes it may mean a shout or cry on the part of a crowd.

What instrument is the Torah referring to? The silver trumpets used by the Israelites in the wilderness were used to sound both a *tekia* and a *terua,* a *tekia* to summon the people and a *terua* to signal that it was time to begin a further journey (Num. 10:1–7). So the *terua* of Rosh HaShana might refer to a trumpet. The sages ruled out this possibility for a simple reason.

Rosh HaShana turns out not to be the only time that a *terua* was sounded in the seventh month. It was also sounded on the tenth of the month, Yom Kippur, in the Jubilee year, when slaves went free and ancestral land returned to its original owners. The Jubilee was the occasion of the famous words, taken directly from the biblical text, written on the Liberty Bell of America, "Proclaim liberty throughout all the land unto all the inhabitants thereof" (Lev. 25:10). The previous verse (25:9) states specifically that one should sound the *terua* with a shofar:

> Then you shall sound the horn loud [*shofar terua*]; in the seventh month on the tenth day of the month, on the Day of Atonement, you shall have the horn sounded throughout the land.

Indeed the Hebrew word for Jubilee, *yovel,* also means a ram's horn (Ex. 19:13). It became a simple inference to conclude that this applied to the *terua* of the first day of the seventh month as well.

What was special about the shofar? In several places in Tanakh it is the sound of battle (see, for example, Josh. 6; I Sam. 4; Jer. 4:19, 49:2). It could also be the sound of celebration. When King David brought the Ark into Jerusalem, he danced and the people rejoiced with *"terua* and the sound of the shofar" (II Sam. 6:15). But in a number of places, especially the historical books, the shofar was sounded at the coronation of a king. So we find at the proclamation of Solomon as king:

> Tzaddok the priest took the horn of oil from the sacred tent and anointed Solomon. Then they sounded the shofar and all the people shouted, "Long live King Solomon!" (I Kings 1:39)

Likewise when Jehu was appointed king:

> They quickly took their cloaks and spread them under him on the bare steps. Then they blew the shofar and shouted, "Jehu is king!" (II Kings 9:13)

When Absalom sought to have himself proclaimed king in the lifetime of his father, David, we read:

> Then Absalom sent secret messengers throughout the tribes of Israel to say, "As soon as you hear the sound of the shofar, then say, 'Absalom is king in Hebron!'" (II Sam. 15:10)

The book of Psalms associates the shofar not with a human king but with the declaration of God as King. A key text is Psalm 47, said in many congregations before the shofar blowing on Rosh HaShana:

> God has been raised up in sound, raised, the Lord, in the voice of the shofar.... For God is King over all the earth.... (Ps. 47:6, 8)

Psalm 98 makes a clear connection between God's kingship and His judgment:

With trumpets and the sound of the shofar, shout for joy before the Lord, the King…. For He is coming to judge the earth. He judges the world with righteousness and all nations with equity. (Ps. 98:6, 9)

We have now arrived at the second great dimension of Rosh HaShana. It is the day on which we celebrate the kingship of God. This has left its mark throughout the Rosh HaShana prayers. The key word is *Melekh*, "King." The leader begins in the morning service with a dramatic rendition of *HaMelekh*. The third blessing of the Amida, which normally ends with the words "the holy God," on Rosh HaShana and throughout the Ten Days of Repentance becomes "the holy King." In particular, Musaf on Rosh HaShana begins with an entire section dedicated to *malkhiyot*, verses relating to divine kingship. Rosh HaShana is the day we celebrate God not just as Creator of the world, but its Ruler also.

The Coronation

The concept of divine kingship sounds simple, even routine, but it is not. It made ancient Israel unique. Eventually it had an impact on the development of freedom in the West. It was a Jewish scholar, Philo, who lived in Alexandria in the first century, who realized how radical it was. Philo was writing about Judaism for a Greek-speaking audience, and when it came to the political structure of Jewry he found that the Greek language had no word for it. The Greeks had words for most things. They were the world's first systematic thinkers, and in Plato's *Republic* and Aristotle's *Politics* they surveyed every known type of political structure – tyranny, monarchy, oligarchy, aristocracy and democracy. But there was no word for the Jewish system, and Philo was forced to invent one to explain it.

The word he chose was *theocracy* – rule by God alone. This was the thought expressed by Gideon, the man who led the Israelites to success in their battle against the Midianites. When the people sought to make him king, he replied: "I will not rule over you, nor will my son rule over you. God will rule over you" (Judges 8:23).

Eventually the Israelites did appoint a king, and in the course of time they developed other systems of governance: judges, elders, patriarchs, exilarchs, city councils and, in the modern State of Israel, democracy. But the ultimate Ruler of the Jewish people was God alone. This meant that no human ruler had absolute authority. Prophets could criticize kings. People could disobey an immoral order. The sovereignty of God meant that there are moral limits to the use of power. Right is sovereign over might. These were, and remain, revolutionary ideas.

They were also responsible for the single most astonishing phenomenon of Jewish history, the fact that Jews retained their identity as a nation for two thousand years in exile, scattered across the world. Wherever they were, God remained their King. They remained His people. Rarely was this better expressed than in the great prayer, *Aleinu*, originally written for Rosh HaShana as a preface to the verses about God's kingship:

He is our God; there is no other. Truly He is our King; there is none else.

There is an integral connection between kingship and creation, and it can be stated simply. God made the universe. Therefore God owns the universe. Therefore God is its ultimate Sovereign since He can specify the terms and conditions under which we exist within the universe. This applies to all humanity.

Hence the second paragraph of *Aleinu*, with its vision and hope of a time "when all humanity will call on Your name," and "all the world's inhabitants will realize and know that to You every knee must bow." The God of revelation and redemption is the God of Israel. The God of creation is the God of all humankind. But they are the same God. Hence the vision of Zechariah with which *Aleinu* ends, when "the Lord shall be King over all the earth; on that day the Lord shall be One and His name One" (Zech. 14:9). Underlying this is perhaps the most remarkable idea of all. "There is no king without a people."[2] The fact that the people of Israel accepted God as their King, and His covenant as their constitution,

---

2. *Kad HaKemah, Rosh HaShana* (2).

means that they bear witness to Him by their very existence and way of life. That is what the psalm means when it says, "You are the Holy One, enthroned on the praises of Israel" (Ps. 22:4). The praises of Israel are the visible symbol of God's majesty. That confers extraordinary dignity on us.

Rabbi Joseph Soloveitchik, doyen of Jewish thinkers in the twentieth century, used to explain this by telling the story of his first Hebrew teacher, a Chabad Hasid who made an indelible impression on him as a child by telling him that Rosh HaShana was God's coronation. "And who puts the crown on His head? We do." He spoke about his memories of praying as a child among the Hasidim on the first night of Rosh HaShana:

> I can feel the unique atmosphere which enveloped these Hasidim as they recited the prayers by which they proclaimed Him their King. The older Hasidim termed this night the "Coronation Night" as they crowned Him as their King. These poor and downtrodden Jews, who suffered so much during their daily existence, were able to experience the enthroning of the Almighty and the true meaning of the Kingship prayers of the Rosh HaShana liturgy.[3]

The shofar on Rosh HaShana is our way of participating in God's coronation.

Exile and Return

The anniversary of creation, a kingship renewal ceremony – there Rosh HaShana might have remained had it not been for one overwhelming historical fact: the Babylonian exile. It is one thing to celebrate the harmony of the created universe when you are at home with the universe, another when you are reminded daily that you are not at home, when you are strangers in a strange land. It is one thing to celebrate divine sovereignty when you enjoy national sovereignty, another when you have lost it and are subject to another power. The destruction of the Temple

---

3. Aaron Rakeffet-Rothkoff, *The Rav*, vol. 2 (Hoboken, NJ: KTAV Publishing House), 171.

and the Babylonian exile were a trauma for the Jewish people, physically and spiritually, and we have an indelible record of how the people felt: "By the rivers of Babylon we sat and wept as we remembered Zion…. How can we sing the Lord's song on foreign soil?" (Ps. 137:1–4).

Judaism and the Jewish people might have disappeared there and then, as had happened to the ten tribes of the northern kingdom, Israel, a century and a half before. There was one difference. The religious identity of the southern kingdom, Judah, was strong. The prophets, from Moses to Jeremiah, had spoken of exile and return. Once before, in the period between Joseph and Moses, the people had experienced exile and return. So defeat and displacement were not final. There was hope. It was contained in one word: *teshuva*.

There is no precise English translation of *teshuva*, which means both "return" – homecoming, a physical act; and "repentance" – remorse, a change of heart and deed, a spiritual act. The reason the Hebrew word means both is because, for the Torah, sin leads to exile. Adam and Eve, after they had sinned, were exiled from the Garden of Eden. Cain, after he had murdered his brother, was punished by being sentenced to eternal exile (Gen. 4:12). The idea of justice in the Torah is based on the principle of *mida keneged mida*, "measure for measure." A sin, *ḥet*, is an act in the wrong place. The result, *galut*, is that the agent finds himself in the wrong place. Sin disturbs the moral harmony of the universe.

But God forgives. That one fact rescues life from tragedy. The sages said that God created repentance before He created humanity (*Nedarim* 39b). What they meant was that God, in creating humanity and endowing the human person with free will, knew that we would make mistakes. We are not angels. We stumble, we sin. We are dust of the earth and to dust we will one day return. Without repentance and forgiveness, the human condition would be unbearable. Therefore God, creating humanity, created the possibility of repentance, meaning that when we acknowledge our failings, we are forgiven. Exile is not an immutable fate. Returning to God, we find Him returning to us. We can restore the moral harmony of the universe.

It follows that on a national scale, *teshuva* means two things that become one: a spiritual return to God and a physical return to the land.

This is how Moses put it in the key text of *teshuva betzibbur,* collective national repentance:

> When all these blessings and curses I have set before you come on you and you take them to heart wherever the Lord your God disperses you among the nations, and when you and your children return to the Lord your God and obey Him with all your heart and with all your soul according to everything I command you today, then the Lord your God will restore your fortunes and have compassion on you and gather you again from all the nations where He scattered you. Even if you have been banished to the most distant land under the heavens, from there the Lord your God will gather you and bring you back. (Deut. 30:1–4)

That was the theory and the hope. The question was: Would it actually happen that way? It did, in the return of the Babylonian exiles to the land of Israel, and it was solemnized in one of the shaping events of Jewish history. It took place in the days of Ezra and Nehemiah on Rosh HaShana itself.

The Great Renewal

Jews, not all but many, had returned from the Babylonian exile. The ruined Temple had been rebuilt. But the nation was in disarray. Religious knowledge was slight. Many had intermarried with local populations. They could not even speak Hebrew. "Half of their children spoke the language of Ashdod, or they spoke the language of one of the other nations, and did not know how to speak the language of Judah" (Neh. 13:24).

On the first day of the seventh month, Ezra the scribe and Nehemiah the governor convened a national assembly at the Water Gate in Jerusalem. Ezra, standing on a wooden platform, publicly read from the Torah while Levites were stationed throughout the crowd to translate and explain what was being said. As they began to realize how far they had drifted from the divine mission, the people started weeping:

And all the people listened attentively to the Book of the Law.... Then Nehemiah the governor, Ezra the priest and teacher of the Law, and the Levites who were instructing the people said to them all, "This day is holy to the Lord your God. Do not mourn or weep." For all the people had been weeping as they listened to the words of the Law. And he [Nehemiah] said, "Go and enjoy choice food and sweet drinks, and send some to those who have nothing prepared. This day is holy to our Lord. Do not grieve, for the joy of the Lord is your strength." The Levites calmed all the people, saying, "Be still, for this is a holy day. Do not grieve." Then all the people went away to eat and drink, to send portions of food and to celebrate with great joy, because they now understood the words that had been made known to them. (Neh. 8:3; 8:9–12)

That Rosh HaShana (which incidentally extended for two days: the people returned the next day to continue the reading) became the start of a period of national rededication, a covenant-renewal ceremony. It was a turning point in Jewish history, and it is not too much to say that we owe to it the survival of Jews and Judaism.

What Ezra and Nehemiah had understood was that religious identity was at the heart of Jewish survival. The Israelites had undergone almost a controlled experiment on what enables a nation to endure. Following the split of the nation into two after the death of Solomon, the northern kingdom had been conquered by the Assyrians. Transported, its people had, for the most part, acculturated into the general population and disappeared, to become known to history as the Lost Ten Tribes. The southern kingdom of Judah, conquered and forced into exile by the Babylonians, had sustained their identity. Inspired by people like Ezekiel, they studied Torah. They prayed. They listened to the prophets, who told them that their covenant with God was still intact. They stayed Jews. Indeed the very fact that we are today called Jews (*Yehudim*, i.e. members of the southern kingdom of Judah) is testimony to this phenomenon.

Ezra and Nehemiah, seeing the sad state of Jewish identity among the Jews of Israel, realized that a major program of religious revival was called for, beginning with the public reading of the Torah that Rosh

HaShana, the first-ever national adult education seminar. The strength of the Jewish nation, they saw more clearly than any of their contemporaries, lay not just in armies and physical defense but in identity and spiritual defense. Ezra was a new type in history: a "scribe," the teacher as hero.

Slowly over the course of the next five centuries, new institutions emerged, most significantly the synagogue and the house of study, which would allow Jewry to survive even military and political defeat. By the first and second century of the common era, when Jews suffered two catastrophes at the hands of the Romans, they had become a people whose heroes were teachers, whose citadels were schools and whose passion was study and the life of the mind. That transformation was responsible for a phenomenon that has no parallel, a people capable of surviving two thousand years of exile, their identity intact. It began with that gathering on the first of Tishrei, when Ezra recalled a people to its ancient mission, and the people wept as they became aware of how far they had drifted from the Torah, their constitution as a nation.

Thus was born the association of the day with *teshuva*, national return. It was Nahmanides in the thirteenth century who most clearly understood that the return of Jews from Babylon and their renewal of the covenant was the historical realization of Moses' prophecy about return, which was itself, for Nahmanides, the source of the command of *teshuva* (commentary to Deut. 30:2).

Individual Responsibility

The Babylonian exile had another effect as well. As a nation in their own land, the Jewish people experienced their fate collectively. War and peace, poverty and prosperity, famine or fruitfulness, these are things a nation experiences as a nation. The Torah is intimately concerned with the fate and dignity of individuals, but it was first and foremost a covenant with the nation as a whole.

Things are different in exile. The nation is no longer in charge of its destiny. It experiences fate primarily as a group of individuals. It remains a nation, but an injured nation, a nation not at home in the world. It was then that an idea present in Judaism from the beginning took on a new significance. The key figure who brought this message to the exiles was a priest and prophet who was with them in Baby-lon: Ezekiel.

Ezekiel reminded the people of the power and possibility of individual responsibility. In so doing, he gave expression to the idea of *teshuva* in a way that has remained salient from his day to now. The first principle he taught the people had already been emphasized by his elder contemporary, Jeremiah. We are each responsible for our own sins, and no one else's:

> The one who sins is the one who will die. The child will not share the guilt of the parent, nor will the parent share the guilt of the child. The righteousness of the righteous will be credited to them, and the wickedness of the wicked will be charged against them. (Ezek. 18:20)

Then he gives precise articulation to the idea of *teshuva*:

> But if a wicked person turns away from all the sins he has com-mitted and keeps all My decrees and does what is just and right, that person will surely live; they will not die. None of the offenses they have committed will be remembered against them. Because of the righteous things they have done, they will live. "Do I take any pleasure in the death of the wicked?" declares the Sovereign Lord. "Rather, am I not pleased when they turn from their ways and live?" (Ezek. 18:21–23)

That is it. No Temple, no sacrifice, no sin offering, no ritual of atonement, but simply the act of turning – *teshuva* – understood as an abandonment of sin and a change of behavior to embrace the holy and the good. These and other verses from Ezekiel became key texts in the rabbinic understanding of *teshuva.*

Ezekiel relates this to the shofar:

> The word of the Lord came to me: Son of man, speak to your people and say to them: When I bring the sword against a land, and the people of the land choose one of their men and make him

their watchman, and he sees the sword coming against the land and blows the shofar to warn the people, then if anyone hears the shofar but does not heed the warning and the sword comes and takes their life, their blood will be on their own head.... (Ezek. 33:1–4)

The task of the prophet is to sound the shofar as a warning to the people that their sins are about to be punished and that they must now do *teshuva* if they are to avert the coming catastrophe. Ezekiel is not the only one to speak of the shofar in these terms. As we read in Isaiah: "Raise your voice like a shofar. Declare to My people their rebellion and to the descendants of Jacob their sins" (Is. 58:1). Hosea (8:1), Joel (2:1, 15) and Amos (3:6) all understood the shofar as the sound of warning of imminent war, itself a sign that the nation had sinned. But Ezekiel, more lucidly than anyone else, set out the doctrine of *teshuva* in the way we understand it today, as something done by individuals as well as a nation, as a change of mind and deed, initiated by the sound of the shofar.

A Day of Judgement

So the basic shape of Rosh HaShana emerged from potentiality to actuality. What was originally a festival of divine creation and sovereignty, accompanied by the shofar as a clarion proclaiming the King, became also – through the prophets, the Babylonian exile and the return – a day of national and individual rededication, a remembrance of sins and a turning with new commitment to the future.

The rabbis fleshed out this sketch with detail and color. First was the name Rosh HaShana itself. The sages knew of four New Years: the first of Nisan as the New Year for kings and festivals, the first of Elul for the tithe of cattle, the first or fifteenth of Shevat for trees, and the first of Tishrei for "years, and Sabbatical years and Jubilees" (*Rosh HaShana* 1:1). However, it was the first of Tishrei that became known as the New Year per se.

The Mishna states that on Rosh HaShana all creatures pass before God (ibid. 1:2). How they do so depends on the precise text of the Mishna, which exists in two variants: *kivnei Maron* or *kivenumeron*.

Numeron is thought to be derived from a Greek word meaning "a troop of soldiers." Accordingly the Talmud reads this as meaning "like the troops of the house of David." The alternative reading, "like the children of Maron," is given two interpretations in the Talmud. One is "like a flock of sheep" passing one by one through a wicket so that they can be counted by the shepherd, or "like the ascent of Beit Maron," a narrow pass through which only one person can go at a time.

The first reading, "like the troops of the house of David," sees the primary meaning of Rosh HaShana as a festival of divine kingship. God is King, the shofar proclaims His presence, and we, His retinue, gather to pay Him homage. The second and third see it as a day on which God judges us, one at a time. The biblical phrase about the land of Israel – "The eyes of the Lord your God are continually on it from the beginning of the year to its end" (Deut. 11:12) – was understood to imply that "from the beginning of the year, sentence is passed as to what the end shall be" (*Rosh HaShana* 8a).

The rabbis also articulated the concept of a book of life. Moses, pleading for the people after the making of the golden calf, says, "But now, please forgive their sin, but if not, then blot me out of the book You have written" (Ex. 32:32). In Psalms 69:29, David says about the wicked, "May they be blotted out of the book of life and not be listed with the righteous."

The book of Esther contains a famous episode: "That night the king could not sleep; so he ordered the book of records [*sefer hazikhronot*] ... to be brought in and read to him" (Est. 6:1). There were times when the king read a record of events that had happened and passed verdict, whether for punishment or reward.

Rabbi Yoḥanan taught that on Rosh HaShana three books lie open in heaven: one for the completely wicked, one for the completely righteous and one for the intermediate. The completely righteous are immediately inscribed in the book of life; the thoroughly wicked are immediately inscribed in the book of death; the verdict on the intermediate is suspended from New Year till the Day of Atonement. If they deserve well, they are inscribed in the book of life; if they do not deserve well, they are inscribed in the book of death (*Rosh HaShana* 16b). It became a particularly beautiful custom to wish people, on the first night of the year, that they be written and sealed immediately for life, implying that those around us are completely righteous. Those who judge others favorably are, we believe, themselves judged favorably.

Both the Babylonian Talmud and the Jerusalem Talmud specify that, whatever the decree, there are certain acts that have the power to avert or annul it, or at least mitigate its harshness. The Babylonian Talmud lists four: charity, prayer, change of name and change of deed; some add a fifth: change of place (*Rosh HaShana* 16b). The Jerusalem Talmud lists three: prayer, charity and *teshuva* (Yerushalmi, *Ta'anit* 2:1), deriving all three from God's answer to Solomon's prayer at the inauguration of the Temple:

> If My people, who are called by My name, will humble themselves and pray [= prayer] and seek My face [= charity] and turn from their wicked ways [= *teshuva*], then I will hear from heaven, and I will forgive their sin and heal their land. (II Chr. 7:14)

All of these motifs – God's kingship, His sitting in the throne of judgment, opening the book in which our deeds and signatures are written, the sound of the shofar that makes even the angels tremble, the shepherd counting his flock, the verdict written on Rosh HaShana and sealed on Yom Kippur, and the power of repentance, prayer and charity to avert the evil decree – are brought together in the liturgical poem *Untaneh Tokef*, one of the great prayers and the most vivid image of Rosh HaShana as we might imagine it in the heavenly court.

We have traveled a long way from the starting point of Rosh HaShana as the anniversary of creation, yet there is a fine rabbinic midrash that brings us back to our starting point. According to Rabbi Eliezer, creation began on 25 Elul, making the first of Tishrei the day on which humanity was created. That day, Adam and Eve were made, and that day they sinned. Yet God forgave them, or at least mitigated their punishment. Initially He had said, "You must not eat from the tree of the knowledge of good and evil, for when you eat from it you will certainly die" (Gen. 2:17). Adam and Eve ate but did not die. Evidently they were forgiven. The midrash continues:

> God said to Adam: This will be a sign to your children. As you stood in judgment before Me this day and were pardoned, so will

your children in the future stand in judgment before Me and will emerge from My presence pardoned. When will that be? *In the seventh month, on the first day of the month.* (Leviticus Raba 29:1)

On Rosh HaShana we are like Adam and Eve, the quintessential representatives of the human condition. We may have sinned. We may have lost the paradise of innocence. We all do. But we are alive. We live in the radiance of God and the generosity of His compassion. In the simplest yet most moving of prayers, Rabbi Akiva turned to God and said, "*Avinu Malkeinu,*" "Our Father, our King" (*Ta'anit* 25a). God is our King, Sovereign of the universe, Author of our laws, the Judge who administers justice. But He is also our Father and we are His children, and can a father withhold compassion from his children? Time and again He forgives us and never loses patience. Human parents may lose faith in a child, but God never does: "Were my father and my mother to forsake me, the Lord would take me in" (Ps. 27:10).

Past, Present and Future

All of these ideas have left their mark on the Maḥzor and appear in our prayers, especially in the central section of the Musaf Amida. On all other festivals, there is one central blessing, *Kedushat HaYom*, "the special sanctity of the day." Uniquely, Rosh HaShana has three central blessings, *Malkhiyot*, Kingship; *Zikhronot*, Remembrances; and *Shofarot*, verses about the Shofar. These correspond to the sentence (not found in Tanakh, but pieced together from biblical phrases), "The Lord is King, the Lord was King, the Lord will be King, forever and all time."

Malkhiyot refers to the present. *Zikhronot* is about memories of the past. *Shofarot* is about the future. The shofar is always a signal of something about to come: the imminent arrival of the king, a warning of impending danger, or the sound of a trial about to begin.

Teshuva sensitizes us to the full significance of time. There are those who live purely in the present, but their lives have no overarching meaning. They react rather than act. They travel with no ultimate destination. They are "like chaff blown by the wind" (Ps. 1:4). To be a Jew is to live poised between past and future: the past and future of our individual lives, of our ancient but still young people and of humanity as a whole.

Teshuva tells us that our past does not determine our future. We can change. We can act differently next time than last. If anything, our future determines our past. Our determination to grow as human beings – our commitment to a more faithful, sensitive, decent life in the year to come – gives us the courage and honesty to face our past and admit its shortcomings. Our *teshuva* and God's forgiveness together mean that we are not prisoners of the past, held captive by it. In Judaism, sin is what we do, not what we are. Therefore we remain intact, able to acknowledge our failures and then move on.

My predecessor Lord Jakobovits made a profound comment about Rosh HaShana. Given that it is the start of the Ten Days of Repentance, surprisingly it contains no explicit confessions, no penitential prayers. These form the text and texture of Yom Kippur but not Rosh HaShana. Why so? Because, he suggested, *teshuva* is driven by two different mindsets: commitment to the future and remorse about the past. Rosh HaShana is about the first, Yom Kippur about the second. *Rosh* means "head" and the default position of the head is looking forward, not back. The placing of Rosh HaShana before Yom Kippur means that our determination to act better in the future should be prior to our feelings of remorse about the past – to which we might add that this is why we blow the shofar on Rosh HaShana. The shofar, too, turns our attention to what lies ahead, not behind.

What Rosh HaShana Says to Us

What then does Rosh HaShana say to us? Of what is it a reminder? How can it transform our lives?

The genius of Judaism was to take eternal truths and translate them into time, into lived experiences. Other cultures have constructed philosophies and theologies, elaborate systems of abstract thought. Judaism prefers truth lived to truth merely thought. Ancient Greece produced the logical imagination. Judaism produced the chronological imagination, truth transposed into the calendar. Rosh HaShana, the anniversary of the creation of humanity, invites us to live and feel the human condition in graphic ways.

The first thing it tells us is that life is short. However much life expectancy has risen, we will not, in one lifetime, be able to achieve everything we might wish to achieve. *Untaneh Tokef* tells the poetry of mortality with haunting pathos:

> Man is founded in dust and ends in dust. He lays down his soul to bring home bread. He is like a broken shard, like grass dried up, like a faded flower, like a fleeting shadow, like a passing cloud, like a breath of wind, like whirling dust, like a dream that slips away.

This life is all we have. How shall we use it well? We know that we will not finish the task, but neither are we free to stand aside from it. That is the first truth.

The second is that life itself, each day, every breath we take, is the gift of God:

> Remember us for life, O King who delights in life, and write us in the book of life – for Your sake, O God of life. (*Zikhronot*)

Life is not something we may take for granted. If we do, we will fail to celebrate it. God gives us one gift above all others, said Maimonides: life itself, beside which everything else is secondary. Other religions have sought God in heaven, or in the afterlife, the distant past or the distant future. Here there is suffering, there reward; here chaos, there order; here pain, there balm; here poverty, there plenty. Judaism has relentlessly sought God in the here-and-now of life on earth. Yes, we believe in life after death, but it is in life before death that we truly find human greatness.

Third, we are free. Judaism is the religion of the free human being freely responding to the God of freedom. We are not in the grip of sin. We are not determined by economic forces or psychological drives or genetically encoded impulses that we are powerless to resist. The very fact that we can do *teshuva*, that we can act differently tomorrow than we did yesterday, tells us we are free. Philosophers have found this idea difficult. So have scientists. But Judaism insists on it, and our ancestors proved it by defying every law of history, surviving against the odds, refusing to accept defeat.

Fourth, life is meaningful. We are not mere accidents of matter, generated by a universe that came into being for no reason and will one day, for no reason, cease to be. We are here because a loving God brought the universe, and life, and us, into existence – a God who knows our fears, hears our prayers, believes in us more than we believe in ourselves, who forgives us when we fail, lifts us when we fall and gives us the strength to overcome despair. The historian Paul Johnson once wrote: "No people has ever insisted more firmly than the Jews that history has a purpose and humanity a destiny." He concluded: "The Jews, therefore, stand right at the center of the perennial attempt to give human life the dignity of a purpose."[4] That too is one of the truths of Rosh HaShana.

Fifth, life is not easy. Judaism does not see the world through rose-tinted lenses. The sufferings of our ancestors haunt our prayers. The world we live in is not the world as it ought to be. That is why, despite every temptation, Judaism has never been able to say the Messianic Age has come, even though we await it daily. But we are not bereft of hope because we are not alone. When Jews went into exile, the *Shekhina*, the Divine Presence, went with them. God is always there, "close to all who call on Him in truth" (Ps. 145:18). He may hide His face, but He is there. He may be silent, but He is listening to us, hearing us and healing us in ways we may not understand at the time but which become clear in retrospect.

Sixth, life may be hard, but it can still be sweet, the way the *ḥalla* and the apple are on Rosh HaShana when we dip them in honey. Jews have never needed wealth to be rich, or power to be strong. To be a Jew is to live for simple things: the love between husband and wife, the sacred bond between parents and children, the gift of community where we help others and others help us and where we learn that joy is doubled and grief halved by being shared. To be a Jew is to give, whether in the form of *tzedaka* or *gemilut ḥasadim* (acts of loving-kindness). It is to learn and never stop seeking, to pray and never stop thanking, to do

---

4. Paul Johnson, *A History of the Jews* (London: Phoenix, 2004), Prologue, 2.

teshuva and never stop growing. In this lies the secret of joy. Throughout history there have been hedonistic cultures that worship pleasure and ascetic cultures that deny it, but Judaism has a different approach altogether: to sanctify pleasure by making it part of the worship of God. Life is sweet when touched by the divine.

Seventh, our life is the single greatest work of art we will ever make. Rabbi Joseph Soloveitchik, in one of his earliest works, spoke about *Ish HaHalakha*, the halakhic personality and its longing to create, to make something new, original. God too longs for us to create and thereby become His partner in the work of renewal. "The most fundamental principle of all is that man must create himself." That is what *teshuva* is, an act of making ourselves anew. On Rosh HaShana we step back from our life like an artist stepping back from his canvas, seeing what needs changing for the painting to be complete.

Eighth, we are what we are because of those who came before us. Our lives are not disconnected particles. We are each a letter in God's book of life. But single letters, though they are the vehicles of meaning, have no meaning when they stand alone. To have meaning they must be joined to other letters to make words, sentences, paragraphs, a story, and to be a Jew is to be part of the strangest, oldest, most unexpected and counterintuitive story there has ever been: the story of a tiny people, never large and often homeless, who nonetheless outlived the greatest empires the world has ever known – the Egyptians, Assyrians, Babylonians, the Greeks and Romans, the medieval empires of Christianity and Islam, all the way to the Third Reich and the Soviet Union. Each in turn thought itself immortal. Each has gone. The Jewish people still lives.

So on Rosh HaShana we remember and ask God to remember those who came before us: Abraham and Isaac, Sarah, Hannah and Rachel, the Israelites of Moses' day, and the Jews of every generation, each of whom left some living legacy in the prayers we say or the melodies in which we sing them. And in one of the most moving verses of the middle section of Musaf we recall the great words said by God through the prophet Jeremiah: "I remember of you the kindness of your youth, your love when you were a bride; how you walked after Me in the desert, through a land not sown" (Jer. 2:2). Our ancestors may have sinned, but they never stopped following God though the way was hard and the destination distant. We do not start with nothing. We have inherited wealth, not material but spiritual. We are heirs to our ancestors' greatness.

Ninth, we are heirs to another kind of greatness too, that of the Torah itself and its high demands, its strenuous ideals, its panoply of mitzvot, its intellectual and existential challenges. Judaism asks great things of us and by doing so makes us great. We walk as tall as the ideals for which we live, and those of the Torah are very high indeed. We are, said Moses, God's children (Deut. 14:1). We are called on, said Isaiah, to be His witnesses, His ambassadors on earth (Is. 43:10). Time and again Jews did things thought impossible. They battled against might in the name of right. They fought against slavery. They showed that it was possible to be a nation without a land, to have influence without power, to be branded the world's pariahs yet not lose self-respect. They believed with unshakable conviction that they would one day return to their land, and though the hope seemed absurd, it happened. Their kingdom may have been bounded by a nutshell, but Jews counted themselves kings of infinite space. Judaism sets the bar high, and though we may fall short time and again, Rosh HaShana and Yom Kippur allow us to begin anew, forgiven, cleansed, undaunted, ready for the next challenge, the next year.

And finally comes the sound of the shofar, piercing our defenses, a wordless cry in a religion of words, a sound produced by breath as if to tell us that that is all life is – a mere breath – yet breath is nothing less than the spirit of God within us: "Then the Lord God formed man from the dust of the ground and breathed into his nostrils the breath of life, and man became a living being" (Gen. 2:7). We are dust of the earth but within us is the breath of God.

And whether the shofar is our cry to God or God's cry to us, somehow in that *tekia, shevarim, terua* – the call, the sob, the wail – is all the pathos of the Divine-human encounter as God asks us to take His gift, life itself, and make of it something holy by so acting as to honor God and His image on earth, humankind. For we defeat death, not by living forever but by living by values that live forever; by doing deeds and creating blessings that will live on after us; and by attaching ourselves in the midst of time to God who lives beyond time, "the King – the living, everlasting God."

The Hebrew verb *lehitpalel,* "to pray," more precisely means "to judge oneself." On Rosh HaShana we stand in judgment. We know what it is to be known. And though we know the worst about ourselves, God sees the best; and when we open ourselves to Him, He gives us the strength to become what we truly are.

Those who fully enter the spirit of Rosh HaShana emerge into the new year charged, energized, focused, renewed, knowing that to be a Jew is to live life in the presence of God, to sanctify life for the sake of God, and to enhance the lives of others – for where we bring blessings into other lives, there God lives.

Yom Kippur

Seeking Forgiveness

Yom Kippur is the holy of holies of Jewish time. Observed with immense ceremony in the Temple, almost miraculously rescued after the Temple was destroyed, sustained ever since with unparalleled awe, it is Judaism's answer to one of the most haunting of human questions: How is it possible to live the ethical life without an overwhelming sense of guilt, inadequacy and failure?

The distance between who we are and who we ought to be is, for most of us, vast. We fail. We fall. We give in to temptation. We drift into bad habits. We say or do things in anger we later deeply regret. We disappoint those who had faith in us. We betray those who trusted us. We lose friends. Sometimes our deepest relationships can fall apart. We experience frustration, shame, humiliation, remorse. We let others down. We let ourselves down. These things are not rare. They happen to all of us, even the greatest. One of the most powerful features of biblical narrative is that its portraits are not idealized. Its heroes are human. They too have their moments of self-doubt. They too sin.

Judaism sets the bar high, expecting great things of us in word and deed. So demanding are the Torah's commandments that we cannot but fall short some, even much, of the time. God asks us in some sense to be like Him: "Be holy for I, the Lord your God, am holy" (Lev. 19:2). Yet how can we be equal to such a challenge when we are, and know we are, human, all too human? How can we fail to disappoint Him? Better surely to accept what we are than aspire to be better than we are. Yet this is a recipe for faint hearts and small spirits, and it is a route Judaism never took. Better to fail while striving greatly than not to strive at all.

Judaism's resolution to this tension is so radical that it transformed the moral horizons of humankind. It says that the God of love and forgiveness created us in love and forgiveness, asking that we love and forgive others. God does not ask us not to fail. Rather, He asks us to acknowledge our failures, repair what we have harmed and move on, learning from our errors and growing thereby. Human life, thus conceived, is neither tragic nor mired in sin. But it is demanding, intensely so. Therefore at its heart there had to be an institution capable of transmuting guilt into moral growth, and estrangement from God or our fellow humans into reconciliation. That institution is Yom Kippur, when in total honesty we fast and afflict ourselves, confessing our failures and immersing ourselves, mystically and metaphorically, in the purifying waters of God's forgiving love.

I want in this chapter to tell the story of the day and the ideas it embodies, for it is one of the most fascinating narratives in the history of ethics and spirituality.

In ancient times the day was celebrated in the form of a massive public ceremony set in the Temple in Jerusalem (see *Yoma*, ch. 1-7). The holiest man in Israel, the High Priest, entered the most sacred space, the Holy of Holies, confessed the sins of the nation using the holiest name of God, and secured atonement for all Israel. It was a moment of intense drama in the life of a people who believed, however fitfully, that their fate depended on their relationship with God, who knew that there is no life, let alone a nation, without sin, and who knew from their history that sin could be punished by catastrophe.

Crowds of people thronged the Temple in Jerusalem, hoping to catch a glimpse of the High Priest as he fulfilled his ministrations. We have eyewitness testimony of a Roman consul, Marcus, who served in Jerusalem at the time of the Second Temple. This is how he describes the procession that made its way to the Temple Mount:

And this I have seen with my own eyes: first to go before [the High Priest] would be all those who were of the seed of the kings of Israel.... A herald would go before them, crying, "Give honor to the house of David." After them came the house of Levi, and a herald crying, "Give honor to the house of Levi." There were thirty-six thousand of them, and all the prefects wore clothing of blue silk; and the priests, of whom there were twenty-four thousand, wore clothing of white silk.

After them came the singers, and after them, the instrumentalists, then the trumpeters, then the guards of the gate, then the incense-makers, then the curtain-makers, then the watchmen and the treasurers, then a class called *chartophylax*, then all the workingmen who worked in the Sanctuary, then the seventy of the Sanhedrin, then a hundred priests with silver rods in their hands to clear the way. Then came the High Priest, and after him all the elders of the priesthood, two by two. And the heads of the academies stood at vantage points and cried, "Lord High Priest, may you come in peace! Pray to our Maker to grant us long life that we may engage in His Torah."[1]

It was a glittering spectacle, the closest of encounters between man and God at the supreme intersection of sacred time and space. The service itself was long and elaborate. The High Priest would be rehearsed in his rituals for seven days beforehand. Five times on the day itself he would have to immerse himself in a *mikveh* and change his robes: gold for his public appearances, plain white for his ministrations within the Holy of Holies. Three times he would make confession, first for himself and his family, then for his fellow priests, and finally for the people as a whole. Each time he used the holy name of God, the watching crowd would prostrate themselves, falling on their faces.

The confession involved a strange and unique ceremony. Two goats, identical in size, height and appearance, would be brought before the High Priest, and with them a box containing two plaques,

---

1.   Solomon ibn Verga, *Shevet Yehuda* (c. 1550), cited in Shmuel Yosef Agnon, *Days of Awe* (New York: Schocken, 1948), 255–258.

one inscribed "To the Lord," the other "To Azazel." Over the goat on which the lot "To Azazel" had fallen, he would confess the sins of the nation, and the goat would then be led by a special person selected for the task into the desert hills outside Jerusalem where it would plunge to its death from a steep precipice. If the confession had been effective, so an ancient tradition states, the red thread it carried would turn white.

After the destruction of the Second Temple there would be no more such scenes. Now there was no High Priest, no sacrifice, no divine fire, no Levites singing praises or crowds thronging the precincts of Jerusalem and filling the Temple Mount. Above all, there was no Yom Kippur ritual through which the people could find forgiveness.

It was then that a transformation took place that must constitute one of the great creative responses to tragedy in history. Tradition has cast Rabbi Akiva in the role of the savior of hope. The Mishna in *Yoma*, the tractate dedicated to Yom Kippur, tells us in effect that Rabbi Akiva could see a new possibility of atonement even in the absence of a High Priest and a Temple. God Himself would purify His people without the need for an intermediary (*Yoma* 8:9). Even ordinary Jews could, as it were, come face to face with the *Shekhina*, the Divine Presence. They needed no one else to apologize for them. The drama that once took place in the Temple could now take place in the human heart. Yom Kippur was saved. It is not too much to say that Jewish faith was saved.

Every synagogue became a fragment of the Temple. Every prayer became a sacrifice. Every Jew became a kind of priest, offering God not an animal but instead the gathered shards of a broken heart. For if God was the God of everywhere, He could be encountered anywhere. And if there were places from which He seemed distant, then time could substitute for place. "Seek God where He is to be found, call on Him where He is close" (Is. 55:6) – this, said the sages, refers to the Ten Days of Repentance from Rosh HaShana to Yom Kippur (*Yevamot* 105a). Holy days became the surrogate for holy spaces. Yom Kippur became the Jerusalem of time, the holy city of the Jewish soul.

Thereafter it never lost its hold on the Jewish imagination. There is a tradition that during the Middle Ages, when Jews were being pressured under threat of expulsion or death to convert to Christianity or Islam, many who did so – the *anusim* or, as they were contemptuously called by the Spanish, *marranos* (swine) – often remained Jews in secret. Some scholars assert that once a year they would make their way to the synagogue on the night of Yom Kippur to reaffirm their Jewish identity.

More recently the story of Franz Rosenzweig (1886–1929) became emblematic. This young German-Jewish intellectual from a highly assimilated family had been persuaded by a friend to convert to Christianity. Insisting on entering the Church not as a pagan but as a Jew, he decided that his last Jewish act would be to go to synagogue. He traveled to Berlin in 1913 to spend Yom Kippur in a small Orthodox synagogue as his last Jewish act.

The experience changed his life. A few days later he wrote that "leaving Judaism no longer seems necessary to me and…no longer possible." He became a *ba'al teshuva*, one of the greatest in the prewar years. On postcards in the trenches of the First World War, he wrote one of the masterpieces of Jewish theology in the twentieth century, *The Star of Redemption*. He became a friend of Martin Buber and founded the *Judisches Lehrhaus*, the House of Jewish Learning, in Frankfurt.[2] For the secular *marranos* of the twentieth century as for their medieval forerunners, Yom Kippur was the day that touched the heart even of those who were otherwise estranged from their faith. It was the day of "coming home," one of the root meanings of the word *teshuva*.

And so it is for us. What has given Yom Kippur its unique place on the map of the Jewish heart is that it is the most intensely personal of all the festivals. Pesah, Shavuot and Sukkot are celebrations of Jewish memory and history. They remind us of what it means to be a member of the Jewish people, sharing its past, its present and its hopes. Rosh HaShana, the anniversary of creation, is about what it means to be human under the sovereignty of God. But Yom Kippur is about what it means to be me, this unique person that I am. It makes us ask:

---

2. Nahum N. Glatzer, *Franz Rosenzweig: His Life and Thought* (New York: Schocken, 1961).

What have I done with my life? Whom have I hurt or harmed? How have I behaved? What have I done with God's greatest gift, life itself? What have I lived for and what will I be remembered for? To be sure, we ask these questions in the company of others. Ours is a communal faith. We pray together, confess together and throw ourselves on God's mercy together. But Yom Kippur remains an intensely personal day of conscience and self-reckoning.

It is the day on which, as the Torah says five times, we are commanded to "afflict" ourselves (Lev. 16:29, 31; 23:27, 32; Num. 29:7). Hence: no eating or drinking, no bathing, no anointing, no sexual relations, no leather shoes. It is customary for men to wear a *kittel*, a white garment reminiscent, some say, of the white tunic the High Priest wore when he entered the Holy of Holies (*Mateh Efrayim* 610:11). Others say it is like a burial shroud (Rema, ibid. 3). Either way, it reminds us of the truths we must face alone. The Torah says that "no man shall be in the Tent of Meeting when [Aaron] comes to make atonement in the holiest place, until he leaves" (Lev. 16:17). Like the High Priest on this holy day, we face God alone. We confront our mortality alone. Outwardly we are in the company of others, but inwardly we are giving a reckoning for our individual life, singular and unique. The fact that everyone else around us is doing likewise makes it bearable.

Fasting and repenting, I stand between two selves, as the High Priest once stood facing two goats, symbolic of the duality of human nature. There is the self I see in the mirror and know in my darkest hours. I know how short life is and how little I have achieved. I remember, with a shame undiminished by the passing of time, the people I offended, wounded, disappointed; the promises I made but did not fulfill; the harsh words I said and the healing words I left unsaid. I know how insignificant I am in the scheme of things, one among billions who will live, die, and eventually vanish from living memory. I am next-to-nothing, a fleeting breath, a driven leaf: "dust you are and to dust you will return" (Gen. 3:19).

Yet there is a second self, the one I see in the reflection of God's love. It is not always easy to feel God's love but it is there, holding us gently, telling us that every wrong we repent of is forgiven, every act of kindness we perform is unforgotten, that we are here because

God wants us to be and because there is work He needs us to do. He loves us as a parent loves a child and has a faith in us that never wavers however many times we fail. In Isaiah's words: "Though the mountains be shaken and the hills be removed, yet My unfailing love for you will not be shaken nor My covenant of peace be removed" (Is. 54:10). God, who "counts the number of the stars and calls each of them by name" (Ps. 147:4), knows each of us by name, and by that knowledge confers on us inalienable dignity and unconditional love. *Teshuva* means "coming home" to this second self and to the better angels of our nature.

The history of Yom Kippur stands in sharp contrast to that of Rosh HaShana. About the New Year, the biblical sources are sparse and enigmatic, but to the Day of Atonement the Torah devotes an entire and detailed chapter, Leviticus 16. On the face of it, there is little left unsaid. This chapter will, however, argue otherwise. The intellectual history of Yom Kippur is still too little understood. Tracing it will take us through a dispute between two of the greatest rabbis of the Middle Ages, a study of the difference between the way priests and prophets understood the moral life, the power of the rabbinic mind to unite two institutions that had remained distinct throughout the whole of the biblical era, and much else besides. First, however, we begin with one of Judaism's greatest innovations, the idea of forgiveness itself.

A Brief History of Forgiveness

There are rare moments when the world changes and a new possibility is born: when the Wright brothers achieved the first man-made flight in 1903; or in 1969 when Neil Armstrong became the first man to set foot on the moon; or when five thousand years ago someone discovered that marks made in clay with a stick could, when the clay dried, become permanent signs, and thus writing and civilization were born.

The birth of forgiveness is one such moment. It is one of the most radical ideas ever to have been introduced into the moral imagination of humankind. Forgiveness is an action that is not a reaction. It breaks the cycle of stimulus-response, harm and retaliation, wrong and revenge, which has led whole cultures to their destruction and still threatens the future of the world. It frees individuals from the burden of their past, and humanity from the irreversibility of history. It tells us that enemies can become friends.

Forgiveness, writes David Konstan in an important philosophical study, did not exist before Judaism.[3] It is, on the face of it, an odd claim to make. Surely every culture has a need to avoid the sheer destructiveness of anger and vengeance that arises in every society when one person wrongs another. That is true, but not every society develops the idea of forgiveness. The ancient Greeks, for example, did not. Instead they had something else often mistaken for forgiveness, namely the *appeasement of anger.*

When someone harms someone else, the victim is angry and seeks revenge. This is clearly dangerous for the perpetrator who will then seek to calm the victim and move on. They may make excuses: It wasn't me, it was someone else. Or, it was me but I couldn't help it. Or, it was me but it was a small wrong, and I have done you much good in the past, so that on balance you should let it pass.

Alternatively, or in conjunction with these other strategies, the perpetrator may beg, plead and perform some ritual of abasement or humiliation. This is a way of saying to the victim, "I am not really a threat." The Greek word *sungnome*, sometimes translated as forgiveness, really means, says Konstan, *exculpation* or *absolution.* It is not that I forgive you for what you did, but that I understand why you did it – you were caught up in circumstances beyond your control – or, alternatively, I do not need to take revenge because you have now shown by your deference to me that you hold me in proper respect. My dignity has been restored. The result of excuse or self-abasement is that, in the phrase of the book of Esther, "the anger of the king abated" (7:10). Appeasement is a way of defusing anger but it is not repentance and it does not lead to forgiveness.

There is a classic example of this in the Torah itself. In Genesis 32–33, Jacob is terrified at the prospect of his meeting with Esau.

---

3. David Konstan, *Before Forgiveness: The Origins of a Moral Idea* (Cambridge: Cambridge University Press, 2010).

Twenty-two years earlier, Jacob had fled into exile after taking Esau's blessing and hearing that his brother had vowed to kill him as soon as their father was dead. Now they are about to meet. Jacob hears that Esau is coming with a force of four hundred men. His response is a paradigm case of appeasement. He sends Esau gifts, accompanied by messengers. When Esau finally appears he abases himself, prostrating himself seven times to the ground. Repeatedly he calls Esau "my lord" and himself "your servant." Esau is placated. The two brothers embrace, weep and go their separate ways. Anger has been averted. But between them there has been appeasement, not forgiveness. Forgiveness plays no part in the story.

I. The Idea of Freedom

Before forgiveness can enter the world, another world-changing idea had to appear: the idea of human freedom. Despite its centrality to Western thought, freedom – the ability to choose between alternatives and act in accordance with one's choices – is anything but self-evident and has been challenged in most cultures and ages.

The ancients did not think about it much, and when they did, they were more inclined to deny it than affirm it. The human person was a boat adrift on the waves of an ocean, chaff blown by the wind, a plaything of the gods, a pawn moved by other hands, a slave, not the master, of his fate. We are what we are and we cannot change what we are.

Once our fate has been decided, there is nothing we can do to avoid it. Laius was told by the Delphic oracle that his son would kill him and take his place. Laius tried every way to ensure this would not come about. So did his son, Oedipus. Yet each plan they made to avoid the outcome helped make it happen. This – the idea of *moira*, inevitability, or *ananke*, blind fate – is at the heart of Greek tragedy and is central to its bleak view of the human situation.

Free will has been denied many times in history. Spinoza did so in the name of natural necessity: our acts are the result of causes beyond our control. For Marx, the shaper of human behavior was economics; for Freud, the play of unconscious drives; for the neo-Darwinians, our genetically encoded instincts. Science has never given a compelling account of free will. For if there can be a complete scientific account of human behavior, it would tell us that our acts have causes such that we could not have acted other than we did.

Radical unconditioned freedom enters Western civilization in the first chapter of Genesis when the free God freely creates the universe, saying, "Let there be." Making humankind in His image, after His likeness (see Gen. 1:26–27), He endowed us too with freedom. We may be dust of the earth but there is within us the breath of God. The human person is, as Pico Della Mirandola put it in his *Oration on the Dignity of Man*, the one being in creation that is neither angel nor beast but can be either depending on his choice. To be human, said Jean-Paul Sartre, is to know that our existence precedes our essence. We have no essence. All we have is choice.

All life was created. Humans alone are creative. Every life-form has drives, inherent instincts of survival. Humans alone are capable of what philosophers call second-order evaluations, deciding which drives to pursue and which not. Other animals act. We alone bear responsibility for our acts because we could have chosen to act otherwise. Freedom is God's greatest gift to humankind but it is also the most fateful and terrifying. For it means that we alone have the power to destroy the work of God.

Genesis tells a troubled story. Gifted with freedom, almost immediately humans betray that gift. Adam and Eve sin. Cain, the first human child, murders Abel his brother. By Genesis 6, the world has become a place of violence and random cruelty, and God regrets He created man. The modern world with its extermination camps and gulags, its oppression and terror, seems hardly to have advanced at all. Technically, humans have excelled. Morally they have failed and continue to fail. For freedom is a double-edged sword. The freedom to do good is inseparable from the freedom to do harm, to commit sin, to practice evil. The problem of evil is *the* problem of humanity.

Yom Kippur is the answer.

For if freedom means that humans will sin, then God must have accepted in advance that they would sin, which means that He provided a mechanism for their forgiveness – a mechanism that, without releasing people from moral responsibility, acknowledges that they can recognize that they did wrong, express remorse for the past and dedicate themselves to learning from it and growing thereby, in short, that they can do *teshuva*. They can repent. This is the meaning of the following remarkable midrash:

> Rabbi Yannai said: From the beginning of creation God foresaw the deeds of the righteous and wicked. *The earth was void* – this refers to the deeds of the wicked. *And God said, "Let there be light"* – this refers to the deeds of the righteous. *And God separated the light from the darkness* – this means, the deeds of the righteous from the deeds of the wicked. *God called the light "day"* – this refers to the deeds of the righteous. *The darkness He called "night"* – this refers to the deeds of the wicked. *And there was evening* – the deeds of the wicked. *And there was morning* – the deeds of the righteous. *One day* – this means that God gave them [both] a single day. Which was it? Yom Kippur. (Genesis Raba 3:8)

The midrash is based on the observation that the Hebrew text of Genesis calls the first day of creation "*yom eḥad*," literally "one day," when it should have said "*yom rishon*," "the first day" (see Numbers Raba 13:6). Evidently, then, the Torah does not mean "the first day." It means the singular, unique day of days, which in Jewish terms means Yom Kippur.

But the midrash is clearly saying something deeper. It is asserting that *divine forgiveness preceded the creation of the first humans,* for without a mechanism for repentance, the creation of Homo sapiens does not make sense. Without it, our guilt would accumulate, as it did in the generation of the Flood. There would be no way of mending the past or moving on from it. The human condition would be tragic. We would live weighed down by the burden of remorse, or worse, we would seek to liberate ourselves from the voice of conscience altogether, and we would then become lower than the beasts.

Repentance and atonement alone redeem the human situation, telling us that though "there is no one on earth who is righteous, does only good and never sins" (Eccl. 7:20), still God accepts our fallibility and failures so long as we acknowledge them as such. Indeed, when we grow through our failures, we become greater than those who never failed. "Where penitents stand," said the sages, "even the perfectly righteous cannot stand" (*Berakhot* 34b).

God gave us freedom, knowing the risks. Because we are free, we bear responsibility for our deeds: we *need* to repent. But because we are free, we can change, so we are *able* to repent. This Jewish insistence on freedom – that morally, we become what we choose to be – is one of its greatest contributions to the ethical imagination. Economics may make us rich or poor. Genetics may make us tall or short. But it is our freely made choices that make us good or bad, honest or deceptive, generous or mean-spirited, altruistic or self-centered, patient or irascible, courageous or cowardly, responsible or feckless. Judaism is the world's great ethic of responsibility, born in the vision of the free God seeking the free worship of free human beings honoring the freedom and dignity of others.

God, who made us in love, forgives. Only on this assumption does the creation of humanity make any sense at all.

II. *Before God Forgives, Man Must Forgive*

Oddly enough, though, it takes time for forgiveness to make its appearance in the Torah. This is strange. If, as the Midrash states and logic dictates, God created forgiveness before He made man, why does it play no obvious part in the early stories of Genesis? Did God forgive Adam and Eve? Did God forgive Cain after he had murdered Abel? Not explicitly. He may have mitigated their punishment. Adam and Eve did not immediately die after eating the forbidden fruit. God placed a mark on Cain's forehead to protect him from being killed by someone else. But mitigation is not the same as forgiveness.

God does not forgive the generation of the Flood, or the builders of Babel, or the sinners of Sodom. Significantly, when Abraham prayed for the people of Sodom he did not ask God to forgive them. His argument was markedly different. He said, "Perhaps there are innocent people there," maybe fifty, perhaps no more than ten. Their merit should, he implied, save the others, but that is quite different from asking God to forgive the others (Gen. 18).

The first time we encounter a clear instance of forgiveness is when Joseph, by now viceroy of Egypt, finally reveals his identity to his brothers. Years earlier, they had contemplated killing him and eventually sold him as a slave. They have come before him in Egypt twice without recognizing who he was. Now he discloses his identity and, while they are silent and in a state of shock, goes on to say these words:

> I am your brother Joseph, whom you sold into Egypt! And now, do not be distressed and do not be angry with yourselves for selling me here, because it was to save lives that God sent me ahead of you. For two years now there has been famine in the land, and for the next five years there will be no plowing and reaping. But God sent me ahead of you to preserve for you a remnant on earth and to save your lives by a great deliverance. So then, it was not you who sent me here, but God. (Gen. 45:4–8)

This is *the first recorded moment in history in which one human being forgives another.*

So astonishing is this forgiveness that the brothers cannot entirely believe it. Years later, after their father Jacob has died, the brothers come to Joseph fearing that he will now take revenge. They concoct a story:

> They sent word to Joseph, saying, "Your father left these instructions before he died: 'This is what you are to say to Joseph: I ask you to forgive your brothers for the sins and the wrongs they committed in treating you so badly.' Now please forgive the sins of the servants of the God of your father." When their message came to him, Joseph wept. (Gen. 50:16–18)

The brothers understand the word "forgive" – they use it in their speech – but they are uneasy about it. Did Joseph really mean it? Does someone really forgive those who sold him into slavery? Joseph weeps that his brothers haven't really understood that he meant it when he said it. But he did, then and now.

David Konstan, in *Before Forgiveness*, identifies this as the first recorded instance of forgiving in history. What he does not make clear is *why* Joseph forgives. There is nothing accidental about

Joseph's behavior. In fact the whole sequence of events, from the moment the brothers appear before him in Egypt for the first time to the moment when he announces his identity and forgives them, is an intricately detailed account of *teshuva*, repentance, the key act of Yom Kippur itself.

Recall what happens. Joseph, having been sold into Egypt as a slave, then thrown into prison on a false charge, eventually rises to become second-in-command in Egypt, having successfully interpreted Pharaoh's dreams. As he predicted, there are seven years of plenty followed by seven years of famine and drought. Lacking food, Jacob sends his sons to Egypt to buy grain, and there they meet the viceroy, not recognizing him as their brother. He is, after all, dressed as an Egyptian ruler and goes by the name Tzafenat-Pane'aḥ. Coming before him, they "bowed down to him with their faces to the ground" (Gen. 42:6).

At this point, by the logic of the story, something should happen. As a young man Joseph had dreamed that one day his brothers would bow down to him. They have just done so. We now expect him to announce his identity and tell the brothers to bring Jacob and the rest of the family to Egypt. His dreams would be fulfilled and the story would reach closure.

Eventually this happens, but not without the longest detour in any narrative in the Torah. Seemingly without reason, Joseph embarks on an elaborate and convoluted stratagem whose purpose is initially far from clear. He keeps his identity secret. He accuses the brothers of a crime they have not committed. He says they are spies. He has them imprisoned for three days. Then, holding Simeon as a hostage, he tells them that they must now return home and bring back their youngest brother, Benjamin.

Slowly as the plot unfolds we begin to get a glimpse of what Joseph is doing. He is forcing the brothers to reenact the earlier occasion when they came back to their father with one of their number, Joseph, missing. Note what happens next:

> They said to one another, "Truly we are guilty [*aval ashemim anaḥnu*] because of our brother. We saw how distressed he was

when he pleaded with us for his life, but we would not listen; that's why this distress has come on us ...." They did not realize that Joseph could understand them, since he was using an interpreter. (Gen. 42:21–23)

An echo of those words, *aval ashemim anaḥnu,* "truly we are guilty," will reverberate throughout our prayers on Yom Kippur. They represent the first stage of repentance. The brothers *admit they have done wrong and demonstrate remorse.*

The brothers duly return with Benjamin. Joseph receives them warmly and has them served with a meal. The food comes from Joseph's own table, a sign of royal favor. There is only one discrepant note. The text says that Benjamin, the youngest, is served with a portion that is "five times the size" of that of the other brothers (Gen. 43:34). At this stage we do not know why.

The next morning, the brothers are on their way home when an Egyptian officer pursues them, accusing them of stealing a precious silver cup. It has been planted deliberately in Benjamin's sack. The cup is found and the brothers are brought back. Benjamin has been found with stolen property in his possession. Judah then says this:

What can we say to my lord? What can we say? How can we prove our innocence? God has uncovered your servants' guilt. We are now my lord's slaves – we ourselves and the one who was found to have the cup. (Gen. 44:16)

This is the second stage of repentance: *confession.* Judah does more. He speaks of collective responsibility. This is important. When the brothers sold Joseph into slavery it was Judah who proposed the crime (Gen. 37:26–27) but they were all (except Reuben) complicit in it.

Joseph dismisses Judah's words: "Only the man who was found to have the cup will become my slave. The rest of you, go back to your father in peace" (42:17). He gives the brothers the opportunity to walk away, leaving Benjamin a slave as they once left Joseph. But Judah, undeterred, mounts a passionate plea to be allowed to take the guilt on himself so that Benjamin can be reunited with his father: "So now let me remain as your slave in place of the lad. Let the lad go back with his brothers!" (42:33). It is at this point that Joseph breaks down, discloses his identity and forgives his brothers.

The reason is clear. Judah, who had many years earlier sold Joseph as a slave, is now willing to become a slave so that his brother Benjamin can go free. He has just demonstrated what the Talmud and Maimonides define as *complete repentance,* namely when circumstances repeat themselves and you have an opportunity to commit the same offense again, but *you refrain from doing so because you have changed.*[4]

We now, in retrospect, understand Joseph's entire strategy. With great care and precision he has set up a controlled experiment to see whether the brothers have changed. Will they abandon Benjamin as they once abandoned Joseph? Like Joseph, Benjamin is a son of Jacob's beloved wife Rachel who died young. The brothers – sons of the less-loved Leah or the handmaids – might be expected to be jealous of Benjamin as they were of Joseph. And just as Joseph had his "many-colored coat" (37:3), so Benjamin at the feast is given five times as much as the others. Will they be provoked by envy yet again?

The parallel is complete. The brothers are free to repeat their crime and no one would blame them. It was, after all, the Egyptian ruler who seized Benjamin through no fault of their own. But they do not repeat the crime. Judah ensures that they do not. He offers to sacrifice his freedom for the sake of Benjamin's. The villain has become a hero. Judah is the first *ba'al teshuva,* the first penitent, the first morally transformed individual in history. Joseph's behavior has had nothing to do with his dreams, or revenge, and everything to do with repentance. Where there is repentance there is forgiveness. The brothers, led by Judah, have gone through all three stages of repentance: (1) admission and remorse (*harata*), (2) confession (*viduy*) and (3) behavioral change (*shinui ma'aseh*).

Forgiveness only exists in a culture in which repentance exists. Repentance presupposes that we are free and morally responsible agents who are capable of change, specifically the change that comes about when we recognize that what we have done is wrong and we are

---

4.   *Yoma* 86b; Maimonides, *Laws of Repentance* 2:1.

responsible for it and must never do it again. The possibility of that kind of moral transformation simply did not exist in ancient Greece or any other pagan culture. Greece was a culture of character and fate. Judaism is a culture of will and choice, the first of its kind in the world.

Forgiveness is not just one idea among many. It transformed the human situation. For the first time it established the possibility that we are not condemned endlessly to repeat the past. When I repent, I show I can change. The future is not predestined. I can make it different from what it might have been. And when I forgive, I show that my action is not mere reaction, the way revenge would be. *Forgiveness breaks the irreversibility of the past.* It is the undoing of what has been done. Repentance and forgiveness – the two great gifts of human freedom – redeem the human condition from tragedy.

Now we can return to our original question. If God created forgiveness before He made man, why does it play no part in the stories of Genesis from Adam and Eve to the patriarchs? We cannot be sure of the answer. The Torah is a cryptic work. It leaves much unsaid. It has, as the sages said, "seventy faces" (Numbers Raba 13:15). More than one interpretation is possible. But one suggests itself overwhelmingly: *God does not forgive human beings until human beings learn to forgive one another.*

Consider the alternative. What would happen if God forgave but humans did not? Then history would be an endless story of retaliation, vendetta, vindictiveness and rancor, violence begetting violence and evil engendering new evil – in short, the world before the Flood, the world that still exists today in the form of tribal warfare and ethnic conflict, the world of Bosnia, Rwanda, Kosovo and Darfur, a world of victims seeking vengeance, thereby creating new victims and new vengeance in a process that, without forgiveness, never ends.

The first act of forgiveness in the Torah is Joseph forgiving his brothers, to teach us that only when we forgive one another does God forgive us. Only when we confess our wrongs to one another does God hear our confession to Him. Only when we repent and show we are worthy of being forgiven do we show that we have learned the responsibility that goes with freedom, without which, as Yeats wrote, "mere anarchy is loosed upon the world."

Humanity changed the day Joseph forgave his brothers. Only when the book of Genesis reaches this note of forgiveness and reconciliation can the drama of Exodus and the first Yom Kippur begin.

Two Types of Atonement

It was the most shocking, unexpected sin in history. The Israelites were encamped near Mount Sinai. They had just been liberated from slavery. No exiled people had ever been freed this way before. The supreme Power had intervened in history to rescue the supremely powerless. The rescue had been accompanied throughout by signs and wonders. Ten plagues had struck the Egyptians until Pharaoh let the people go.

Even then the wonders did not cease. When the people were thirsty on their journey through the desert, God sent them water from a rock. When they were hungry, he gave them manna from heaven. When they came up against the impassable barrier of the Sea of Reeds, God divided the waters so that they could cross on dry land. More than three thousand years later we have not stopped telling the story, the greatest narrative of hope the world has ever known.

Then, at Mount Sinai, the people had experienced the greatest revelation in history, when God spoke to an entire nation and made a covenant with them, promising to be their Sovereign and Protector, inviting them to become a kingdom of priests and a holy nation, a nation unlike any other, constituted by its faith.

Now, forty days later, after the memory of that moment had receded, the people wondered what had become of their leader. Moses had climbed the mountain to receive a record of the covenant on tablets of stone, and had not returned. The people panicked. What were they to do in the absence of the man who led them out of Egypt and communicated with God on their behalf? They felt the need for a substitute. They clamored around Aaron. They made a golden calf. Even today, reading the story, it remains a shocking moment. From the heights they had descended to the depths. God, aware of what was happening, told Moses: "Go down, because your people, whom you brought up out of Egypt, have become corrupt" (Ex. 32:7).

Moses prays. Never had there been a prayer as long, protracted, passionate, as this. "I fell prostrate before the Lord for forty days and forty nights; I ate no bread and drank no water, because of all the sin you had committed, doing what was evil in the Lord's sight and so arousing His anger" (Deut. 9:18). In the end God relented. He agreed to forgive the people, and promised Moses a new set of tablets to replace those he had broken in his anger and now lay in fragments beyond repair.

The new tablets symbolized a new beginning. For another forty days Moses was with God. He then descended the mountain, holding the tablets. The people saw him and what he was carrying and knew that they had been forgiven. When Moses came down the mountain with the second tablets, that day became the enduring image of forgiveness. Moses descended on the tenth of Tishrei, and thereafter, the anniversary of that day would become established as a time of forgiveness for all generations.

There is a daring midrash on this, taking as its point of departure the line from Psalm 61, "Hear my cry, O God; listen to my prayer." The psalm, like many others, begins with the word *LaMenatze'aḥ*, literally, "For the conductor, the director of music." The word could be read, however, as "For the victor," and with a truly remarkable inversion, the midrash interprets this as "For the victor who sought to be defeated":

> For the victor who sought to be defeated, as it is said [Is. 57:16], *I will not accuse them forever, nor will I always be angry, for then they would faint away because of Me – the very people I have created.* Do not read it thus, but, *I will accuse in order to be defeated.* How so? Thus said the Holy One, blessed be He: When I win, I lose; and when I lose, I win. I defeated the generation of the Flood, but I lost thereby, for I destroyed My own creation, as it says [Gen. 7:23], *Every living thing on the face of the earth was wiped out.* The same happened with the generation of the Tower of Babel and the people of Sodom. But in the days of Moses who defeated Me [by persuading Me to forgive the Israelites whom I had sworn to destroy], I gained for I did not destroy Israel. (*Pesikta Rabati* 9)

Moses is the hero who defeated God – which turned out to be God's own deepest victory. When Moses came down with the symbol of the power of penitential prayer, that day became the first Yom Kippur.

I. The Aftermath of Sinai: Penitential Prayer

That is not the only legacy of that moment, however. Something else happened that has had a decisive impact on Jewish prayer. To understand it we must turn to the great scene when Moses, having secured the people's forgiveness, asks God to show him His glory (Ex. 33:18). God tells Moses to stand in the crevice of a rock. There God will cause His glory to pass by. Moses will not be able to see God directly, "for no one may see Me and live," but he will come as close as is possible for a human being:

> And the Lord descended in the cloud and stood with him there, and proclaimed in the name of the Lord. And the Lord passed by before him and proclaimed: "The Lord, the Lord, compassionate and gracious God, slow to anger, abounding in loving-kindness and truth, extending loving-kindness to a thousand generations, forgiving iniquity, rebellion and sin, and absolving [the guilty who repent] ...." (Ex. 34:5–7)

Note that God speaks these words, which became known as the Thirteen Attributes of Mercy, not Moses. What is God doing at this point? God Himself says, "I am making a covenant with you" (Ex. 34:10). But it is not yet clear what this means. After all, God had just made a covenant with the people. They had endangered it by their sin, but Moses had prayed for and achieved their pardon. What then is this new covenant with Moses? The answer to all these questions becomes clear only two books later, in the book of Numbers.

It is then that the people commit another sin as grievous as the making of the golden calf. Moses had sent spies to look at the land. They had come back with a demoralizing report. The land is indeed good, they said, flowing with milk and honey. But the people are strong. Their cities are highly fortified. We will not be able to defeat them. They are giants. We are grasshoppers (Num. 13).

At this point the people, despondent and hopeless, say, "Let's choose a leader and go back to Egypt" (Num. 14:4). As He did at the time of the golden calf, God threatens to destroy the people and begin a nation anew with Moses. Again Moses prays to God to forgive the people, for His sake if not for theirs. Then he adds a new element to his prayer:

> Now may the Lord's strength be displayed, just as You have declared: "The Lord is slow to anger, abounding in loving-kindness, forgiving iniquity and rebellion." Yet He does not leave the guilty unpunished; He punishes the children for the sin of the parents to the third and fourth generation. In accordance with Your great love, forgive the sin of these people, just as You have pardoned them from the time they left Egypt until now. (Num. 14:17–19)

Moses is doing something he has not done before. Previously he has prayed on the basis of how God's acts will look to the world, and on the basis of His covenant with the patriarchs. Now he is praying on the basis of God's own nature. He is, as it were, recalling God to Himself. Essentially he is repeating what God Himself had said at Mount Sinai. He says so. He says, "as You have declared," as if to say, "These are Your words, not mine."

Only now do we fully understand what God was doing on that previous occasion. *He was teaching Moses how to pray.* This is how the sages put it, with their characteristic daring:

> Were it not written in the Torah it would be impossible to say it, but this teaches that God wrapped Himself in a tallit like a leader of prayer and taught Moses the order of prayer. He said: Whenever Israel sin, say these words and I will forgive them. (*Rosh HaShana* 17b)

That is what Moses inferred, and what he did during the episode of the spies. We now understand what God meant earlier when He said, "I am making a covenant with you." This was a covenant specifically about the Thirteen Attributes of Mercy. God was saying that when Israel said these words, He would relent and forgive. As for the anthropomorphic idea that God "wrapped Himself" in a tallit, the sages are translating the words *"vaya'avor... al panav"* (Ex. 34:6) not as "God passed before him [Moses]" but rather, "God passed [a cloak, a cloud] over His face" – so that Moses would not see His face (Malbim). The tallit is the screen separating us from God, the distance that allows God to be God and humans to be human.

No sooner does Moses pray this prayer, than God says two momentous words that will be repeated time and again during Yom Kippur: *Salaḥti kidvarekha,* "I have forgiven, as you asked" (Num. 14:20). So forgiveness for the sin of the golden calf was more than a one-time event. It gave Moses and his successors the words needed to secure divine forgiveness on other occasions also. The Thirteen Attributes of Mercy are the prayer God taught humanity, the prayer Moses used successfully after the episode of the spies.

The dual episode of the calf and the spies became an essential element of our devotions on Yom Kippur and other penitential days, the prayers we know as *Seliḥot.* Every time we say them we reenact the drama of Moses pleading for his people. *Seliḥot* take us back to the scene of Moses in the crevice of a rock at Mount Sinai as God's glory passed by. It was one of the great moments in the history of the prophets.

II. The Second Yom Kippur

But prophets are not the only type of religious leader in Judaism, and for a compelling reason. There was only one Moses. Not every generation produces a prophet. We have not had them in Judaism since Malachi two and half millennia ago.

Judaism begins in a series of transfiguring moments of epiphany. Something momentous happens. The world seems lit as if by a heavenly light. God has entered the human arena. People glimpse new possibilities. The world will never be quite the same again. So it was when Abraham first heard the call of God, when Moses encountered God in the burning bush, when the Israelites left Egypt on their way to freedom, and when the sea divided and they passed through on dry land. But how do you turn unique moments into ongoing continuity? How do you translate them into the biorhythms of succeeding generations? How do you prevent epoch-making moments fading into the distant past?

That is when we need memory and ritual. You take a unique event and turn it into a recurring ceremony. You turn linear time into cyclical time. You reenact history by writing it into the calendar. The Hebrew word for calendar, *luah*, also means "tablet." The tablets of stone are written onto the tablet of the year and thus into the tablet of the heart. The descent of Moses from the mountain in a blaze of divine light was to become not a once-only event but a regularly repeated one. Thus Yom Kippur as an annual event, the Sabbath of Sabbaths of the Jewish year, was born.

But that required someone other than a prophet. The prophet lives in the immediacy of the moment, not in the endlessly reiterated cycles of time. This required religious leadership of a different order, namely, the priest. The priest represents order, structure, continuity, the precisely formulated ritual followed in strict, meticulous obedience. Max Weber called this the routinization of charisma. The first Day of Atonement needed the intercession of a Moses, but the second and subsequent occasions required the agency of an Aaron, a High Priest. That is indeed how the Torah describes it in Leviticus 16.

The service of the High Priest on Yom Kippur was high drama. It was an event like no other. It involved strange rituals performed at no other time, such as the casting of lots on two animals, one of which was offered as a sacrifice to God, the other of which was led, bearing the sins of the people, "to Azazel." There is nothing remotely comparable in any of the other Temple rituals.

This was the moment of supreme solemnity when, each year, the High Priest atoned for the sins of the entire nation. He prepared for it for seven days in advance. Elaborate contingency measures were taken in case at the last moment he was unable to officiate. It involved an elaborate choreography of ritual and changes of garments. There were public moments when the High Priest appeared before the people robed in gold and splendor. There were also intensely private ones, as when he entered the Holy of Holies alone, dressed in a simple white tunic, and communed with God.

The transition from the first to the second Yom Kippur involved a move from prophet to priest. This is a huge difference. Prophets and priests were different kinds of people who served God in different ways. What was appropriate to one was inappropriate, even forbidden, to the other. Judaism is a religion of distinctions and differences. Only thus do we bring order to the world. Judaism radically distinguishes between priestly and prophetic sensibilities. Each has its place in the religious life. Each receives eloquent expression on Yom Kippur. But they are different, especially when it comes to atonement and sin.

III. Priests and Atonement

Some of the differences between priests and prophets are obvious. Priesthood was dynastic. It passed from father to son, from Aaron to his descendants. Prophecy was not. Moses' children did not succeed him. The son of a prophet is not necessarily a prophet. In general, the prophets were drawn from no particular tribe, class, region or occupational group. Prophecy is a uniquely individual gift that you do not inherit.

The priesthood was exclusively masculine, whereas there were women prophets as well as men. Tradition counts seven: Sarah, Miriam, Deborah, Hannah, Abigail, Huldah and Esther. Priests wore robes of office; prophets had none. Priests functioned within the precincts of the Temple; prophets lived among the people.

The authority of the priest was official, while that of the prophet was personal. That is why the prophets were so distinctive. Their personalities shaped their perception and message. Hosea was not Amos. Isaiah was not Jeremiah. Prophet and priest exemplified Max Weber's famous distinction between charismatic and traditional-legal authority.

What I want to explore here, though, is the difference between *Torat Kohanim* and *Torat Nevi'im* – the codes that guided priestly and prophetic sensibilities – in their response to the religious life, obedience and sin, atonement and repentance. We are used to thinking about these things as if they all belonged to a single system. They do now, but they did not always. When prophets and priests were the active Jewish religious leaders, they had different ways of thinking about the life of faith, so far apart that they hardly overlapped at all.

For the priest, the key words of the religious life are *kadosh*, holy, and *tahor*, pure. To be a Jew is to be *set apart*: that is what the word *kadosh*, holy, actually means. This in turn has to do with the special closeness the Jewish people have to God. Because of this we are bound to a special code of conduct that gives expression to this singularity.

It means, for example, eating only certain kinds of food and being bound to a strict discipline of sexual ethics. In *Torat Kohanim*, the priestly law, there are statutes, *ḥukkim*, that do not seem to make obvious sense in terms of conventional ethics, such as not eating meat and milk together, or not wearing clothes of mixed wool and linen, or not sowing fields with mixed seeds. All these laws have to do with the special perspective of *Torat Kohanim*.

They have to do with order. The priestly mind sees the universe in terms of distinctions, boundaries and domains, in which each object or act has its proper place and must not be mixed with another. The priest's task is to maintain boundaries and respect limits. For the priest, goodness equals order. We learn this from the way God created the world. He took chaos – *tohu vavohu* – and turned it into a finely tuned universe with its myriad life-forms, each with its ecological niche, its place in the scheme of things. A world that is ordered is good. One that is chaotic is bad and unsustainable.

So Jews are charged to respect and honor boundaries and differences by obeying the will of God, Creator of the world and Architect of its order. Priests see the world in terms of strictly defined categories: *kodesh* and *ḥol*, holy and profane; *tahor* and *tameh*, pure and impure. The key priestly verbs are *lehavdil*, "to distinguish," "to separate," "to demarcate," and *lehorot*, "to teach" in the sense of giving halakhic rulings.

Priests have a strong moral sense. The commands to love your neighbor and the stranger as yourself occur, in the Torah, in the most priestly of the books, Leviticus, and are taught alongside the *ḥukkim*, the statutes, that have no apparent moral content. The highest virtue for the priest is obedience: doing exactly as God told us to do. Prophets often acted on the spur of the moment. That is what Moses did when he smashed the tablets on seeing the golden calf. But there is absolutely no place for spontaneity in the world of the priest.

Nadav and Avihu, two of Aaron's sons, spontaneously made a fire offering at the consecration of the Tabernacle and died as a result. When priests, charged with maintaining order, act spontaneously, it is like mixing milk and meat, or matter and anti-matter. It creates disorder, and disorder in the moral universe is like entropy in the physical universe.

It means a loss of energy, a diminution of the presence of God. So when people sin, they have to restore order through the appropriate ritual.

When the Temple stood, this involved purification if you had become defiled, or the bringing of a sacrifice if you had done wrong. You had to come to the Temple because that, in the world of the priest, is where humans meet God. God is everywhere, but we meet Him only in special places at special times. Each time has its appropriate sacrifice and service, just as each prayer has its appropriate words. It is through acting exactly as God has prescribed that we restore the order we have damaged through our sins.

Listening carefully to how the Torah describes the ritual of the High Priest on Yom Kippur, we hear the key terms of the priestly sensibility:

> When he finishes bringing atonement for the holiest place and the Tent of Meeting and the altar, he shall offer up the living goat. Aaron shall press his hands onto the head of the living goat and confess all the guilt of Israel, and all of their rebellions, all of their sins…. For you will be atoned on this day and made pure; of all your sins before the Lord you shall be purified. (Lev. 16:20–21, 30)

The key themes are confession, purification and atonement, the last of which occurs a sizable twenty-three times in the space of a single chapter. The day itself, the tenth of Tishrei, is described three times in the Torah as *Yom (Ha)Kippurim*, the "Day of Atonements."

The root *k-p-r*, "atone," has a variety of meanings. It means "to cover over": Noah was told to cover (*vekhafarta*, Gen. 6:14) the ark with pitch. The gold covering of the Ark in the Tabernacle was called a *kaporet*. A *kofer* was also a ransom, a sum paid to redeem a debt or avoid a hazard (see Ex. 21:30).

Guilt, therefore, is seen as a kind of debt incurred by the sinner to God and must be redeemed by the performance of a ritual, confession, and the payment of a ransom, the sin offering. This "covers over" or obliterates the sin. It also cleanses the sinner since sin leaves a mark on the soul. It is a kind of defilement (see Nahmanides to Lev. 4:2).

Sin, for the priest, is the transgression of a boundary, and there are specific names for the different kinds of sin: *ḥet*, for an unintentional sin, *avon* for a deliberate sin, and *pesha* for a sin committed as a rebellion. All sin threatens the Divine-human harmony on which the universe depends. Confession accompanied by sacrifice restores that harmony, and the ritual itself must follow a highly structured procedure. Structure is of the essence, for the priest is the guardian of order, and only by obediently following divine instructions do we honor the order God made in creating the universe. Note that the fundamental concern of the priest is the relationship between the people and God.

Note also what is missing from the priestly account. There is nothing here about the relationship of human beings with one another. The verb *shuv*, to "return" or "repent," does not appear at all. The priest is engaged in *kapara* and *tahara*, atonement and purification, not with *teshuva*, repentance and return.

IV. Prophets and Repentance

The prophets are quite different. They use different words. They think in different ways. Here, for example, are Isaiah, Jeremiah, Hosea and Joel on the subject of repentance:

> Wash and make yourselves clean. Take your evil deeds out of My sight; stop doing wrong. Learn to do right; seek justice. Defend the oppressed. Take up the cause of the fatherless; plead the case of the widow. Come now, let us reason together, says the Lord: If your sins are like scarlet, they shall be whitened like snow; should they be as red as crimson, they shall become like wool. (Is. 1:16–18)

> Now reform your ways and your actions and obey the Lord your God. Then the Lord will relent and not bring the disaster He has pronounced against you. (Jer. 26:13)

> Return, Israel, to the Lord your God. Your sins have been your downfall! Take words with you and return to the Lord. Say to Him: "Forgive all our sins and receive us graciously, that we may offer the fruit of our lips." (Hos. 14:2–3)

Rend your heart and not your garments. Return to the Lord your God, for He is gracious and compassionate, slow to anger and abounding in loving-kindness, and He relents from sending calamity. (Joel 2:13)

This is a completely different way of thinking. The prophets are intensely concerned with social morality. They regard injustice, corruption, the neglect of the poor and the oppression of the weak as national catastrophes. They are not indifferent to the relationship between the people and God – far from it. They constantly castigate idolatry. But they see this in moral terms. It is an act of betrayal, disloyalty, faithlessness. Also they are concerned less with outward ritual than with inner remorse: "Rend your heart and not your garments." They are not opposed to ritual and sacrifice, but they are outraged when it is used as an attempt, as it were, to bribe God to avert His eyes from evil and injustice.

Note also that the prophets speak from and in the midst of history. Sin is not something that has consequences only for the spiritual relationship between the people and God. It damages the nation's fate. It threatens its future. When drought, famine, war and defeat happen it is because the people have sinned, and if they continue to do so, worse will follow.

The language the prophets use is quite different from that of the priests. Time and again they use the word the priests never use, namely "return," *shuv*, from which we get the word *teshuva*. Return to God, they say, and He will return to you. The priestly word *k-p-r*, "atone," plays almost no role whatsoever in the prophetic literature. Isaiah uses it rarely, Jeremiah only once and negatively ("Do not forgive their crimes or blot out their sins from Your sight" [18:23]). The twelve minor prophets do not use it at all (Amos uses it once [5:12] to mean a bribe). This is particularly noticeable in the book of Jonah whose entire theme is repentance.

There is one other difference between the language of priests and prophets. They both make use of the verb *s-l-ḥ*, to forgive. But the prophets use it always and only in the active form: God forgives. Priests use it exclusively in the passive form: *venislaḥ*, "it will be forgiven."

So we have two types of religious leader, the priest and the prophet, both of whom serve the same God as part of the same faith and the same people, whose visions of the spiritual-moral life are quite different. The priest thinks of sin primarily in terms of the relationship between humans and God. The prophet sees the effects of sin on society. He or she knows that if you dishonor God you will eventually dishonor human beings.

What angers the prophet is seeing people trying to have it both ways – honoring God by bringing sacrifices at the Temple while exploiting or oppressing their fellow humans. Don't think you can fool God, the prophet says. You cannot ignore Him and survive as a nation. The prophet speaks not in the language of holy and profane, pure and defiled, commandment and sin, but in terms of the great covenantal virtues: *tzedek*, righteousness, *mishpat*, justice, *hesed*, love, and *rahamim*, compassion.

The prophet does not speak about putting things right by sacrifice and confession but by a change of heart and deed, abandoning evil and returning to God. The one exception was Ezekiel, the only person to use both a prophetic and a priestly vocabulary. The reason is simple: Ezekiel was that rare phenomenon, a prophet who was also a priest (unlike Jeremiah, both roles are evident in the language of Ezekiel).

Priests and prophets belong to different worlds. The only reason we think of them together is because of the history of Yom Kippur. The first Yom Kippur was brought about by Moses, the greatest of the prophets. The second and subsequent Days of Atonement belonged to Aaron and his descendants, the High Priests.

It took historical catastrophe and a religious genius to bring the two worlds together. The catastrophe was the destruction of the Second Temple. The genius was Rabbi Akiva.

The Two Hemispheres United

It was one of the most turbulent periods in history. An ancient order was coming to an end, and almost everyone knew it. With the death of Herod in 4 BCE, Israel came under direct Roman rule. There was unrest throughout the land. Jews and Greeks vied for influence, and conflict often flared into violence. There were Jewish uprisings, brutally suppressed. Throughout Israel there were sects convinced they were living through the End of Days. In Qumran on the shores of the Dead Sea, a group of religious pietists was living in expectation of the final confrontation between the sons of light and the sons of darkness. A whole series of messianic figures emerged, each the harbinger of a new "kingdom of heaven." All were killed.

In the year 66 CE the tension erupted. Provoked by persecution, buoyed by messianic hope, Jews rose in rebellion. A heavy contingent of Roman troops under Vespasian and Titus was sent to crush the uprising. It took seven years. In 70 CE the Temple was destroyed. Three years later the last remaining outpost of zealots in the mountain fastness of Masada committed suicide rather than allow themselves to be taken captive by the Romans. Some contemporary estimates put the number of Jewish casualties during this period at over a million. It was a devastating blow.

In the year 132 there was another uprising, this time under Shimon bar Kosiva, known as Bar Kokhba and considered by some of the rabbis to be the Messiah. For a while it was a success. For two years Jews regained a fragile independence. The Roman reprisal, when it came, was merciless. The Roman historian Dio estimated that in the course of the campaign, 580,000 Jews were killed and 985 Jewish settlements destroyed. Almost an entire generation of Jewish leaders and teachers, sages and scholars, was put to death. Hadrian had Jerusalem leveled, then rebuilt as the Roman city Aelia Capitolina. Jews were forbidden entry on pain of death. It was the end of resistance and the beginning of what would eventually become the longest exile ever suffered by a people. Within a century the center of Jewish life had moved to Babylon.

All the institutions of national Jewish life were now gone. There was no Temple, no sacrificial order, no priests, no kings, no prophets, no land, no independence, and no expectation that they might soon return. With the possible exception of the Holocaust it was the most traumatic period in Jewish history. A passage in the Talmud records that at the height of the Hadrianic persecutions there were rabbis who taught that "by rights we should issue a decree that Jews should not marry and have children, so that the seed of Abraham comes to an end of its own accord" (*Bava Batra* 60b). To many it seemed as if the Jewish journey had reached its close. Where in the despair was there a route to hope?

In the encompassing turmoil one problem was acute for those whose religious imagination was most sensitive. What, in the absence of a Temple and its sacrifices, would now lift the burden of sin and guilt? Judaism is a system of high moral and spiritual demands. Without some way of resolving the tension between the ideal of perfection and the all-too-imperfect nature of human conduct, the weight of undischarged guilt would be immense.

So long as the Temple stood, the service of the High Priest on Yom Kippur was designed to secure atonement for all Israel (Lev. 16:2–34). Already, though, even before the destruction of the Temple, the priesthood no longer commanded the respect of all sections of the population. For several generations it had become enmeshed in politics. Some Hasmonean kings had served as High Priests, transgressing against the principled separation of powers in Judaism. There were times under Greek and Roman rule when the office went to the highest bidder. There were other times when the priesthood was caught up in the conflict between Pharisees and Sadducees, a serious rift in late Second Temple times. All too often the office of High Priest became a pawn in a game of power.

Many sages wrestled with this problem. One in particular, though, is associated with the conceptual revolution that occurred in the post-Temple age. Rabbi Akiva had an almost legendary life. He had grown up as an illiterate shepherd with a violent dislike of rabbis and their culture. At the insistence of his wife, he undertook a course of study and eventually became prodigiously learned, a leader of Jewish scholarship and one of its most heroic figures. Amid the despair at the destruction of the Temple, his was one of the great voices of hope. In old age he gave his support to the Bar Kokhba rebellion, and was put to a cruel death by the Romans. He remains a symbol of Jewish martyrdom.

His response to the end of the Temple and its Day of Atonement rites was not one of mourning, but a paradoxical sense of uplift. Tragedy had not defeated hope. It could even be used to bring about a spiritual advance. The Temple rites might be lost, but in their place would come something even deeper and more democratic. Far from being separated from God, the sinner was now able to come closer to the Divine Presence.

His words were these: "Happy are you, Israel: before whom do you purify yourselves, and who purifies you? Your Father in heaven" (*Yoma* 8:9).

He meant this: Now that there was no Temple and no High Priest, atonement need no longer be vicarious. The sinner could obtain forgiveness directly. All he or she needed to do was confess the sin, express remorse and resolve not to repeat it in the future. Atonement was no longer mediated by a third party. It needed no High Priest, no sacrifice and no Temple ritual. It was a direct relationship between the individual and God. This was one of rabbinic Judaism's most magnificent ideas. Jews continue to mourn the loss of the Temple and pray for its restoration, but their ability to transform grief into growth, defeat into spiritual victory, remains awe-inspiring.

I. Uniting Priest and Prophet

Essentially what Rabbi Akiva and the sages did was to bring together the priestly and prophetic ideas of atonement and return. They took from *Torat Kohanim*, the law of the priests, the idea of Yom Kippur itself – a special day in the Jewish calendar dedicated to fasting, self-affliction and the rectification of sin. The prophets never thought in terms of specific days of the year when they spoke about repentance. Any day was a good day when it came to abandoning evil and returning to God.

They also took from the service of the High Priest the idea of *viduy*, confession. The High Priest confessed three times on Yom Kippur: first for himself and his family, then for his fellow priests, then for the people as a whole. We too confess on Yom Kippur – ten times, corresponding to the ten times the High Priest used the most holy name of God.

To be sure, confession was not strictly confined to priests or the Temple. Saul and David both confessed, using the word *ḥatati*, "I have sinned," when confronted with their sins by a prophet. But the formal act of confession was mainly associated with the bringing of a sin or guilt offering, and collective confession with the service of the High Priest. Note that in confession there is no direct address to God, no argument, no pleading, no case for the defense, no plea in mitigation. Instead there is ritual. We have done wrong. We are guilty. We now wish to undergo the process that will allow us to be atoned for and cleansed.

There are other elements unique to Yom Kippur, designed to reenact the service of the Temple. During the Repetition of Musaf, we recount the whole of the High Priest's service – something we do at no other time – telling the story much as we relate the Exodus at the Seder table on Pesaḥ. Even the account, said during Musaf, of the "ten martyrs," the sages who died for their faith during the Roman era, has a priestly undertone, as if to say: Let all those who died *al Kiddush Hashem*, for the sanctification of God's name, count as our people's sacrifices to You. Let their deaths atone for our sins.

We say aloud the line, "Blessed be the name of His glorious kingdom for ever and all time," immediately after the first verse of the Shema (said silently the rest of the year) because in ancient times it was said aloud in the Temple in place of the word "Amen," which was never used in the Temple service. We prostrate ourselves four times during Musaf, something we only do on one other occasion, Rosh HaShana, again in memory of the Temple. The custom of men wearing the *kittel*, a white tunic, on Yom Kippur recalls the white robe the High Priest wore on that day when he entered the Holy of Holies. All of this is priestly.

But we also say *Seliḥot*, direct prayers to God asking for forgiveness. This, as we saw in the last section, is a supremely prophetic act, going back to Moses' two great prayers on behalf of the Jewish people, after the golden calf and the episode of the spies.

Equally prophetic are the two Haftarot we say on Yom Kippur. The first, in the morning, comes from one of the most prophetic of all utterances, the fifty-eighth chapter of Isaiah, with its insistence that true repentance is measured by the way we treat our fellow humans:

> Is this the fast I have chosen – a day when a man will oppress himself? When he bows his head like a rush in the wind, when he lays his bed with sackcloth and ashes? Is this what you call a fast, "a day for the Lord's favor"? No; this is the fast I choose: Loosen the bindings of evil, and break the slavery chain. Those who were crushed, release to freedom; shatter every yoke of slavery. Break your bread for the starving, and bring dispossessed wanderers home. When you see a person naked, clothe him: do not avert your eyes from your own flesh. (Is. 58:5–7)

This is an astonishing passage to read on a day in which we *are* fasting, humbling ourselves and bowing our heads. The afternoon Haftara, the book of Jonah, is no less of a counterintuitive choice since it concerns the repentance, not of Israel but of Israel's enemies, the Assyrians in Nineveh. Yet it too makes the point that it is not fasting as such that constitutes repentance but rather a change of heart and deed: "[All] shall cry out to God with a powerful cry; let every man turn back from his evil way, and from the violence that fills his hands. Who knows – perhaps God, too, will turn back and relent; will turn back from His burning rage, before we are all lost" (Jonah 3:8–9).

Equally striking is the following paradox. The sages ruled that Yom Kippur atones only for the sins between us and God, not for those between us and our fellow humans. *Kol Nidrei*, the legal procedure for the annulment of vows, refers only to vows between us and God. Yet the confessions, both the shorter *Ashamnu*, "We have sinned," and especially the longer *Al ḥet*, "For the sin," speak mainly of sins between us and our fellows. This is a prophetic perspective translated into the language of the priest, that is, into *viduy*, the confession that accompanied sacrifices for wrongdoing. So Yom Kippur as it developed from the days of Rabbi Akiva succeeded in uniting two religious mindsets, that of the priest and the prophet, that had been distinct and separate for more than a thousand years. It was an immense achievement.

II. Maimonides and Nahmanides on Repentance

We can gain a deeper insight into this synthesis by looking closely at a major disagreement between two of the greatest rabbis of the Middle Ages, Maimonides and Nahmanides.

Maimonides was one of the most polymathic minds the Jewish people has ever produced. Born in Spain (c. 1135) to Rabbi Maimon, a rabbi and religious judge, he spent his childhood in Cordoba, then enjoying the brief period of relative tolerance known as the *Convivencia* when Muslims, Christians and Jews lived together in relative harmony. In 1148 a radical Islamic sect, the Almohads, came to power, instituting religious persecution and forcing the Maimon family into flight. Originally they went to Fez in Morocco, then to Israel, but the Jewish community, devastated by the Crusades, offered no possibility of a livelihood, and the family eventually settled in Fustat, near Cairo, where Maimonides was to live out the rest of his days until his death in 1204. There he wrote some of the greatest works of Jewish scholarship, including the unsurpassed code of law, the *Mishneh Torah*, and the sublime if enigmatic philosophical masterpiece, *The Guide for the Perplexed.*

Nahmanides, born in Gerona, Catalonia, in 1194, was, like Maimonides, a physician as well as the greatest rabbi of his time, equally adept at Jewish law and biblical interpretation. In 1263 in Barcelona he was enlisted into one of the great confrontations between Judaism and Christianity: the public disputation, in the presence of King James I of Aragon, with Pablo Christiani, a Jewish convert to Christianity. Nahmanides spoke brilliantly, but was forced into exile in 1265 when the king was put under pressure by the Christian authorities. He traveled to Israel and set about strengthening the Jewish community in Jerusalem, establishing a yeshiva and a synagogue. It was the beginning of the recovery of a Jewish presence in the holy city.

Both men were concerned with finding the source of the command at the heart of Yom Kippur, namely *teshuva*, the duty to repent one's sins and "return" to God, but they differed utterly in their analyses. Here is Maimonides' account:

> In respect of all the commands of the Torah, positive or negative, if a person transgressed any of them, deliberately or in error, and repents and turns away from his sins, he is under a duty to confess before God, blessed be He, as it is said, "If a man or a woman sins against his fellow man, thus being untrue to God, and becoming guilty of a crime, he must confess the sin he has committed" [Num. 5:6–7]. This means verbal confession, and this confession is a positive command.
>
> How does one confess? The penitent says, "I beg of You, O Lord, I have sinned, I have acted perversely, I have transgressed before You and have done such and such; and behold, I repent

and am ashamed of my deeds and I will never do this again."
This constitutes the essence of confession. The fuller and more
detailed the confession one makes, the more praiseworthy he is.
(*Laws of Repentance* 1:1)

Note how circuitous Maimonides' prose is: *If* one commits a
sin, and *if* one then repents, *then* one must confess. It sounds as if the
command is the confession, not the repentance that precedes it. In the
superscription to the *Laws of Repentance* he puts it slightly differently.
There he says that the command is "that the sinner repent of his sin
before God and confess," as if the mitzva were *both* the repentance and
the confession.

What Maimonides is saying is that the actual command is the
confession, a verbal declaration. But confession must be sincere in order
to count, and a sincere confession presupposes that you repent of the
sin, meaning, (1) you know it was a sin, (2) you feel remorse that you
committed it, and (3) you are now formally declaring your guilt and your
determination not to repeat the offense. Repentance, for Maimonides, is
not directly commanded in the Torah. It is commanded obliquely. You
have to have it in order to fulfill the command of confession. Confession is the *ma'aseh mitzva*, the physical act, while *teshuva* is the *kiyum
mitzva*, the mental component necessary to make the act the fulfillment
of a command.

Note that Maimonides locates the mitzva in the world of the
Temple and its sacrifices. It was there that individuals confessed when
they brought sin or guilt offerings. It was there that the High Priest
confessed his and the people's sins on Yom Kippur. We might have
thought that, since confession was an accompaniment of sacrifices, when
the sacrifices ceased, so too did confession itself. However, elsewhere
(*Sefer HaMitzvot*, positive command 73) Maimonides cites the *Sifri*, an
authoritative halakhic midrash, to prove that the command of confession still holds, even though we lack the sacrifices that accompanied it
in Temple times.

In short, for Maimonides, repentance belongs to *Torat Kohanim*,
the law of the priests. It derives, ultimately, from the Sanctuary and its

rituals, the world over which Aaron and his descendants officiated. It is what we have left from the Temple.

The view of Nahmanides could not be more different. Searching for the basis of the command of *teshuva*, he turns to one of the great prophetic visions Moses outlined at the end of his life:

> When all these blessings and curses I have set before you come upon you and you take them to heart wherever the Lord your God disperses you among the nations, and when you and your children return to the Lord your God and obey Him with all your heart and with all your soul according to everything I command you today, then the Lord your God will restore your fortunes and have compassion on you and gather you again from all the nations where He scattered you. Even if you have been banished to the most distant land under the heavens, from there the Lord your God will gather you and bring you back.... The Lord will again delight in you and make you prosperous, just as He delighted in your ancestors, if you obey the Lord your God and keep His commands and decrees that are written in this Book of the Law and turn to the Lord your God with all your heart and with all your soul. (Deut. 30:1–10)

This is the passage in which Moses, lifting his eyes to the furthermost horizon of prophecy, foresees a time when the Israelites will be defeated and forced into exile. There they will come to the conclusion that this was no mere happenstance. It occurred because they had sinned and forsaken God and He in return had forsaken them. They would then return to God. He would return to them and they would return to their land.

Note that the entire passage does not mention sin or transgression, confession or sacrifice. It makes no mention of any ritual or verbal declaration. Nor does it mention the key word, *k-p-r*, "atonement," in any of its forms or inflections. There is not a single hint of *Torat Kohanim*, the world and mindset of the priest. It is a vast conspectus of history, a portrait of national decline and restoration, exile and a new beginning.

What is missed in almost every English translation is the fact that the key word in the passage is the verb *shuv*, "to return," from which the word *teshuva*, repentance, is derived. It appears no fewer than eight times in ten verses. This was clearly the decisive consideration as far as Nahmanides was concerned. If we are looking for a source of the command of *teshuva*, then we must seek a passage in which the verb occurs. Nahmanides then notes that immediately after this vision Moses adds:

> *This command* I am prescribing to you today is not too difficult for you or beyond your reach. It is not in heaven, so [that you should] say, "Who shall go up to heaven and bring it to us so that we can hear it and keep it?" It is not over the sea so [that you should] say, "Who will cross the sea and get if for us, so that we will be able to hear it and keep it?" It is something that is very close to you. It is in your mouth and in your heart, so that you can keep it. (Deut. 30:11–14)

Which is "This command"? asks Nahmanides, and answers: "This is the command of *teshuva*, repentance."

Note how very different Nahmanides' view of repentance is from that of Maimonides. For him repentance is part of the historical drama of the Jewish people. The punishment for sin is exile. Adam and Eve were exiled from the Garden of Eden. Cain was condemned to permanent exile ("You shall be a restless wanderer" [Gen. 4:12]) after murdering his brother Abel. So would the Israelites, if they sinned, suffer defeat and displacement. Hence the rich double meaning of the word *teshuva*, signifying both spiritual and physical return. If they came home spiritually to God He would bring them home physically to their land.

It would be hard to find a wider disagreement not only on the source but also the nature of the command. For Nahmanides repentance is not about a ritual of atonement but about the complete reorientation of an individual, or the people as a whole, from estrangement from God to rededication and return. Nahmanides' account locates repentance not in *Torat Kohanim*, the law of the priests, but in *Torat Nevi'im*, the world of the prophet. It is the prophet who relates spirituality to history, the state of a nation's soul to its fate in the vicissitudes of time. Where Maimonides finds *teshuva* in the world of Aaron and the priests, Nahmanides locates it in the mind of Moses and the prophets.

In the light of all we have said, we can see that Maimonides and Nahmanides were both right because they were speaking about different things. Maimonides tells us that the origin of *kapara*, atonement, is priestly. Nahmanides tells us that the basis of *teshuva*, repentance-and-return, is prophetic. It was the genius of the sages to bring these two processes together, strengthening the connection between honoring God and honoring the image of God that is our fellow human.

That, then, is Yom Kippur, a day of restoring our relationship with God, with our fellows and with the better angels of our nature. Rabbinic Judaism integrated the twin hemispheres of the Jewish brain, the priestly and prophetic mindsets. Yom Kippur still bears traces of its dual origin in the prophetic moment of the first year when Moses achieved divine forgiveness for the Israelites' sin, and the priestly nature of the second, when Aaron secured atonement for the people by his service in the Sanctuary.

III. A Republic of Free and Equal Citizens

The following speech, adapted from Ansky's play *The Dybbuk*, expresses beautifully the revolution wrought by rabbinic Judaism:

> At a certain hour, on a certain day of the year, the four supreme sanctities met together. On the Day of Atonement, the holiest day of the year, the holiest person, the High Priest, entered the holiest place, the Holy of Holies in Jerusalem, and there pronounced the holiest word, the Divine Name. Now that there is no Temple, wherever a person stands to lift his eyes to heaven becomes a Holy of Holies. Every human being created by God in His own likeness is a High Priest. Each day of a person's life is the Day of Atonement. Every word he speaks from the heart is the name of God.

At Mount Sinai in the days of Moses, God invited the Israelites to become "a kingdom of priests and a holy nation" (Ex. 19:6). All would be priests. The nation as a whole would be holy. Under the sovereignty of

God, there would be a republic of free and equal citizens held together not by hierarchy or power but by the moral bond of covenant.

It did not happen, at least not literally. Throughout the biblical era there were hierarchies. There were kings, prophets and priests. Yet ideals, repeatedly invoked, do not die. They lie like seeds in parched earth waiting for the rain. It was precisely at Israel's bleakest moment that something like the biblical vision did emerge. Monarchy, priesthood and prophecy ceased, and were succeeded by more egalitarian institutions. Prayer took the place of sacrifice. The synagogue replaced the Temple. Repentance substituted for the rites of the High Priest.

Judaism, no longer a religion of land and state, kings and armies, became a faith built around homes, schools and communities. For eighteen hundred years without a state Jews were a nation linked not by relationships of power but by a common commitment to the covenant. Jewry, no longer a sovereign nation, became a global people. From that point onward every Jew in politics became a king, in study a prophet, and in prayer, especially on Yom Kippur, a priest.

Out of catastrophe, the Jewish people, inspired by sages like Rabbi Akiva, brought about a revolution in the life of the spirit, foreshadowed at Mount Sinai but not fully realized until more than a thousand years later, and perhaps not fully appreciated even now. The Judaism of the sages – a Judaism without the revelatory events or manifest miracles of the Bible – achieved what no other religion has ever done, sustaining the identity of a people, dispersed, stateless and largely powerless, everywhere a minority and often a despised one, for two millennia, leading it in generation after generation to heights of scholarship and piety that transfigured lives and lit them with an inner fire of love and longing and religious passion that turned pain into poetry and transformed Yom Kippur from a day on which one man atoned for all, into one on which all atoned for each in a covenant of human solidarity in the direct unmediated presence of God.

New Insights into Ancient Texts

Three passages in the Yom Kippur prayers have occasioned much speculation, and in this section I offer a new interpretation of each. First is *Kol Nidrei*, the prayer-that-is-not-a-prayer with which Yom Kippur begins. Second is the service of the High Priest, in the Tabernacle and later the Temple, especially the rite of the goat sent to Azazel, the original "scapegoat." What was the meaning of this strange procedure? Third is the poem said on *Kol Nidrei* night, "Like clay in the potter's hands," misunderstood by many commentators and translators.

I. Kol Nidrei

Kol Nidrei is the strangest prayer ever to capture the religious imagination. First, it is not a prayer at all. It is not even a confession. It is a dry legal formula for the annulment of vows. It is written in Aramaic. It does not mention God. It is not part of the service. It does not require a synagogue. And it was disapproved of, or at least questioned, by generations of halakhic authorities.

The first time we hear of *Kol Nidrei*, in the ninth century, it is already being opposed by Rav Natronai Gaon (Responsa 1:185), the first of many sages through the centuries who found it problematic. In their view, one cannot annul the vows of an entire congregation this way. Even if one could, one should not, since it may lead people to treat vows lightly. Besides which, there has already been an annulment of vows ten days earlier, on the morning before Rosh HaShana. This is mentioned explicitly in the Talmud (*Nedarim* 23b). There is no mention of an annulment on Yom Kippur.

Rabbeinu Tam, Rashi's grandson, was particularly insistent in arguing that the kind of annulment *Kol Nidrei* represents cannot be retroactive. It cannot apply to vows already taken. It can only be a preemptive qualification of vows in the future. Accordingly, he insisted on changing its wording so that *Kol Nidrei* refers not to vows from last year to this, but from this year to next (*Sefer HaYashar* 100). However, the custom developed to say both – a compromise at the cost of coherence. It is one thing to seek to undo vows we have already made, quite another to preclude vows we might make in the future.

Disturbingly, *Kol Nidrei* created hostility on the part of non-Jews, who said it showed that Jews did not feel bound to honor their promises since they vitiated them on the holiest night of the year. In vain it was repeatedly emphasized that *Kol Nidrei* applies only to vows between us and God, not those between us and our fellow humans. Throughout the Middle Ages, and in some places until the eighteenth century, in lawsuits with non-Jews, Jews were forced to take a special *Oath More Judaico*, because of this concern.

So there were communal and halakhic reasons not to say *Kol Nidrei*, yet it survived all the doubts and misgivings. It remains the quintessential expression of the awe and solemnity of the day. Its undiminished power defies all obvious explanations. Somehow it seems to point to something larger than itself, whether in Jewish history or the inner heartbeat of the Jewish soul.

Several historians have argued that it acquired its pathos from the phenomenon of forced conversions, whether to Christianity or Islam, that occurred in several places in the Middle Ages, most notably Spain and Portugal in the fourteenth and fifteenth century. Jews would be offered the choice: convert or suffer persecution. Sometimes it was: convert or be expelled. At times it was even: convert or die. Some Jews did convert. They were known in Hebrew as *anusim* (people who acted under coercion). In Spanish they were known as *conversos*, or contemptuously as *marranos* (swine).

Many of them remained Jews in secret, and once a year on the night of Yom Kippur they would make their way in secret to the synagogue to seek release from the vows they had taken to adopt another faith, on the compelling grounds that they had no other choice. For them, coming to the synagogue was like *coming home*, the root meaning of *teshuva*.

There are obvious problems with this hypothesis. Firstly, *Kol Nidrei* was in existence several centuries *before* the era of forced conversions. So historian Joseph S. Bloch suggested that *Kol Nidrei* may have originated in the much-earlier Christian persecution of Jews in Visigoth Spain, when in 613 Sisebur issued a decree that all Jews should either convert or be expelled, anticipating the Spanish expulsion of 1492. Even so, it is unlikely that *conversos* would have taken the risk of being discovered practicing Judaism. Had they done so during the centuries in which the Inquisition was in force, they would have risked torture, trial and death.

Yet the connection between *Kol Nidrei* and Jews estranged from the community continues to tantalize, and may be the explanation for the preceding passage introduced by Rabbi Meir of Rothenburg in the thirteenth century: "By the authority of the heavenly and earthly court we grant permission to pray with the transgressors." This constitutes the formal lifting of a ban of excommunication and was a way of welcoming outcasts back into the community. The fact remains, though, that the text of *Kol Nidrei* makes no reference to conversion, return, identity or atonement. It is what it is: simply an annulment of vows.

Others have suggested that it is not the words of *Kol Nidrei* that have ensured its survival, but the music, the ancient, moving melody that immediately evokes a mood of drama and expectancy as the leader of prayer turns toward heaven, pleading on behalf of the congregation. The tune of *Kol Nidrei* is one of those known as *miSinai*, "from Sinai," meaning in this context, of great antiquity, though probably it was composed in Rhineland Germany in the age of the Crusades. The music is indeed uniquely soulful. Beethoven chose the same opening sequence of notes for the sixth movement of his *String Quartet in C sharp minor, opus 131*, one of his most sublime compositions. Already in the fifteenth century we read of rabbis who sought to rectify the text of *Kol Nidrei*, only to find their suggestions rejected on the grounds that they would interfere with the melodic phrasing.

The Ashkenazi melody, rising from diminuendo to fortissimo in the course of its threefold repetition, has intense power. Music, since the Israelites sang a song to God at the Reed Sea, has been the language of the soul as it reaches out toward the unsayable. Yet rather than solve the problem, this suggestion only deepens it. Why chant a melody at all to a text that is not a prayer but a legal process?

So the theories as they stand do not satisfy.

To understand *Kol Nidrei* we need to go back to a unique feature of Tanakh, without counterpart in any other religion. Time and again we find that the dialogue between God and the prophets takes the form of a legal challenge. Sometimes, especially in the books of Hosea and Micah, the plaintiff is God and the accused, the children of Israel. At other times, as when Abraham argues with God over the fate of Sodom, or Jeremiah or Habakkuk or Job protest the sufferings of the innocent, the roles are reversed. Always the subject is justice, and the context, the covenant between God and Israel. This genre – the dialogue between God and humanity structured as a courtroom drama – is known as the *riv* ("contention, dispute, accusation") pattern, and it is central to Judaism.

It emerges from the logic of *covenant*, Judaism's fundamental idea. A covenant is an agreement between two or more parties who, each respecting the dignity and freedom of the other, come together to pledge their mutual loyalty. In human terms the closest analogy is a marriage. In political terms it is a treaty between two nations. Only in Judaism is the idea given religious dignity (Christianity borrowed the idea of covenant from Judaism but gave it a somewhat different interpretation). It means that God, having liberated the Israelites from slavery in Egypt, adopts them as His *am segula*, His specially cherished nation, while the Israelites accept God as their Sovereign, the Torah as their written constitution and their mission as "a kingdom of priests and a holy nation" (Ex. 19:6) or, as Isaiah puts it, God's "witnesses" in the world (Is. 43–44).

The covenant bestows an unrivaled dignity on humans. Judaism acknowledges, as do most faiths, that God is infinite and we infinitesimal, God is eternal and we ephemeral, God is everything and we next to nothing. But Judaism makes the momentous claim in the opposite direction, that we are "God's partners in the work of creation" (*Shabbat* 10a and 119b). We are not tainted by original sin; we are not incapable of greatness; we are God's stake in the world. Tanakh tells an astonishing love story: about God's love for a people to whom He binds Himself in covenant, a covenant He never breaks, rescinds or changes however many times we betray it and Him. The covenant is law as love and loyalty.

Hence the model of the courtroom drama when either partner feels that the other has not honored the terms of the agreement. Before the impersonal bar of justice, God may accuse Israel of abandoning Him, or sometimes the roles are reversed and the prophets challenge God on what they perceive as a lack of justice in the world. This is a consistent theme in both Tanakh and the rabbinic literature. It also had a major practical influence on synagogue life.

Any Jew who felt he or she had suffered an injustice could interrupt the reading of the Torah in synagogue (*ikuv keria*) and present their case before the congregation. The plaintiff would mount the *bima*, bang three times on the table and say, "I am delaying the Torah reading." He would explain why he had chosen to present his case directly to the community instead of a court or Beit Din. He would then tell the members of the community that he was depending on them for truth and justice, and one of the leaders of the congregation would accept the responsibility.

The case would be discussed, the *gabbai* would mount the *bima* and announce the names of three arbitrators (*borerim*) who had been chosen to hear the case, and the deadline for settling the disagreement. Usually this was accepted, but if the plaintiff still felt unfairly treated, he could continue to delay the Torah reading. Yaffa Eliach, who describes how this worked in Poland in the interwar years, says that it "proved a potent social weapon, quite often providing the community with a satisfactory and speedy resolution to extremely knotty problems."[5]

The synagogue, in other words, could be turned into a court of law. That is the function of *Kol Nidrei*. Precisely because it is not a prayer but a legal process, it signals that what is about to happen in the next twenty-five hours is something more and other than prayer in the conventional sense.

The prayers of Yom Kippur are different from those of any other festival. They include a legal act, confession, a plea of guilt that rightly belongs in a court of law. Physically, the synagogue looks like it does the rest of the year, but functionally it has changed. The Beit Knesset has become a Beit Din. The synagogue is now a court of law. Sitting on the Throne of Justice is God Himself and we are the prisoners at the bar. The trial that began on Rosh HaShana has reached its last day. We are the accused, and we are about to be judged on the evidence of our lives. So *Kol Nidrei*, the prayer-that-is-not-a-prayer, transforms the house of prayer into a law court, providing the setting and mood for the unique drama that will reach its climax at Ne'ila when the court rises, the Judge is ready to leave and the verdict, written, is about to be sealed.

5. Yaffa Eliach, *There Once Was a World* (New York: Little, Brown and Company, 1998), 84–87.

That is the first dimension of *Kol Nidrei,* but we can go a level deeper.

How, after all, does *teshuva* work? We confess our wrongs, express remorse and resolve not to repeat, but how can we undo the past? Surely, what's done is done. The asymmetry of time means that we can affect the future but not the past. However, it is not quite so. *The release of vows that takes place through* Kol Nidrei *constitutes a legal precedent – the only one – for what we seek, through* teshuva, *to achieve for our sins.* The ground on which we seek annulment of vows is *ḥarata,* "remorse." The fact that we now regret having taken the vow is the reason the sages were able to say that full intent – an essential element of a valid vow – was lacking from the outset.

But this is precisely what we do when we confess our sins and express our remorse for them. We thereby signal retroactively that full intent was lacking from our sins. Had we known then what we know now, we would not have acted as we did. Therefore we did not really mean to do what we did. This is what Resh Lakish meant when he said that *teshuva* has the power retroactively to turn deliberate sins into inadvertent ones (*Yoma* 86b), and inadvertent sins can be forgiven. In fact this is why, immediately after *Kol Nidrei,* we recite the biblical verse that says: "All the congregation of Israel will be forgiven…for they sinned without intent [*bishgaga*]" (Num. 15:26). So both the annulment of vows and *teshuva* share the power of remorse to change or mitigate the past and liberate us from its bonds.

But there is a third level of significance to *Kol Nidrei* that is deeper still. Recall that Yom Kippur only exists in virtue of the fact that Moses secured God's forgiveness of the Israelites after the sin of the golden calf, descending from the mountain on the tenth of Tishrei with a new set of tablets to replace those he had smashed in anger at their sin.

How did Moses secure God's forgiveness of the people? The text introducing Moses' prayer begins with the Hebrew words, *Vayeḥal Moshe.* Normally these are translated as "Moses besought, implored, entreated, pleaded or attempted to pacify" God (Ex. 32:11). However, *the same verb is used in the context of annulling or breaking a vow* (Num. 30:3). On this basis the sages advanced a truly remarkable interpretation:

[*Vayehal Moshe* means] "Moses *absolved God of His vow.*" When the Israelites made the golden calf, Moses sought to persuade God to forgive them, but God said, "I have already taken an oath that *whoever sacrifices to any god other than the Lord must be punished* [Ex. 22:19]. I cannot retract what I have said." Moses replied, "Lord of the universe, You have given me the power to annul oaths, for You taught me that one who takes an oath cannot break his word but a scholar can absolve him. I hereby absolve You of Your vow." (Abridged from Exodus Raba 43:4)

According to the sages, *the original act of divine forgiveness on which Yom Kippur is based came about through the annulment of a vow,* when Moses annulled the vow of God.

If this is so, we understand precisely why *Kol Nidrei* was chosen to introduce the prayers of Yom Kippur:

1. It transforms the synagogue into a courtroom, and prayer into a trial.
2. It establishes the logic of atonement through the power of *harata,* "remorse," retroactively to vitiate the intention behind the deed, thus rendering our sins unwitting (*beshogeg*) and hence forgivable.
3. An act of annulment of a vow – the sages' interpretation of Moses' daring plea to God after the sin of the golden calf – constitutes the historical precedent for Yom Kippur.

Judaism has been accused over the centuries of being a religion of law, not love. This is precisely untrue. Judaism is a religion of law *and* love, for without law there is no justice, and even with law (indeed, *only* with law) there is still mercy, compassion and forgiveness. God's great gift of love was law: the law that establishes human rights and responsibilities, that treats rich and poor alike, that allows God to challenge humans but also humans to challenge God, the law studied by every Jewish child, the law written in letters of black fire on white fire that burns in our hearts, making Jews among the most passionate fighters for justice the world has ever known.

Law without love is harsh, but love without law is anarchy and eventually turns to hate. So in the name of the love-of-law and the law-of-love, we ask God to release us from our vows and from our sins for the same reason: that we regret and have remorse for both. The power of *Kol Nidrei* has less to do with forced conversions, or even music, than with the courtroom drama, unique to Judaism, in which we stand, giving an account of our lives, our fate poised between God's justice and compassion.

II. The Scapegoat

The strangest element of the service on Yom Kippur in Temple times was the ritual of the two goats, one offered as a sacrifice, the other sent away into the desert "to Azazel." They were brought before the High Priest, to all intents and purposes indistinguishable from one another: they were chosen to be as similar as possible to one another in size and appearance. Lots were drawn, one bearing the words "To the Lord," the other, "To Azazel." The one on which the lot "To the Lord" fell was offered as a sacrifice. Over the other, the High Priest confessed the sins of the nation and it was then taken away into the desert hills outside Jerusalem where it plunged to its death. Tradition tells us that a red thread would be attached to its horns, half of which was removed before the animal was sent away. If the rite had been effective, the red thread would turn to white.

Sin and guilt offerings were common in ancient Israel, but this ceremony was unique. Normally confession was made over the animal to be offered as a sacrifice. In this case confession was made over the goat *not* offered as a sacrifice. Why the division of the offering into two? Why two identical animals whose fate, so different, was decided by the drawing of a lot? And who or what was Azazel?

The word Azazel appears nowhere else in Scripture, and three major theories emerged as to its meaning. According to the sages and Rashi it meant "a steep, rocky or hard place," in other words a description of its destination. According to Ibn Ezra (cryptically) and Nahmanides (explicitly), Azazel was the name of a spirit or demon, one of the fallen angels referred to in Genesis 6:2. The third interpretation is that the word simply means "the goat [*ez*] that was sent away [*azal*]." Hence the English word "(e)scapegoat" coined by William Tyndale in his 1530 English translation of the Bible.

Maimonides offers the most compelling explanation, that the ritual was intended as a symbolic drama:

> There is no doubt that sins cannot be carried like a burden, and taken off the shoulder of one being to be laid on that of another being. But these ceremonies are of a symbolic character, and serve to impress men with a certain idea, and to induce them to repent; as if to say, we have freed ourselves of our previous deeds, have cast them behind our backs, and removed them from us as far as possible. (*Guide for the Perplexed*, III:46)

This makes sense, but the question remains. Why was this ritual different from all other sin or guilt offerings? Why two goats rather than one?

The simplest answer is that the High Priest's service on Yom Kippur was intended to achieve something other and more than ordinary sacrifices occasioned by sin. The Torah specifies two objectives, not one: "For on this day you will be atoned and made pure; of all your sins before the Lord you shall be purified" (Lev. 16:30). Normally all that was aimed at was atonement, *kapara*. On Yom Kippur something else was aimed at: cleansing, purification, *tahara*. Atonement is for acts. Purification is for persons. Sins leave stains on the character of those who commit them, and these need to be cleansed before we can undergo catharsis and begin anew.

Sin defiles. King David felt stained after his adultery with Bathsheba: "Wash me thoroughly of my iniquity and cleanse me of my sin" (Ps. 51:4). Shakespeare has Macbeth say, after his crime, "Will these hands ne'er be clean?" The ceremony closest to the rite of the scapegoat – where an animal was let loose rather than sacrificed – was the ritual for someone who was being cleansed of a skin disease:

> If they have been healed of their defiling skin disease, the priest shall order that *two live clean birds* and some cedar wood, scarlet yarn and hyssop be brought for the person to be cleansed. Then

the priest shall order that *one of the birds be sacrificed* over fresh water in a clay pot. He is then to take the live bird…. And he is *to release the live bird in the open fields.* (Lev. 14:4–7)

The released bird, like the scapegoat, was sent away carrying the impurity, the stain. Clearly this is psychological. A moral stain is not something physical. It exists in the mind, the emotions, the soul. It is hard to rid oneself of the feeling of defilement when you have committed a wrong, even when you know it has been forgiven. Some symbolic action seems necessary. The survival of such rites as *Tashlikh,* the "casting away" of sins on Rosh HaShana, and *Kaparot,* "atonements, expiations," on the eve of Yom Kippur – the first involving crumbs, the second a live chicken – is evidence of this. Both practices were criticized by leading halakhic authorities yet both survived for the reason Maimonides gives. It is easier to feel that defilement has gone if we have had some visible representation of its departure. We feel cleansed once we see it go somewhere, carried by something. This may not be rational, but then neither are we, much of the time.

That is the simplest explanation. The sacrificed goat represented *kapara,* atonement. The goat sent away symbolized *tahara,* cleansing of the moral stain. There is however an additional suggestion made by the Midrash, the *Zohar* and the fifteenth-century Spanish commentator Abrabanel that takes us to an altogether deeper level of symbolism. All three note a series of connections, verbal or visual, between the two goats and the sibling rivalry between Jacob and Esau.

Two identical goats suggest twins, and Jacob and Esau are the Torah's most notable (if non-identical) twins. Two goats also play a part in their story. When Rebecca hears that Isaac is about to bless Esau, she tells Jacob, "Go out to the flock and bring me *two choice young goats,* so I can prepare some tasty food for your father, such as he likes" (Gen. 27:9).

The Hebrew word used for "goat" in Leviticus 16 is *se'ir,* which also means "hairy." This is the word used to describe Esau at birth ("His whole body was like a hairy garment" [Gen. 25:25]) and later when Jacob was about to take Esau's blessing ("But my brother Esau is a hairy man" [Gen. 27:11]). Esau's territory throughout the Bible is Mount Seir. The red thread attached to the goat also has Esau connections. His alternative name, Edom, means "red," either because his hair was red at birth (Gen. 25:25) or because of the red lentil soup for which he traded his birthright (25:30). The keyword of Leviticus 16 is *k-p-r*, "atone." It appears twenty-three times in this one chapter. Significantly, the only time it appears in the sense of "atone" in Genesis is when Jacob, about to meet Esau after an absence of twenty-two years, sends messengers with gifts, saying, "I will pacify him [*akhapra panav*] with these gifts I am sending on ahead; later, when I see him, perhaps he will receive me" (32:20).

If there *is* a connection between the scapegoat and the rivalry between Jacob and Esau, what is it? A clue is offered by the analysis of sacrificial rites by the French scholar Rene Girard in his classic work, *Violence and the Sacred*. Girard argues that (1) the primary religious act is sacrifice; (2) sacrifice is always an attempt to curb violence within society; and (3) the primary source of violence is sibling rivalry.

Girard takes issue with Freud who argued that violence is born in the tension between fathers and sons: the Oedipus and Laius complexes. Genesis supports Girard. One of its key themes is sibling rivalry – between Cain and Abel, Isaac and Ishmael, Jacob and Esau, and Joseph and his brothers. In at least three of these cases, violence is waiting in the wings and in one, Cain and Abel, there is actual fratricide.

Girard suggests that the origin of violence is "mimetic desire," that is, *the desire to be someone else, to have what they have*. The classic instances of this in literature usually have to do with twins. Non-biblical examples are, in Greek myth, Oedipus' sons Eteocles and Polynices, and in Roman folklore, Romulus and Remus. Girard states that "the proliferation of enemy brothers in Greek myth and in dramatic adaptations of myth implies the continual presence of a sacrificial crisis" – that is, without sacrifice there is violence between siblings, at least one of whom wants what the other has.

Turning to Esau and Jacob, this is the dominant theme of their early life. Jacob buys Esau's birthright, takes Esau's blessing and when asked by his blind father Isaac, "Who are you, my son?" replies, "I am Esau your firstborn" (Gen. 27:18–19). Even when the twins were born, Jacob was clinging to Esau's heel. Jacob is the supreme instance in the Torah of mimetic desire.

It can be hard for us today to realize that there was once a time when Jacob and Esau were not seen in black-and-white terms. Rabbinic tradition tends to give Jacob all the virtues, Esau all the vices (except in honoring his father, where all agree that he was exemplary). Already in Tanakh we find this contrast in the statement of Malachi (1:2–3) that God loves Jacob and hates Esau. But Malachi was the last of the prophets, and two earlier prophets, Hosea and Jeremiah, saw matters in a very different light.

Hosea says: "The Lord has a charge to bring against Judah; He will punish Jacob according to his ways and repay him according to his deeds. In the womb he grasped his brother's heel" (Hos. 12:3–4). Jeremiah says, in a passage laden with echoes of the Jacob story, "Beware of your friends; do not trust your brothers, for every brother behaves like Jacob [*kol aḥ akov Yaakov*]" (Jer. 9:3). Hosea and Jeremiah are criticizing Jacob for his behavior toward Esau. Both are speaking about sin and the need for repentance. The Jeremiah passage is the Haftara for Tisha B'Av, the saddest day of the year.

In the haunting passage (Gen. 32:24–32) in which Jacob wrestles, alone at night, with an unnamed adversary, he finally throws off his mimetic desire to be like Esau. The stranger, who refuses to be named, was identified by the sages as "the guardian angel of Esau" ("*saro shel Esav*," Genesis Raba 77:3, 78:3). He asks Jacob to let him go. Jacob says, "I will not let you go until you bless me." The stranger then gives him a new name, Israel. A new name in this context means a new identity. Jacob will no longer be *Yaakov*, the child who would not let go of his brother's heel (Gen. 25:26). He will be content to be himself, "the man who wrestles with [or, who has become great before] man and God" (Gen. 32:28). At that point, Jacob lets go. It is the turning point in his life.

The next morning he meets Esau after their long separation. He bows down to him seven times, calls him "my lord," and himself "your servant," and says about the huge gift of cattle which Esau is reluctant to accept, "Please *take my blessing* that is brought to you, for God has shown me favor and I have everything" (33:11). The reference is to the blessing Jacob took pretending to be Esau, in which Isaac said, "May nations serve you and peoples *bow down to you*. Be *lord over your brothers*, and may the sons of your mother bow down to you" (Gen. 27:29). By bowing down to Esau and calling him "my lord," Jacob is showing that he no longer wants his brother's blessing and is content with his own ("I have everything").

Putting all this together we arrive at a dramatic conclusion. (1) *The worst sin – it caused the Flood – is violence;* (2) *the greatest source of violence in Genesis is sibling rivalry, one person wanting the blessing that rightly belongs to another;* (3) *the antidote to violence is to stop wanting to be someone else and to be content to be yourself.* Jacob and Esau were able to meet, embrace and peaceably go their separate ways as soon as Jacob was content to be himself and no longer wanted Esau's blessings. So it is with us. We can live at peace with the world when we are at peace with ourselves. If we seek to cure ourselves of the will to sin, we must let go of the desire to have someone else's blessings.

The ritual of the two identical goats, one of which was sent away bearing with it our sins, can then be seen to symbolize the two identities that live in every troubled heart: the one that is myself and the one that is not-myself. *When I learn to let the "not-myself" go, as the goat was let go on Yom Kippur, I find inner peace and can live at peace with the world.* The goat sent away is the Esau that lived in Jacob's mind until, one night wrestling with a stranger, Jacob learned to let go, and in that act became Israel, the father of the Jewish people, content to be itself, no longer seeking the identity or the blessings of others.

III. Of Potters and Clay

One poem said on *Kol Nidrei* night has long confused commentators and translators, the one beginning, "Like clay in the potter's hands." What has puzzled them is the refrain, "Look to the covenant and disregard our inclination." Many have understood "the covenant" to be a reference to the Thirteen Attributes of Mercy, about which the Talmud says that God made a covenant that this prayer would not go unanswered (*Rosh HaShana* 17b). They have interpreted *Yetzer* as "the Accuser," that is, the angel, Satan, who is prosecuting counsel on the Day of Judgment.

However, the poem is in fact about an earlier covenant, and the word *yetzer* means "inclination," not "Accuser." The refrain is based on a remarkable midrash that weaves together four biblical verses – two from the story of Noah and the Flood, and two from the prophets Isaiah and Jeremiah – to provide a stunning account of the human condition and a powerful plea for the defense of those who sin.

The story begins with the moment in the book of Genesis when God decided to bring a flood:

> God saw that man's wickedness on earth was increasing. Every inclination [*yetzer*] of his innermost thought was only for evil, all day long. God regretted that He had made man on earth, and He was pained to His very core. (Gen. 6:5–6)

God then brought a flood that wiped out everything He had made other than Noah, his family and the animals he brought with him into the ark. Eventually the flood ended, the waters receded, and Noah and his entourage set foot on dry land to begin the story again. Noah made an offering to God, which moved God to vow that never again would He punish humanity in this wholesale way:

> God said to Himself, "Never again will I curse the soil because of man, for the inclination [*yetzer*] of man's heart is evil from his youth. I will never again strike down all life as I have just done." (Gen. 8:21)

The contradiction between the two passages is glaring. In Genesis 6, man's inclination was a reason for God to bring a flood. In Genesis 8, it has become a reason for God *not* to bring another flood. How are we to understand this?

The sages made an intuitive connection between the word *yetzer*, "inclination," and *yotzer*, "creator," "former," "molder," "shaper." The verb *y-tz-r* is the one used in Genesis 2:7 to describe the creation of the first man: "Then the Lord God formed [*vayitzer*] the man from the dust of the earth and breathed into his nostrils the breath of life." More specifically, *yotzer* also means "potter," and this led the sages to two other biblical verses. One appears in the book of Jeremiah. The prophet has been told by God to go the house of the local potter and watch him as he shapes the clay. Then Jeremiah hears God saying:

> "Can I not do with you, Israel, as this potter does?" declares the Lord. "Like clay in the hand of the potter [*yotzer*], so are you in My hand, Israel." (Jer. 18:6)

Jeremiah heard this as a warning of imminent catastrophe. The people were sinning and they were about to suffer defeat and exile at the hands of the Babylonians. Israel could do nothing to avoid this fate except to repent. Without God, all attempts to defeat their enemy would fail. They were in God's hands, like the clay on the potter's wheel.

Isaiah, however, took the same image and gave it a quite different slant:

> Yet You, Lord, are our Father. We are the clay, You are our Potter [*Yotzreinu*]; we are all the work of Your hand. Do not be angry beyond measure, Lord; do not remember our sins forever. (Is. 64:7–8)

Forgive us, says Isaiah, for we are what You made us. If we do wrong, it is because You gave us the freedom to do wrong. If we disappoint You, remember it is You who shaped us, formed us, made us what we are. You are the Potter, we merely the clay in Your hands.

Out of this array of verses spanning the centuries, and playing on the connection between *yetzer* and *yotzer*, "inclination" and "potter," the sages constructed the following remarkable midrash:

> What is the meaning of "*We are the clay, You are our Potter*"? Israel said: "Master of the universe, You have caused it to be written about us, '*Like clay in the hand of the potter, so are you in My hand, Israel.*' Therefore do not leave us even though we sin and provoke You, for we are merely the clay and You are the Potter. Consider: If a potter makes a jar and leaves a pebble in it, when it comes out of the furnace it will leak from the hole left by the pebble and lose

the liquid poured into it. Who caused the jar to leak and lose its liquid? The potter who left the pebble in the jar as it was being made." This is how Israel pleaded before God: "Master of the universe, You created in us an evil inclination from our youth, as it says, *for the inclination of man's heart is evil from his youth*, and it is this that has caused us to sin, since You have not removed from us the inclination that instigates us to sin." (Exodus Raba 46:4)

We now see how the sages understood the change in God's relation to the world before and after the Flood. Before the Flood, God was exasperated at the human capacity for evil, the *yetzer*. After the Flood, however, seeing Noah's devotion, God realizes that it is not the human capacity for evil that is remarkable. It is our capacity for good. We do evil because we are flesh and blood. We are physical. We have instinctual drives. We are clay, not fire; mortals, not angels. God formed us from the dust of the earth. Dust we are, and to dust we return.

"How then can I punish them for their *yetzer* if I am their *Yotzer*?" That is the thought God had after the Flood. It was then that He made a covenant with Noah that He would never again destroy humanity. Many centuries later the same dialectic occurs in the prophecies of Jeremiah and Isaiah. He reminds Jeremiah of His total power over the fate of nations. But the powerlessness of humanity in the face of God serves Isaiah as the great plea for the defense: How can You blame us for what we are if You made us what we are?

Isaiah's prayer serves as the basis for the poet to say we are "like clay in the potter's hands…look to the covenant and disregard our inclination." We have a *yetzer* because God is the *Yotzer*. We have instinctual drives that lead us to sin because that is how we were made, creatures of earth with earthly passions, physical beings imprisoned in our physicality. We are, said Hamlet, the "quintessence of dust." The poet throws himself on the mercy of God expressed in the covenant He made with Noah after the Flood when He said, "Never again will I curse the soil because of man, for the inclination of man's heart is evil from his youth."

Is this, considered impartially, an adequate defense? Can we blame our sins on God who made us? In general terms, no. For God gave us the power to defeat the inclination. That is what He said to Cain at the dawn of the human story: "Sin is crouching at your door; it desires to have you, but you can master it" (Gen. 4:7).

Nonetheless, tonight we are on trial, and the poet is concerned less to state a metaphysical truth than to throw himself on the mercy of the Judge, reminding Him of the time when He first made a covenant of compassion and forbearance with humankind. This is, in short, a plea in the great Judaic tradition of audacity in prayer, about which the Talmud says, "*Ḥutzpa*, even toward Heaven, helps" (*Sanhedrin* 105a).

As with *Kol Nidrei* so with "Like clay in the potter's hands," this is less a conventional prayer than a judicial hearing in which counsel for the defense pleads with every argument at his disposal, from confession to self-abasement, to the annulment of vows, to a reminder of the great moment of divine compassion after the Flood when God forgave humanity for merely being human. An ultimate truth? No. Rather a prayer said in the confidence borne of the love God has for us, His human children, the work of His hands.

Yom Kippur – How It Changes Us

To those who fully open themselves to it, Yom Kippur is a life-transforming experience. It tells us that God, who created the universe in love and forgiveness, reaches out to us in love and forgiveness, asking us to love and forgive others. God never asked us not to make mistakes. All He asks is that we acknowledge our mistakes, learn from them, grow through them and make amends where we can.

No religion has held such a high view of human possibility. The God who created us in His image gave us freedom. We are not tainted by original sin, destined to fail, caught in the grip of an evil only divine grace can defeat. To the contrary, we have within us the power to choose life. Together we have the power to change the world.

Nor are we, as some scientific materialists claim, mere concatenations of chemicals, a bundle of selfish genes blindly replicating themselves into the future. Our souls are more than our minds, our minds are more than our brains, and our brains are more than mere chemical impulses responding to stimuli. Human freedom – the freedom to choose to be better than we were – remains a mystery but it is not a mere given. Freedom is like a muscle and the more we exercise it, the stronger and healthier it becomes.

Judaism constantly asks us to exercise our freedom. To be a Jew is not to go with the flow, to be like everyone else, to follow the path of least resistance, to worship the conventional wisdom of the age. To the contrary, to be a Jew is to have the courage to live in a way that is not the way of everyone. Each time we eat, drink, pray or go to work, we are conscious of the demands our faith makes on us, to live God's will and be one of His ambassadors to the world. Judaism always has been, perhaps always will be, countercultural.

In ages of collectivism, Jews emphasized the value of the individual. In ages of individualism, Jews built strong communities. When most of humanity was consigned to ignorance, Jews were highly literate. When others were building monuments and amphitheaters, Jews were building schools. In materialistic times they kept faith with the spiritual. In ages of poverty they practiced *tzedaka* so that none would lack the essentials of a dignified life. The sages said that Abraham was called *haIvri*, "the Hebrew," because all the world was on one side (*ever ehad*) and Abraham on the other (Genesis Raba 42:8). To be a Jew is to swim against the current, challenging the idols of the age whatever the idol, whatever the age.

So, as our ancestors used to say, "*S'iz schver tzu zein a Yid*" – "It is not easy to be a Jew." But if Jews have contributed to the human heritage out of all proportion to our numbers, the explanation lies here. Those of whom great things are asked become great – not because they are inherently better or more gifted than others but because they feel themselves challenged, summoned, to greatness.

Few religions have asked more of their followers. There are 613 commandments in the Torah. Jewish law applies to every aspect of our being, from the highest aspirations to the most prosaic details of quotidian life. Our library of sacred texts – Tanakh, Mishna, Gemara, Midrash, codes and commentaries – is so vast that no lifetime is long enough to master it. Theophrastus, a pupil of Aristotle, sought a description that would explain to his fellow Greeks what Jews are. The answer he came up with was, "a nation of philosophers."

So high does Judaism set the bar that it is inevitable that we should fall short time and again. This means that forgiveness was written into the script from the beginning. God, said the sages, sought to create the world under the attribute of strict justice but He saw that it could not stand. What did He do? He added mercy to justice, compassion to retribution, forbearance to the strict rule of law. God forgives. Judaism is a religion, the world's first, of forgiveness.

Not every civilization is as forgiving as Judaism. There were religions that never forgave Jews for refusing to convert. Many of the greatest European intellectuals – among them Voltaire, Fichte, Kant, Hegel, Schopenhauer, Nietzsche, Frege and Heidegger – never quite forgave Jews for staying Jews, different, angular, countercultural, iconoclastic. Yet despite the tragedies of more than twenty centuries, Jews and Judaism still flourish, refusing to grant victory to cultures of contempt or the angel of death.

The majesty and mystery of Judaism is that, though at best Jews were a small people in a small land, no match for the circumambient empires that periodically assaulted them, Jews did not give way to self-hate, self-disesteem or despair. Beneath the awe and solemnity of Yom Kippur, one fact shines radiant throughout: that God loves us more than we love ourselves. He believes in us more than we believe in ourselves. He never gives up on us, however many times we slip and fall. The story of Judaism from beginning to end is the tale of God's love for a people who rarely fully reciprocated that love, yet never altogether failed to be moved by it.

Rabbi Akiva put it best in a mere two words: *Avinu Malkeinu* (*Ta'anit* 25b). Yes, You are our Sovereign, God Almighty, Maker of the cosmos, King of kings. But You are also our Father. You told Moses to say to Pharaoh in Your name: "My child, My firstborn, Israel" (Ex. 4:22). That love continues to make Jews a symbol of hope to humanity, testifying that a nation does not need to be large to be great, nor powerful to have influence. Each of us can, by a single act of kindness or generosity of spirit, cause a ray of the divine light to shine in the human darkness, allowing the *Shekhina*, at least for a moment, to be at home in our world.

More than Yom Kippur expresses our faith in God, it is the expression of God's faith in us.

I. Shame and Guilt

Judaism is the world's greatest example of a guilt-and-repentance culture as opposed to the shame-and-honor culture of the ancient Greeks.

In a shame culture such as that of Greek tragedy, evil attaches to the person. It is a kind of indelible stain. There is no way back for one who has done a shameful deed. He is a pariah and the best he can hope for is to die in a noble cause. In a guilt culture like that of Judaism, evil is an attribute of the act, not the agent. Even one who has done wrong has a sacred self that remains intact. He may have to undergo punishment. He certainly has to make amends. But there remains a core of worth that can never be lost. A guilt culture hates the sin, not the sinner. Repentance, rehabilitation and return are always possible.

A guilt culture is a culture of responsibility. We do not blame anyone else for the wrong we do. It is always tempting to blame others – it wasn't me, it was my parents, my upbringing, my friends, my genes, my social class, the media, the system, "them." That was what the first two humans did in the Garden of Eden. When challenged by God for eating the forbidden fruit, the man blamed the woman. The woman blamed the serpent. The result was paradise lost.

Blaming others for our failings is as old as humanity, but it is disastrous. It means that we define ourselves as victims. A culture of victimhood wins the compassion of others but at too high a cost. It incubates feelings of resentment, humiliation, grievance and grudge. It leads people to rage against the world instead of taking steps to mend it. Jews have suffered much, but Yom Kippur prevents us from ever defining ourselves as victims. As we confess our sins, we blame no one but ourselves.

That is demanding, psychologically and spiritually. Yet it is the price we must pay for freedom. Other ancient literatures record the successes of rulers and empires. The Hebrew Bible is a unique chronicle of failures. No one in its pages is perfect, not the patriarchs and matriarchs, not priests or prophets, not kings or the ruling elite. No history is as painfully honest as that of Tanakh, and it was possible only in the deep belief that God forgives. God pardons; God atones; God is holding out His hand, calling us back with inextinguishable love. That allows us to be honest with ourselves.

II. The Growth Mindset

It also allows us to grow. We owe a debt to cognitive behavioral therapy for reminding us of a classic element of Jewish faith, that when we change the way we think, we change the way we feel. And when we feel differently, we live differently. What we believe shapes what we become.

At the heart of *teshuva* is the belief that we can change. We are not destined to be forever what we were. In the Torah we see Judah grow from an envious brother prepared to sell Joseph as a slave, to a man with the conscience and courage to offer himself as a slave so that his brother Benjamin can go free.

We see Moses grow from a man lacking the confidence to lead – "Who am I?" (Ex. 3:11), "They will not believe in me" (Ex. 4:1) – to become the greatest leader of all time. The man who once stammered and said of himself, "I am not a man of words" (Ex. 4:10), becomes by the end of his life the most eloquent and visionary of all the prophets.

We see remarkable women transcend their social situation. Tamar, the woman Judah mistakes for a prostitute, eventually teaches him to have the courage to admit he was wrong, reinforcing his role as the first *ba'al teshuva* in history. Ruth, the woman from Moab, Israel's enemy, displays such growth through her loyalty to Naomi that she becomes the great-grandmother of David, Israel's greatest king.

We see Hosea, Jeremiah, Jonah and Job wrestle with themselves and with God. That, after all, is what the name Israel means: one who wrestles, not one who accepts the status quo. The figures of the Hebrew Bible are not two-dimensional figures who remain at the end of their lives what they were at the beginning. Theirs may be a painful, but not a tragic, fate.

We know that some people relish a challenge and take risks, while others, no less gifted, play it safe and ultimately underachieve. Psychologists tell us that the crucial difference lies in whether you think of your ability as a fixed quantum or as something developed through effort and experience. *Teshuva* is essentially about effort and experience. It assumes we can grow.

Teshuva means I can take risks, knowing that I may fail but knowing that failure is not final. Time and again Moses failed to engender in his people a clear sense of history and destiny, even a basic gratitude for what God had done for them. But failing a hundred times does not make a failure. Indeed in God's eyes none of us is a failure so long as we still have breath to breathe and a life to live.

Teshuva means that if I get it wrong and make mistakes, God does not lose faith in me even though I may lose faith in myself. "Were my father and my mother to forsake me, the Lord would take me in" (Ps. 27:10). Some of the greatest heroes in the Bible did not believe in themselves. Isaiah said, "I am a man of unclean lips" (Is. 6:5). Jeremiah said, "I cannot speak for I am a child" (Jer. 1:6). Jonah, given a mission by God, ran away. God believes in us, even if we do not. That alone is a life-changing fact if we fully open ourselves to its implications.

Teshuva means that the past is not irredeemable. Through *teshuva* undertaken in love, said Resh Lakish, "even deliberate sins may be transformed into merits" (*Yoma* 86b). Resh Lakish himself was a *ba'al teshuva*, a reformed bandit who used the strength he had once devoted to robbery to instead save people held hostage. King David, another *ba'al teshuva*, drew some of his deepest poetry from the pain of his personal abyss.

Teshuva means that from every mistake, I grow. There is no failure I experience that does not make me a deeper human being; no challenge I accept, however much I fall short, that does not develop in me strengths I would not otherwise have had.

That is the first transformation of Yom Kippur: a renewed relationship with myself.

III. Our Relationships with Others

The second is a renewed relationship with others. We know that Yom Kippur atones only for sins between us and God, but that does not mean that these are the only sins for which we need to seek atonement. To the contrary: many, even most, of the sins we confess on Yom Kippur are about our relationships with others. Rabbi Ḥanina ben Dosa taught: "In one whom people delight, God delights" (*Avot* 3:13). Throughout the prophetic and rabbinic literature it is assumed that as we act to others so God acts to us. Those who forgive are forgiven. Those who condemn are condemned.

The days from Rosh HaShana to Yom Kippur are a time when we try to mend relationships that have broken. It takes one kind of moral courage to apologize, another to forgive, but both may be necessary.

Failure to heal relationships can split families, destroy marriages, ruin friendships and divide communities. That is not where God wants us to be. As the sages pointed out, God allowed His own name to be blotted out to make peace between husband and wife. They also said that after Sarah died, Abraham took back Hagar and Ishmael into his family, mending the rift that had occurred many years before. Aaron, according to tradition, was loved by all the people because he was able to mend fractured friendships.

Writing as a self-confessed secular Jew, the philosopher Alain de Botton says that Yom Kippur is "one of the most psychologically effective mechanisms ever devised for the resolution of social conflict." He explains:

> The Day of Atonement has the immense advantage of making the idea of saying sorry look like it came from somewhere else, the initiative of neither the perpetrator nor the victim. It is the day itself that is making us sit here and talk about the peculiar incident six months ago when you lied and I blustered and you accused me of insincerity and I made you cry, an incident that neither of us can quite forget but that we can't quite mention either and which has slowly been corroding the trust and love we once had for each other.[6]

Without a designated day, would we ever get around to mending our broken relationships? Often we do not tell people how they have hurt us because we do not want to look vulnerable and small-minded. In the opposite direction, sometimes we are reluctant to apologize because we feel so guilty that we do not want to expose our guilt. As De Botton puts it: "We can be so sorry that we find ourselves incapable of saying sorry." He adds: "So cathartic is the Day of Atonement, it seems a pity that there should be only one of them a year."

That is the second transformation of Yom Kippur: a renewed relationship with others.

6. Alain de Botton, *Religion for Atheists: A Non-Believer's Guide to the Uses of Religion* (London: Hamish Hamilton, 2012).

IV. Coming Home

The third is a renewed relationship with God.

On Yom Kippur, God is close. Admittedly in Judaism we prefer to talk *to* God than *about* God. Hence we have relatively little theology. We know that God is beyond our understanding. If I could know God, said one Jewish philosopher, I would be God. Yet Jewish life is full of signals of transcendence, intimations of eternity. We encounter God in three ways: through creation, revelation and redemption.

Through creation: the more we understand of cosmology, the more we realize how improbable the universe is. According to Lord Rees, former president of the Royal Society and Britain's most distinguished scientist, the margin of error in the six mathematical constants that determine the shape of the physical universe is almost infinitesimally small. The universe is too finely tuned for the emergence of stars, planets and life to have come into existence by chance. The only alternative hypothesis is that there is an infinity of parallel universes of which we happen to inhabit the one congenial to the emergence of life. That raises as many questions as it solves, if indeed it solves any. The more we understand of the sheer improbability of the existence of the universe, the emergence of life from inanimate matter, and the equally mysterious appearance of Homo sapiens, the only life-form capable of asking the question "Why?" the more the line from Psalms rings true: "How numerous are Your works, Lord; You made them all in wisdom" (Ps. 104:24).

Through revelation: the words of God as recorded in the Torah. There is nothing in history to compare to the fact that Jews spent a thousand years (from Moses to the last of the prophets) compiling a commentary to the Torah in the form of the prophetic, historical and wisdom books of Tanakh, then another thousand years (from Malachi to the Babylonian Talmud) compiling a commentary to the commentary in the form of the vast literature of the Oral Torah (Midrash, Mishna and Gemara), then another thousand years (from the *Geonim* to the Aharonim, the later authorities) writing commentaries to the commentary to the commentary.

No people has so loved a book, declaring that its study is a higher religious experience than prayer. In the land of Israel it was their written constitution as a nation. In the Diaspora it was, as Heine put it, the "portable homeland" of the Jews. It remains the source and wellspring from which the West has drawn its great ideals of the sanctity of life, the twin imperatives of justice and love, personal and social responsibility, peace as an ideal, *tzedaka* as an imperative, the importance of equal access to knowledge and dignity, our duties as guardians of the natural world, and many other ideals without which the West would not be what it is. If we search anywhere for the voice of God, it is here, in the Book of books.

And through history: many great thinkers, including Blaise Pascal and Leo Tolstoy, believed that Jewish history was the most compelling evidence of the existence of God. Nikolai Berdyaev (1874–1948) was a former professor of philosophy at the University of Moscow who eventually rejected Marxism and devoted the rest of his life to religion. In *The Meaning of History* he explains why:

> I remember how the materialist interpretation of history, when I attempted in my youth to verify it by applying it to the destinies of peoples, broke down in the case of the Jews, where destiny seemed absolutely inexplicable from the materialistic standpoint…. Its survival is a mysterious and wonderful phenomenon demonstrating that the life of this people is governed by a special predetermination, transcending the processes of adaptation expounded by the materialistic interpretation of history. The survival of the Jews, their resistance to destruction, their endurance under absolutely peculiar conditions and the fateful role played by them in history: all these point to the particular and mysterious foundations of their destiny.[7]

But perhaps such reflections are beside the point. For it can sometimes be that God comes to us not as the conclusion of a line of reasoning but as a feeling, an intuition, a sensed presence, as we stand in the synagogue on this holy day – listening to our people's melodies, saying the words Jews have said from Barcelona to Bergen-Belsen to

---

7. Nikolai Berdyaev, *The Meaning of History* (New Brunswick, NJ: Transaction, 2009), 86–87.

Benei Berak, from Toledo to Treblinka to Tel Aviv – knowing that we are part of an immense story that has played itself out through the centuries and continents, the tempestuous yet ultimately hope-inspiring love story of a people in search of God and God in search of a people.

There has never been a drama remotely like this in its ups and downs, triumphs and tragedies, its songs of praise and lamentation, and we are part of it. For most of us it is not something we chose but a fate we were born into. But as Winston Churchill put it, "Some people like the Jews, and some do not. But no thoughtful man can deny the fact that they are beyond question the most formidable and the most remarkable race which has ever appeared in the world." Or as the Oxford literary scholar A.L. Rowse wrote toward the end of his life, "If there is one honor in the world I should like, it would be to be an honorary member of the Jewish people."

V. What Chapter Will We Write in the Book of Life?

In 1888, Alfred Nobel, the man who invented dynamite, was reading his morning papers when, with a shock, he found himself reading his own obituary. It turned out that a journalist had made a simple mistake. It was Nobel's *brother* who had died.

What horrified Nobel was what he read. It spoke about "the dynamite king" who had made a fortune from explosives. Nobel suddenly realized that if he did not change his life, that was all he would be remembered for. At that moment he decided to dedicate his fortune to creating five annual prizes for those who'd made outstanding contributions in physics, chemistry, medicine, literature and peace. Nobel chose to be remembered not for selling weapons of destruction but for honoring contributions to human knowledge. The question Yom Kippur forces on us is not so much "Will we live?" but "*How* will we live?" For what would we wish to be remembered?

On this day of days we are brutally candid: "Before I was formed I was unworthy, and now that I have been formed it is as if I had not been formed. I am dust while alive, how much more so when I am dead." Yet the same faith that inspired those words also declared that we should see ourselves and the world as if equally poised between merit and guilt, and that our next act could tilt the balance, for my life and for the world (Maimonides, *Laws of Repentance* 3:4). Judaism lives in this dialect between our smallness and our potential greatness. We may be dust, but within us are immortal longings.

Yom Kippur invites us to become better than we were in the knowledge that we can be better than we are. That knowledge comes from God. I remember as a student hearing a witty put-down of a brash business tycoon: "He is a self-made man, thereby relieving God of a great responsibility." If we are only self-made, we live within the prison of our own limitations. The truly great human beings are those who have opened themselves to the inspiration of something greater than themselves.

"Wherever you find the greatness of God," said Rabbi Yoḥanan, "there you find His humility" (*Megilla* 31a). Yom Kippur is about the humility that leads to greatness: our ability to say, over and over again, "We have sinned," and yet know that this is not a maudlin self-abasement, but rather, the prelude to greater achievement in the future, the way a champion in any sport, a maestro in any field, reviews his or her past mistakes as part of the preparation for the next challenge, the next rung to climb.

Jews had a genius for spiritual greatness. Even Sigmund Freud, hostile as he was to religion in general, could not but express admiration in the last book he wrote, *Moses and Monotheism*, for the way Judaism produced not one charismatic figure but generation after generation of them. The philosopher Ludwig Wittgenstein, even more ambivalent about his Jewish ancestry, wrote in his notebook in 1931, "Amongst Jews 'genius' is found only in the holy man."[8] Jews had this genius not because they are better than others – often, reading the prophets, you get the impression that the opposite was sometimes true – but because they worked harder at it. The Hebrew word for serving God, *avoda*, also means "hard work."

Judaism takes the simple things of life and makes them holy. *Kashrut* makes eating holy. *Kiddush* makes drinking holy. The laws of family purity make the physical relationship between husband and wife holy. Study sanctifies the intellect. Prayer reconfigures the mind.

---

8. Ludwig Wittgenstein, *Culture and Value* (Chicago: University of Chicago Press, 1980), 18e.

Constant acts of generosity and care sharpen our emotional intelligence, honing our skills of empathy. Judaism, as Rabbi Joseph Soloveitchik put it, sees creativity as the essence of humanity, and our greatest creation is our self. We forge our life in the fire of love: love of God, the neighbor and the stranger. And by sanctifying family and community, Judaism sacralizes the bonds of belonging that make us who we are.

The power of Yom Kippur is that it brings us face to face with these truths. Through its words, music and devotions, through the way it focuses energies by depriving us of all the physical pleasures we normally associate with a Jewish festival, through the sheer driving passion of the liturgy with its hundred ways of saying sorry, it confronts us with the ultimate question: How will we live? Will we live a life that explores to the full the capacity of the human mind to reach out to that which lies beyond it? Will we grow emotionally? Will we learn the arts of loyalty and love? Will we train our inner ear to hear the cry of the lonely and the poor? Will we live a life that makes a difference, bringing the world-that-is a little closer to being the world-that-ought-to-be? Will we open our hearts and minds to God?

It is possible to live a lifetime without asking any of these questions. It is the genius of Judaism that it makes us do so once a year, when God is close to us because we are close to Him. Yom Kippur retains the traces of those two great figures, Moses the prophet and Aaron the priest, who between them created a tension between spontaneity and structure, passion and order, which continues to vitalize the Jewish spirit, giving it the blessings of both restlessness and rest. Alone with God, together with our people, singing the songs and praying the prayers they said in every age under the most diverse circumstances, we find ourselves questioned, challenged, summoned, inspired.

Like Moses on the mountain, like Aaron in the Holy of Holies, we come as near as we can to being face to face with God, and after it we are not the same as we were before. That personal transformation, the ability to make our tomorrow greater than our yesterday, is the essence of *teshuva* and of Yom Kippur.

The most demanding day of the Jewish year, a day without food and drink, a day of prayer and penitence, confession and pleading, in which we accuse ourselves of every conceivable sin, still calls to Jews, touching us at the deepest level of our being. It is a day in which we run toward the open arms of God, weeping because we may have disappointed Him, or because sometimes we feel He has disappointed us, yet knowing that we need one another, for though God can create universes, He cannot live within the human heart unless we let Him in.

It is a day not just of confession and forgiveness but of a profound liberation. Atonement means that we can begin again. We are not held captive by the past, by our failures. The book is open and God invites us – His hand guiding us the way a scribe guides the hand of those who write a letter in a Torah scroll – to write a new chapter in the story of our people, a chapter uniquely our own yet one that we cannot write on our own without being open to something vaster than we will ever fully understand. It is a day on which God invites us to greatness.

May He forgive us. May we, lifted by His love, rise to meet His call.

Sukkot

Season of Joy

It was a sight that, once seen, was never forgotten. Jerusalem was thronged with pilgrims. For days there had been a noise and energy about the streets and arcades that you never felt at other times of the year. People were busy constructing their sukkot in courtyards and on the level roofs of their houses, and bringing foliage for the covering through which they would see the stars and which, some said, were reminders of the clouds of glory that accompanied their ancestors on their epic trek through the desert. In the markets people had been busy buying the palm branches, citrons and twigs of myrtle and willow, examining each for perfection of form so that they could celebrate the festival with what King David had called *hadrat kodesh*, the beauty of holiness (Ps. 29:2).

The courtyard of the Temple was more crowded than at any other time of the year. People were excited. You could feel the anticipation, the barely suppressed exuberance. It was an emotion woven of many strands. The great Days of Awe, with their intense solemnity, were over. The great shofar had sounded, heralding the New Year. On Yom Kippur the High Priest had officiated, confessing the sins of the people and symbolically laying them on one of two goats, chosen by lot, that was then sent out into the desert, a visible symbol of guilt being carried away. The High Priest had atoned for the people. The slate had been wiped clean. Now, less than a week later, there was a palpable feeling of release and a new beginning.

Then there was the mood of thanksgiving. The harvest had been gathered. The fields and groves and vineyards had yielded their produce. It was a time to thank God for His many blessings: the land, the earth, the sun, the rain, the fields and yields, the freedom. People recalled the words of Moses even before they had entered the land: If you love the Lord your God and worship Him with all your heart and soul, then He would send rain in its due season, in autumn and spring, and they would gather in grain, grapes for wine and olives for oil. There would be grass in the fields for the cattle. "You will eat and be satisfied." So he had said (Deut. 8:10), and so it had been. In Israel you could never take rain for granted. When it came it felt like a blessing from heaven.

The stalls were overflowing with produce. The rabbis had specifically ordained that those who lived within a day's distance from Jerusalem should bring to the city the fruit of the fourth year and the produce set aside for the second tithe, and not redeem it for money, so that "the markets of Jerusalem would be decorated with fruit" (*Beitza* 5a).

The Temple courtyard was packed with people who had come from all parts of the land to be here for these holy days. This was the sight that made the sages say that it was one of the miracles that happened regularly at the Temple: "the people stood crowded together, yet there was ample space when they prostrated themselves" (*Avot* 5:7). There were processions round the altar all seven days of the festival, with people carrying their palm branches, citrons, myrtle and willows. The atmosphere rose to a crescendo when the Levites sang the Hallel and the entire crowd, waving their palm branches, roared their responses: "His loving-kindness is forever" and "Lord, please save us." It was this litany, with its repeated refrain *Hosha na*, "Please save" (an abbreviation of the biblical "*hoshia na*"), that gave the Western world the word "hosanna" for a shout of jubilation.

There were aspects of the Temple service on Sukkot that happened at no other time of the year. There were processions around the altar, not just with the four kinds but also with branches of willow, *arava*.

Accompanying the sacrifices was not just the usual libation of wine but also a special water libation. Every morning at dawn, in a special ceremony, priests and Levites would leave the Temple courtyard and walk south to the Shiloah stream from which they drew water, which was then placed into a golden bowl. As they entered the Temple, shofar blasts were sounded.

So significant was this entire ceremony that, at night on the intermediate days of the festival, in preparation for the next morning's events, a celebration took place in the Temple courtyard known as *Simhat Beit HaSho'eva*, "Rejoicing in the House of the Water-Drawing." So euphoric was the mood on those nights that the sages said, "One who did not see the Rejoicing in the House of the Water-Drawing [*Simhat Beit HaSho'eva*] never saw celebration in his days" (*Sukka* 5:1).

The mood was like a wedding. Some played the flute, others harps, lutes and cymbals. People sang, danced and clapped. The leading religious figures in the land, sages, heads of yeshivot, members of the high court, the pious, elders, and men of renown all joined the celebrations. It was said that the *nasi*, Rabban Shimon ben Gamliel, used to juggle flaming torches (*Sukka* 53a). Sages became acrobats. Scholars did somersaults. They considered it the ultimate dignity to sacrifice your dignity in the sacred cause of joy. So lighthearted and exuberant were the celebrations that people began to be concerned that they might turn into the kind of revelry associated with the Greek Dionysia and the Roman Bacchanalia, where a combination of drink and mixing of the sexes led to the kind of debauchery alien to Judaism, all the more so in the precincts of the Temple. So to prevent the mixing of the sexes, a ladies' gallery was erected in the Temple, the first of its kind, so that the women could watch and see the dancing below. The celebrations went on throughout the night, and there were sages who said that during Sukkot they never slept, so continuous were the celebrations.

To illuminate the Temple at night, three giant candelabra were lit, each with four gold basins and multiple wicks, filled with oil by young men from priestly families. They used to say that the whole of Jerusalem was lit by the radiance that emanated from these lamps (*Sukka* 5:3). The singing and dancing went on until dawn, when the shofar was blown to signal that the time had come for the procession to collect the water from the Shiloah spring to begin (*Sukka* 5:4).

There was no other moment in the Jewish year quite like Sukkot. Even before the building of the Temple, we read of an annual "festival for God at Shilo" at which young women danced in the vineyards (Judges 21:19–20). Some scholars surmise that it was this festival on which Elkanah would go each year to the sanctuary at Shilo, and it was for this reason – Sukkot being among other things a festival celebrating the wine vintage – that Eli the priest, seeing Hannah praying, thought she was drunk (I Sam. 1:3–18).

The harvest had been gathered, work in the field was for the time being over, and people had both reason and time to celebrate. This meant that the crowds were larger at this festival than at any other time of the year, even Pesaḥ. During the Roman campaign against Israel in the Great Revolt of 66–70 CE, Cestius Gallus approached the city of Lydda, only to find it almost completely deserted because virtually the whole town had traveled to Jerusalem to celebrate Sukkot there (*Wars of the Jews*, II:19:1).

It was the obvious time to choose for great national ceremonies. The Torah states that every seven years, at the end of the year of release, the king must convene a national assembly and read Torah to the people (Deut. 31:10–13). This was, in effect, a covenant renewal ceremony, reminding the people of their past, their collective raison d'être and their commitments to God. The Torah specifies that this was a family celebration to which men, women and children should come. It was a solemn reminder of who the people were, and why.

For the same reason, Solomon chose this time for the consecration of the Temple: the project his father David had conceived, only to be told by God that it would not be he, but his son, who would do it. The task was immense and deeply symbolic. The book of Kings tells us that the work was begun "in the four hundred and eightieth year after the Israelites left Egypt" (I Kings 6:1), the only event in post-Mosaic history to be dated by reference to the Exodus. The number (forty, the number of the wilderness years, multiplied by twelve, the number of the tribes) is itself symbolic. It had taken centuries to settle the land, build towns, unite the tribes into a single kingdom under a single king, and establish Jerusalem as the nation's capital. The building took seven years, and required vast amounts of quarried stone (shaped into blocks at the quarry so that no sound of hammer or chisel would be heard in the sacred precincts of the Temple itself) together with cedarwood and pinewood imported from Lebanon.

The celebrations were launched by a historic speech from Solomon, and went on for two weeks, the second of which was Sukkot. On the eighth day, Solomon told the people that on the morrow they were to return home. The people "blessed the king, going back to their tents happy and buoyant of heart over all the goodness that the Lord had performed for His servant, David, and for His people, Israel" (I Kings 8:66).

Centuries later, in a much more low-key ceremony, the Second Temple was also dedicated on Sukkot, the celebrations led by the governor Zerubavel and the High Priest Joshua (Ezra 3:1–6). Work on the Temple was desultory because of active opposition on the part of the Samaritans. The entire project lapsed for some seventeen years. Eventually, Jewish life, and with it the restoration of the Temple as the spiritual heart of the nation, was re-energized by two remarkable leaders who had recently arrived from Babylon: Ezra and Nehemiah. Together they convened a new national assembly, one of the most important in Jewish history.

It began on the first of Tishrei, on the day we now know as Rosh HaShana. In a conscious echo of the septennial address by the king, Ezra stood on a wooden platform in front of the Water Gate in Jerusalem and read the Torah to the assembly. As it dawned on them how far they had drifted from the covenant their ancestors had made with God, the people started weeping. Ezra and Nehemiah, however, stilled the crowd, saying: "Go and enjoy choice food and sweet drinks, and send some to those who have nothing prepared. This day is holy to our Lord. Do not grieve, for the joy of the Lord is your strength" (Neh. 8:10; see "The Great Renewal" in the previous chapter).

The next day they returned and Ezra read further from the Torah. In the course of the reading, the people heard the command to celebrate Sukkot, a practice that had evidently been neglected for generations. Word spread throughout the crowd, and within days it had been carried throughout the country. Everywhere, people could be seen collecting branches from olive trees, palms and myrtles to make coverings for the sukkot that they proceeded to build locally and in Jerusalem itself by two of its gates. The book of Nehemiah records that "the whole company that had returned from exile built temporary shelters and lived in them. From the days of Joshua son of Nun until that day, the Israelites had not celebrated it like this. And their joy was very great" (8:17). The celebrations lasted seven days and "on the eighth day, in accordance with the law, there was an assembly" (8:18) – in other words they celebrated Shemini Atzeret.

That moment was a turning point in Jewish history, the start of a long revolution in Jewish life, in which a vision intimated long before by Moses began to become real in the life of the nation. The nation had become, in effect, the People of the Book, whose citadels were houses of study, whose heroes were teachers and scribes and whose passion was learning and the life of the mind. What Ezra and Nehemiah understood, and would be proved true many times in the following centuries, was that the real battle faced by Israel was less military than spiritual. Jews might lose everything else, but if they kept their identity, they would outlive the mightiest of empires.

Sukkot became not just the festival of ingathering, but also the great moment of national rededication. So it is not surprising that when, several centuries later, the Maccabees celebrated their victory over the Seleucid Greeks and their Hellenized Jewish sympathizers, and reconsecrated the Temple, they modeled their celebrations on Sukkot, in the form of the festival we now call Hanukka. Despite the fact it takes place at a quite different time of the year, beginning on 25 Kislev, the letter they sent to the Jews of Egypt requests them to celebrate at that time "the festival of Sukkot and the festival of the fire given when Nehemiah, who built the Temple and the altar, offered sacrifices" (II Macc. 1:18).

The same book later describes the first time Hanukka was observed by the Maccabees, the year they defeated the Greeks: "They celebrated it for eight days with rejoicing in the manner of Sukkot, remembering how not long before, during the festival of Sukkot, they had been wandering in the mountains and caves like wild beasts" (II Macc. 10:6). In other words, they had been unable to celebrate Sukkot properly that year while they were in hiding during the war itself. "Therefore, carrying ivy-wreathed wands and beautiful branches, and also fronds of palms, they offered hymns of thanksgiving to Him who had given success to the purifying of His own holy place" (ibid. 10:7). In other words, Ḥanukka itself was modeled on Sukkot, which had become not only the festival of joy, but supremely the festival of the Temple and national rededication.

Already in Leviticus and Deuteronomy, Sukkot had been singled out for special celebration. "And you shall rejoice on your festival," said Moses in connection with Sukkot, "and you will be truly joyful" (Deut. 16:14–15). So it seemed natural to call these days *zeman simḥateinu*, "our time of rejoicing."

Joy is at the heart of Judaism. "Serve the Lord with joy," said the psalm (100:2), "come before Him with jubilation." Israel would come to know more than its share of sufferings, defeats, destructions and exiles. Yet what sustained it was not sadness but gladness, a deep religious joy. In the last month of his life, Moses had warned the people not to take the land, its freedoms or its produce for granted, nor to forget their origins. The land was not theirs but God's, and therefore the right way to celebrate it was by gratitude. Bad things would happen, he warned, if people ever lost their capacity for joy. Curses would strike the nation, "because you did not serve the Lord your God with joy and gladness of heart out of the abundance of all good things" (Deut. 28:47).

The one defense against national entropy – the loss of collective energy over time – would be joy itself, a combination of thanksgiving, humility, gratitude and memories of the suffering that had to be endured in the course of arriving at this place and this estate. Judaism is not a religion of austerity, self-denial and stoic endurance. It is not a faith that allowed itself to be overwhelmed by tragedy. Time and again it arose, phoenix-like, from catastrophe, demoralization and defeat, and each time renewed itself, gathering ever-greater strength in the process. True faith, in Judaism, is marked by the capacity for joy.

That, however, is only the first and outermost layer of a festival of unusual complexity and depth. In the following sections I want to explore the meaning of Sukkot at deeper levels, for it will turn out to be, perhaps more than any other, the festival that tells us what it is to be a Jew, and what difference faith makes to the human condition itself.

Our journey begins with one of the last voices of the great tradition of Israel's prophets, the man we know as Zechariah.

The Dual Festival

The defeat of the southern kingdom by the Babylonians in the sixth century BCE was the deepest, most defining trauma of the biblical age. We can still feel the overpowering grief of the book of Lamentations, its raw pain undiminished by the intervening millennia, as the prophet sees the defeat of his people and the ruins of the Temple. We can still hear the despair of the exiles who, "by the rivers of Babylon," sat and wept as they remembered Zion (Ps. 137:1). Yet, as the two great prophets of exile, Jeremiah and Ezekiel, had promised, the people did return. The Babylonian empire was defeated by a newer superpower, Persia, under whose enlightened leader, Cyrus, Jews were given permission to return.

The situation they found in the Holy Land was devastating. The people had lost almost all contact with their religious heritage. As Nehemiah later wrote, they no longer observed the Sabbath. They had intermarried with neighboring people. They no longer knew how to speak Hebrew: "Half of their children spoke the language of Ashdod, or they spoke the language of one of the other nations" (Neh. 13:24). Work had begun on rebuilding the Temple, but it hit a series of difficulties, and the returning exiles turned instead to rebuilding their homes and farms. The unfinished Temple was a visual reminder of Israel's broken state, politically, culturally and religiously.

One prophet who undertook the task of kindling a spark of hope from the dying embers of national identity was Zechariah. His message, astonishing in the circumstances, was that despite its forlorn state, the people of the covenant would revive, and then inspire not only themselves, but the world. The day would come when "ten people from all languages and nations will take firm hold of one Jew by the hem of his robe and say, 'Let us go with you, because we have heard that God is with you'" (Zech. 8:23). Zechariah also gave expression to one of the briefest and best summaries ever given of Jewish history: "'Not by might nor by power, but by My Spirit,' says the Lord Almighty" (4:6).

All the prophets had foreseen that the nation would be punished for its sins but would eventually return to God. Beginning with Ezekiel in exile in Babylon, prophecy now took on a darker complexion, as if the road from here to the Messianic Age could no longer pass through the normal processes of history. Israel's glory would be restored, but this would happen only through divine intervention into the human script, shaking the foundations of the world. Eschatology, *Aḥarit HaYamim*, the vision of the End of Days, began to grow more disturbing.

Zechariah was the first prophet to say that even after Jews returned to their land, this would not be the end of their troubles. The nations of the world would form an alliance and wage war against the Jewish people in Jerusalem. God Himself would be forced to intervene to defend His people and defeat their enemies. The earth would shake. God would crush the Mount of Olives and flatten the surrounding countryside. Mount Zion would tower alone, streams of water issuing from it, bringing fertility to the land. After these momentous events, the nations would come to acknowledge that there is only one God: "Then the Lord shall be King over all the earth: on that day the Lord shall be One and His name One" (14:9) – a verse now one of the best-known lines of Jewish prayer.

It was in the course of this prophecy that Zechariah made a unique prediction. Not only would Jerusalem be the capital of Israel, it would become the spiritual center of the world. The nations would gather there once a year on Sukkot:

> And it will be: those remaining from all the nations who came up against Jerusalem will go up year upon year to bow down to the King, Lord of hosts, and to celebrate the festival of Sukkot. And it will be: those from the earth's families who do not go up to Jerusalem and bow down to the King, Lord of hosts – rain shall not fall for them; and if the family of Egypt does not go up, does not come – they will have no [overflow]. This will be the plague that the Lord will bring upon the nations who do not go up to celebrate the festival of Sukkot; such will be the punishment of Egypt and the punishment of all the nations who do not come up to celebrate the festival of Sukkot. (14:16–19)

There is no other prophecy quite like this anywhere else in Tanakh: none that says that a Jewish festival will one day be global, observed by all the nations. The pilgrimage festivals were part of Israel's unique heritage, not its universal truths. They are about Israel and its seasons, and about the formative moments of Jewish history: the Exodus from Egypt, the Giving of the Torah at Mount Sinai and, in the case of Sukkot, the forty years of wandering in the desert without a permanent home. Zechariah was thus making an unprecedented assertion when he spoke of Sukkot as a festival not just for Israel but for everyone.

What led him to do so? There was one unusual feature of the Sukkot sacrifices that might have inspired this thought. Whereas in the case of the other seven-day festival, Pesaḥ, on which the offerings were the same each day, on Sukkot they were different. On the first day, thirteen young bulls were offered, on the second twelve, and so on until the seventh day, when there were seven – making a total of seventy in all (Num. 29:12–34). Seventy in the Torah corresponds to the number of nations into which humanity was divided according to Genesis 10. The sages drew the conclusion that in making an offering of seventy young bulls on Sukkot, the Israelites were in effect sacrificing and praying on behalf of humanity as a whole (*Sukka* 55b.) Zechariah may thus have been inspired by an idea implicit in the Torah itself.

Hence the paradox: Sukkot is the most universalistic of the festivals, the only one that will one day be celebrated by all humanity. As Zechariah makes clear, this has to do with its association with rain, and there is nothing distinctively Jewish about the need for rain. All countries, especially in the Middle East, need it. At the same time it is also the most particularist of festivals. No other nation took as a symbol not a castle, a fortress or a triumphal arch, but a fragile tabernacle. No other nation was born, not in its land, but in the desert. Far from being universal, Sukkot seems intensely particularistic, the festival of a people like no other, whose only protection was its faith in the sheltering wings of the Divine Presence.

There are other unusual features of Sukkot. In the list of holy days in Deuteronomy 16, rejoicing is not mentioned in connection with Pesaḥ. It is mentioned once in connection with Shavuot, but twice in the context of Sukkot:

You shall rejoice [*vesamaḥta*] on your festival…. You shall celebrate for seven days for the Lord your God in the place which the Lord shall choose, for the Lord your God shall bless you in all of your produce and all that you do; and you will be truly joyful [*vehayita akh same'aḥ*]. (Deut. 16:14–15)

It was this that led to the description of Sukkot as *zeman simḥateinu,* "our time of rejoicing." But why a double joy?

Turning to the account of the festivals in Leviticus 23, we notice something else unusual about Sukkot. It is defined not in terms of *one* overriding symbol, but *two.* The first is the command to take the "four kinds" of fruit and foliage:

On the first day, you shall take for yourselves a fruit of the citron tree, palm fronds, myrtle branches and willows of the brook, and be joyous in the presence of the Lord your God for seven days. (Lev. 23:40)

The second command is quite different:

You shall dwell in booths for seven days; all those born among Israel shall dwell in booths, so that your descendants will know that I settled the children of Israel in booths when I brought them out of the land of Egypt; I am the Lord your God. (Lev. 23:42–43)

It was this command – to leave our homes and live in a temporary dwelling – that gave the festival its name.

No other festival has this dual symbolism, and their juxtaposition is curious. Not only are the "four kinds" and the sukka different in character: in a sense they conflict with one another. The "four kinds" are associated with the land of Israel. The sukka is the opposite, a reminder of exodus, exile, the desert and no-man's-land. In practical terms also they conflicted. The four kinds were, as the sages said, symbols of and a mode of intercession for rain (*Ta'anit* 2b). Indeed the rabbis said that rainfall for the coming year was determined on the first day of Sukkot (*Rosh HaShana* 1:2). But the command to live for seven days in a sukka with only leaves for a roof presupposes the absence of rain. If it rains on Sukkot, with the exception of the first night, we are exempt from the command for as long as the rain lasts, if it is heavy enough to spoil the food on the table (*Sukka* 2:9).

All this conveys the impression that Sukkot represents two festivals, not one. In fact it does, and therein lies its uniqueness. Though the festivals are often listed together, they represent two quite different cycles of time. First is the annual cycle of the pilgrimage festivals: Pesaḥ, Shavuot and Sukkot. These tell the singular story of Jewish identity and history: the Exodus, the revelation at Mount Sinai and the long journey through the wilderness. Celebrating them, we reenact what made Israel the particular people it is. The central section of the Amida prayer on these festivals begins with the classic statement of Jewish particularity: "You have chosen us from among all peoples."

There is a second cycle – the festivals of the seventh month, Rosh HaShana, Yom Kippur and Sukkot. Just as the seventh day, Shabbat, is *zekher lema'aseh bereshit*, a memorial of creation, so is the seventh month. *Hayom harat olam*, "This day is the birth of the world," we say in our prayers on Rosh HaShana. When it comes to creation, we are all created, and we are all accountable to our Creator, Jew and non-Jew alike. That is why the Mishna says that on Rosh HaShana, "All who have come into this world pass before Him like sheep" (*Rosh HaShana* 1:2). All humanity is judged. The language of the prayers on the Days of Awe is markedly more universal than at other times. The central section of the Amida begins by speaking not about Israel, the chosen people, but about humankind as a whole: "And so place the fear of You...over all that You have made." Rosh HaShana and Yom Kippur are about the sovereignty of God over all the world. We reflect on the human, not just the Jewish, condition.

The two cycles reflect two quite different aspects of God as He relates to the world: as Creator and Redeemer. As Creator we relate to God through nature. As Redeemer we relate to God through history. As Creator, God is universal. We are all in God's image, formed in His likeness. We share a covenant of human solidarity, made by God with Noah and through him all humankind after the Flood. We are fellow citizens of the world under the sovereignty of God. As Redeemer, however, God is particularistic. Whatever His relationship with other nations (and He has a relationship with other nations: so the prophets insist), Jews know Him through His saving acts in Israel's past: the Exodus, the revelation and the journey to the Promised Land.

It is now obvious what makes Sukkot unique. It is the only festival that is part of both cycles. It belongs to the yearly cycle of Jewish history – Pesaḥ, Shavuot and Sukkot – the year that begins in Nisan, the month of the Exodus in which Jewish national history began. But it also belongs to the seventh-month cycle that represents creation and nature: Rosh HaShana, Yom Kippur and Sukkot. The year of nature begins on Rosh HaShana, the anniversary of creation itself. Hence the double joy, and the twofold symbolism.

The "four kinds" represent what is universal about Sukkot. They are about nature. They are the only time we do a mitzva with natural objects: a lulav, etrog, and myrtle and willow leaves. They are about humanity's dependence on nature, and nature's need for rain. That is why Zechariah foresaw that when all nations acknowledged God, they would come together in the seventh month to pray for rain on Sukkot. The sukka, by contrast, has nothing to do with rain. It has to do with history and what makes Jewish history unique. We have undergone repeated experiences of exile. Too often Jews have known that where they are is only a temporary dwelling. Jewish history has often been a long journey across the wilderness of time.

Something else about Sukkot, in this case common to both the "four kinds" and the sukka, also points to this duality. The "four kinds" are unprocessed products of nature. The covering of the sukka must also be made of materials that were once growing and are now detached but not yet turned into crafted objects of a kind capable of contracting *tum'a*, impurity (*Sukka* 1:4). Both the "four kinds" and the sukka covering represent the boundary between nature and culture, what Lévi-Strauss called the "raw" and the "cooked." Nature is universal. Culture is not. Once again we feel the tension between our common humanity and our religious specificity, between what makes us the same and what makes us different.

More than any other festival, Sukkot represents the dual character of Jewish faith. We believe in the universality of God, together with the particularity of Jewish history and identity. All nations need rain. We are all part of nature. We are all dependent on the complex ecology of the created world. We are all threatened by climate change, global warming, the destruction of rain forests, the overexploitation of non-renewable energy sources and the mass extinction of species. But each nation is different. As Jews we are heirs to a history unlike that of any other people: small, vulnerable, suffering repeated exile and defeat, yet surviving and celebrating.

Sukkot thus represents the tension at the heart of Judaism in a way not shared by any other faith. The God of Israel is the God of all humanity. But the religion of Israel is not, and will not be, the religion of all humanity. Even in the Messianic Age, Zechariah tells us, the nations will celebrate only Sukkot together with Israel, not the other festivals – despite the fact that on that day God will be One and His name One.

This is one of the most important truths Judaism offers the world: humanity is formed out of our commonalities and differences. Our differences shape our identity. Our commonalities form our humanity. We are neither completely different, nor all the same. If we were completely different, we could not communicate. If we were all alike, we would have nothing to say. Our differences matter. But so too does the truth that despite our religious differences, we share a common humanity. Sukkot is thus the festival of a double joy: at being part of this people, yet also participating in the universal fate of humankind.

The Strangest Book of the Bible

Our real journey into the meaning of Sukkot, however, begins with a book that is not merely the strangest in Tanakh, but also one of the most unlikely ever to have been included in a canon of sacred texts: Kohelet, known in English through its Greek translation as Ecclesiastes, meaning "one who addresses an assembly."

Kohelet is a strange, bewildering and much debated book. It was one of the last to be canonized, though it was widely known and studied long before its status was finalized. It was included in the Septuagint, the first translation of the Hebrew Bible into Greek. It is presupposed by the book known as Ben Sira (also known as Ecclesiasticus), written in the late second century BCE. Fragments of Kohelet were found among the Dead Sea Scrolls. Nonetheless, there were rabbis who found it problematic. A minority held that it was not to be included in Tanakh. For them it represented merely the human wisdom of Solomon, not a text inspired by *ruaḥ hakodesh*, the holy spirit, a precondition of being included in the Bible.

A homily in the Talmud (*Shabbat* 30a) tells us some of the problems the sages had with the book.

> O Solomon, where is your wisdom? Where is your understanding? Not only do your words contradict those of your father David, but they also contradict themselves. Your father David said, "It is not the dead who praise the Lord" [Ps. 115:17], but you said, "I thought the dead more fortunate, who have died already, than the living who yet live" [Eccl. 4:2], and then you said, "Better to be a living dog than a dead lion" [9:4].

Is it better to be alive than dead? Kohelet answers both yes and no.

Other rabbis pointed out other contradictions. Ibn Ezra counted nine of them and said that the attentive reader would find more. Kohelet praises joy (8:15) and derides it (2:2). He values wisdom (2:13) and denigrates it (6:8). He says things will go well for those who are God-fearing (8:12) and then says that there are righteous people who suffer the fate of the wicked, and wicked people who receive the reward of the righteous (8:14). Such were the internal contradictions in the book that some sages sought not merely to exclude it from the canon but to have it banned (*Shabbat* 30b).

Kohelet's tendency to say one thing and then the opposite makes the book hard to understand, but this alone would not have justified excluding it from the canon. The sages were adroit in resolving apparent contradictions, of which there are many in the Hebrew Bible. Kohelet uses contradiction the way Socrates used questions, to force his listeners to think beyond conventional wisdom, and understand the complexity and many-sidedness of life. He understood what Niels Bohr famously said, that the opposite of a superficial truth is a falsehood, but the opposite of a profound truth may well be another profound truth. The use of contradiction is common within the wisdom literature. One example comes from the book of Proverbs: "Do not answer a fool according to his folly, or you yourself will be just like him. Do answer a fool according to his folly, or he will be wise in his own eyes" (Prov. 26:4–5). It was not its internal contradictions that made some think Kohelet did not belong in the Hebrew Bible, but something far more consequential.

It was that many of the views expressed by Kohelet seem to verge on heresy.[1] The same fate, he says, awaits the righteous and the wicked, the pure and impure, the good and the sinner (9:2). There is no correlation between effort and reward. The race is not to the swift, nor bread to the wise, nor grace to the learned: time and chance happen to them all (9:11). Kohelet sees "the victims' tears and none to console them; power at the hands of their oppressors, and none to console them" (4:1). Where then is justice and the Judge?

"The fate of man is the fate of cattle; the same fate awaits them both," hence "the pre-eminence of man over beast is nothing" (3:19). What then becomes of the idea of the uniqueness of the human person made in the image and likeness of God Himself? Don't be too righteous or too wicked, says Kohelet (7:16–17). What then should we do: be a little righteous and a little wicked? "Follow your heart where it leads you, your eyes where they allure you," he says to the young man (11:9). What then happens to the third paragraph of the Shema which tells us not to stray "after your heart and after your eyes" (Num. 15:39)?

Kohelet says not a word about Jewish particularity. Scholars have long noted its similarity to other wisdom literature of the ancient Near East, Egyptian, Mesopotamian, even Canaanite. It would not have been out of place in Greece in the third century BCE: in places it reads like a Stoic or Epicurean text. Though it contains many references to God, it never once uses the four-letter name we refer to as Hashem, that is, God as He relates specifically to the Jewish people. Kohelet speaks only of Elokim, that is, the God of creation, nature and humankind as a whole.

The most important feature of Kohelet that makes it seem so remote from faith is his repeated use of the word *hevel*. It occurs no fewer than thirty-eight times in the course of the book, more than half of its

---

1. See Leviticus Raba 28:1; Ecclesiastes Raba 1:4, 11:9; *Midrash Mishlei* 25:1.

incidences in Tanakh as a whole. *Hevel* has traditionally been understood to mean futile, meaningless, empty, pointless, "absurd" in the existentialist sense, and most famously in the King James translation: "Vanity of vanities, saith the Preacher, vanity of vanities; all is vanity."

This is what makes the book so challenging. Religion in general, Judaism specifically, is the attempt to find meaning in the cosmos and in human life. Faith is the attempt to hear the music beneath the noise, discern the path amidst the undergrowth, to sense the destination of the long journey of which our lives are a part. Judaism is the bold attempt to address directly what Viktor Frankl called "Man's Search for Meaning." To see life as meaningless – *hevel* – seems in the most profound sense to part company with Jewish tradition.

Thus Kohelet, despite its invocations of God and its pious ending, reads at first like a subversive book. If there is no justice in history, if the strong crush the weak, and power is in the hands of the oppressor, if the wise man who saves the city is forgotten while evil reigns in place of judgment, why are we here at all? We live, we suffer, then we die. That seems to be Kohelet's philosophy. Homo sapiens, however "noble in reason and infinite in faculty," is ultimately no more than the "quintessence of dust." But this is Hamlet, not Judaism. And even if a case can be made for its inclusion in the library of sacred texts, why, of all the books, was it chosen for Sukkot, *zeman simḥateinu*, "our time of rejoicing"? Of all our holy books it seems the most bleak and depressing.

Kohelet is a puzzle to be solved, a mystery to be decoded. If we do so, we will discover not only that it is a profound statement of faith, one of the deepest in literature, but also that it is the key to understanding Sukkot itself.

I. *Who Was Kohelet?*

Fortunately, the book gives us the clue that allows us to unpack its meaning in its second word, the one that gives it its title as well as the name of its author: Kohelet. Who was he? There is only one possible answer: Kohelet was Solomon. The opening sentence states: "The sayings of Kohelet son of David, King of Israel in Jerusalem." The only son of David who became king was Solomon. The rest of Kohelet confirms this identification. Solomon was the only king of Israel whose life matches the description in chapter two, of a man who amassed a great estate, built palaces, planted vineyards, orchards and gardens, had vast numbers of slaves and servants, accumulated silver and gold, and had many wives and concubines.

Kohelet's claim to have gathered more wisdom than any other king before him (1:16) parallels the description of Solomon in I Kings 5:9, in which "God gave Solomon wisdom and very great insight, and a breadth of understanding as measureless as the sand on the seashore." The statement at the end of the book, that Kohelet "weighed and explored and assembled many wise sayings" (12:9), matches the statement in the book of Kings that Solomon "spoke three thousand proverbs," and was so famous for his wisdom that "people from all nations came to listen" to him (5:12–14).

If Kohelet was Solomon, why is he not called Solomon? This is the first indication that the book is not a treatise to be read, but an encrypted text to be deciphered. Note that the question is not the historical one: who actually wrote Kohelet? Whoever wrote Kohelet, without a shadow of doubt it is meant to be read as the reflections of the man known as Israel's wisest king. In which case, the book should mention Solomon. That is the case with the two other books traditionally ascribed to him, the Song of Songs and Proverbs. The name Solomon appears nowhere in Kohelet. What is more, the word "Kohelet" appears nowhere else in Tanakh. This strongly suggests that Kohelet is more than the name of the author. It is a clue to the interpretation of the book.

The point is often missed in translation, because it is difficult to convey in other languages the density of associations often carried by a single Hebrew word. That is clearly the case here. The word "Kohelet" comes from the root *k-h-l*, meaning "to gather people together." Thus it is usually translated as "preacher," "teacher" or "convener of an assembly." However, what matters here is not what the word means, but rather the associations it carries with it. As soon as we turn to the other key instances of the verb, a fascinating picture begins to emerge.

The first connection is with the mitzva known as *Hak'hel*: the command that the king was to assemble the people every seven years at a national assembly on Sukkot at the end of a sabbatical year.

Every seventh year, in the scheduled year of release, during the festival of Sukkot, when all Israel comes to appear before the Lord your God at the place that He will choose, you shall read this law before all Israel in their hearing. Assemble the people – men, women and children, as well as the aliens residing in your towns – so that they may hear and learn to fear the Lord your God and to observe diligently all the words of this law, and so that their children, who have not known it, may hear and learn to fear the Lord your God, as long as you live in the land that you are crossing over the Jordan to possess. (Deut. 31:10–13)

Here then is an immediate connection between Sukkot, a king, an assembly, an act of teaching, and the verb *hak'hel*, from the same root as the word "Kohelet." This connection was not lost on the sages, who explained that Solomon was called Kohelet precisely because of this role, and suggested that the book is based on what Solomon taught at these gatherings (Ecclesiastes Raba 1:2). Something of this is hinted at the very end of the book: "Kohelet's wisdom went further than this; he taught the people understanding always, and weighed and explored and assembled many wise sayings" (12:9). We do not find in the story of Solomon that he "taught the people." Hence it was not absurd to suggest that this happened at the septennial gathering of the nation on Sukkot.

There is, as we noted in the first section, another connection between Solomon and Sukkot, namely the dedication of the Temple, which took place over a fourteen-day period, the last seven of which coincided with Sukkot. If we turn to I Kings 8, the chapter that describes the consecration of the Temple, we find that the verb *k-h-l* plays a key role in the text. It appears seven times, and a seven-fold repetition is often used in biblical prose to indicate a key word. The chapter tells how Solomon assembled the elders of Israel and all the heads of the tribes to bring up the Ark of the Covenant of the Lord out of the city of David, which is Zion. Again we find a connection between a national assembly, the king and Sukkot.

There is a third connection, more oblique, but one that will eventually prove highly consequential. The Temple was the successor to the *Mishkan*, the Tabernacle or Sanctuary that the Israelites made in the desert, their first collective house of worship. Construction began immediately after Moses descended from Mount Sinai with the second set of tablets, having broken the first after the sin of the golden calf. In this narrative, too, the key word is *k-h-l*. At the making of the calf we read that "when the people saw that Moses delayed to come down from the mountain, the people gathered themselves together [*vayikahel*] around Aaron, and said to him, 'Come, make gods for us, who shall go before us...'" (Ex. 32:1). After securing atonement for the people, Moses commanded them to build the Sanctuary. The narrative begins, "Moses assembled [*vayak'hel*] all the congregation of the Israelites..." (35:1). Again the key word is *k-h-l*.

The assembly Moses convened to set in motion the building of the Sanctuary was a *tikkun*, a setting-right, of the assembly that had committed the sin in the first place. According to tradition, Moses descended the mountain with the second tablets – the sign that the people had been forgiven and the covenant between them and God was still in place – on Yom Kippur. That is why the anniversary of that day became, throughout the generations, the day of forgiveness and atonement. The next day, work on the Sanctuary began (see Rashi to Ex. 35:1). Still today the custom is to begin making the sukka immediately after Yom Kippur.

So there is a whole series of connections between the word "Kohelet," from the root *k-h-l*, and a king, a national assembly, the Sanctuary in the wilderness, the Temple in Jerusalem, and Sukkot. Indeed the prophet Amos calls the Temple *Sukkat David*, "David's Tabernacle" (Amos 9:11). These echoes and evocations are too strong to be coincidental. The key to understanding Kohelet is Sukkot, and the key to understanding Sukkot is Kohelet. Nor is the root *k-h-l* the only link between the book and the festival.

II. Wisdom, the Universal Heritage

Recall Zechariah's prophecy that one day Sukkot would be celebrated by all the nations on earth, and the sages' understanding that the seventy bullocks offered during the festival were on behalf of the seventy nations, that is, on behalf of humanity as a whole. Sukkot is the most universalist of the festivals, and Kohelet is by far the most universalist of the five "scrolls" – the Megillot. Ruth, Esther and Lamentations tell highly particularist narratives about characters and events in Jewish history. The Song of Songs is about the particularity of love: what makes this lover and this beloved unique. But Kohelet is consistently, even surprisingly, universal. The word "Israel" only appears twice, and then in the form of an editorial aside, "I Kohelet was king of Israel in Jerusalem" (1:12, and compare 1:1). The four-letter name of God, Hashem, indicating His specific I-Thou relationship with the people Israel, never appears in the book. Instead, forty-two times the word "Elokim" is used: that is, God in His relationship with humanity as a whole.

The reason for this is that Kohelet is supremely written in the wisdom voice. There are three primary voices in Tanakh. Each corresponds to a different way in which we encounter God, and each is embodied in a different kind of leadership role. Respectively, they are the king, the priest and the prophet, and they correspond to the three modes of God's relationship with the world: creation, revelation and redemption.

The priest speaks the language of revelation, that is, God's word in the form of law. The priest's key roles are *lehavdil*, "to distinguish," "to separate," and *lehorot*, "to instruct," "to give a legal ruling." The priest sees distinctions in the world invisible to the naked eye. They are not part of the physical world as such; they are, rather, part of the sacred ontology, the underlying divine order, of the universe. The key words in the priest's vocabulary are *tahor* and *tameh*, pure and impure, and *kodesh* and *ḥol*, holy and profane. He (priests in Judaism were always male) lives within a structure of time wholly determined by divine service: originally the sacrificial service of the Temple. The priest represents the holy in Jewish life. Halakha, Jewish law, belongs to the priestly voice.

The prophet hears and speaks God's word, not for all time but for this time: this place, this context, this circumstance, the today that is different from yesterday and tomorrow. He or she (prophets could be either) senses the presence of God in history, specifically history as a journey toward redemption, that is to say, a society that honors God by honoring His image, humankind. While the priest looks at the sacred nature of things, the prophet is concerned with relationships between persons, and between the individual and God. His or her key words are *tzedek*, fairness, *mishpat*, retributive justice, *ḥesed*, covenant love, and *raḥamim*, compassion. While the world of the priest never changes, the prophet's world is constantly changing, depending on where the people are and in which direction society is moving. The prophet is concerned with faithfulness in Jewish life: loyalty, integrity and honesty between the people and God and between one another.

Wisdom in the Hebrew Bible is very different from the worlds of the priest and the prophet. It is almost always associated with kings and royal courts, and it is universal, not specific to Judaism. It is part of the human heritage: it is part of what it means to be created in the image and likeness of God. Thus the sages said: "If you are told that there is wisdom among the nations, believe it. If you are told there is Torah among the nations, do not believe it" (Lamentations Raba 2:13). The sages coined a blessing on seeing "a great sage from the [other] nations" (*Berakhot* 58a). The wisdom literature of Tanakh – Kohelet, Proverbs, Job and some Psalms – is recognizably similar to the wisdom literature of the ancient Near East as well as the philosophers and moralists of ancient Greece and Rome. Whereas priestly and prophetic consciousness lives in particularity, the essence of wisdom is universality.

If the priestly voice is about revelation and the prophetic about redemption, wisdom belongs to the realm of creation. It is about what we would nowadays call the natural and social sciences. Wisdom and Torah are very different. Wisdom is about facts, Torah is about laws. Wisdom is about what is, Torah about what ought to be. Wisdom is descriptive while Torah is prescriptive. Wisdom is acquired through observation and reflection. Torah is acquired through revelation and tradition. In relation to wisdom, what matters is the truth of a proposition, not its source. Hence Maimonides' famous axiom: "Accept the truth, whoever says it" (Introduction to *Pirkei Avot*). In the case of Torah, however, source is of the essence. Does it come from the revelation at Sinai, or from the Oral Law, faithfully transmitted? Hence the rabbinic rule: "Whoever reports a saying in the name of the one who said it brings deliverance to the world" (*Avot* 6:6).

The words *ḥakham*, a wise person, and *ḥokhma*, wisdom, appear fifty-three times in Kohelet, as against a mere thirty-three times in the entire Mosaic books, where (with the exception of Deuteronomy) they are almost entirely used in connection with the royal court in Egypt – Pharaoh and his advisers – or the Sanctuary, where *ḥokhma* is used in the sense of craftsmanship.

It is therefore no accident that the most universal of books, Kohelet, is read on the most universal of pilgrimage festivals, Sukkot. Wisdom, the knowledge of God in creation, belongs to the seventh month, the month of creation (Rosh HaShana as the anniversary of the birth of the world and humankind). And just as Zechariah said that there would come a time when "those remaining from all the nations... will go up year upon year to bow down to the King, the Lord of hosts, and to celebrate the festival of Sukkot" (Zech. 14:16), so the book of Kings says, "From all nations people came to listen to Solomon's wisdom, sent by all the kings of the world, who had heard of his wisdom" (I Kings 5:14). That is the second connection between Kohelet and Sukkot. But it is the third that is the most surprising.

III. The Structure of Joy

Kohelet is often seen as a depressing, despairing, almost nihilistic book. The author is old, disillusioned, skeptical about the ability of humans to change the world or institute justice in the affairs of men, disinclined to find any redemptive quality in life itself. So, of all biblical books, it seems the least appropriate to read on Sukkot, "the season of our joy." Yet, counterintuitively, it turns out that this is precisely what Kohelet is about.

The root *s-m-ḥ*, meaning joy or rejoicing, appears no fewer than seventeen times in the course of the book. To put this in context, the same root appears only once in each of the first four Mosaic books, Genesis, Exodus, Leviticus and Numbers, and twelve times in Deuteronomy. There are more references to joy in Kohelet than in all the Mosaic books combined

Nor is this all. The references to joy are carefully structured. The overall development of the book is not clear, but one thing is: seven times, after a sequence of dispiriting reflections, Kohelet interrupts his theme with a reference to joy:

1. There is no good for man to find, but that he eat and drink and show himself some good of all his labor; this I saw to be a gift from God.... He gave wisdom and insight and joy to those who are satisfied with what they have. (2:24–26)

2. And so I know that there is no good for them but to be happy and to do what is good in their lifetime. And if any man eats and drinks and sees some good of all his labor – that is a gift from God. (3:12–13)

3. I saw that there is no good at all but for man to take pleasure in his works; for that is his share. (3:22)

4. This is what I have seen that is good: the beauty of eating and drinking and seeing some good of all the labor one toils over beneath the sun, all the days of the life God has given one – for this is one's share. For if God gives any man wealth and belongings, and grants him the power to eat of them, to take hold of what is his, to take pleasure in his labors – that is a gift from God. For he will not think too much about the days of his life; for God has given him the joy of his heart to be occupied with. (5:17–19)

5. And so I praise joy – for there is no good for man beneath the sun, but to eat and drink and be happy. This is what he has to accompany him in his labors, through that life that God has given him beneath the sun. (8:15)

6. Go, eat your bread in joy, and drink your wine with a joyful heart, for God has accepted your deeds.... Live well, with the woman you love, all the days of the shallow breath He has given you here beneath the sun. (9:7–9)

7. There is a sweetness in the light; it is good for the eyes to see the sun. And should a man live many years he should rejoice in all of them, remembering, too, the days of darkness, for there will be many. All that comes is but a breath. (11:7–8)

Then comes the ten-line coda, precisely symmetrical with the ten-line introduction to the book. The closing movement, a long adagio beginning with the words, "Young man, rejoice now in your youth" (11:9), is one of the most moving descriptions of age and physical decline in all literature, comparing it to the darkening of the sun, the slow decay of an old house, a well that no longer yields water, a shattered lamp, a broken pitcher, and dust returning to the earth as it was, ending with the words, "'Shallowest breath,' said Kohelet, 'It is all but shallow breath'" (12:8). The introduction begins with almost identical words, "'Shallowest breath,' said Kohelet, 'The shallowest breath, it is all but breath'" (1:2), and then describes the endless cycles of nature in which "one age departs, another comes" (1:4). Between the beginning and the end, we have moved from abstract to concrete, from a general statement about the human condition to the intensely personal pattern as the dying author urges the young man to rejoice while he can.

We see here something fascinating. The main text reads almost like a dialogue between the author's jaded persona and his other voice that keeps saying, "Rejoice." It is no accident that this happens seven times. The number seven is a key figure in relation to Solomon. The building of the Temple took seven years (I Kings 6:38). The celebrations were in the seventh month (I Kings 8:2). They lasted for "seven days and another seven days" (I Kings 8:65). In his prayer at the dedication, Solomon made seven petitions to God (I Kings 8:30–53). So the sevenfold interruption of joy in Kohelet is not random. It is a feature of the text that the author expects sensitive readers to notice. These seven injunctions to joy coincide with the seven days of the festival of joy.

The coda corresponds to the eighth day, on which Solomon took his leave of the people: "On the eighth day he let the people go. They blessed the king and returned home, joyous and glad of heart for all the good which God had shown His servant David and His people Israel" (I Kings 8:66). That day was, of course, Shemini Atzeret. Not only, then, is Kohelet the only book of the Hebrew Bible that is a treatise on joy. Even its structure precisely parallels that of Sukkot and Shemini Atzeret, seven days of joy plus one.

We have now established three sets of connection between Kohelet and Sukkot. One is the name Kohelet itself, with its multiple associations with kings, the Temple, the Tabernacle and Sukkot. A second relates to *hokhma*, wisdom, its universality and its connection to creation. The third has to do with *simha*, joy, the theme both of the festival and the book. We can now hazard a hypothesis: this is the interpretive key that unlocks the book and its teachings.

Kohelet has been analyzed by scholars as an isolated text. As such, we cannot begin to say what it means because of its internal contradictions and because we do not know precisely when it was written and why. Who was the intended audience? What were they expected to draw from the book? Which is the real Kohelet, the voice of despair or the counter-voice of joy? Considered in and of itself, the book could mean almost anything.

But placing it within the canon and the calendar, and associating it with Sukkot – an association, we have argued, that is anything but random – it ceases to be a work in and of itself. It is part of a larger pattern. That is what we will argue in the chapter on Pesah about another perplexing work, *Shir HaShirim*, the Song of Songs. Considered in itself, it reads like a series of secular love songs. But considered in its calendrical and canonical context, it resolves one of the most fundamental questions in Judaism: Where is the answering response on the part of the Israelites to God's freely given love? A single verse from Jeremiah makes the connection: "I remember of you the kindness of your youth, your love when you were a bride; how you walked after Me in the desert, through a land not sown" (Jer. 2:2). The Song of Songs is the record of that love.

Kohelet has a similar function within the Hebrew Bible. What, though, is the question to which it is an answer?

IV. Breath

The meaning of Kohelet hinges on one word: *hevel*. As we saw, it occurs thirty-eight times, more than half of all its occurrences in Tanakh. No other book announces its theme more emphatically, by using one word five times in a single sentence, the second in the book. "'*Hevel* of *hevels*,' says Kohelet, '*Hevel* of *hevels*, all is *hevel*.'"

The word has been translated many ways: "pointless," "meaningless," "futile," "empty," "vapor," "smoke," "insubstantial," "absurd," "vanity." There is something to these translations, but they do not represent the word's primary meaning. It means "breath." The Hebrew words for soul – among them *nefesh*, *ruah* and *neshama* – all have to do with the act of breathing. The same is true in other ancient languages. "Psyche," as in psychology, also derives from the Greek word for breath. *Hevel* specifically means a shallow breath.

What obsesses Kohelet is that all that separates life from death is a shallow breath. He is obsessed by the fragility and brevity of life, as contrasted with the seeming eternity of the universe. The world endures forever. But we are, as we say in our prayers on Rosh HaShana and Yom Kippur, "like a broken shard, like grass dried up, like a faded flower, like a fleeting shadow, like a passing cloud, like a breath of wind, like whirling dust, like a dream that slips away." Dust we are and to dust we return. Take breath away and a living body becomes a mere corpse. Reading Kohelet reminds us of the scene in Shakespeare's *King Lear*, when the aged king holds in his arms the dead body of his daughter Cordelia, the only one who truly loved him, and whose faithfulness he discovered too late, and says, "Why should a dog, a horse, a rat have breath, and thou no breath at all?" Or it recalls the verse of T.S. Eliot: "I will show you something different from either / Your shadow at morning striding behind you / Or your shadow at evening rising to meet you; / I will show you fear in a handful of dust."

Kohelet is a sustained meditation on mortality, one of the most profound in all literature. He is traumatized by the "unbearable lightness of being," the fact that life is lived toward death, that our days are numbered, that like Moses, for each of us there will be a Jordan we will not cross, a fulfillment we will not live to see. We do not, cannot, know how long we will live, but life will always seem too short.

This single fact, for Kohelet, overshadows all human existence. It mocks all achievement and aspiration. We may accumulate wealth, but who knows what those who come after us will do with it? We may achieve power, but it will pass, on our demise, to other people – as Solomon's kingdom fell to his son Rehoboam, whose failure to heed his father's advisers caused the kingdom to split into two, a division from which it never fully recovered, and which undid all that his father and grandfather had striven to do.

Who knows how posterity will judge us? Who knows if we will be remembered at all? And if we are not remembered, of what consequence is our life? It is a mere pattern drawn in sand that will be dissolved by the next high tide. Whatever we achieve in this life will not save us from oblivion. Naked we came into the world and naked we will return.

That is the overwhelming fact for Kohelet. That is why he says that there is no ultimate difference between the righteous and the wicked, or between man and the animals. We will all die in the end, and that is the most important fact about us.

We can now state, simply and boldly, the connection between Kohelet and Sukkot. A sukka is a *dirat arai*, a temporary dwelling. Kohelet is about the fact that the human body is a temporary dwelling. Life is a sukka. We are strangers and temporary residents on earth. As Rilke said, "even the noticing beasts are aware that we don't feel very securely at home in this interpreted world" (*Duino Elegies*, 1). We seek the security of a house, a home, and find there is none to be had. There is no way of making human life everlasting. We cannot banish risk and uncertainty. Time is a desert, a wilderness, and all we have as we journey is a hut, a booth, a tent. Kohelet is a philosophical statement of life seen as a sukka.

As such it is not a unique voice in Tanakh. We find something similar in the book of Psalms:

> You have made my days mere handbreadths;
> the span of my years is as nothing before You.
> Mere breath is each man standing…
> Man walks like a shadow,
> He goes as a breath,
> Storing without knowing who will gather…
> Surely everyone is but a breath…
> I dwell with You as a stranger,
> a temporary resident, like all my fathers. (Ps. 39:6–13)

Likewise in the book of Job:

> Remember, O God, that my life is but a breath;
> Not again will my eyes see good…
> I despise my life; I will not live forever.
> Let me alone, for my days are mere breath. (Job 7:7, 16)

Kohelet was thus not the first to feel that death cast its shadow over the whole of life. Nor was he the last. In 1879, having reached his fiftieth birthday, Leo Tolstoy had achieved success and acclaim. He had published two of the greatest novels ever written, *War and Peace* and *Anna Karenina*. He owned a vast estate, was married, and had fourteen children. Yet he succumbed to precisely the thoughts that had driven Kohelet to despair.

He recounts his crisis by way of a story. A traveler is crossing the steppes when he encounters a ferocious wild animal. To escape, he hides in an empty well. But at the bottom of the well he sees a dragon, its jaws open, ready to eat him. He cannot leave the well for fear of the beast. He cannot drop to the bottom because of the dragon. He seizes hold of the branch of a bush growing in a crevice in the well's wall. It is all that is saving him from death. His arms are growing weak, but still he holds on. Then he sees two mice, one black, the other white, gnawing at the branch. Soon they will eat through it, and he will fall into the dragon's mouth. He sees some drops of honey on the leaves of the bush and stretches out his tongue to lick them.

That, says Tolstoy, is how his life feels to him. He has almost no strength left, he is about to fall, the black and white mice – nights and days – are gnawing away at his future and even the drops of honey no longer give him pleasure. The question that haunted him was simply this: "Is there any meaning in my life that the inevitable death awaiting me does not destroy?" (Tolstoy, *A Confession*).

Like Kohelet, Tolstoy searched for an answer in wisdom, that is, in science and philosophy, and like Kohelet he found none. Science could not understand the question, and philosophy could only repeat it. For Tolstoy, like Kohelet, the fundamental human question is simply: Why live?

We now sense the depth of the drama of Sukkot seen through the eyes of Kohelet. For ten days, beginning on Rosh HaShana and reaching a climax on Yom Kippur, we have prayed, "Remember us for life, O King who desires life, and write us in the book of life – for Your sake, O God of life." Now, having survived the trial, we are faced with the deepest question of all. What is life? What is this gift we have been granted? What gives life meaning, purpose, substance? What will redeem us from the shadow of death?

V. A Critique of Pure Happiness

Kohelet's answer, in a word, is joy. That, as we have seen, is the repeated refrain of the counter-voice within the book. Kohelet's alter ego knows that, yes, life is short, knowledge painful and the ruling powers corrupt. The righteous sometimes die young, and evildoers sometimes reach old age. If you make justice – visible, manifest justice, down here on earth – your precondition for making a blessing over life, you will wait a long time, and you will die disappointed. Kohelet tells us these truths with brutal honesty. But he has grown older, wiser. He has passed through the valley of disillusion and emerged on the other side.

What redeems life and etches it with the charisma of grace is joy: joy in your work ("The sleep of a worker is sweet" – 5:11), joy in your marriage ("See life with the woman you love" – 9:9), and joy in the simple pleasures of life. Take joy in each day. Above all, rejoice when you are young. Kohelet is an old man. No one has written a more moving description of the dying of the light in old age than does Kohelet in the last chapter of the book. Yet his conclusion yields to neither cynicism nor despair. You do not need to be blind to the imperfections of the human world or the slow ravages of age in order to rejoice. You can know life with all its flaws and still have joy.

Aristotle in the *Nicomachean Ethics* said that happiness is that at which all people aim. It is the one thing good in itself and not as a means to some other end. Judaism in general, and Kohelet specifically, disagree. Yes, happiness – *osher* in Hebrew – is a value in Judaism. Its derivative *ashrei* is the first word in the book of Psalms. We say the prayer we call *Ashrei* three times each day. Yet it is not the supreme value. *Simḥa*, joy, is. As we noted, it appears twelve times in Deuteronomy, seventeen times in Kohelet. What is the difference?

Happiness in the classic sense, *eudaemonia* in Greek, *felicitas* in Latin, and *ashrei* in Hebrew, means doing well and faring well. The good person acts morally and is respected by others for doing so. Barring accidents or misfortune, he or she is blessed with a good marriage, children, a reputation for integrity ("the crown of a good name" – *Avot* 4:17), an honored place within the community and the feeling of a life well lived. He sleeps well at night, knowing he has done nothing of which to be ashamed. That is the happy individual of Psalm 1. He is like a tree planted by streams of water that gives forth fruit in its due season and whose leaves do not wither. Psalm 92, the Psalm of the Sabbath day, deepens the imagery. The wicked are like grass: they grow fast but are soon cut down. The righteous are like a tree, giving fruit and shade like a palm, growing tall like a cedar in Lebanon. Happiness is the outcome of a moral life.

But happiness depends on many external circumstances. What of the poor, the exploited, the unemployed? What, asks the Torah repeatedly, of the orphan, the widow and the stranger within the gates? What, asks Kohelet, of the tears of the oppressed who have no comforter? What of the wise man who saved the city only to be unthanked, ignored, forgotten? What, we might ask nowadays, of the victims of terror, or those who live under tyranny? To speak of happiness under such circumstances is almost to mock the afflicted.

When the world is in a state of order, when there is peace and good governance and accountability, when there are shared values within a society, and those who are blessed share their blessings with the vulnerable and the destitute, when the great and the good are indeed great and good, yes, one can speak of happiness as a central value. What, though, survives when none of these preconditions are met? What is left when the world we live in looks less like a house than a sukka, open to the wind, the rain and the cold? What remains, other than fear, in a state of radical insecurity?

The answer is *simha*, joy. For joy does not involve, as does happiness, a judgment about life as a whole. Joy lives in the moment. It asks no questions about tomorrow. It celebrates the power of now. The Talmud says that each Sunday, Shammai, the great sage of the late Second Temple period, was already preparing for Shabbat. Hillel, however, lived by a different principle: "Blessed be God day by day" (*Beitza* 16a). Joy blesses God day by day. It celebrates the mere fact of being here, now, existing when we might not have existed, inhaling to the full this day, this hour, this eternity-in-a-moment that was not before and will not be again. Joy embraces the contingency of life. It knows that yesterday has gone and tomorrow is unknown. It does not ask what was or will be. It makes no calculations. It is a state of radical thankfulness for the gift of being. Even in an age too fraught for happiness, there can still be joy.

Rainer Maria Rilke wrote in one of his letters, "The reality of joy in the world is indescribable; only in joy does creation take place (happiness, on the contrary, is only a promising, intelligible constellation of things already there); joy is a marvelous increasing of what exists, a pure addition out of nothingness." He added, "How superficially must happiness engage us, after all, if it can leave us time to think and worry about how long it will last." What saved Kohelet was his belated realization that joy, not happiness, is what redeems life from the shadow of death. Joy does not ask how long it will last. It discovers epiphany in the here and now.

Joy is the antidote to the sickness we sense in the great autobiographical section of Kohelet chapter two. There is no passage like it anywhere else in Tanakh. Kohelet is speaking about how he acquired houses, vineyards, orchards, male and female servants, silver, gold, wives and concubines. He had everything. Except meaning. Except purpose. Except joy. What makes the text unique is its double use of the first person singular. "I built for myself...I planted for myself...I collected for myself...I acquired for myself..." (Eccl. 2:4–8). Kohelet's error was spelled out in the Mishna centuries later by Hillel: "If I am not for myself, who will be for me? And if I am only for myself, what am I?" (*Avot* 1:14).

Happiness is something I can feel on my own. But joy in the Torah is essentially shared. A husband must make his wife rejoice (Deut. 24:5). Festivals were to be occasions of collective rejoicing, "you and your sons and daughters, your male and female slaves, and the Levite, the stranger and orphan and widow that dwell within your gates" (Deut. 16:11). Bringing first fruits to the Temple involved collective celebration: "You and the Levites and the strangers in your midst shall rejoice in all the good things the Lord your God has given to you and your household" (Deut. 26:11). Unlike happiness, *simḥa* only exists in virtue of being shared. It is a form of social emotion.

It is also a religious one. Kierkegaard once wrote, "It is moral to grieve; it is religious to rejoice." Joy is a form of thanksgiving. It is a way of acknowledging life as a gift – and if it is a gift, there must be a Giver. Joy is King David dancing before God the day the Ark was brought to Jerusalem. It is the "righteous and men of good deeds" doing somersaults and juggling with flaming torches in the Temple courtyard during *Simḥat Beit HaSho'eva*. Joy is a Jewish wedding. It is dancing in the presence of the Divine. There is nothing in it of pride or self-satisfaction. It defeats the fear of death by turning our attention outward. For a moment the "I" is silent and we become part of the celebrating "We," our voice merging with others in the song creation sings to its Creator, the nation to its sovereign God, and we to God for "keeping us alive and sustaining us and bringing us to this day." The *Shekhina*, said the sages, does not live in sadness or depression, but in the joy of fulfilling God's command (*simha shel mitzva*).

Unlike happiness, joy is not conditional on things going well. No one put this better than the prophet Habakkuk, in one of the most moving passages in the prophetic literature:

> Though the fig tree does not blossom,
>   and no fruit is on the vines;
> though the produce of the olive fails
>   and the fields yield no food;
> though the flock is cut off from the fold
>   and there is no herd in the stalls,
> yet I will rejoice in the Lord;
> I will exult in the God of my salvation. (Hab. 3:17–18)

Joy alone, Kohelet realized at the end of a long life, has the power to defeat despair. It does not speak the language of reason. It does not answer the existential questions of a disillusioned philosopher-king. Joy belongs to an older, deeper part of the brain. Like music, it gives expression to the inexpressible. It says, yes, life is sometimes unfair and the world unjust, but the very brevity of life makes each moment precious. It says: stop thinking of tomorrow. Celebrate, sing, join the dance however undignified it makes you look. Joy bathes life with light. It liberates the soul from the prison of the self. Joy is Jerusalem on Sukkot. Joy solves no problems but it gives us the strength to keep searching. It sustains the faith we need if we are, in the year ahead, to face the future without fear and heal some of the fractures of our injured world.

VI. The Limits of Wisdom

Kohelet ends with an epilogue, written as if by another hand. It says: "The final word: it has all been said. Hold God in awe, and heed His commands, for that is all man has." It was this sentence that warranted the book's inclusion in Tanakh. Some of the sages questioned Kohelet's place among the sacred scriptures. They held it should be banned ("hidden") because its teachings could lead to heresy. Those who argued for its inclusion said that it began and ended with words of Torah. So this penultimate sentence of the book can look contrived, as if it were added as an afterthought, the intellectual equivalent of a *kashrut* certification. But this is to misjudge the book as a whole.

On the surface it reads like a subversive book. It challenges conventional religious faith at many points. It questions whether there is justice in the world, whether there is a real difference between the righteous and the wicked, or even between Homo sapiens and the animals. It hints that there are limits to our freedom: what is crooked can never be straightened (1:15; the source of Kant's famous remark that "out of the crooked timber of humanity no straight thing was ever made"). Nothing is really new, "that which is to be is what has been already" (1:9), and try as we might to change the world, it stays as it always was.

God exists – Kohelet uses the word more than forty times – but in the book He seems a long way away. He is in heaven, we are on earth, and there seems to be no contact between us. But this, to repeat, is on the surface. Kohelet is really subversion of a second order. It undermines those who undermine, critiques the critics, subverts the subversion and shows how too much reliance on intellect and wisdom can lead to nihilism.

It is one of those rare books that refutes itself. Yehuda HaLevi in the *Kuzari* wrote a critique of philosophy in the language of philosophy. Ludwig Wittgenstein did something similar in his *Tractatus Logico-Philosophicus*. He showed that the ultimate truths of philosophy were inexpressible in philosophy. "Of what we cannot speak, thereof we must be silent." Philosophy is like a ladder on which we climb to a higher plane and then find that we must throw the ladder away. Kohelet is Tanakh's most powerful critique of wisdom spoken in the voice of wisdom itself.

Kohelet is not negative about it. He says that wisdom stands to folly as does light to darkness (2:13). It is a shelter, an estate (7:11–12). It "gives the wise man more power than ten rulers in a city" (7:19). It lights up a person's face (8:1). But it fails to uncover meaning in life. It tells us how but not why. It gives us prudence and pragmatism, not moral passion. If you want this, do that. If you want to avoid this, guard yourself from that. It constantly asks, "What is the *yitaron*, the advantage, the return on investment, the cost-benefit ratio?" It speaks of profits, not prophets. It tells us which pitfalls to stay clear of, but not who we are or why we are here.

Recall what we said about wisdom in Tanakh. It sees God not in revelation or redemption, but in creation. It speaks the truths that are universal, not those that are particular. It relates to Elokim, not Hashem, or as Yehuda HaLevi put it, the God of Aristotle, not the God of Abraham (*Kuzari* IV:16). It belongs not to the priest in the Temple nor the prophet in the town square, but to the court and advisers of the king. It speaks the language of realpolitik. Don't criticize a king. Don't curse a rich man. Diversify your investments. When evil is abroad, stay at home. But it fails to give an answer to the most basic of questions: Why live? The best answer it can come up with is that life is *hevel*. It is empty, meaningless, futile, as pointless as trying to chase and hold the wind, but at least it is short.

If the only way we seek to encounter God is through creation, we will discover the deep truth embedded in biblical Hebrew, that *olam*, meaning "universe," comes from the same root as *ne'elam*, "hidden." Nature is not transparent to the purposes and presence of God. By and large, and with some notable exceptions, mainstream Judaism did not follow Christianity in predicating faith in the existence of God on natural theology, itself built on the Aristotelian premise that purposes are inherent in nature. In the Hebrew Bible nature does not prove the existence of God. It sings the praises of God, and that is something else altogether. If all we have are universal laws and personal choices – as we have today in our secular, scientific, individualistic culture – we will not discover meaning. We will land up where Kohelet found himself after pursuing possessions, power and a thousand women: pronouncing life *hevel*, a mere shallow, fleeting, insubstantial breath.

There is a reason for this. The meaning of a system lies outside the system. The meaning of chess is not contained in the rules of chess. You can know all the rules by heart and still have no idea why people play it and are so absorbed by it. The meaning of the universe lies outside the

universe. That is why Abrahamic monotheism was so transformative –
not because it reduced the many gods of paganism to one, but because
it spoke about a God outside nature who created nature, a God beyond
the universe who made the universe. For the first time it showed that
there is meaning to life, not one we invent but one we discover. It was
this that rescued the human condition from the tragic sense of life.

But meaning cannot be accessed by pure reason, by "wisdom."
That is because, as Kohelet says no fewer than thirty-two times, wisdom
tells us what exists "under the heavens," or "under the sun." Like science,
it establishes connections between different empirical phenomena. If
X then Y. It does not, cannot, reach beyond the physical universe to that
which lies beyond. Wisdom is neither the revelation of the priest nor
the word of the prophet. Wisdom can tell us where, when and how, but
not why. Questions of meaning will systematically elude it. Wisdom will
always conclude, in the words of the late Sir Bernard Williams, one of
the wisest of his generation, "that the world was not made for us, or we
for the world, that our history tells no purposive story, and that there is
no position outside the world or outside history from which we might
hope to authenticate our activities." In short, all is *hevel*.

Meaning is not engraved in nature. It is not written in the galax-
ies with their billions of stars, nor is it inscribed in the 3.1 billion letters
of the human genome. Meaning is not universal but particular. It lives
in stories, memories, rituals, songs, in collective acts of worship, and in
communities bound together by shared history and the bonds of collective responsibility. It is something we inherit from our parents and
hand on, if we are blessed, to our children.

Meaning is more like music than words, more like poetry than
prose, more like home than a hotel. It lives in stories, not scientific
formulae. Wisdom can give us stoic acceptance or epicurean pleasure,
but not meaning. For meaning, we need the priest and the prophet.
We need revelation and redemption. We need the word from beyond
the universe that created the universe and is capable of inspiring us to
change the universe. We need a sense of the sacred and a feeling, however inchoate, for God's purposes in history. That is why, in ancient Israel,
there was not one kind of leader but three, and why Tanakh is written
in a multiplicity of voices, each with its own perspective and sensibility.

After Tolstoy had experienced his own dark night of the soul, what restored him was neither philosophy nor science but the faith of the workers on his estate, simple people leading ordinary lives, who suffered without life losing its meaning for them. Tolstoy eventually came to the conclusion that what they had was faith. "If a man lives, he believes in something.... If he understands the illusory nature of the finite, he must believe in the infinite. Without faith he cannot live."

That is the meaning of the penultimate sentence of Kohelet. Note that wisdom almost invariably uses the metaphor of seeing. We speak of insight, foresight, hindsight, vision. We make an observation. We adopt a perspective. When we understand, we say, "I see." Kohelet uses the word *ra'iti*, "I saw," eighteen times. But revelation, the source of meaning, is not something we see. It is something we hear. That is why *shema* is the key word of Deuteronomy, where it occurs ninety-two times. As Moses said about the revelation at Mount Sinai, "You heard the sound of words but saw no form; there was only a voice" (Deut. 4:12). That is what the penultimate sentence is saying: "The final word: it has all been said. Hold God in awe, and heed His commands, for that is all man has." Meaning is what we hear, not see.

The divine word is what links the finite – us – to the Infinite, God. In the beginning was the word: "And God said, 'Let there be....'" And, concludes Kohelet, "*Sof davar*," "In the end is the word." Seeing makes us wise, but it is listening that gives life meaning.

VII. *The Freedom of Insecurity*

Kohelet is a commentary, oblique and subtle to be sure, to the life of Solomon. It is an answer to the questions that anyone who reads Solomon's story in the book of Kings must ask. What went wrong? How did the wisest man on earth go so far astray? How did the man who built the Temple become the one who, through his myriad wives from many nations, admitted idolatry into the national life of Israel? How did the king whose name means "peace" and whose reign was marked by peace, become the figure who generated so many tensions within the nation that, shortly after his death, it split into two and never in all the subsequent centuries recovered the greatness it once had?

The story of Solomon is the most perplexing in Tanakh. It starts with immense promise. God, through the prophet Nathan, had told David that he would not build the Temple, but his son would. He would have what David lacked: peace. God said that He would adopt David's son as His own: "I will be to him a Father, and he shall be to Me a son" (II Sam. 7:14). It is a uniquely auspicious beginning.

That mood is maintained when David dies and Solomon inherits his throne. God appears to Solomon in a dream and offers him anything he wishes. Solomon asks for only one thing: "an understanding heart, to judge Your people and discern between good and evil" (I Kings 3:9). Pleased with this reply, God says that He will indeed give him wisdom, but also in addition, "riches and honor, so that no other king shall compare with you, all your days" (ibid. 13).

So it was. Solomon had, says Kings, "wisdom and understanding beyond measure, and breadth of mind like the sand on the seashore." His acumen surpassed that of "all the people of the East and all the wisdom of Egypt." He composed three thousand proverbs. His fame spread throughout the region and "people of all nations came to hear" his wisdom (5:9–14). No other figure in Tanakh is spoken of in these terms.

When the fall came, therefore, it was serious and surprising. Deuteronomy contains three commands about a king of Israel. He should not "acquire many horses for himself or cause the people to return to Egypt" to buy them. He should not have many wives, nor should he accumulate "much silver and gold" (Deut. 17:16–17).

Solomon broke all three. He had twelve thousand horses (I Kings 10:26). He "exceeded all the kings of the earth in riches" (10:23). He had seven hundred wives and three hundred concubines including, says the text, many from "the nations concerning which the Lord had said to the people of Israel, 'You shall not enter into marriage with them, neither shall they with you, for surely they will turn away your heart after their gods'" (I Kings 11:1–8). The result was that idolatry was introduced into Israel at the highest level.

The Talmud (*Sanhedrin* 21b) is candid. It says that Solomon fell because these commands were given a reason by the Torah itself. The king should not own too many horses because that will cause him to return to Egypt to buy them. He should not have too many wives "lest his heart turn away." Solomon thought he was clever enough to break the law without suffering the consequences: buying horses from Egypt or being led astray by his wives. He was wrong in both cases. Tanakh leaves us in no doubt as to his epitaph: "Solomon did evil in the sight of the Lord" (I Kings 11:6).

Much though the narrative tries to skirt around it, one of the precipitating factors was the building of the Temple itself. In a sentence that proved retrospectively to be deeply ironic, the text says that "in the four hundred and eightieth year after the people of Israel came out of the land of Egypt," Solomon "began to build the House of the Lord" (I Kings 6:1). It was a way of saying that the act of Temple-building was about to bring the long Jewish journey to closure.

The idea that there would one day be a central sanctuary in the Promised Land goes back to the song at the Reed Sea: "You will bring them and plant them on the mountain of Your inheritance – the place, Lord, You made for Your dwelling, the Sanctuary, Lord, Your hands established" (Ex. 15:17). It had taken centuries for the land to be conquered and settled, the tribes united under a single king and Jerusalem made the capital city. Building the House of God was now all that remained to be done.

But there are ominous notes throughout the narrative. The building involved a treaty with Lebanon in exchange for the large amount of cedar wood involved in the construction. A labor force was drafted of thirty thousand men working in monthly shifts for the wood alone, together with eighty thousand stone-cutters, seventy thousand men employed to transport the stone and 3,300 officers to supervise the work (I Kings 5:15–25).

The local non-Israelite population – the remaining Amorites, Hittites, Perizzites, Hivites and Jebusites – were taken as slaves. The text adds that "of the people of Israel, Solomon made no slaves" (I Kings 9:22). That this needed to be said is alarming. The entire narrative echoes the experience of the Israelites in Egypt, sometimes using the same words. We now realize the significance of a fact told at the very beginning of the story, that "Solomon made an alliance with Pharaoh king of Egypt and married his daughter" (I Kings 3:1). What was a king of Israel doing by forging an alliance, in the form of a marriage, with the imperial power that had once turned his ancestors into slaves? By turning his own people into a corvée, an unpaid, conscripted labor force, Solomon had in effect transformed Israel into a second Egypt.

The consequences were far-reaching. After Solomon's death the people came to his son and successor Rehoboam, complaining, "Your father put a heavy yoke on us, but now lighten the harsh labor and the heavy yoke he put on us and we will serve you" (I Kings 12:4). Rehoboam consulted his father's advisers, who told him in effect: if you serve the people, they will serve you. He did not listen, preferring instead the advice of his own friends who told him to assert his authority by making the burden heavier still. Instead of serving the people, Solomon's son expected them to serve him. This was the single most fateful moment in Israel's history. The people rebelled, the kingdom divided and the nation never fully recovered.

What went wrong? That is Kohelet's question. To understand his answer we must turn to Sigmund Freud's most brilliant disciple, Otto Rank. Rank's most original contribution to the study of human nature was his insight that we are torn between two fears: the fear of living and the fear of dying.

The fear of living is what we experience in early childhood, namely separation anxiety. The young child knows how vulnerable and dependent he or she is, especially in relation to the mother. We fear being alone. We need the protective embrace of human others. It is for this reason that we seek to identify with a group, a team, a community or a nation. We merge our identity with theirs. It is the anxiety about being singular, different, individuated, that Rank called the fear of living.

No sooner do we identify with a group, however, than we fear the opposite: losing our individuality. When the "I" is wholly subordinated to the "We," we feel stifled, submerged, suffocated. This is what Rank called the fear of dying. Rank's view was that it was this second fear that led people with a strong sense of self to seek immortality through heroic acts of death-defying courage, or by creating works of art that will live forever (Shakespeare's "Not marble, nor the gilded monuments / of princes, shall outlive this powerful rhyme"). In ancient times rulers sought immortality by building imperishable monuments – temples, pyramids and palaces that would stand forever. The stronger the "I" and the greater the refusal to merge into the "We," the deeper becomes the fear of death, and the more powerful the temptation to defeat it by a personal immortality project, something that will allow my name to live forever.

That is what Kohelet is telling us about Solomon. As we have already seen, no other book in Tanakh uses the first person singular as often as does Kohelet: "I built for myself... I made for myself... I gathered for myself... I acquired for myself" (Eccl. 2:4–9). These are the words of someone obsessed with I-me-mine. And, as Rank said, one with an exaggerated sense of self supremely fears death. That is Kohelet, telling us thirty-eight times how haunted he is by the realization that life is *hevel*, a mere breath that will one day cease, returning us naked to the grave, and turning our bodies to dust. Kohelet does not speak about the Temple, or how Solomon spent thirteen years – almost twice as long as the seven years it took to build the Temple – building a palace for himself (I Kings 7:1–12). But these facts hover in the background, unmistakably there.

The rabbis said something very acute about Solomon's Temple. They understood Psalm 24 – "Who may ascend the mountain of the Lord? Who may stand in His holy place?" – as referring to the Temple dedication ceremony. The psalm ends with an odd repetition:

> Lift up your heads, O gates; be uplifted, eternal doors,
> so that the King of glory may enter.
> Who is the King of glory? It is the Lord, strong and mighty,
> the Lord mighty in battle.
> Lift up your heads, O gates; be uplifted, eternal doors,
> so that the King of glory may enter.
> Who is He, the King of glory?
> The Lord of hosts, He is the King of glory, Selah. (Ps. 24:7–10)

This is how they interpreted these lines: When Solomon tried to take the Ark into the Holy of Holies, the doors refused to open. Hence his command, "Lift up your heads, O gates." The gates then asked him, "Who is the King of glory?" Solomon replied, "The Lord." Yet the doors still refused to open. So Solomon had to ask again, and still they did not open (*Shabbat* 30a). In other words, the sages attributed to gates the suspicion that Solomon regarded himself, not God, as "the king of glory." A man who spends almost twice as long building a palace for himself as building a house for God lays himself open to the suspicion that the Temple was Solomon's own immortality project, the building he believed would make his name live forever.

Those who fear death spend their lives in a futile quest for security, for something they can attach themselves to that will not die. That, suggests the psalm, is the allure of idols: "They have mouths but cannot speak, eyes but cannot see. They have ears but cannot hear" (Ps. 115:5–6). You know where you are with an idol. It does not move. It does not breathe. It does not change. Hence the sin of the golden calf. Recall that it began with the people panicking because of the absence of Moses. They needed a leader. Why did they not do the obvious and turn to Aaron, Moses' brother, his partner, spokesman, colleague and companion? Why an object made of gold? Because they wanted something predictable, something that did not get angry with them, challenge them, urge them to ever-greater heights. Bricks, mortar, stone, marble, cedar, silver, gold: these are things you can safely worship because they make no demands. They are there, unchanging, forever.

Implicit in Kohelet is a story about Solomon's life as a search for security in terms of what we have, what we own and what we can control. That is a temptation that has led astray some of the most gifted leaders of all times. But it is a false quest. Sukkot tells us why: you can live in a hut with only leaves for a roof, exposed to the wind, the cold and the rain, and still rejoice.

And it is joy, not monumental architecture, that defeats the fear of death, because it lifts us beyond the self, the insistent, interminable "I." Joy is something we share with others. Joy is gratitude for the gift of life that we feel in the presence of the Giver of life. We become eternal not by constructing buildings, but by opening ourselves up, making ourselves vulnerable, to the Eternal, to God Himself.

God brought the Israelites from slavery to freedom. But freedom requires the ability to live with insecurity. It means making space for other people to express their freedom in different, unpredictable ways. It means empowering your children, as God empowered Abraham, saying "Walk on ahead of Me" (Gen. 17:1). It means not seeking to turn those around you into clones of yourself or servants of your will. It means, in Judaism, living with an unpredictable God who, when asked by Moses for His name, said, "I will be what I will be" (Ex. 3:14). It means living with God who made every human being in His image, yet who does not have an image. Without the courage to live with insecurity, even the wisest of men, King Solomon, can go astray.

Sukkot is the festival of insecurity. It is the festival of a people who know they will never be entirely safe, surrounded as they are by larger, stronger nations, assaulted as they have so often been for having the courage to be different. Sitting in the sukka, *betzila demehemnuta*, "under the shadow of faith" (*Zohar, Emor* 103a), is all the security we need. As David said in Psalm 27:5, "He will keep me safe in His pavilion [lit. sukka] on the day of trouble." If God is our refuge, who then shall we fear? We do not need what Solomon made for himself: a palace of cedar. A sukka is the polar opposite. It is spiritual security in the midst of physical vulnerability. The most monumental building, even the Temple itself, will not guarantee the safety of the nation, if what matters is the building, not the builders, and if we think we are "the king of glory."

Solomon's Temple, the noblest of projects executed in the wrong way for the wrong reason, did not make the king immortal, or the nation invulnerable. It left Solomon with a terrible epitaph, and divided the nation, leaving it very vulnerable indeed.

What Is a Sukka?

Now we are in a position to ask, what exactly is a sukka? What does it represent, symbolize, recall? What message is it meant to convey? There is only one passage in the Torah relating to the command, and it is brief to the point of obscurity: "You shall dwell in booths [*sukkot*] for seven days; all those born among Israel shall dwell in booths, so that your descendants will know that I settled the children of Israel in booths when I brought them out of the land of Egypt: I am the Lord your God" (Lev. 23:42–43).

The problems are obvious. First, the word "sukka" or "sukkot" is not used at any stage to describe the living conditions of the Israelites during the wilderness years. A sukka is a temporary, portable dwelling, a hut or booth. *Nowhere, except in this verse, were the Israelites in the wilderness spoken of as living in sukkot.* Instead they lived in tents. "How goodly are your tents, O Jacob," said the pagan prophet Balaam (Num. 24:5).

After the revelation at Mount Sinai, God told Moses to tell the people to "return to their tents" (Deut. 5:27). When the people complained about the manna, Moses heard them "weeping at the entrance to their tents" (Num. 11:10). During the Koraḥ rebellion, Moses said to the people, "Move away from the tents of these evil men" (Num. 16:26).

And so on.

Tents are made of fabric or animal skins. They do not have coverings of foliage. Where in any case would the people find vegetation in the desert for forty years? Tents are not booths. Not surprisingly, therefore, a dispute arose among the sages as to what exactly a sukka represents.

The dispute appears both in the halakhic midrash, the *Sifra* (to Lev. 23), and also in the Talmud (*Sukka* 11b), but with the names of the rabbis reversed. According to the *Sifra*, Rabbi Eliezer says it means *sukkot mamash*, booths in the literal sense of the word. A sukka is a sukka is a sukka: nothing more, nothing less. Rabbi Akiva says that the sukka represents the clouds of glory that accompanied the Israelites on their journeys through the desert.

There are obvious difficulties with either interpretation. For the one who says it means literally booths, what then is there to celebrate? There was nothing miraculous, or even out of the ordinary, about a group of people on a journey living in temporary shelter. That is what happens to many nomadic populations. Booths are still used by some Bedouin today. The Exodus from Egypt and the Giving of the Torah at Mount Sinai – commemorated respectively on Pesaḥ and Shavuot – were clearly epoch-making events, occurrences out of the ordinary, encounters with the Divine. Not so a shed, a hut, a booth.

No less problematic is the view that the sukka represents the clouds of glory. If so, why not say so? Let the verse say, "so that future generations will know that I surrounded the Israelites with clouds of glory when I brought them out of the land of Egypt." The point is serious and substantive. In general we say that *mitzvot einan tzerikhot kavana*, "the fulfillment of a command is not conditional on specific intention" (*Tosafot, Sukka* 42a). But in this case the intent is written into the text of the command itself. It says, "so that future generations will know." The Talmud tells us that this has halakhic consequences. According to one view a sukka whose roof is higher than twenty cubits from the ground is invalid because at that height you are not conscious of the roof, and therefore the sukka is not fulfilling its function of reminding you, "so that future generations will know" (*Sukka* 2a). *How then can there be a command whose purpose is to remind you of something, if the thing it is supposed to remind you of is not stated in the text, and is not even clear to the sages of the Mishna?*

In any case, what is the connection between a booth and clouds? The one does not naturally evoke thoughts of the other. A booth is a humble, fragile, temporary shelter. The clouds of glory were radiant, majestic, an unmistakable sign of the presence of God. There is an obvious dissonance between the two ideas.

To be sure, Rabbi Akiva bases his interpretation on a text, a messianic vision from the book of Isaiah: "Then the Lord will create over the whole site of Mount Zion and over her assemblies a cloud by day, and smoke and the shining of a flaming fire by night; for over all the glory there will be a canopy. There will be a sukka for shade by day from the heat, and for a refuge and a shelter from the storm and rain" (Is. 4:5–6). This passage does indeed bring together the idea of clouds, shelter, glory and sukka. Yet the sukka of which Isaiah speaks belongs to the future, not to the past, of which the festival is a memorial.

Let us therefore recall what we have learned thus far from our study of Kohelet. First we noted that the name Kohelet is a key to the decryption of the book and of the festival itself. We saw that the root of the word, *k-h-l*, strikes multiple connections between the festival and the nation's collective house of worship, the *Mishkan* in the desert and the Temple in Jerusalem. *Hak'hel* is the command (Deut. 31:10–13) that once every seven years on Sukkot, someone (assumed to be the king) was "to address the nation when all Israel comes to appear before the Lord your God *at the place He will choose*," meaning the Temple. The root *k-h-l* is the first word the Torah uses when Moses commands the Israelites to build the *Mishkan* (Ex. 35:1) – on the day after Yom Kippur just before Sukkot. It is also a key word in the story of the golden calf, for which the *Mishkan* itself was a *tikkun*, an act of repair. Also, the root appears seven times in I Kings 8, the account of Solomon dedicating the Temple on Sukkot. All of these suggest a Temple connection.

Now consider the clouds of glory themselves. The actual phrase "clouds of glory" appears nowhere in Tanakh. We hear of a divine cloud in several contexts. God guided the Israelites through the desert in a pillar of cloud by day and fire by night (Ex. 13:21). A cloud positioned itself at the Reed Sea between the Israelites and the pursuing Egyptians, to protect the people from Pharaoh's army (Ex. 14:19–20). The glory of God appeared in a cloud when manna fell for the people to eat (Ex. 16:10). A cloud covered the top of Mount Sinai when God revealed Himself to the people (Ex. 19:16).

However, the most significant accounts of God's glory appearing in a cloud occur in connection with the *Mishkan* and the Temple. Here is the description of the *Mishkan*:

> Then the cloud covered the Tent of Meeting, and the glory of the Lord filled the Tabernacle. And Moses was not able to enter the Tent of Meeting because the cloud settled on it, and the glory of the Lord filled the Tabernacle. (Ex. 40:34–35)

And this is the description of the Temple:

> And when the priests left the Holy Place, the cloud filled the House of the Lord. And the priests could not stand up to serve because of the cloud – for the Presence of God filled the House. (I Kings 8:10–11)

We begin to sense a significant connection. Sukkot, as we noted in the first section, was the Temple festival par excellence. It was also the time of the year when the First Temple was consecrated, and also the Second. It was the festival celebrated in the days of Ezra and Nehemiah after the people had gathered in the Temple to hear the Torah read in public. Immediately after Sukkot that year, the people renewed their covenant with God. Even the rededication of the Temple in the days of the Maccabees, though it took place at a different time of the year, was explicitly modeled after Sukkot.

Note also how the Temple connection persisted even after the building itself was destroyed. In this context there is a pointed contrast between Pesaḥ and Sukkot. After the destruction of the Temple, the Seder ritual changed dramatically. No longer was the central act the offering of the Paschal Lamb. Instead the ritual was focused on matza, the unleavened bread. There was almost no attempt to replicate the Temple ritual outside its precincts. In the case of Sukkot however, many customs that were practiced *only* in the Temple when it stood – taking the four kinds on the second and subsequent days of the festival, the circuits around the altar and the beating of the willow branches – were transferred everywhere after the destruction as *zekher leMikdash*, a "reminder of the Temple" (*Rosh HaShana* 4:3).

And so a significance appears. *The connection between Sukkot and the clouds of glory has to do with the* Mishkan *or the Temple.* There are other connections as well. The verb *s-kh-kh*, "to cover," from which "*sukka*" is derived, and which in rabbinic Hebrew designates the roof of the sukka, *appears in the Torah only in connection with the* Mishkan. It says about the Cherubim, the angelic, childlike figures above the Ark, that their wings "overshadowed" it (*sokhekhim*, Ex. 25:20). The same verb is used about the *parokhet*, the veil, curtain or canopy that "covered" the Ark (Ex. 40:3).

Now consider the differences between the Sanctuary in the wilderness and the Temple built by Solomon in Jerusalem. Two are fundamental. The first is that the Sanctuary was built entirely by voluntary contributions of money or materials or time. The text in Exodus emphasizes repeatedly that contributions were to be received from every man and woman "whose heart moved them to give" (Ex. 35:21 et al.). The Temple, by contrast, was built on the basis of conscripted labor. There was nothing voluntary about the efforts of the hundreds of thousands of people involved in the construction.

Second, *the Sanctuary was portable.* It was built of a framework and drapes that could be dismantled and carried by the Levites when the time came for the people to travel onward on the next stage of their journey. The Temple, of course, was not portable. It was built in Jerusalem and could not exist anywhere else.

Now let us go back and revisit the scene that transpired when David first expressed his wish to build the Temple. God sent him the following message via the prophet Nathan:

> Go and tell My servant David, "This is what the Lord says: Are you the one to build Me a house to dwell in? I have not dwelt in a house from the day I brought the Israelites up out of Egypt to this day. I have been moving from place to place with a tent as My dwelling. Wherever I have moved with all the Israelites, did I ever say to any of their rulers whom I commanded to shepherd My people Israel, 'Why have you not built Me a house of cedar?'" (II Sam. 7:5–7)

Now we can state precisely what a sukka is. *A sukka stands in the same relationship to a house that the* Mishkan *in the desert did to the Temple in Jerusalem.* A sukka moves. A house does not. Those who live in a sukka are on a journey. Those who live in a house have arrived. A sukka suggests a person or nation on the move. A house is what you build when you have come to the end of your wanderings and you want to settle down.

As long as the Temple stood, and even after it was destroyed, God wanted the people never to forget the original *Mishkan* in the desert. Indeed many English Bibles translate the word *Mishkan* as "Tabernacle" from the Latin *taberna* meaning a hut, a shed, a booth, understanding instinctively that the most important thing about it was that it was temporary, portable, the symbol of a people who had not yet arrived.

More than that: it was the symbol of God Himself. Recall that the first time we hear the word "cloud" mentioned in connection with God, it is *already the symbol of a journey*: "By day the Lord went ahead of them in a pillar of cloud to guide them on their way, and by night in a pillar of fire to give them light, so that they could travel by day or night" (Ex. 13:21). God does not stand still. The God beyond the universe is not a God confined to one place, even the holiest. He is the God whose *Shekhina*, His immanent Presence, is in every place where His people travel. The *Mishkan* was small, fragile, movable. It was the very opposite of the temples of Egypt and ziggurats of Babylon. *But it was filled with the clouds of glory.*

In the last month of his life, as the new generation was about to cross the Jordan and enter the land he could only see from afar, Moses wanted them to understand one thing above all others. The real trial, he said, was not in the past but in the future, not in the desert but in the Promised Land. The greatest challenge to faith would be not poverty but affluence, not slavery but freedom, not exile but home. People who believe that they have arrived become complacent, self-satisfied, self-congratulatory, and that is the beginning of the end of national greatness:

> Be careful that you do not forget the Lord your God, failing to observe His commands, His laws and His decrees that I am giving you this day. Otherwise, when you eat and are satisfied, when you build fine houses and settle down, and when your herds and flocks grow large and your silver and gold increase and all you have is multiplied, then your heart will become proud and you will forget the Lord your God, who brought you out of Egypt, out of the land of slavery…. You may say to yourself, "My power and the strength of my hands have produced this wealth for me." (Deut. 8:11–17)

God wanted us never to take security for granted. Civilizations, as the historian Giambattista Vico documented in *Scienza Nuova* (1725), start by being young and energetic, then become successful and wealthy, then self-indulgent and decadent, and eventually fall to younger, hungrier powers.

The only way to avoid this is, for one week in every year, to remind yourself of where you came from and how you once lived. *Those were the days when God Himself lived in your midst in a temporary, portable dwelling.* It was made not of bricks or stone but of hangings and drapes. But it was full of the clouds of glory. The word *Mishkan*, from the root *sh-kh-n*, means "to dwell." When God says to Moses, "Make Me a sanctuary that I may dwell [*shakhanti*] among them" (Ex. 25:8), this is the first time we have heard the verb in connection with God. It is, in this context, a very odd word. Recall that God told Moses at the burning bush that when the Israelites were about to leave Egypt, each woman should "ask of her neighbor [*mishekhenta*]" (Ex. 3:22). A *shakhen* is a neighbor. There were times when God revealed Himself in signs, wonders and miracles. But when the Israelites made the *Mishkan* and God dwelled there in clouds of glory, *He was as close to the people as a next-door neighbor.*

On Sukkot, the Temple festival par excellence, the temptation was at its height to believe that what makes a house of God is architectural magnificence on a monumental scale. *That has been true about virtually every religion, ancient and modern, since the dawn of time. But it is not true of Judaism.* God does not live in buildings but in the open heart, the heart that makes itself vulnerable the way the covering of a sukka is vulnerable. If the covering of the sukka is thick enough to keep out the rain, it is invalid (*Mishna Berura* 631:6). If a human heart is thick enough to keep out the word of God that is like rain (Deut. 32:2), then it too will lose its holiness: "Yeshurun grew fat and kicked; you grew fat, thick, gross; then he forsook God who made him" (Deut. 32:15).

For seven days we are commanded to live in a sukka to remind us that *this is how God lived in our ancestors' midst* when they journeyed from Egypt to the Promised Land. It was not just the Israelites who lived in temporary dwellings when God brought them out of the land of Egypt. So did God Himself. *That was the miracle*: that the Creator of heaven and earth lived among the people so closely that, homeless and vulnerable though they were, they could feel the *Shekhina* in their midst.

So Rabbi Eliezer and Rabbi Akiva were both right. The sukka really was a sukka: a portable shrine, a movable sanctuary, a temporary temple. But it was filled with clouds of glory. Not even Solomon's Temple made the people feel as close to God as did the *Mishkan*. A nation that seeks security in stone eventually grows old. A people that never stops traveling, spiritually if not physically, will never grow old.

There is an extraordinary intimation of all this early on in the Torah. If we examine Genesis carefully, we will discover that the patriarchs did not live in houses. When the word "house" is used in a patriarchal context, it means not a building but rather "family" or "household."

Others lived in houses. The patriarchs lived in tents. The contrast is often striking. In Genesis 18, when angels visit Abraham, he is sitting at the entrance of his *tent*. In the next chapter, they come to his nephew Lot in Sodom and find that he is living in a *house* (Gen. 19:2, 4). The first patriarch described as living in a house is Jacob.

The verse that says so is little short of astonishing. "Jacob went to Sukkot, where he built a house for himself and made sheds [*sukkot*] for his livestock. That is why he called the place Sukkot" (Gen. 33:17). This is the first time one of the patriarchs is spoken of as building a house, yet he does not call the place "house" (as in Beit-El or Beit-Leḥem for example). Instead he calls it Sukkot *in honor of the sheds he has made for his cattle!* How are we to explain this?

The only plausible explanation is that at the very moment Jacob sought to settle in a permanent home, he wished never to forget that he remained, in some sense, a nomad as Abraham and Isaac were. He was on a journey. To be a Jew is to be on a journey. Judaism was born in two journeys, Abraham and Sarah's from Mesopotamia, Moses and the Israelites' from Egypt. Mesopotamia and Egypt, the world's two first great civilizations, worshiped the gods in monumental buildings, to construct which they turned whole populations into slaves. This, says the Torah, is to betray both God and humanity. God does not need that kind of house. Recall what He said to David: "Wherever I have moved with all the Israelites, did I ever say to any of their rulers ... 'Why have you not built Me a house of cedar?'" God moves. Israel moves. God does not seek, nor is Israel called on to build, statements in stone. Other nations may do so. But that, says God, is not who I am, nor is it who I want you to be.

The sentence in the Torah which describes the first house ever built by a Jew is also the first place in which the word "Sukkot" appears – and it appears not once but three times. If you want to understand Sukkot, meditate on this verse.

Recall too the first time the word "house" is used in connection with God (other than as the place name Beit-El). It happens when Jacob is in the middle of a journey, fleeing home and not yet arrived at his destination. Alone at night, Jacob sleeps and dreams of a ladder connecting earth and heaven. He wakes and says, "How awesome is this place! *This is none other than the house of God;* this is the gate of heaven" (Gen. 28:17). There was no house there, only a dream and a vision glimpsed in the midst of a journey. Recall too that as the Israelites began their journey out of Egypt toward the Promised Land, their first stop was at a place called Sukkot (Num. 33:5). Those who live in sukkot are on a journey. God's first words to Abraham were *"Lekh lekha"*: Move. The definition of a Jew is: one-who-is-on-a-journey.

However humble our sukka, when we invite guests they turn out to be *Ushpizin* – the heroes of our people – just as Abraham and Sarah welcomed anonymous strangers and discovered they were angels. When we sit in a sukka under the shelter of faith, we find ourselves surrounded by the *Shekhina*, God's clouds of glory. In Judaism, as Rabbi Yoḥanan said about God: greatness is humility (*Megilla* 31a). So it is with buildings when they become symbols. The humblest can be the greatest. That is why on Sukkot, the supreme Temple festival, God wanted us to remember the time He lived in our ancestors' midst in a sukka. Never was He closer to them or they to Him than when, using only materials they had donated, and time and skills they had volunteered, they built the *Mishkan*, the Tabernacle, so that the *Shekhina* could live in their midst.

So on this month of months, Tishrei, we begin with the anniversary of the creation of the universe – the home God made for us. But we then go on to remember the *Mishkan*, the home our ancestors made for God. The Torah spends only thirty-four verses describing the creation of the universe, but almost a third of the book of Exodus describing the building of the *Mishkan*, as if to say that it is easy for an infinite, omnipotent God to make a home for us, but His real pleasure – His *naḥat ruaḥ* – lies in the home we build for Him, with one condition, that it is built with humility – not the hubris that turned the wisest of Israel's kings almost into a pharaoh, and led eventually to the division of the kingdom and the destruction of the Temple itself.

The universe is the space God makes for us. The sukka, with its incomplete roof and its door open to strangers, is the space we make for God.

The Four Kinds

The other major symbol on Sukkot is the "four kinds," defined in the Torah in these words: "And on the first day, you shall take for yourselves a fruit of the citron tree, palm fronds, myrtle branches and willows of the brook, and be joyous in the presence of the Lord your God for seven days" (Lev. 23:40).

Uniquely in the case of symbolic objects, the Torah does not tell us why we are to take these four. It intimates why the matza and the Paschal Lamb on Pesaḥ, and why the sukka itself on Sukkot, but not the four kinds. It is not clear what they are, why we take them, or what we do with them. There is even a tantalizing passage in the book of Nehemiah which seems to suggest that, for some at least, they were understood as materials for use in constructing the sukka:

> And they found written in the law which the Lord had commanded by Moses, that the children of Israel should dwell in booths in the feast of the seventh month: and that they should publish and proclaim in all their cities, and in Jerusalem, saying, "Go forth unto the mount, and fetch olive branches, and pine branches, and myrtle branches, and palm branches, and branches of thick trees, to make booths, as it is written." So the people went forth, and brought them, and made themselves booths, every one upon the roof of his house, and in their courts, and in the courts of the House of God, and in the street of the water gate, and in the street of the gate of Ephraim. (Neh. 8:14–16)

To be sure, there are differences between this list and that in Leviticus, which does not mention olive branches and pine branches. But there was at least one sage of the mishnaic period who held that the covering of the sukka should be made of the same materials as the four kinds (*Sukka* 37a).

It was here that the Oral tradition proved vital. The fruit of the citron tree (*hadar* tree in Hebrew) was identified with the etrog, the palm fronds with the lulav. The "leafy tree" (as it is called in Hebrew) was the myrtle, and the willow was self-explanatory. "You shall take" was understood as holding them in the hand, most importantly during the recital of Hallel. The tension in the verse between "On the first day you shall take" and "You shall rejoice before the Lord for seven days" was easily resolved. In the Temple, that is, "before the Lord," the four kinds were to be taken all seven days, while elsewhere only on the first day. So it was until the destruction of the Second Temple, when Rabban Yoḥanan ben Zakkai ordained that they be taken on all seven days (except Shabbat) everywhere, "in memory of the Temple" (*Rosh HaShana* 4:3).

There was also a procession around the altar holding the four kinds, once each day, seven times on the seventh day. The Book of Jubilees, dating from the second century BCE, even attributes this custom to Abraham: "And Abraham took branches of palm trees and the fruit of *hadar* trees and every day, going round the altar with the branches seven times in the morning, he praised and gave thanks to God for all things in joy" (Jubilees 16:31). The Talmud also mentions another, more stringent custom:

> This was the custom of the men in Jerusalem: When a man left his house he carried his lulav in his hand. When he went to the synagogue, his lulav was in his hand. When he said the Shema and the Amida his lulav was still in his hand.... If he went to visit the sick or comfort mourners he would go with his lulav in his hand. (*Sukka* 41b)

Rabbinic sources provided a variety of symbolic explanations. One well-known account said that the four kinds represented different kinds of Jews. The etrog has fragrance and fruit; the palm, fruit but no fragrance; the myrtle, fragrance but no fruit; and the willow has neither. Fragrance means Torah knowledge. Fruit means good deeds. Some Jews have both, some have one but not the other, and some have neither. God said: In order to make it impossible for Israel to be destroyed, let them be bound together so that the righteous atone for the others. The four kinds thus became a symbol of Jewish unity (Leviticus Raba 30:12). Another source related them to four parts of the body. The lulav was the spine, the myrtle the eyes, the willow leaves the mouth and the etrog the heart. Together they amounted to the statement that we worship God "with all my bones," or alternatively that they atoned for the sins we committed with the different limbs (Leviticus Raba 30:14).

However, these are secondary elaborations. The Talmud itself says that the four kinds were taken as part of the process of asking God to send rain (*Ta'anit* 2b). That the festival had to do with rain was already clear in Zechariah's prophecy that in the Messianic Age the nations of the world would come to Jerusalem on Sukkot so that their lands would be blessed by rain. The Mishna (*Rosh HaShana* 1:2) says that on Ḥag, the festival par excellence, the rabbinic name for Sukkot, the world is judged in relation to rain. Essentially, the four kinds are all forms of vegetation that require water. The palm tree is associated with an oasis in a desert; the willow usually signifies that there is running water nearby; and the etrog and myrtle both need significant rainfall. Accordingly, Maimonides gave the following explanation in his *Guide for the Perplexed*:

> I believe that the four species are a symbolic expression of our rejoicing that the Israelites were taken from the wilderness, "no place of seed, or of figs, or of vines, or of pomegranates, or of water to drink" [Num. 20:5], and brought to a country full of fruit trees and rivers. In order to remember this we take the fruit which is the most pleasant of the fruit of the land, branches which smell best, most beautiful leaves, and also the best of herbs, that is, the willows of the brook. (*Guide*, III:43)

The reason behind these specific plants was straightforward, even prosaic. First, says Maimonides, they were plentiful in Israel in biblical times, so that everyone could easily obtain them. Second, they have a good appearance, they are green, and some have a pleasant smell. Thirdly, they keep fresh for seven days, "which is not the case with peaches, pomegranates, quinces, pears and the like."

There were other ceremonies performed in the Second Temple that were also related to rain. The first was the water libations. Throughout the year a libation of wine accompanied the sacrifices, but on Sukkot there was a water libation also. Each morning there would be a ceremonial procession from the Temple to the Shiloaḥ pool just outside the city, to collect the water to be used in the libations. So intense was the atmosphere surrounding this practice that, as we noted in the first section, all-night celebrations known as *Simḥat Beit HaShoʼeva*, "Rejoicing in the House of the Water-Drawing," took place on the nights beforehand in the Temple.

Another was the willow ceremony. Each day of the festival except Shabbat, people would go to Motza, a town close to Jerusalem, where they would cut willow branches which they brought to the Temple and stood them around the altar. Some believe there is a reference to this in Hallel itself, in Psalm 118:27, translated as: "Bedeck the festival with branches at the corners of the altar" (see *Sukka* 45a). The processions around the altar reached a crescendo on the seventh day when there were seven circuits with willow branches (some say with the lulav) which were then struck. The day was known as "the day of beating" – a custom we still observe on Hoshana Raba.

Because these additional ceremonies had no explicit source in Scripture, they became a source of contention between the Pharisees, who believed in an authoritative Oral Law dating back to Moses, and the Sadducees, who denied the Oral Law, and who were also the group most closely associated with the Temple priesthood. There was an occasion, the Talmud says, when a Sadducee priest decided to pour the water libation on his feet rather than on the altar, apparently as a personal protest against what he saw as an unwarranted practice. This led to a riot in which the outraged crowd pelted the hapless priest with their etrogs, and a section of the altar itself was damaged (*Sukka* 48b).

Rain-making ceremonies are not unusual in religions of the ancient world. What made Israel different, however, was a phenomenon disclosed by Moses only at the end of his life. Until then the land had been described as "flowing with milk and honey." What Moses revealed in the last month of his life was something different and more challenging:

> The land you are entering to take over is not like the land of Egypt, from which you have come, where you planted your seed and irrigated it by foot as in a vegetable garden. But the land you are crossing the Jordan to take possession of is a land of mountains

and valleys that drinks rain from heaven. It is a land the Lord your God cares for; the eyes of the Lord your God are continually on it from the beginning of the year to its end. (Deut. 11:10–12)

Israel would not have a regular, predictable water supply like the Tigris-Euphrates valley or the Nile delta. It depends on rain, and in Israel rain is not something that can be taken for granted. Drought and famine led Abraham, Isaac and Jacob into exile at some time in their lives.

The result is the second dimension of insecurity that frames Sukkot as a festival: the uncertainty of rain. This meant that the natural focus of attention for those who live in the land is to look up to the heaven, rather than down to the naturally fertile earth. It meant the strongest possible connection between faith itself and the rainfall needed for the land to yield its produce, and for the nation to be able to celebrate a harvest of plenty.

This is a central theme of the passage in Deuteronomy that became the second paragraph of the Shema:

> If you indeed heed My commandments with which I charge you today, to love the Lord your God and worship Him with all your heart and with all your soul, I will give rain in your land in its season, the early and late rain; and you shall gather in your grain, wine and oil. I will give grass in your field for your cattle, and you shall eat and be satisfied. Be careful lest your heart be tempted and you go astray and worship other gods, bowing down to them. Then the Lord's anger will flare against you and He will close the heavens so that there will be no rain. The land will not yield its crops, and you will perish swiftly from the good land that the Lord is giving you. (Deut. 11:13–17)

Israel is a land where the very climate itself becomes a commentary on the faithfulness of the nation to God. Israel is the land of promise, but it will always depend on He-who-promises.

In the Holy Land, geography becomes destiny. So argued the great Jewish poet and philosopher Yehuda HaLevi:

[Israel's] fertility or barrenness, its happiness or misfortune, depend upon the divine influence which your conduct will merit, whilst the rest of the world will continue its natural course. For if the Divine Presence is among you, you will perceive by the fertility of your country, by the regularity with which your rainfalls appear in their due seasons, by your victories over your enemies in spite of your inferior numbers, that your affairs are not managed by simple laws of nature, but by the Divine Will. You will also see that drought, death and wild beasts pursue you as a result of disobedience, although the whole world lives in peace. This shows you that your concerns are arranged by a higher power than mere nature. (*Kuzari*, I:109)

Unpacking this in non-mystical terms, HaLevi is saying that the topography and climate of a country affects the culture and ethos of those who live there. In Mesopotamia and Egypt, the most powerful reality was the regularity of nature, the succession of the seasons which seemed to mirror the slow revolution of the stars. The cultures to which these cradles of civilization gave rise were cosmological and their sense of time cyclical. The universe seemed to be ruled by the heavenly bodies whose hierarchy and order was replicated in the hierarchy and order of life on earth.

Israel, by contrast, was a land without regularities. There was no guarantee that next year the rain would fall, the earth yield its crops, and the trees their fruit. So in Israel a new sense of time was born – the time we call historical. Those who lived, or live, in Israel exist in a state of radical contingency. They can never take the future for granted. They depend on something other than nature. Even the secular David Ben-Gurion, the State of Israel's first prime minister, said: "In Israel, in order to be a realist, you must believe in miracles." In Egypt, where the source of life was the Nile, you looked down. In Israel, where the source of life is rain, you had no choice but to look up.

When Moses told the Israelites the full story about the land, he was telling them that it was a place where not just wheat and barley, but the human spirit also, grew. It was the land where people are lifted beyond themselves because, time and again, they have to believe in something and some One beyond themselves. Not accidentally but essentially, by its climate, topography and location, Israel is the land where, merely to survive, the human eye must turn to heaven and the human ear to heaven's call.

Shemini Atzeret

In February 1997, then-president of the State of Israel, Ezer Weizman, paid the first, and thus far the only, state visit to Britain as the guest of Her Majesty the Queen. The custom is that on the first night of such a visit the queen hosts a state banquet at Buckingham Palace. It was, for the Jews present, a unique and moving moment to hear *HaTikva* played in the banqueting hall of the palace, and to hear the queen propose a toast to the president with the word *LeHayyim*.

There is a protocol for such visits. Present are many representative figures, ambassadors, members of the government and other members of the royal family. At the end of the evening, after most of the guests have taken their leave, there is a small and intimate gathering for just a few individuals, on that occasion the Queen, Prince Philip, the Queen Mother, the prime minister and a few others, for a more relaxed and personal conversation with the guest of honor. It was this kind of occasion with its royal protocol that led the sages to their particular understanding of Shemini Atzeret.

It is a strange, even unique day in the Jewish calendar. It is described as the eighth day, and thus part of Sukkot, but it is also designated by a name, Atzeret, of its own. Is it, or is it not, a separate festival in its own right? It seems to be both. How are we to understand this fact?

What guided the sages was the detail that whereas on the seven days of Sukkot seventy young bulls were offered, on Atzeret, the eighth day, there was only one. Connecting this to Zechariah's prophecy that in the Messianic Age all nations would celebrate Sukkot, they concluded that the seventy sacrifices of Sukkot represented the seventy nations of the world as described in Genesis 10. Even though Zechariah's vision had not yet been realized, it was as if all humanity were in some sense present in Jerusalem on the festival, and sacrifices made on their behalf. On the eighth day, as they were leaving, it was as if God were inviting the Jewish people to a small private reception. The word *Atzeret* itself was interpreted to mean, "Stop, stay a while." Shemini Atzeret was private time between God and His people. It was a day of particularity after the universality of the seven days of Sukkot.

In some versions of this narrative the emphasis was on the length of time before the people would return to the Temple, virtually half a year until Pesaḥ. Others stressed the sudden shift from seventy sacrifices to one. The memorable phrase, though, that shines through, is the one mentioned by Rashi (commentary to Lev. 23:36), in which God says to Israel, "It is hard for Me to see you go." This is the language of intimacy.

As we noted earlier, Sukkot represents more clearly than any other festival the dualities of Judaism. The four kinds are a symbol of the land of Israel, while the sukka reminds us of exile. The four kinds are a ritual of rain, while eating in the sukka depends on the absence of rain. Above all, though, there is the tension between the universality of nature and the particularity of history. There is an aspect of Sukkot – rainfall, harvest, climate – to which everyone can relate, but there is another – the long journey through the wilderness – that speaks to the unique experience of the Jewish people.

This tension between the universal and the particular is unique to Judaism. The God of Israel is the God of all humanity, but the religion of Israel is not the religion of all humanity. It is conspicuous that while the other two Abrahamic monotheisms, Christianity and Islam, borrowed much from Judaism, they did not borrow this. They became universalist faiths, believing that everyone ought to embrace the one true religion, their own, and that those who do not are denied the blessings of eternity. *Extra ecclesiam non est salus*, "Outside the church none is saved."

Judaism disagrees. For this it was derided for many centuries, and to some degree still today. Why, if it represents religious truth, is it not to be shared with everyone? If there is only one God, why is there not only one way to salvation? There is no doubt that if Judaism had become an evangelizing, conversion-driven religion – as it would have had to, had it believed in universalism – there would be many more Jews than there are today. As I write, there are an estimated 2.4 billion Christians, 1.6 billion Muslims and only 13 million Jews. The disparity is vast.

Judaism is the road less traveled, because it represents a complex truth that could not be expressed in any other way. The Torah tells a simple story. God gave humans the gift of freedom, which they then used not to enhance creation but to endanger it. Adam and Eve broke the first prohibition. Cain, the first human child, became the first murderer. Within a remarkably short space of time, all flesh had corrupted its way on earth, the world was filled with violence, and only one man, Noah, found favor in God's eyes. After the Flood, God made a covenant with Noah, and through him with all humanity, but after the hubris of the builders of the Tower of Babel, God chose another way. Having established a basic threshold in the form of the Noahide laws, He then chose one man, one family, and eventually one nation, to become a living example of what it is to exist closely and continuously in the presence of God. There are, in the affairs of humankind, universal laws and specific examples. The Noahide covenant constitutes the universal laws. The way of life of Abraham and his descendants are the example.

What this means in Judaism is that the righteous of all the nations have a share in the world to come (*Sanhedrin* 105a). In contemporary terms it means that our common humanity precedes our religious differences. It also means that by creating all humans in His image, God set us the challenge of seeing His image in one who is not in my image: whose color, culture, class and creed are not mine. The ultimate spiritual challenge is to see the trace of God in the face of a stranger.

Zechariah, in the vision we read as the Haftara for the first day, puts this precisely. He says that in the End of Days, "The Lord shall be King over all the earth; on that day the Lord shall be One and His name One" (1:49), meaning that all the nations will recognize the sovereignty of a single transcendent God. Yet at the same time Zechariah envisages the nations participating only in Sukkot, the most universal of the festivals, and the one in which they have the greatest interest since they all need rain. He does not envisage their becoming Jews, accepting the "yoke of the commands," all 613 of them. He does not speak of their conversion. The practical outcome of this dual theology – the universality of God and the particularity of Torah – is that we are commanded to be true to our faith, and a blessing to others, regardless of their faith. That is the way of Abraham.

Shemini Atzeret reminds us of the intimacy Jews have always felt in the presence of God. The cathedrals of Europe convey a sense of the vastness of God and the smallness of humankind. The small synagogues of Tzefat, where Isaac Luria and Joseph Karo prayed, convey a sense of the closeness of God and the greatness of humankind. Jews, except when they sought to imitate the gentiles, did not build cathedrals. Even the Temple reached its greatest architectural grandeur under Herod, a man better known for his political ruthlessness than his spiritual sensibilities.

So, when all the universality of Judaism has been expressed, there remains something that cannot be universalized: that sense of intimacy with and closeness to God that we feel on Shemini Atzeret, when all the other guests have left. Shemini Atzeret is chamber music, not a symphony. It is quiet time with God. We are reluctant to leave, and we dare to think that He is reluctant to see us go. Justice is universal, love is particular. There are some things we share because we are human. But there are other things, constitutive of our identity, that are uniquely ours – most importantly our relationships to those who form our family. On Sukkot we are among strangers and friends. On Shemini Atzeret we are with family.

When the Temple stood, it was as if God had said to His people: Stop. Pause. Stand in My courtyard, in Jerusalem the holy city, and feel My presence in the quiet of the day, the still blue sky, and the breeze gently rustling the trees. And even though the Temple has not been rebuilt, and Israel remains surrounded by enemies, and all we have of the Temple Mount is a wall, the most abstract of all religious symbols, yet still today in Jerusalem you can feel the Divine Presence as nowhere else on earth, a presence that does not have to be announced with clarions, robes and rituals, and we know that though God is God of all the world, to us He is also father, husband, neighbor, shepherd, king, and we are His children, and this is our private time together, breathing each other's being, blessed by the gift of being present to one another.

Simḥat Torah

One of the more amusing scenes in Anglo-Jewish history occurred on 14 October 1663. Seven years had passed since Oliver Cromwell had found no legal bar to Jews living in England (hence the so-called "return" of 1656). A small synagogue was opened in Creechurch Lane in the City of

London, forerunner of Bevis Marks (1701), the oldest still-extant place of Jewish worship in Britain.

The famous diarist Samuel Pepys decided to pay a visit to this new curiosity, to see how Jews conducted themselves at prayer. What he saw amazed and scandalized him. As chance or providence had it, the day of his visit turned out to be Simḥat Torah. This is how he described what he saw:

> And anon their Laws that they take out of the press [i.e. the Ark] are carried by several men, four or five several burthens in all, and they do relieve one another; and whether it is that every one desires to have the carrying of it, I cannot tell, thus they carried it round about the room while such a service is singing…. But, Lord! to see the disorder, laughing, sporting, and no attention, but confusion in all their service, more like brutes than people knowing the true God, would make a man forswear ever seeing them more and indeed I never did see so much, or could have imagined there had been any religion in the whole world so absurdly performed as this.

This was not the kind of behavior he was used to in a house of worship. It was conduct unbecoming. It was the kind of joy that does not translate easily into other languages of the spirit. It wasn't English.

Simḥat Torah is unique among festivals. It is not mentioned in the Torah, nor in the Talmud. Unlike Purim and Ḥanukka, it was not formalized by any decision on the part of the religious authorities, nor does it commemorate any historical deliverance. It is the supreme example of what the mystics called an *itaruta deletata*, "an awakening from below." It grew from the grassroots, slowly developing over time. It is the only festival that is celebrated as a distinct day only in the Diaspora: in Israel it is subsumed as part of the celebration of Shemini Atzeret. It affords, in other words, a rare glimpse into the reflexes of the collective Jewish soul.

It was born in Babylon, probably at the end of the period of the *Amora'im*, the rabbis of the Talmud, in the fifth or sixth century. The Babylonian custom – now universal – was to divide the Torah into fifty-four portions to be read in the course of a year. The *Eretz Yisrael* custom was to divide it into 155 or 175 portions, to be read in a three- or three-and-a-half-year cycle. On the second day of Shemini Atzeret in Babylon (there was no second day in Israel), the custom was to read the passage in which King Solomon blesses the people at the end of the Temple consecration ceremony and sends them on their way home. Normally the Torah reading on a festival has to do with the festival itself, but on this day it became a custom to read the last portion of the Torah, in which Moses blessed the nation at the end of his life. The day was thus known as *Yom Berakha*, "the day of blessing" (*Siddur Rav Sa'adia Gaon*).

It had long been the custom to make a celebration on completing a section of study, a talmudic tractate or an order of the Mishna (*Shabbat* 118b). This too was attributed to Solomon, who made a feast after God had granted him wisdom (I Kings 3:15). Thus the custom evolved to make a celebration at the completion of the Mosaic books, and it was considered a great honor to be called to the Torah for this last portion. The celebration became known as *Simḥat Torah*, "rejoicing in the Torah," though this was not yet the name given to the day.

No sooner had this custom developed than there was a feeling that it would be wrong to conclude the Torah without also immediately beginning it again. This was expressed in the form of the idea that Satan (prosecuting counsel in the heavenly court) might bring an accusation against the Jewish people that having reached the end of the book, they stopped at that point (*Seder Trois*, 4). Thus it became the norm to begin again with the opening of *Parashat Bereshit*. How this was to be done became the subject of many different customs. Some said the Genesis passage by heart. Others read it from a second *Sefer Torah*. In some places only one person was called to the two readings; in others two were called, one for the end, the other for the beginning, but without a blessing in between. The first said the blessing before reading, the second the blessing after. Eventually a consensus emerged. There would be two separate *aliyot*, one for the close of Deuteronomy, the other for the opening of Genesis.

Meanwhile other customs developed in the spirit of the day. The first was to call up many more people to the Torah than on usual occasions. Soon all men in the synagogue received *aliyot*, the portion being read multiple times. Then by the eleventh century the custom appeared of calling up *kol hane'arim*, all the children, with an adult saying the blessing, and the children gathered together under a tallit spread over them like a wedding canopy.

Only in the twelfth century do we find the two key honors, being called to the end and the beginning, being described as *Hatan Torah*, bridegroom of the law, and *Hatan Bereshit*, bridegroom of the beginning. Abraham Yaari, who has written the standard history of Simhat Torah, speculates the original title was *Hatam* or *Hotem Torah*, literally the one who "seals" or "concludes" the Torah. Nonetheless, once the word *Hatan*, bridegroom, appeared, it soon won universal approval. As early as the eighth century in Babylon the custom had been that on this day people adorned the Torah scroll with women's scarves and ornaments. Thus the Torah had long been treated as a bride, and it became logical to describe those who honored it as bridegrooms. Only much later, under the influence of the mystics in Tzefat associated with Rabbi Isaac Luria, did the custom evolve to do *Hakafot*, circuits around the *bima*, with multiple Torah scrolls.

Simhat Torah did not develop in Israel, firstly because there was no second day of Shemini Atzeret, secondly and more importantly because they did not complete the Torah reading in a single year. The Jewish community in Israel was devastated by the Crusades. In 1099, virtually the entire community in Jerusalem was massacred by the Christians. The city, said some observers, was knee-deep in blood. It was this almost total destruction of Israeli Jewry that finally brought the three-year cycle to an end. Nonetheless, even in the twelfth century, when Moses Maimonides was living in Fostat near Cairo, there were two synagogues, one of which followed the Babylonian custom, the other of which still maintained the Israeli one of a triennial lection. Despite this split, which Maimonides lamented, the traveler Benjamin of Tudela tells us that the members of the Israeli synagogue joined the Babylonian-oriented community to celebrate the ending of the Torah, so unity prevailed at least one day a year.

Thus far, history. But the very emergence of Simhat Torah signals something remarkable. Recall that Sukkot and Shemini Atzeret are both described as *zeman simhateinu*, the season of our joy. The nature of that joy was clear, and signaled in different ways both by the sukka and by the four kinds. The sukka reminded the people how blessed they were to be living in Israel when they recalled how their ancestors had to live for forty years without a land or a permanent home. The lulav, etrog, myrtle and willows were a vivid demonstration of the fruitfulness of the land under the divine blessing of rain. The joy of Sukkot was the joy of living in the Promised Land.

But by the time Simḥat Torah had spread throughout the Jewish world, Jews had lost virtually everything: their land, their home, their freedom and independence, the Temple, the priesthood, the sacrificial order – all that had once been their source of joy. A single devastating sentence, in one of the *piyutim* of Ne'ila at the close of Yom Kippur, summed up their situation: *Ein shiur rak haTorah hazot*, "Nothing remains but this Torah." All that remained was a book.

Sa'adia Gaon, writing in the tenth century, asked a simple question. In virtue of what was the Jewish people still a nation? It had none of the normal preconditions of a nation. Jews were scattered throughout the world. They did not live in the same territory. They were not part of a single economic or political order. They did not share the same circumambient culture. They did not speak the same language of everyday speech. Rashi spoke French, Maimonides Arabic. Yet they were, and were seen to be, one nation, bound by a bond of collective destiny and responsibility. Hence Sa'adia concluded: our people is a people only in virtue of our Torah (*Beliefs and Opinions*, 3). In the lovely rabbinic phrase about the Ark, which contained the tablets, "It carried those who carried it" (*Sota* 35a). More than the Jewish people preserved the Torah, the Torah preserved the Jewish people.

It was, as we say in our prayers, "our life and the length of our days." It was their marriage contract with God, the record of the covenant that bound them unbreakably together. They had lost their world but they still had God's word, and it was enough.

More than enough. On Simḥat Torah, without their being commanded by any verse in the Torah or any decree of the rabbis, Jews throughout the world sang and danced and recited poems in honor of the Torah, exactly as if they were the "men of renown" dancing in the courtyard of the Temple at the *Simḥat Beit HaSho'eva*, or as if they were King David bringing the Ark to Jerusalem. They were determined to show God, and the world, that they could still be *akh same'aḥ*, as the Torah said about Sukkot: wholly, totally, given over to joy. It would be hard to find a parallel in the entire history of the human spirit of a people capable of such joy at a time when they were being massacred by Christians in the name of the God of love, or brutalized by Muslim radicals like the Almohades in the name of the God of compassion.

A people that can walk through the valley of the shadow of death and still rejoice is a people that cannot be defeated by any force or any fear. King David was despised by his wife, Saul's daughter, Michal, for abandoning his dignity as a king when he danced and leaped with all his might before the Lord (II Sam. 6:14–16). The Spanish and Portuguese Jews of the Creechurch Lane synagogue in 1663 were equally looked down on by Samuel Pepys, who thought their conduct unbecoming in a house of God. Maimonides, however, writes (*Laws of Shofar* 8:15) that to experience joy in the fulfillment of a mitzva out of the love of God is to touch the spiritual heights. Whoever stands on his dignity and regards such things as beneath him is, he says, a sinner and a fool, and whoever abandons his dignity for the sake of joy is thereby elevated "because there is no greatness or honor higher than celebrating before God."

Simḥat Torah was born when Jews had lost everything else, but they never lost their capacity to rejoice. Nehemiah was right when he said to the people weeping as they listened to the Torah, realizing how far they had drifted from it: "Do not grieve, for the joy of the Lord is your strength" (Neh. 8:10). A people whose capacity for joy cannot be destroyed is itself indestructible. Zechariah was right: "'Not by might nor by power, but by My Spirit,' says the Lord Almighty" (Zech. 4:6).

Sukkot for Our Time

Of all the festivals, Sukkot is surely the one that speaks most powerfully to our time. Kohelet could almost have been written in the twenty-first century. Here is the ultimate success, the man who has it all – the houses, the cars, the clothes, the adoring women, the envy of all men – who has pursued everything this world can offer from pleasure to possessions to power to wisdom, and yet who, surveying the totality of his life, can only say, in effect, "Meaningless, meaningless, everything is meaningless."

Kohelet's failure to find meaning is directly related to his obsession with the "I" and the "Me": "I built for myself. I gathered for myself. I acquired for myself." The more he pursues his desires, the emptier his life becomes. There is no more powerful critique of the consumer society, whose idol is the self, whose icon is the "selfie" and whose moral code is "Whatever works for you." This is the society that achieved unprecedented affluence, giving people more choices than they have ever known, and yet at the same time saw an unprecedented rise in alcohol and drug abuse, eating disorders, stress-related syndromes, depression, attempted suicide and actual suicide. A society of tourists, not pilgrims, is not one that will yield the sense of a life worth living. Of all things people have chosen to worship, the self is the least fulfilling. A culture of narcissism quickly gives way to loneliness and despair.

Kohelet was also, of course, a cosmopolitan: a man at home everywhere and therefore nowhere. This is the man who had seven hundred wives and three hundred concubines but in the end could only say, "Woman is more bitter than death" (7:26). It should be clear to anyone who reads this in the context of the life of Solomon that Kohelet is not really talking about women but about himself.

In the end Kohelet finds meaning in simple things. Sweet is the sleep of a laboring man. Enjoy life with the woman you love. Eat, drink and enjoy the sun. That ultimately is the meaning of Sukkot as a whole. It is a festival of simple things. It is, Jewishly, the time we come closer to nature than any other, sitting in a hut with only leaves for a roof, and taking in our hands the unprocessed fruits and foliage of the palm branch, the citron, twigs of myrtle and leaves of willow. It is a time when we briefly liberate ourselves from the sophisticated pleasures of the city and the processed artifacts of a technological age, and recapture some of the innocence we had when we were young, when the world still had the radiance of wonder.

The power of Sukkot is that it takes us back to the most elemental roots of our being. You don't need to live in a palace to be surrounded by clouds of glory. You don't need to be rich to buy yourself the same leaves and fruit that a billionaire uses in worshiping God. Living in the sukka and inviting guests to your meal, you discover – such is the premise of *Ushpizin*, the mystical guests – that the people who have come to visit you are none other than Abraham, Isaac and Jacob and their wives. What makes a hut more beautiful than a home is that when it comes to Sukkot, there is no difference between the richest of the rich and the poorest of the poor. We are all strangers on earth, temporary residents in God's almost eternal universe. And whether or not we are capable of pleasure, whether or not we have found happiness, we can all feel joy.

Sukkot is the time we ask the most profound question of what makes a life worth living. Having prayed on Rosh HaShana and Yom Kippur to be written in the book of life, Kohelet forces us to remember how brief life actually is, and how vulnerable. "Teach us rightly to number our days, that we may gain a heart of wisdom" (Ps. 90:12). What matters is not how long we live, but how intensely we feel that life is a gift we repay by giving to others. Joy, the overwhelming theme of the festival, is what we feel when we know that it is a privilege simply to be alive, inhaling the intoxicating beauty of this moment amidst the profusion of nature, the teeming diversity of life and the sense of communion with those many others with whom we share a history and a hope.

Most majestically of all, Sukkot is the festival of insecurity. It is the candid acknowledgment that there is no life without risk, yet we can face the future without fear when we know we are not alone. God is with us, in the rain that brings blessings to the earth, in the love that brought the universe and us into being and in the resilience of spirit that allowed a small and vulnerable people to outlive the greatest empires the world has ever known. Sukkot reminds us that God's glory was present in the small, portable Tabernacle that Moses and the Israelites built in the desert even more emphatically than in Solomon's Temple with all its grandeur. A temple can be destroyed. But a sukka, broken, can be rebuilt tomorrow. Security is not something we can achieve physically but it is something we can acquire mentally, psychologically, spiritually. All it needs is the courage and willingness to sit under the shadow of God's sheltering wings.

The sukka became in the course of time a symbol, not only of forty years in the wilderness, but of centuries of exile and dispersion. In the Middle Ages alone, Jews were expelled from England in 1290, from France several times (1182, 1322, 1394), from Vienna in 1421, Cologne in

1424, Bavaria in 1442, Milan in 1489 and most traumatically, from Spain in 1492. In the 1880s a wave of pogroms in Eastern Europe sent millions of Jews into flight to the West, and these migrations continue even today. Jewish history reads like a vast continuation of the stages of the Israelites' journey in the thirty-second chapter of the book of Numbers: "They traveled...and they encamped.... They traveled...and they encamped." Too often, home turned out to be no more than a temporary dwelling, a sukka. More than most, whether in the land of Israel or elsewhere, Jews have known the full force of insecurity.

Yet with its genius for the unexpected and its ability to rescue hope from tragedy, Judaism declared this festival of insecurity to be *zeman simhateinu*, the season of our rejoicing. For the sukka, that quintessential symbol of vulnerability, turns out to be the embodiment of faith, the faith of a people who forty centuries ago set out on a risk-laden journey across a wilderness of space and time, with no more protection than the sheltering presence of the *Shekhina*. Sitting in the sukka under its canopy of leaves, I often think of my ancestors and their wanderings across Europe in search of safety, and I begin to understand how faith was their only home. It was fragile, chillingly exposed to the storms of prejudice and hate. But it proved stronger than superpowers and outlived them all.

Toward the end of his great *History of the Jews*, Paul Johnson wrote:

> The Jews were not just innovators. They were also exemplars and epitomizers of the human condition. They seemed to present all the inescapable dilemmas of man in a heightened and clarified form.... The Jews were the emblem of homeless and vulnerable humanity. But is not the whole earth no more than a temporary transit camp?

Those words go to the heart of Sukkot. To know that life is full of risk and yet to affirm it, to sense the full insecurity of the human situation and yet to rejoice: this, for me, is the essence of faith. Judaism is no comforting illusion that all is well in this dark world. It is instead the courage to celebrate in the midst of uncertainty, and to rejoice even in the transitory shelter of the Tabernacle, the Jewish symbol of home.

Pesaḥ

Finding Freedom

Pesaḥ and the Jewish Task

Pesaḥ is the oldest and most transformative story of hope ever told. It tells of how an otherwise undistinguished group of slaves found their way to freedom from the greatest and longest-lived empire of their time, indeed of any time. It tells the revolutionary story of how the supreme Power intervened in history to liberate the supremely powerless. It is a story of the defeat of probability by the force of possibility. It defines what it is to be a Jew: a living symbol of hope.

Pesaḥ tells us that the strength of a nation does not lie in horses and chariots, armies and arms, or in colossal statues and monumental buildings, overt demonstrations of power and wealth. It depends on simpler things: humility in the presence of the God of creation, trust in the God of redemption and history, and a sense of the non-negotiable sanctity of human life, created by God in His image, even the life of a slave or a child too young to ask questions. Pesaḥ is the eternal critique of power used by humans to coerce and diminish their fellow humans.

It is the story more than a hundred generations of our ancestors handed on to their children, and they to theirs. As we do likewise, millennia later, we know what it is to be the people of history, guardians of a narrative not engraved in hieroglyphics on the walls of a monumental building but carried in the minds of living, breathing human beings who, for longer than any other people, have kept faith with the future and the past, bearing witness to the power of the human spirit when it opens itself to a greater power, beckoning us to a world of freedom, responsibility and human dignity.

Pesaḥ is more than simply one festival among others in the Jewish calendar, more even than the anniversary of Israel's birth as a free people setting out on its journey to the Promised Land. In this section, I want to show how it emerged, in four ways, as the central event around which most of Judaism turns.

First, close examination shows us that the Torah narrative of Genesis from Abraham to Jacob is a series of anticipations of the Exodus, focusing our attention on, and heightening our anticipation of, what would eventually take place in the days of Moses.

Second, remembering "that you were once slaves in Egypt" is the single most frequently invoked "reason for the commands." The Exodus was not *just* an event in history – though it *was* an event in history.[1] It forms an essential part of the logic of Jewish law.

Third, key elements of Jewish law and faith are best understood as a protest against and alternative to the Egypt of the pharaohs even where the Torah does not state this explicitly. Knowledge of that ancient world gives us fresh insights into why Judaism is as it is.

Fourth, sustained meditation on the contrast between Egypt and the society the Israelites were called on to create reveals a fundamental choice that civilizations must make, then, now and perhaps for all time. There is nothing antiquarian about the issues Pesaḥ raises: slavery, freedom, politics, power, state, society, human dignity and responsibility.

---

1. On the historicity of the Exodus, see among others, James K. Hoffmeier, *Israel in Egypt: The Evidence for the Authenticity of the Exodus Tradition* (Oxford: Oxford University Press, 1996); Colin J. Humphreys, *The Miracles of Exodus* (London: Continuum, 2003).

These are as salient today as they were in the days of Moses. Pesaḥ can never be obsolete.

At the heart of the festival is a concrete historical experience. The Israelites, as described in the Torah, were a fractious group of slaves of shared ancestry, one of a number of such groups attracted to Egypt from the north, drawn by its wealth and power, only to find themselves eventually its victims. The Egypt of the pharaohs was the longest-lived empire the world has known, already some eighteen centuries old by the time of the Exodus. For more than a thousand years before Moses, its landscape had been dominated by the great pyramid of Giza, the tallest man-made structure in the world until the construction of the Eiffel Tower in 1889. The discovery in 1922 by the English archeologist Howard Carter of the tomb of a relatively minor pharaoh, Tutankhamun, revealed the astonishing wealth and sophistication of the royal court at that time. If historians are correct in identifying Rameses II as the pharaoh of the Exodus, then Egypt had reached the very summit of its power, bestriding the narrow world like a colossus.

At one level it is a story of wonders and miracles. But the enduring message of Pesaḥ is deeper than this, for it opens out into a dramatically new vision of what a society might be like if the only Sovereign is God, and every citizen is in His image. It is about the power of the powerless and the powerlessness of power. Politics has never been more radical, more ethical or more humane.

Heinrich Heine said, "Since the Exodus, freedom has spoken with a Hebrew accent." But it is, as Emmanuel Levinas called it, a "difficult freedom," based as it is on a demanding code of individual and collective responsibility. Pesaḥ makes us taste the choice: on the one hand the bread of affliction and bitter herbs of slavery; on the other, four cups of wine, each marking a stage in the long walk to liberty. As long as humans seek to exercise power over one another, the story will continue and the choice will still be ours.

Prefigurations of the Exodus

Almost at the beginning of the Jewish story, something surpassingly strange happens. The initial sequence is clear. God calls Abraham to leave his land, his birthplace and his father's house and travel "to the land I will show you" (Gen. 12:1). Abraham does so immediately, without delay or demur, and arrives in the land of Canaan.

It is then that something unexpected happens. No sooner has he arrived than he is forced to leave: "There was a famine in the land" (ibid. 10). Abraham must travel to Egypt where there is food. Sarah is a beautiful woman; Abraham fears he will be killed so that Sarah can be taken into the royal harem. He asks her to pretend to be his sister, which she does, and Pharaoh takes her into the palace. Plagues then strike him and his household. He intuits – the text is not clear how – that this has something to do with Abraham and Sarah. He summons Abraham who tells him the truth, whereupon Pharaoh sends both of them away. Meanwhile, in Egypt, Abraham has grown wealthy. The story then resumes where we left it, with Abraham and his household in the land of Canaan.

What is this story doing here? It is not there simply because it happened. The Torah never records events merely because they happened. It omits vast tracts of the patriarchs' lives. Later, it omits thirty-eight of the forty years of the Israelites in the wilderness. If an event is told in the Torah, it is there to teach us something. "Torah" means teaching. What, then, is the lesson we are meant to learn?

A midrash (Genesis Raba 40:6) gives us the answer. Abraham's forced descent into Egypt is an intimation of, and rehearsal for, what would eventually happen to his descendants. The parallels are many and precise. Here are some:

Abraham	The Israelites
There was a famine in the land (Gen. 12:10)	For two years now there has been famine in the land (Gen. 45:6)
and Abram went down to Egypt (ibid.)	Our forefathers went down into Egypt (Num. 20:15)
to live there for a while (ibid.)	We have come to live here awhile (Gen. 47:4)
because the famine was severe (ibid.)	because the famine is severe (ibid.)

"They will kill me but will let you live" (Gen. 12:12)	"Every boy that is born you must throw into the Nile, but let every girl live" (Ex. 1:22)
The Lord plagued Pharaoh and his house with great plagues (Gen. 12:17)	The ten plagues
Pharaoh gave orders about Abram to his men, and they sent him on his way (Gen. 12:20)	The Egyptians urged the people, that they might send them out of the land in haste (Ex. 12:33)
Abram had become very wealthy in livestock and in silver and gold (Gen. 13:2)	He brought out Israel, laden with silver and gold (Ps. 105:37)

The similarities are so exact and multiple as to be unmistakable. Even the verb *sh-l-ḥ*, "to send," in the penultimate parallel means, among other things, to liberate a slave. Abraham was not a slave but he was, in a certain sense, a captive. The midrash explains: "The Holy One said to our father Abraham: 'Go forth and tread a path for your children.' For you find that everything written in connection with Abraham is written in connection with his children." The exile and exodus were not accidental. They were rehearsed at the very beginning of the Jewish journey.

In case we should miss the point, the story is repeated twice more with minor variations, first with Abraham and Sarah in Gerar in the land of the Philistines (Gen. 20), then with Isaac and Rebecca in the same place with the same key figure, King Avimelekh (Gen. 26). There is the same emphasis on danger, the same circumstance of the key figures, Abraham and Sarah, Isaac and Rebecca, being forced into a lie to save a life, the same discovery of the facts just in time, the same anxious release. Something is taking shape.

So it was in the life of the first two generations of the family of the covenant. What about the third, Jacob? Jacob too is forced, by famine, to send members of his family to Egypt for food. Eventually he and the rest of the family join them. But this was not a rehearsal for exile. It was the exile itself. Did something similar happen earlier in Jacob's life?

It did, and the Haggada in a famous passage points this out: "Go and learn what Laban the Aramean sought to do to our father Jacob."

On the face of it, there is no connection between the events of Pesaḥ and the earlier life of Jacob. The Israelites were forced into Egypt because of famine; Jacob fled his home because his brother Esau was threatening to kill him. Yet it is Jacob's life with Laban that presents many other parallels to the events that would later take place in Egypt. Just as Pharaoh was generous in offering hospitality to Joseph's family, so Laban welcomed Jacob: "You are my own flesh and blood" (Gen. 29:14). Just as the Israelites multiplied in Egypt, so Jacob had many children. He "grew exceedingly prosperous and came to own large flocks, and maidservants and menservants, and camels and donkeys" (Gen. 30:43). Just as the political climate in Egypt changed – a new king arose who "knew not Joseph" (Ex. 1:8) – so the climate in Laban's family changed: "Jacob noticed that Laban's attitude toward him was not what it had been" (Gen. 31:2).

Moses asks Pharaoh: "Let my people go" (Ex. 5:1). Jacob asks Laban: "Send me on my way so I can go back to my own homeland" (Gen. 30:25). Pharaoh refuses. Laban is reluctant. Jacob then works for Laban for a further six years – the length of service after which, in Jewish law, a slave goes free (Ex. 21:2). The Israelites and Jacob eventually leave, against the will of their hosts. Pharaoh and Laban both follow in pursuit. In both cases divine intervention protects pursued from pursuer: an impenetrable cloud comes between the Israelites and the Egyptians. God Himself appears to Laban telling him not to harm Jacob (31:24). Again the parallels are clear. The Haggada is drawing our attention to a connection we might otherwise have missed.[2]

Over and above all these events is one scene in which the entire drama of exile and exodus is foretold, long in advance, to Abraham:

> As the sun was setting, Abram fell into a deep sleep, and a thick and dreadful darkness came over him. He [God] said to Abram, "Know that your descendants will be strangers in a land not their own, and they will be enslaved and oppressed for four hundred

2. See David Daube, *The Exodus Pattern in the Bible* (London: Faber and Faber, 1963).

years; but know that I shall judge the nation that enslaves them, and then they will leave with great wealth. You, however, will go to your ancestors in peace and be buried at a good old age. In the fourth generation your descendants will come back here, for the sin of the Amorites has not yet reached its full measure." (Gen. 15:12–16)

This scene, "the Covenant between the Pieces," makes it clear that the entire sequence of events leading up to exile and exodus did not simply happen. They were pre-scripted. They were meant to be. That is what the Haggada means when it says that God "calculated the end," and that Jacob "went down to Egypt – compelled by what had been spoken." Despite the apparently free actions of human agents, there was a Providence at work behind the scenes. This is as close as Judaism gets to Greek tragedy.

The story of Pesaḥ is thus understood by the Torah not as just a historical event, not even an event that involved signs and wonders and miraculous deliverances. It always was meant to be part of the journey, prefigured five times in advance by four exiles and a nighttime vision before there even was a Jewish people. *The way to the Promised Land passes through Egypt and exile.* This was not a detour but part of the route itself, anticipated at the very outset. Why so? The answer lies in the inner logic of the Torah as a set of commands and a way of life, not just for individuals but as a nation in its land.

Reasons for the Commands

The journey to the Promised Land had to pass through Egypt because Israel was to construct a society that would be the antithesis of Egypt. Therefore they had to know Egypt, experience Egypt, feel it in their bones, carry it with them as an indelible memory that they would hand on to all future generations. They had to experience what it was like to be on the wrong side of power: strangers, outsiders, metics, *apiru* as they were known in Egypt in those days, people without rights who were subject to the whim of a merciless ruler. The taste of that affliction was never to be forgotten.

To this day, the temples, colossi and pyramids of Egypt are awe-inspiring. They were meant to be, and they succeeded. But there is a question to be asked about monumental architecture through the ages, much of it religious: at whose cost was it built? Virtually none was produced without exploitation on a massive scale: treasures won through war, wealth through taxes on subject populations, and forced labor, the corvée, the earliest and most primitive form of taxation, imposed by rulers on the ruled almost from the dawn of civilization. The Giza pyramid, for example, with its 2,300,000 blocks of stone, each weighing on average more than a ton, was built during the twenty years of Pharaoh Khufu's reign (c.2545–2525 BCE). A simple calculation shows that the builders would have had to set one stone in place every two minutes for ten hours each day for two decades. This suggests forced labor of the most extensive kind involving tens of thousands of people at any time.

It is against this feature of the first great civilizations – Mesopotamia from which Abraham's family came, and the Egypt Moses and the Israelites left – that the Torah is a protest. In Genesis and Exodus we hear little about the idolatry and pagan rituals that were later to earn the scorn of the prophets. We hear much, however, about something else, namely the hierarchical society by which some presume to rule over others. This, to the Torah, is the unforgivable. In *Paradise Lost*, Milton, like the sages, traces this back to Nimrod, the first great ruler of Assyria and by implication the builder of the Tower of Babel (see Gen. 10:8–11). Milton writes that when Adam was told that Nimrod would "arrogate dominion undeserved," he was horrified:

> O execrable son so to aspire Above his Brethren, to himself assuming Authority usurped, from God not given: He gave us only over beast, fish, fowl Dominion absolute; that right we hold By his donation; but man over men He made not lord; such title to himself Reserving, human left from human free. (*Paradise Lost*, Book XII:64–71)

To question this – the right of humans to rule over other humans, without their consent, depriving them of their freedom – was, at that time and for most of history, utterly unthinkable. All advanced societies were like this. How could they be otherwise? Was this not the very structure of the universe? Did the sun not rule the day? Did the moon not rule the night? Was there not in heaven itself a hierarchy of the gods?

Monotheism is a theology, but it is also and no less fundamentally a political philosophy with revolutionary implications. If there is only one God, then there is no hierarchy in heaven. And if He set His image on human beings as such, then there is no justified hierarchy-without-consent on earth either. But to say this is one thing; to live it, breathe it, feel it, was another. There is only one way of so doing. A nation in exile must experience what it feels like to be on the wrong side of power. Why not a nation in its own land? Because a nation in its land cannot but assume that the way things were is the natural course of things. To create a new society you have to leave an old one. That is why Abraham had to leave behind all that was familiar to him. That is why the Israelites could be charged to construct a different social order, because they knew they were not Egyptians. They did not think they were. The Egyptians did not think they were. Outsiders can see the relativity of social structures that insiders believe to be inscribed in the nature of the human condition itself.

Time and again, when Moses explains to the Israelites the reason for the commands, he does so by asking them to *remember what it felt like* to live in a society where matters were arranged otherwise:

> Observe the Sabbath day by keeping it holy, as the Lord your God has commanded you. Six days you shall labor and do all your work, but the seventh day is a sabbath to the Lord your God. On it you shall not do any work, neither you, nor your son or daughter, nor your male or female servant, nor your ox, your donkey or any of your animals, nor any foreigner residing in your towns, so that your male and female servants may rest as you do. *Remember that you were slaves in Egypt* and that the Lord your God brought you out of there with a strong hand and an outstretched arm. It is for this reason that the Lord your God has commanded you to observe the Sabbath day. (Deut. 5:12–15)

> And you shall love the stranger, for *you yourselves were strangers* in the land of Egypt. (Deut. 10:19)

If your Hebrew kinsman or kinswoman is sold to you, he shall work for you for six years, and in the seventh year, you must release him from your service, free. When you set him free from your service you must not send him away empty-handed. You must give generously to him of your flock, your granary and your wine vat with which the Lord your God has blessed you; so you shall give him. And *you shall remember that you were once a slave in the land of Egypt* and the Lord your God redeemed you; this is why, today, I command you thus. (Deut. 15:12–15)

Do not deprive the foreigner or the fatherless of justice, or take the cloak of the widow as a pledge. *Remember that you were slaves in Egypt* and the Lord your God redeemed you from there. That is why I command you to do this. (Deut. 24:17–18)

When you harvest the grapes in your vineyard, do not go over the vines again. Leave what remains for the foreigner, the fatherless and the widow. *Remember that you were slaves in Egypt.* That is why I command you to do this. (Deut. 24:21–22)

As the instances accumulate, the plan of the Torah becomes clear. The Exodus functions not simply as a fact of history, but also and primarily as the fundamental principle of jurisprudence, the logic and justification of the Law.

The Israelites were commanded to create *a society that was not Egypt*, that was different, opposite, countercultural. It would be a society in which even slaves rested every seventh day and breathed the wide air of freedom. It would be one in which no one was destitute, no one deprived of the basic necessities of life. It would be one in which no one became trapped endlessly in debt, or forced irretrievably to sell ancestral property. Everyone would have access to justice. Those at the margins of society – the widow, the orphan, the Levite, the stranger – were to be treated with dignity and included in national festivals and celebrations.

This made sense because the Israelites had been on the receiving end of Egypt. They knew what it felt like to be poor, to be deprived of justice, to be treated as less than human. They knew what it felt like to work without cease. In the words of Exodus, they "knew the soul of a stranger" (23:9). They knew from the inside what powerlessness feels like.

Scholars have drawn attention to the fact that what makes Torah law different from other law codes in the ancient world is its appeal to reason. Ancient law in general was "apodictic, without justification and without persuasion." Its style is "categorical, demanding and commanding." It "enjoins, prescribes and orders, expecting to be heeded solely on the strength of being an official decree." It seeks no understanding and solicits no consent.[3] Against this the Torah represents "the Jewish predilection for justified law."

It is a point made by the great medieval commentator Ralbag (Gersonides, 1288–1344) who also argues that this is what makes the Torah different:

> Behold our Torah is unique among all the other doctrines and religions that other nations have had, in that our Torah contains nothing that does not originate in equity and reason. Therefore this Divine Law attracts people in virtue of its essence, so that they behave in accordance with it. The laws and religions of other nations are not like this: they do not conform to equity and wisdom, but are foreign to the nature of man, and people obey them because of compulsion, out of fear of the threat of punishment but not because of their essence.[4]

We now begin to see something singular about the Jewish experience. For as long as human beings have thought about morality, they have asked the question: Why be moral? Why act for the benefit of others if it is to your advantage to behave otherwise? We are self-seeking creatures, driven by desire. Why then desist from something you want to do and can do, merely because you ought not to? Plato, in *The Republic*, uses a thought experiment. He recalls the legend of Gyges' ring which had the power to make anyone who wore it invisible. One who had such

---

3.   David Weiss Halivni, *Midrash, Mishnah, Gemara: The Jewish Predilection for Justified Law* (Cambridge, MA: Harvard University Press, 1986), 5.

4.   Gersonides, Commentary to *Va'etḥanan*, par. 14.

a ring could commit any crime and get away with it. Why then would such a person be moral?[5]

Many answers have been given in the history of thought, none of them wholly satisfactory. The most famous attempt in the second half of the twentieth century was John Rawls' principle of "the veil of ignorance."[6] What kind of society would you construct if you did not know in advance who you would be: black or white, rich or poor, upper or lower class, gifted or otherwise? You would, he says, choose a society with equal liberties for all – precisely the kind of society the Torah seeks to create within the constraints of the human, political and social realities of its time.

The trouble with Rawls' principle is that social structures are created by real people in real positions of privilege and power. Outside the classroom there is no veil of ignorance. We are born into the world as this, not that; with these parents, this history, this ethnicity, in this specific place and time. We make decisions on the basis of what we are, not on hypothetical consideration of what, in another life, we might have been.

The Torah gives the most powerful grounding ever contemplated for a moral system. It provides not a veil of ignorance but a sustaining stream of knowledge – acquired through experience, nurtured by memory, enacted in ritual, retold in sacred story, tasted on the tongue, never to be forgotten. Indeed, says God through the prophets from Moses to Jeremiah, if you ever forget it, you will be forced to relive it, through further exiles, other persecutions.

Egypt was, for the Israelites, the school of the soul. They knew what it was like to be on the receiving end of absolute power: Rameses II, the greatest ruler of the longest-lived empire the world has ever known. They had then experienced something that would serve as a source of wonder from that day to this. They had been rescued by the Creator of heaven and earth who had brought them from slavery to freedom, taken them through the sea on dry land, given them bread from heaven and water from a rock, and then made a covenant with them, not for His

5. Plato, *The Republic*, Book II:359a–360d

6. John Rawls, *A Theory of Justice* (Cambridge, MA: Harvard University Press, 1971).

sake but for theirs, inviting them under His sovereignty to build a society that would use their God-given freedom to honor the liberty of others.

However, as we will now see, it is not just the commands that explicitly refer to "remembering Egypt" that were shaped by the Egyptian experience. So were many other features of Jewish law and belief.

Ozymandias

Stimulated by Napoleon's Egyptian campaign, Europe in the early nineteenth century was intrigued by the rediscovery of the magnificence of the civilization that once dominated the world but now lay in ruins, leading the young English poet Shelley to publish, in 1818, the most famous and haunting of all critiques of self-aggrandizing rulers:

> I met a traveller from an antique land
> Who said: Two vast and trunkless legs of stone
> Stand in the desert. Near them, on the sand,
> Half sunk, a shattered visage lies, whose frown,
> And wrinkled lip, and sneer of cold command,
> Tell that its sculptor well those passions read
> Which yet survive, stamped on these lifeless things,
> The hand that mocked them and the heart that fed.
> And on the pedestal these words appear:
> "My name is Ozymandias, king of kings:
> Look on my works, ye Mighty, and despair!"
> Nothing beside remains. Round the decay
> Of that colossal wreck, boundless and bare
> The lone and level sands stretch far away.

Ozymandias was the Greek name for the most famous pharaoh of all, third ruler of the nineteenth dynasty who dominated Egypt for some sixty-six years and is thought by many scholars to be the pharaoh of the Exodus, Rameses II. To the extent that the Torah is a deliberately contrarian work, a protest against and conscious alternative to the great civilizations of its day, it is worth reflecting more fully on who Rameses was and what he represented.

Early in his reign, in 1274 BCE, he fought a well-documented campaign to reconquer the strategic town of Kadesh in what is now western Syria. Some years earlier it had been taken by the Hittites. Rameses himself led the Egyptian army, and was informed that the Hittites, hearing of his advance, had fled. Approaching the town he discovered that he had been misinformed and that the Hittites were actually hiding behind the town, preparing to make a preemptive strike. A ferocious battle ensued, with the Egyptians initially suffering devastating losses. The arrival of reinforcements just saved the day. The next day, the two forces clashed again, but both were too weakened to achieve a decisive result and a peace treaty was signed. Rameses had barely avoided humiliating defeat, but on returning to Egypt declared that he had won a momentous victory, accounts and depictions of which were, during the ensuing years, inscribed on temple walls throughout the land.

In a culture in which truth took second place to royal glory, it is perhaps not surprising that no record of either the Israelites or the Exodus survives in Egyptian inscriptions, with one exception. It is contained in the Merneptah stele inscribed in the reign of Rameses II's successor Merneptah IV. It contains the following line:

Israel is laid waste, her seed is destroyed.

The first-ever reference to Israel outside the Bible is an obituary: another triumph of wishful thinking over reality.

No one in history constructed more monuments to his glory than Rameses II. His architectural ambitions were vast, his self-adulation even more so. He undertook huge building projects at Luxor, where he enlarged the already spacious temple, as well as constructing new temples throughout his realm from Lebanon to Sudan. One of his most grandiose projects was the temple of Rameses-beloved-of-Amun at Abu Simbel. The entrance to the smaller of the two buildings has, on each side, a statue of Queen Nefertari, flanked by two giant statues of Rameses thirty feet high. The facade of the larger temple has four vast statues of the seated king, each seventy feet high (three-and-a-half times as tall as the Lincoln Memorial in Washington). Inside, the pillared hall – each column adorned with a statue of Rameses depicted as Osiris, the

Egyptian god of the afterlife – leads to four vast statues of Egypt's main gods, Ptah, Amun, Ra-Horakhty, the sun god, and Rameses himself. As one scholar writes, "Few autocrats in human history have conceived a more dramatic expression of their personality cult."[7] It is clear that when Pharaoh responds angrily to Moses' request in God's name to let the Israelites go, saying, "Who is the Lord that I should obey His voice to let Israel go? I do not know the Lord," what he means is, "Here, I am god."

It was Rameses II who constructed an entirely new city near Hutwaret where his father Seti I had built a summer palace. It was a vast panoply of mansions, storehouses and barracks which took two decades of construction to complete. The royal quarter alone covered four square miles, and the steps leading to the throne were adorned with images of the king's enemies so that he could symbolically tread on them each time he ascended to the throne. He called it Per-Rameses, "the house of Rameses," and it is one of the two cities mentioned in Exodus 1:11 as being built by the Israelites. The other, "Pithom," or Per-Atum (Tell el-Maskhuta), was in the eastern Nile delta, a day's journey away.

By the time of Moses, Egypt of the pharaohs was eighteen centuries old, already longer lived than any subsequent empire. Its wealth and military power were unsurpassed, but it was not altogether unassailable. The Egyptians had, in the sixteenth century BCE, endured the rule of foreigners, the Hyksos, a fact that gives an edge to the statement of Pharaoh at the beginning of Exodus, "Look, the people of the children of Israel are more and mightier than we" (Ex. 1:9). This was not a theoretical fear. The Egyptians knew themselves to be vulnerable to incursion especially, though not only, from the north. Egypt had many gods, some 1,500 of them according to recent estimates. But by Rameses' day the real gods of Egypt were its rulers. It was they who were divine, who had communication with the gods and ruled even after death, whose buildings testified to their immortality, whose colossi dominated the landscape, striking fear in all who passed by. Rameses ruled Egypt as the sun ruled the sky.

The wealth of the royal court was astonishing, as became clear after the 1922 discovery of the tomb of Tutankhamun, with its coffin of pure gold, its funerary mask of gold, lapis lazuli, carnelian, quartz,

7. Toby Wilkinson, *The Rise and Fall of Ancient Egypt* (London: Bloomsbury, 2010), 332.

obsidian and turquoise, and its treasury of precious objects. At the same time the population as a whole lived a wretched existence. Remains of human skeletons show that they suffered not infrequently from starvation. There were regular epidemics among the urban population living crammed together in unsanitary conditions. Hepatitis, amoebic dysentery and schistosomiasis were common. Those who did not die were often disfigured. Contemporary documents speak of whole villages of people with impaired eyesight, the bleary-eyed, the one-eyed and the blind.

Farming at best yielded subsistence. Taxes had to be paid on all produce. Defaulters were thrown into prison. The vast majority of the population were illiterate, and virtually all able-bodied men were subject to the corvée, forced to work when the Nile flooded and fields were inundated, on the pharaoh's latest building extravaganza. The corvée was not abolished in Egypt until 1889. The conditions under which the Egyptians worked were not significantly better than those suffered by the Israelites. Their rations were barely enough to sustain life, and the backbreaking work under a sweltering sun with little food and less water meant that many died in the course of the great constructions.

Infant mortality was high, even in royal circles. We do not have independent evidence of what happened during the plagues, but we do know that Rameses II prematurely lost his twelve eldest sons, because his successor, Merneptah, was his thirteenth. Mortality was one of the central preoccupations of ancient Egypt: it was, in T.S. Eliot's phrase, "much possessed with death." Pharaohs, however, even those who did not see themselves as gods, on death joined the gods and became immortal. That is what the pyramids were initially: buildings through which the soul of the departed pharaoh ascended to heaven to join the immortals. Temples, although not themselves mausoleums (pharaohs were buried in tombs in the Valley of the Kings on the west bank of the Nile), were nonetheless intended to be eternal memorials, for even deceased pharaohs continued to rule over the destiny of Egypt from their court in heaven. Not until much later was the promise of immortality extended to ordinary people.

Against this background certain features of the Torah appear in a new or stronger light. First and most obvious is the sharpest possible *rejection of permanent economic hierarchy*, of a society in which some are fabulously rich while others are desperately poor. Even a king in Israel was not allowed to accumulate "much silver and gold" (Deut. 17:17). The entire welfare structure of the Torah, the corner of the field, other parts of the harvest, the tithe for the poor in the third and sixth years, the release of debts in the seventh and so on were intended to prevent the despair and destitution that existed in Egypt. "The great concern of Moses," wrote Henry George, "was to lay the foundation of a social state in which deep poverty and degrading want should be unknown."[8] When the wealth of the rich led to indifference to the poor, the prophets were incensed:

> You lie on beds adorned with ivory and lounge on your couches. You dine on choice lambs and fattened calves...but you do not grieve over the ruin of Joseph. (Amos 6:4–6)

Isaiah says, "The Lord enters into judgment with the elders and princes of His people: 'It is you who have devoured the vineyard, the spoil of the poor is in your houses. What do you mean by crushing My people, by grinding the face of the poor?' says the Lord God of hosts" (Is. 3:14–15). Jeremiah says simply of the reforming king Josiah, "He judged the cause of the poor and needy; then it was well. Is this not to know Me? says the Lord" (Jer. 22:16). Judaism is not socialism or communism. It distrusts the power of governments and sees private property as one of the primary safeguards of liberty. But deep-seated economic inequity offends against the fundamental values of *tzedaka* and *mishpat*, social and legislative justice, deemed by God Himself to be "the way of the Lord" (Gen. 18:19).

Second, in reaction against Rameses II specifically and rulers of the ancient world generally, the Tanakh redefines the institution of monarchy. Leaving aside the well-known ambivalence of the Torah about monarchy altogether, two features in particular of the Jewish law of kings were unique for their time and significant for all time. One was that the king had no major religious role whatsoever.[9] He was not the High Priest; he was not the performer of key rituals; he was not the

---

8. Henry George, *Moses: A Lecture* (Berlin: J. Harrwitz, 1899).
9. To be sure, the king officiated at *Hak'hel*, the septennial public reading of the Torah, but this was not a sacramental function, a form of worship.

intermediary of the nation in relation to the gods; he had no privileged access to their will or favor. The sages famously objected to the later Hasmonean kings because they broke this rule: they said to Alexander Jannaeus (king of Judea, 103–76 BCE), "Let the crown of kingship be sufficient for you; leave to the descendants of Aaron the crown of priesthood" (*Kiddushin* 66a).

The other was that the king had no legislative power. As many scholars have shown, there are parallels between the Israelite system of law and that of other ancient Near-Eastern powers. But everywhere else, acts like the remission of debts or the restoration of ancestral property were within the grant of the king. In Israel all such acts were in the power of God alone. God alone is the legislator. So unique was this that Josephus, trying to explain it to the Romans, had to coin a word for it – there was no other system like it. The word he coined was *theocracy*, "rule by God," but since, in the course of time, the term has come to mean rule by clerics, a better word would be *nomocracy*, "the rule of laws, not men." The king was neither the author of the law nor above the law. As the prophets made clear – Nathan to David, Elijah to Ahab – when it came to the pursuit of private interest rather than the public good, there was no royal prerogative in Israel.

The effect of these two principles was to *secularize* power. The king rules; he is entitled to honor and has many rights, but the power he holds is conditional: first on God, second on God's law, third on the will of the people. Divine sovereignty and human freedom are the fundamental realities in the politics of covenant. To these, monarchy (except in later messianic interpretations) comes a poor third. Michael Walzer puts it slightly differently: the Hebrew Bible "relativizes" all political regimes.[10] None is sacrosanct; none is written into the scheme of things. Ideally there would be no politics at all, just a vertical relationship between the people and God and a horizontal relationship of mutual responsibility between the people and one another. *The secularization and relativization of power in Judaism are a direct and specific rejection of the politics of the ancient world, never more clearly exemplified than by Rameses II, the ruler who turned himself into a god.*

---

10. Michael Walzer, *In God's Shadow: Politics in the Hebrew Bible* (New Haven, CT: Yale University Press, 2012), 204.

Perhaps most significantly of all, Egypt left its mark on the Hebrew Bible in its unerring focus on life, not death. Given the obsession of ancient Egypt with the realm of death and the afterlife, the almost complete absence of these subjects from Tanakh is astonishing. There is no mention of it where we would most expect it. Kohelet, for example, is a sustained meditation on mortality; everything is meaningless because we are all going to die. All the questions asked by Job could be answered in a single sentence: "Though you have suffered in this world you will receive your reward in the World to Come." The problematics of both books would be removed at a stroke by reference to the afterlife, but it is not there. Instead, says Moses, "This day I call the heavens and the earth as witnesses against you that I have set before you life and death, blessings and curses. Therefore choose life, that you and your children may live" (Deut. 30:19).

It is not that Judaism denies the afterlife or the resurrection of the dead. These are central to its faith. They emerge from their concealment, as it were, in the later prophets and the post-biblical sages. But it is impossible to read the Torah without realizing that it is, at specific points and to a high degree, a polemic against beliefs about the afterlife and the practices and cultures to which they give rise that it finds profoundly objectionable. There is almost no injustice that cannot be justified by reference to life after death. Terrorist suicide bombing is the latest example. When Karl Marx called religion "the opium of the people," this is what he had in mind: that the promise of bliss in an afterlife makes people accept chains and injustices in this life.

Nikolai Berdyaev in *The Meaning of History* argues that this is Judaism's fundamental error of judgment: its belief that perfect justice can ever be found in this world. That, he says, is what gives Judaism its eternal restlessness. It is why people dislike it so much. Christianity, he believes, made the better choice, by transferring its vision of justice, peace and perfection to life after death.

Berdyaev may or may not be right in his characterization of Judaism and Christianity, but the Jewish reply is compelling and unfaltering. If this physical life, set in this physical universe, is to be forever fraught with pain, cruelty, injustice and betrayal; if humans are doomed in advance by original sin to fail in all their moral aspirations; if life down here is to be endured rather than perfected, then why did God create the universe in the first place? Why was He not content with the angels? Why did He make man? To create a being destined to suffer, fated to fail, unable to achieve anything on his own, briefly granted God's image only to have it snatched away after the first sin – this, to Jews, is not the work of a loving Creator. If all hope belongs in heaven, why do we strive on earth? Berdyaev's is not the Jewish voice in Christianity but the unmistakable accent of ancient Greece, with its orphic cults and Gnostic mysticism and Platonic devaluation of the physical world. Rejecting Egypt's cult of death, Judaism commands, "Choose life."

We will understand more of Judaism the more we know about what it was a reaction against,[11] and in this equation the figure of Rameses II plays a key role. There are two features in particular of the story of Moses that cannot be understood other than in this light. One is the statement, at the end of Deuteronomy, that Moses was buried by God Himself, in the Plain of Moab, opposite the Holy Land, and that "no one knows his burial place to this day" (Deut. 34:6). This is directed against the monuments and mausoleums of ancient Egypt. It says in effect: no one needs to know, let alone stand in awe, of the place where you are buried for you to be immortal. "We do not make monuments for the dead; their words are their memorial" (Yerushalmi, *Shekalim* 2:5).

The other is a curious feature of the narrative of Moses' birth. We recall that he was placed in a basket and set afloat on the Nile where he was seen and subsequently adopted by Pharaoh's daughter. She gives him the name Moshe (Moses), saying, "I have drawn him [*meshitihu*] from the water" (Ex. 2:10). It takes a while before we realize that there is something strange about this sentence. It presupposes that Pharaoh's daughter spoke Hebrew. It also makes the impossible assumption that not only would she adopt a Hebrew child in direct contravention to her father's decree that every male child be killed, but would advertise the fact by giving him a Hebrew name. In short, the Hebrew etymology of the name is only half of the story.

---

11. This, of course, is Maimonides' approach in *The Guide for the Perplexed.* See also Jan Assmann, *Moses the Egyptian* (Cambridge, MA: Harvard University Press, 1997).

Moses – in the form Mose, Mses or Messes – is in fact an Egyptian word. It figures in the names of several Pharaohs, including Thutmose, and most significantly Rameses himself. The word means "child." Understanding this we stand before one of the Torah's boldest and most revolutionary strokes. Years later, two men are to be involved in a monumental confrontation: Rameses and Moses. Their names tell us what is at stake. Rameses means "child of the sun god Ra." Rameses, as we have seen, saw himself as a god and erected a temple at Abu Simbel to that proposition. Moses was simply, anonymously, "a child" – with no more identification than that, exactly as there is no name given to his parents when we first encounter them in the biblical text, other than the bare description, "A man of the tribe of Levi married a Levite woman" (Ex. 2:1).

It is not one man, a supreme ruler, who is in the image of God, but every man, woman and child on the face of the earth. It is not one infant who is a child of God but all infants: "My child, My firstborn, Israel," as God tells Moses to tell Pharaoh on their first meeting (Ex. 4:22). The greatest ruler, if he holds himself to be a god, stands lower in the true order of things than any child who serves God rather than making God serve him. Moses means "a mere child." Nothing could be more skewed than the various commentators, most famously Otto Rank and Sigmund Freud, who read the story of the childhood of Moses as a variant on the "birth-of-the-hero myth" to be found in the ancient world in endless versions, among them the stories about Sargon, Oedipus, Paris and many others. What they failed to see is that the story of the birth of Moses is *a polemic against such myth*: an anti-myth, a sharp, stinging rejection of the idea that every hero is really of noble blood, raised by commoners, but truly royal and destined by birth to conquer and rule. This is not the world of Israel. It is the world Israel rejects.

Rameses II, worshiped in his lifetime, revered ever since, left gigantic statues of himself all over Egypt and beyond. One of the greatest of these was the huge granite colossus that stood in the mortuary temple he built in his own honor at Thebes. It was eventually destroyed by an earthquake. The account of the shattered fragments, inscribed with Rameses' throne name Usermaatra – rendered in Greek as Ozymandias – inspired Shelley's famous poem, testimony to the iron law of history that the greatest empire will eventually crumble and fall. It was not this, however, that had a lasting impact on the Hebraic mind but something else altogether: that when humans try to be more than human they end up less than human. Only when God is God can we be us. Only under divine sovereignty can a truly humane social order be built.

Exodus Politics

The political vision to emerge from the crucible of exile was unique, an ideal never fully realized yet never ceasing to make Jewish life different from the way other societies have structured themselves. Essentially it is a sustained critique of power at every level: political, economic, military, even demographic.

The use of power by one human over another is a form of violence. It diminishes victim and perpetrator alike. Power is a zero-sum game. I use it to buy my freedom at the cost of yours. It is a way of getting you to do my will despite your will. It turns you into a means to my end. Dominance, the use of force, brutality, whether raw as in primitive societies, or cultivated as in the case of hierarchical, class- or caste-based social orders, is an act of defiance against the principle of the first chapter of Genesis, that we are all created equally in the image and likeness of God.

So ideally Israel would not have a power structure in the form of kings at all. As Gideon the judge said when the people sought to make him king, "I will not rule over you, nor will my son rule over you. God will rule over you" (Judges 8:23). Israel's army will not rely on force of arms or brute strength. God "does not take delight in the strength of horses, nor pleasure in the fleetness of man" (Ps. 147:10). Whether it is Joshua against Jericho, Gideon against the Midianites, David against Goliath, or Elisha predicting the sudden end of an Aramean siege, the emphasis is always on the few against the many, the weak against the strong, intelligence against brute force, the unexpected outcome through unconventional means.

Wealth may be as much of a danger as poverty: "When you build fine houses and settle down, and when your herds and flocks grow large and your silver and gold increase and all you have is multiplied, then your heart will become proud and you will forget the Lord your God, who brought you out of Egypt, out of the land of slavery" (Deut. 8:12–14). Nor, despite the repeated promises in Genesis of as many children as the stars of the sky, the dust of the earth or the sand on the seashore, would Israel find strength in numbers: "The Lord did not set His affection on you and choose you because you were more numerous than other peoples, for you were the fewest of all peoples" (Deut. 7:7).

The political structure envisaged by the Torah emerges out of a profound meditation – beginning in the opening chapters of Genesis – on the tension between freedom and order. God creates order, calling the universe into being day after day by mere speech ("And God said"); for the first three days creating carefully differentiated domains: night and day, upper and lower waters, sea and dry land; then for the next three days furnishing them with the appropriate forms: sun and moon, birds and fish, animals and humans. This finely tuned order, seven times pronounced "good," is disrupted because of the freedom God has bestowed on man, sin leading to murder and from there to a Hobbesian state of nature, a war of all against all in which life is nasty, brutish and short. The human alternatives set out in Genesis and Exodus are stark. There is freedom without order – the world before the Flood – and there is order without freedom – the Egypt of the pharaohs.

How then can there be both? This is the problem and it is not simple. The sages had a tradition that the question, "What is this service to you?" (Ex. 12:26), was asked by "the wicked son." The Haggada attributes this to the phrase "to you" – implying "but not to me." Other commentators[12] point to the verb used in the verse. Normally a question is *asked*, but here it is *said* ("And if your children should *say* to you…"). When you ask a question, you seek an answer, but when you state a question you merely seek to challenge and undermine.

The Talmud Yerushalmi (*Pesaḥim* 10:4), though, has a quite different explanation. It focuses on the word "service," and has the child asking, "What is the point of all this effort at which you are toiling?" What the Yerushalmi is alluding to is that the word the Torah uses for the enslavement of the Israelites to Pharaoh, *avoda*, is exactly the same as it uses for serving God. In what sense, then, were the Israelites liberated

12. Rabbi Moshe Silber, *Ḥashukei Kesef* to Exodus 12:26.

from slavery to freedom? Before the Exodus they were *avadim*. After the Exodus they were *avadim*. The only difference was to whom. Before it was to Pharaoh, thereafter it was to God. On the face of it, this looks less like freedom than a mere change of masters. One may be cruel, the other benign, but *avdut*, service or servitude, is still the opposite of freedom. Where then does liberty enter the human condition?

The Torah's answer consists of three elements. First is the principle of consent. Read the Torah carefully and we see that God binds Himself to make a covenant with the Israelites only if they agree. He tells Moses to make a proposal to the people. God will take them as His *am segula*, favored people, if and only if they willingly assent to become "a kingdom of priests and a holy nation" (Ex. 19:5–6). Both before and after the revelation at Mount Sinai the people give their consent. Note the wording. Before the revelation:

> All the people answered as one and said, "All that God has spoken, we will do." (Ex. 19:8)

Afterward, we read:

> Moses came and told the people all of God's words and all the laws. The people *all responded with a single voice*, "We will keep every word that God has spoken" [...]. He took the book of the covenant and read it aloud to the people. They replied, "We will do and obey all that God has declared." (Ex. 24:3, 7)

Unlike all other covenants in the ancient world this was not made on behalf of the people by their ruler. Moses is not empowered to speak on behalf of the Israelites. They all have to be asked; they all have to give their consent. This, argues political philosopher Michael Walzer, is part of what makes the political structure of the Torah an "almost democracy."[13]

Note also that God insists on asking the people whether they agree to the covenant and its terms, despite the fact that He has rescued them from slavery, and that they have already called themselves, in the

---

13. Walzer, *In God's Shadow*, 200.

Song at the Sea, "the people You acquired" (Ex. 15:16). Implicit in this strong insistence on voluntary agreement is the principle (stated in the American Declaration of Independence[14]) that *there is no government without the consent of the governed, even when the governor is God Himself.* The presence or absence of assent is what makes the difference between freedom and slavery.[15]

The second is that throughout Deuteronomy, the Torah's key covenantal document, the commandments are not given as "decrees of the king" to be obeyed merely because they have been ordained. Reasons are constantly given, usually in terms of the phrase, "remember that you were slaves in the land of Egypt." By this appeal to reason, God "invites the receiver of the law to join in grasping the beneficent effect of the law, thereby bestowing dignity upon him and giving him a sense that he is a partner in the law."[16]

There is a fundamental difference between a parent teaching a child why certain things are wrong, and a commander instructing those under his command not to do this or that. The one is a form of education; the other is a relationship of command-and-control. Education is an apprenticeship in liberty; command-and-control is a demand for obedience, pure and simple. One of the most striking facts about biblical Hebrew is that, despite the Torah containing 613 commandments, it contains no word that means "to obey." Modern Hebrew had to adopt the Aramaic word *letzayet*. The word the Torah uses instead of "to obey" is *shema*, a word that means "to listen, to hear, to understand, to internalize, and to respond." God does not call for blind submission to His will. As the sages said, "God does not act like a tyrant to His creatures" (*Avoda Zara* 3a).

God wants us to keep His laws freely and voluntarily because we understand them. Hence the unique insistence, throughout the Torah, on the importance of education as the constant conversation between the generations. Parents are to talk to their children repeatedly about

14. "To secure these rights, Governments are instituted among Men, deriving their just powers from the consent of the governed."
15. The Talmud (*Shabbat* 88a) famously questions whether the consent given at Mount Sinai was truly free. The covenant however was subsequently renewed several times under different circumstances.
16. Halivni, *Midrash, Mishnah, Gemara,* 14.

them, "when you sit at home and when you travel on the way, when you lie down and when you rise" (Deut. 6:7).

> When your children ask you, "What are the testimonies, the statutes and laws that the Lord our God has commanded you?" tell them: "We were slaves of Pharaoh in Egypt, but the Lord brought us out of Egypt with a strong hand.... The Lord commanded us to obey all these decrees and to fear the Lord our God, so that we might always prosper and be kept alive, as is the case today." (Deut. 6:20–24)

Third is the radical alternative to a hierarchical society: the horizontal society formed by the covenant, through which each is responsible for playing his or her part in the maintenance of a just and gracious order – by helping the poor, acting justly, honestly and compassionately, educating children, not neglecting marginal members of society and so on, the principle later formulated by the sages as "all Israel are sureties for one another" (*Sanhedrin* 27b; *Shevuot* 39a).

This is a radically devolved leadership that Exodus calls "a kingdom of priests and a holy nation" (Ex. 19:6), and to which Moses alludes when he says, "Would that all God's people were prophets" (Num. 11:29). Covenant, as set forth in the Hebrew Bible, is the dramatic idea that the people, individually and together, accept responsibility for determining their fate by acting righteously with one another, relying on the God of justice to secure justice in the arena of history. They have autonomy; only God has sovereignty. If the people act well, God will ensure that they fare well. If they act badly, it will end badly. All depends on faithfulness to God and decency to people. All else – governments, rulers, armies, alliances, strategy, warfare, the entire repertoire of power – will prove illusory in the long run.

The politics of the Torah are unlike any other in the emphasis they place on society rather than the state; "we the people" rather than governments, monarchs or rulers; voluntary welfare rather than state-based taxation; devolved rather than centralized authority; education and social sanction rather than the coercive use of power. It never fully succeeded in biblical times. The reluctant conclusion of the book of Judges is that "in those days there was no king in Israel; everyone did what was right in his own eyes" (Judges 17:6 and 21:25). Without government there is anarchy. Even the Israelites were forced to this Hobbesian conclusion ("Pray for the welfare of the government, for were it not for fear of it, people would swallow one another alive" [*Avot* 3:2]). Thus monarchy was born and with it the corruptions of power.

Yet the ideal remained and gained in strength after the reforms of Ezra, the growth of rabbinic Judaism and its academies, and the dispersion of Jewry after the collapse of the Bar Kokhba rebellion. What emerged was a unique collection of semi-autonomous communities, each with its own religious, educational and welfare institutions, self-funded and self-governing, with fellowships, *ḥevrot*, for almost every conceivable communal need – supporting the poor, visiting the sick, performing last rites for the dead, helping families who had suffered bereavement, and so on through the catalogue of requirements of dignified life as a member of the community of faith. The educational structure, lynchpin of the entire system, worked on the assumption that everyone was expected to be learned in the law – to know it, understand it, keep it and ensure that it was kept by others.

In a manuscript found among his papers after his death, the French political philosopher Jean-Jacques Rousseau expressed amazement at the power of this "astonishing and truly unique spectacle," an exiled, landless and often persecuted people, "nonetheless preserving its characteristics, its laws, its customs, its patriotic love of the early social union, when all ties with it seem broken." Athens, Sparta and Rome, he says, "have perished and no longer have children left on earth; Zion, destroyed, has not lost its children." He continues:

> What must be the strength of legislation capable of working such wonders, capable of braving conquests, dispersions, revolutions, exiles, capable of surviving the customs, laws, empire of all the nations, and which finally promises them, by these trials, that it is going to continue to sustain them all, to conquer the vicissitudes of things human, and to last as long as the world?[17]

17. Quoted in Leon Poliakov, *The History of Anti-Semitism*, vol. III (London: Routledge and Kegan Paul, 1975), 104–5.

The short answer is that in its unique political structure, in which all sovereignty belongs to God and where the other covenantal partner is not the king, High Priest or prophet but the nation as a whole, responsibility is maximally diffused and ethics does the work of what in other systems is done by politics. The opposite of one man ruling over a nation is a nation ruling over itself, under the eye of, following the laws of, and accountable to, God Himself. Utopian to be sure and never fully realizable in a world of wars, yet it remains the greatest experiment ever undertaken in the idea of politics without power, the rule of right not might.

The Future of the Past

As we noted above, the Exodus happened five times *before* it happened. First Abraham and Sarah went into exile in Egypt, then Abraham foresaw the fate of his descendants in a night vision, then he and Sarah were forced into exile to Gerar, then Isaac and Rebecca suffered the same fate, then Jacob went into exile to Laban: four journeys and a prophecy, each prefiguring what the Israelites would have to endure, but each also a kind of assurance that they would survive and return.

So it came about that the Exodus also happened *after* it happened. In one of his most remarkable flights of prophecy, Moses warned the people even before they had entered the land that one day they would dishonor the covenant and be forced into exile again. There, far from home, they would reflect on their fate and come to the conclusion that defeat and disaster were not the mere happenstance of history but the result of their faithlessness to God. If they would return to God then God would return to them and bring them back to their land:

> Then the Lord your God will restore your fortunes and have compassion on you and gather you again from all the nations where He scattered you. Even if you are scattered to the furthermost lands under the heavens, from there the Lord your God will gather you and take you back. (Deut. 30:3–4)

It was an astonishing vision but, as it happened, a necessary one. Israel's existence as a nation in its land could never be taken for granted.

It was a small country, surrounded not only by other small nations but by large and hungry empires. It was also fractious. The tribal confederation that lasted throughout the period of the judges gave way to a monarchy, but the nation was imperfectly united and after a mere three generations of kings it split into Israel and Judah, north and south. Most of the literary prophets either anticipated defeat and exile, or experienced it. Yet they had hope.

Theirs was not *mere* hope, optimism, wishful thinking. It was grounded in historical experience and theological principle. God had redeemed the people in the past. He would do so again in the future. Partly because the people, sobered by suffering, would repent. Partly because God had given His word and would not break it. Partly because the bond between God and the people was unbreakable, like that between a father and a son, or as the prophets preferred to see it, like that between a husband and a faithless wife he cannot bring himself to divorce because he still loves her. But fundamentally, because the Exodus is the shape of Jewish time. Sin brings exile. Repentance brings return. So it was; so it will be.

The prophets foresaw a second exodus. Hosea did, long in advance:

> "They shall come trembling like a bird from Egypt, like a dove from the land of Assyria. And I will let them dwell in their houses," says the Lord. (Hos. 11:11)

Likewise Amos:

> I will bring back the captives of My people Israel; they shall build the waste cities and inhabit them; they shall plant vineyards and drink wine from them; they shall also make gardens and eat fruit from them. I will plant them in their land…. (Amos 9:14–15)

Amos and Hosea both prophesied in the eighth century BCE and both directed their words to the northern kingdom, which did indeed fall to the Assyrians as they had foreseen. A century and a half later the southern kingdom of Judea also fell, this time to the Babylonians.

There in exile it was Ezekiel who gave the people hope, though his was a dark hope.

In one of the most haunting of all prophetic visions – we read it on Shabbat Ḥol HaMo'ed – Ezekiel sees his people as a landscape of corpses, a valley of dry bones. They are devastated. They say *avda tikvateinu,* "our hope is gone." God then asks him: "Son of man, can these bones be revived?" The prophet does not know what to say. Then he sees the bones slowly come together and grow flesh and skin and come to life again. Then he hears God say:

> Son of man, these bones are all the house of Israel: behold, they say, "Our bones have dried, our hope is lost, our decree has been sealed." Therefore, prophesy, saying to them, "Thus spoke the Lord God: 'Behold, I shall open your graves and lift you out of your graves, My people; I shall bring you to the land of Israel. And you will know that I am the Lord when I open your graves and lift you out of your graves, My people.'" (Ezek. 37:11–13)

Isaiah, the poet laureate of hope, had a more positive vision – we read it as the Haftara for the eighth day. The prophet foresaw a day in which "the Lord will reach out His hand a second time to reclaim the surviving remnant that is left of His people from Assyria, from Lower Egypt, Pathros, Cush, from Elam, Shinar, Hamath and the islands of the sea." Once again He would prevail over the waters, drying up "the gulf of the Egyptian sea" and the Euphrates river, so that the Israelites will once again walk through waters that have become dry land, and "there will be a highway for the remnant of His people that is left from Assyria, as there was for Israel when they came up from Egypt" (Is. 11:11–16).

Isaiah's younger contemporary Micah put it most simply: "As in the days of your exodus from Egypt, so I will show you wonders" (Mic. 7:15). And so it happened. Barely half a century after conquering Judea and destroying the Temple, Babylon fell to the Persians. First Cyrus, then Darius, gave the Jews permission to return, rebuild the Temple and reestablish their national life. It may have been less miraculous than the prophets hoped: not all the people returned, nor was there true political independence. But it was a second exodus.

Then came Greece, the empire of Alexander the Great, and then Rome. There were times when these Hellenistic powers allowed Jews a measure of autonomy and religious freedom, but others when that freedom was denied. Three times Jews rose in revolt, once successfully against Antiochus IV, twice unsuccessfully against Rome, the Great Revolt of 66–73 and the Bar Kokhba rebellion of 132–135. These were two of the greatest disasters of Jewish history. In the first, the Temple was destroyed again. In the second, the whole of Judea was devastated (see "Surviving Grief," below).

Jews went into exile again, some to Babylon, others to Egypt, yet others to Rome and other parts of the Mediterranean and beyond. A rabbinic midrash,[18] commenting on Jacob's dream of a ladder stretching from earth to heaven with angels ascending and descending, interprets it as a reference to the empires that would conquer Jacob's children. He saw the angels of Babylon, the Medes and Persians, and Greece rise and then come down, but the angel of Rome kept rising, showing no sign of decline, and Jacob was afraid. This was an exile seemingly without end.

For the first time we hear a note of absolute despair. In the wake of the Hadrianic persecutions that followed the defeat of Bar Kokhba, we find the following statement in the Talmud: "By rights we should issue a decree that no Jew should marry and have children, so that the seed of Abraham might come to an end of its own accord" (*Bava Batra* 60b). Rarely before and rarely since have such words been said, let alone recorded in one of Judaism's canonical texts.

Yet despair did not prevail. From Babylon in talmudic or early post-talmudic times, we begin to hear of a new custom, of saying at the beginning of the Seder service in Aramaic: "This is the bread of oppression our fathers ate in the land of Egypt. Let all who are hungry come in and eat; let all who are in need come and join us for the Pesaḥ. Now we are here; next year in the land of Israel. Now – slaves; next year we shall be free." As if to say: Yes, we are in exile again. But we have been here before, and we have returned before. Next year.

The centuries passed. Then came the 1860s and the childhood of a young member of a highly assimilated family in Austro-Hungary,

---

18. Leviticus Raba, *Emor* 29.

Theodor Herzl. Previously, in the atmosphere of European nationalism and the unification of Italy, rabbis like Zvi Hirsch Kalischer and Yehuda Alkalai had begun to advocate a return to Zion. Moses Hess, a secular Jew and one-time companion of Karl Marx, had found himself drawn back to the fate of his people by the Damascus blood libel of 1841, and he too had become a Zionist. Herzl knew none of this at the time, but in later life, he recalled the following childhood dream:

> One night, as I was going to sleep, I suddenly remembered the story of the Exodus from Egypt. The story of the historical exodus and the legend of the future redemption, which will be brought about by King Messiah, became confused in my mind…. One night I had a wonderful dream: King Messiah came…. On one of the clouds we met the figure of Moses…and the Messiah… turned to me: "Go and announce to the Jews that I will soon come and perform great miracles for my people and for the whole world."[19]

Herzl's parents had given him little Jewish instruction and he grew up to be somewhat dismissive of religion. But this he knew: that once there was an exodus and there would be again.

At the end of the Second World War, as in Moses' day, the Jewish people had barely survived attempted genocide. As the scale of the Final Solution became clear, the Jewish people were closer to Ezekiel's vision than ever before. A third of them had become a valley of dry bones. Now in a last-ditch effort to restore to the Jewish people its ancient, ancestral home, David Ben-Gurion stood to address the United Nations Commission charged with deciding the fate of the land to which Moses had led his people those many centuries before. If it voted for partition, then in effect the United Nations would be deciding to bring into being the modern State of Israel, restoring sovereignty to the people that had lost it two thousand years earlier. Ben-Gurion must have known that it was the most important speech of his life and that the fate of the Jewish people rested on its outcome. In the course of his remarks he said this:

19. Quoted in T. Herzl, *The Jewish State* (Borgo Press, 2008), intro. Alex Bein, 17.

Three hundred years ago a ship called the Mayflower set sail to the New World. This was a great event in the history of England. Yet I wonder if there is one Englishman who knows at what time the ship set sail? Do the English know how many people embarked on this voyage? What quality of bread did they eat? Yet more than 3,300 years ago ... the Jews left Egypt. Every Jew in the world, even in America or Soviet Russia, knows on exactly what day they left – the fifteenth of the month of Nisan – and everyone knows what kind of bread the Jews ate.[20]

The United Nations voted, with the requisite majority, for partition. Seven months later the State of Israel was reborn. The third exodus had taken place.

The narrative arch is vast, from the banks of the Jordan to Babylon to Austro-Hungary to the United Nations in New York, spanning more than half the history of civilization. Yet the Pesaḥ story lived on, time and again rescuing a people from despair.

There is no proof of hope, no scientific theory on which it can be grounded, no compelling, unequivocal historical evidence that the human story is destined to end well. The optimistic reading, which used to be called the Whig theory of history, was dealt a catastrophic blow in the twentieth century: two world wars, a hundred million deaths, and two evil empires, the Third Reich and the Soviet Union, as bestial as any the world has ever known. The end of the Cold War and the fall of the Berlin Wall led to vicious ethnic conflict in Bosnia, Kosovo, Chechnya and elsewhere. The "Arab Spring" of 2011 has not, as I write, yet led to the spread of freedom, civil rights and the rule of law in the Middle East. There is no straight inference from the past to optimism about the human future. But there are grounds for hope: the story of Israel, its exiles, its exoduses, its survival against the odds, its refusal to despair.

Israel's existence has never been easy: not in biblical times and not today. It has always been a small country surrounded by large empires, without the natural resources, the wealth, the landmass or the

20. Quoted in Lawrence Hoffman, *Israel: A Spiritual Travel Guide* (Woodstock, VT: Jewish Lights, 2005), 114–15.

demographic strength ever to become, in worldly terms, a superpower. All it had, then and now, was the individual strength and resourcefulness of its people – that and its faith and way of life. The relationship between God and the Jewish people has been fraught. There were times when the people turned away from God. There were times when God "hid His face" from the people. But the name "Israel" itself, according to the Torah (Gen. 32:28), means one who wrestles with God and with man and prevails. We never stop wrestling with God, nor He with us.

Reading the story of the Exodus against the history of the Jewish people through the ages, one thing shines with greater intensity than all others: the way that monotheism confers dignity and responsibility on the individual, every individual equally. There is no hierarchy in heaven; therefore there is, ideally, no hierarchy on earth. We are each called on to be holy, to be knowledgeable like priests, visionary like prophets, willing to fight battles like kings.

The ideal society is one formed by covenant, in which we each accept responsibility for the fate of the nation. That is not democracy in the Greek sense, which is about government and power. It is about society as a moral enterprise. It is about freedom-as-responsibility, not freedom-as-autonomy. It is, as John Locke put it, about liberty, not license. It is about freedom as the collective achievement of a people who know what it tastes like to eat the bread of affliction and know also that a society of everyone-for-himself is less like the route to the Promised Land than like the way back to Egypt. It is a difficult freedom, but it is one worth having.

Societies where everyone is valued, where everyone has dignity, where there may be economic differences but no class distinctions, where no one is so poor as to be deprived of the essentials of existence, where responsibility is not delegated up or down but distributed throughout the population, where children are precious, the elderly respected, where education is the highest priority, and where no one stands aside from his duties to the nation as a whole – such societies are morally strong even if they are small and outnumbered. That is the Jewish faith. That is what Israel, the people, the land and their story mean.

There is one passage missing from the Haggada that, perhaps, deserves to be reinstated. It occurs at the point where Rabbi Elazar ben

Azaria has compared himself to a seventy-year-old man (the burdens of leadership made his hair turn gray overnight [*Berakhot* 28a]) but he never understood until now why we must mention the Exodus from Egypt at night until Ben Zoma explained it to him. Ben Zoma inferred it from the phrase, "so that you may remember the day of your Exodus out of Egypt *all* the days of your life." The word "all," says Ben Zoma, comes to include nights. Not so, said the sages. It comes to include the Messianic Age.

There the text breaks off. It is, in fact, an extract from the Mishna. However, the Talmud (*Berakhot* 12b) tells us how the conversation continued. Ben Zoma said to the sages:

> Will we remember the going out of Egypt in the Messianic Age? Did not the prophet Jeremiah say otherwise? For he said, "The days are coming," declares the Lord, "when people will no longer say, 'As surely as the Lord lives, who brought the Israelites up out of Egypt,' but they will say, 'As surely as the Lord lives, who brought the descendants of Israel up out of the land of the north and out of all the countries where He had banished them.' Then they will live in their own land" (Jer. 23:7–8).

The sages concurred, adding simply that when that time comes we will still remember the Exodus from Egypt, even though we will have another and larger exodus for which to thank God.

So it has come to pass, and it is wondrous in our eyes. There are stories that change the world, none more remarkable than that of Pesaḥ, the master-narrative of hope.

The Omer: Three Studies

Pesaḥ, as befits a celebration of beginnings, is not only a self-contained festival in its own right. It also looks forward. It is the start of a journey through space and time. Hence the command, associated with the bringing of the grain offering known as the Omer, to *count time*, numbering the days and weeks until the next festival, Shavuot. The following three sections are about this command. The first is about a famous controversy that arose between different Jewish groups in the late Second Temple period. The second is about a later disagreement, in the era of the *Geonim* (c.589–1038). The third is about the post-talmudic custom to mark this time, or at least a major portion of it, as a period of collective mourning.

I. *New Light on an Old Controversy*

One feature of Pesaḥ occasioned intense controversy between the various factions in the Second Temple period and in early medieval Jewish life. It concerned the offering known as the Omer and the count it initiated to the next festival, Shavuot. Here is the law as stated in Leviticus:

> When you enter the land which I am giving you, and you harvest its grains, you shall bring the first Omer measure of your harvest to the priest. He shall wave the Omer in the presence of the Lord so that it may be accepted from you; the priest shall wave it on the day following the [Pesaḥ] rest day…. And you shall count seven complete weeks from the day following the [Pesaḥ] rest day, when you brought the Omer as a wave-offering. To the day after the seventh week you shall count fifty days. Then you shall present a meal-offering of new grain to the Lord. (Lev. 23:10–11, 15–16)

The passage raises obvious questions. What did the Omer offering signify? What did it have to do with Pesaḥ, or for that matter with Shavuot? Why the counting of the days between, something we do not find in connection with any other festival?

The real historical controversy however, and it was prolonged and acrimonious, was about the phrase "the day following the [Pesaḥ] rest day." What does this mean? If we translate *maḥarat haShabbat* as "the day following the Sabbath," then the plain sense is Sunday. But which Sunday? And why? And did it really mean Sunday here? There are, after all, two cycles of time in the Jewish year. There is weekly time, determined by the cycle of seven days culminating in the Sabbath, set by God Himself in the act of creation. And there is monthly time, entrusted by God in His first command to the Israelites themselves (Ex. 12:2), to determine the calendar in a complex synthesis between the sun that gives rise to seasons and the moon that gives rise to months. So the reference to the Sabbath in the context of Pesaḥ and Shavuot seems discordant, a confusion of two time modes – God's time (the Sabbath) and Israel's time (the festivals).

There was a tension here and it highlighted the deep schisms in Jewish life in the late Second Temple period between Pharisees on the one hand, and other groups like the Boethusians, Sadducees, Samaritans and the Qumran sect on the other. Later in the period of the *Geonim*, from the eighth century onward, a similar controversy arose between the followers of the rabbis and the Karaites. The Pharisees and the rabbis held, as we do, that there is an Oral tradition, the *Torah Shebe'al Peh*, of equal authority with the Torah's written text, the *Torah Shebikhtav*. That tradition said that "the day following the rest day" meant "the day after the first day of the festival," which, being a day of rest, could also be called Shabbat.

The other groups, denying the Oral tradition, held that the word "Shabbat" was to be construed literally. For them the Omer was offered on a Sunday, and Shavuot would fall on Sunday seven weeks later. The Boethusians, Sadducees and Karaites understood the phrase to mean "the day after the Shabbat *during* Pesaḥ." The Qumran sect understood it to refer to the Shabbat *after* Pesaḥ. The Jews of Ethiopia held a fourth view, understanding it to mean the last day of the festival, so for them Shavuot fell six days later than for the Pharisees and rabbis. The result was chaos: different groups celebrating a major festival on different days.

Almost certainly the controversy arose because of an ambiguity that developed in post-biblical Judaism. Two concepts that in the Torah are quite distinct became blurred: the word *Pesaḥ* and the phrase *Ḥag HaMatzot*, "the festival of unleavened bread." *Pesaḥ* in the Torah refers to the fourteenth day of Nisan, on the afternoon of which the Paschal offering (the Pesaḥ) was brought. *Ḥag HaMatzot* is the name of the seven-day festival that begins the next day, on the fifteenth of Nisan (see Lev. 23:5–6). Pesaḥ itself was not a day of rest, but the first day of *Ḥag HaMatzot* was (Lev. 23:7). That is why in this chapter, Leviticus 23, the Torah uses the phrase "the day after the Sabbath," meaning "the day after the day of rest," to make it clear that it does *not* mean, "the day after Pesaḥ," that is, the day after the fourteenth, but rather, "the day after the fifteenth, which is a day of rest." Only in post-biblical usage, when Pesaḥ began to be used as a synonym for *Ḥag HaMatzot*, did the confusion, and thus the controversy, arise.

Why, though, did it take the shape it did? I will argue in this section that a different issue was at stake than the authority of the Oral Law. But first, though, the count itself. What did it represent? There were two types of approach, depending on whether we understand the festivals seasonally or historically. Historically, Pesaḥ was the anniversary of the Exodus, Shavuot the anniversary of the Giving of the Torah on Mount Sinai.[21] On this reading, the counting of days has to do with the journey between Egypt and Sinai, between liberation on the one hand and the making of the covenant – the constitution of liberty – on the other. The count is a way of marking the significance of this key seven-week journey, italicizing time for emphasis.

The rationalist and mystical traditions, in the form of Maimonides and the *Zohar*, understood this in their respective ways. For Maimonides (*Guide for the Perplexed*, III:43), it was a counting-to. The Israelites keenly anticipated their encounter with God at Sinai and counted the days as they traveled to the destination. For the *Zohar*, it was a counting-from. The Israelites, defiled by their long stay in Egypt, were engaged in a process of purification.[22]

The festivals, though, also have a seasonal dimension, relating to the agricultural year. The Omer was an offering of the first produce of the barley harvest. It was this that allowed the people to eat from the new produce of the field – until then it was forbidden to do so. The following seven weeks were the most intensive time of the farmer's year, the period of the grain harvest, culminating in Shavuot with its offering of two loaves of bread made of leavened wheat.

---

21. Note, however, that the association of Shavuot and the Giving of the Torah at Sinai is nowhere mentioned in Tanakh. This too is part of the Oral tradition.
22. *Zohar, Emor* 97a. This difference neatly coincides with two other commands of counting in Jewish law. A *nidda*, a woman who has menstruated, counts the days until she can become purified again – a counting-from (Lev. 15:28). And in biblical times the court counted the seven cycles of seven years to the Jubilee – a counting-to (Lev. 25:8). The former corresponds to the *Zohar*'s reading of the Omer count, the latter to Maimonides' interpretation.

From this perspective, counting the days had to do with the extended period of the grain harvest. It was a way of praying for a good crop (Abudraham), or of giving thanks for God's blessings in the fields (Sforno). Probably it was both. There is a further theory that the counting was necessary because people were in the fields, away from the town. There was a danger that people might forget when the festival was due. Hence the count so as not to lose track of the fact that Shavuot was imminent (*Roke'aḥ*).

To return now to the phrase "the day following the rest day": those who understood it literally as Sunday had some compelling arguments in their favor. First, that is what the phrase usually means. If the Torah meant, as the Pharisees said, "the day after the first day of the festival," why did it not say so? Besides which, only by starting the count on the first day of the week does a count of forty-nine days yield "seven complete weeks" in the usual sense, namely a seven-day period beginning on Sunday and ending on Shabbat. One Boethusian reported in the Talmud (*Menaḥot* 65a) offered a third and touchingly human consideration. Moses, he said, was "a lover of Israel." Realizing that after seven exhausting weeks in the field, farmers would be tired, Moses (or rather, God) had compassion on them and gave them a festival that immediately followed Shabbat – in other words, a long weekend!

However there is a further reason, not mentioned in the talmudic sources but clearly hovering in the background. The word "omer," in addition to meaning "sheaf," has a highly significant connotation in the context of the Exodus. It was the measure of the manna that fell for the Israelites when they had exhausted the matza they had brought with them from Egypt. The Torah (Ex. 16:1–18) tells us that the food ran out, the people were starving, they complained to Moses and God sent them the manna, one of whose miraculous properties was that however much people collected they always found that they had an Omer's quantity (one tenth of an ephah).

This suggests that the Boethusians and other sectarians may have had a specific historical understanding of the Omer. It was a way of remembering the manna itself – the bread of freedom they ate in the wilderness once the unleavened bread of affliction had been consumed. This is not absurd: still today we observe the custom of having two loaves of bread on Shabbat to recall the double portion of manna that fell on Friday in honor of Shabbat. If this is so, then the Boethusians would have had another and yet more powerful argument to deploy in their debate with the Pharisees: *the manna first fell on a Sunday!* On this even the Talmud, the classic text of rabbinic Judaism, agrees.[23] That, the Boethusians might have argued, is why the Omer is always offered on Sunday: it recalls the manna that first fell on Sunday.

The mention of manna, however, brings us to one of the simplest and most compelling arguments against the Boethusians. It is given by Maimonides.[24] He refers to the passage in the book of Joshua that we read as the Haftara for the first day of Pesaḥ:

> The children of Israel camped at Gilgal and they made the Pesaḥ offering on the fourteenth day of the month in the evening, on the plains of Jericho. They ate of the produce of the land on the day after the Pesaḥ, matzot and roasted grain, on that very day. And the manna ceased [to come down] the next day, when they ate of the produce of the land, and the children of Israel no longer had manna; they ate of the crops of the land of Canaan that year. (Josh. 5:10–12)

Here we see the Israelites eating from the new produce "the day after the Pesaḥ (*mimaḥarat haPesaḥ*)," not "the day after the Sabbath." New produce may only be eaten after the Omer has been brought. Clearly then the Omer was brought on the day after the festival, rather than on a Sunday. The proof is impressive.[25] But Maimonides is implicitly telling us something more. *The offering of the Omer recalls not the beginning but the end of the manna.* If this is so, the implications are immense.

The differences between the manna and the new produce of the land, the food Joshua and his contemporaries were the first to eat, were these:

---

23. *Shabbat* 87b; Rashi to Ex. 16:1.
24. *Laws of Daily and Additional Offerings* 7:11. See also Ibn Ezra to Lev. 23:11; Judah HaLevi, *Kuzari*, III:41.
25. Note, however, Ibn Ezra's critique of this proof in his commentary to Lev. 23:11.

- The manna came from the wilderness; the new grain came from the land of Israel.
- The manna was in many respects miraculous; the new grain was not.
- The manna was the gift of God; the new grain involved the work of humans, farmers.[26]
- The manna is described in the Torah as "bread from heaven" (Ex. 16:4); the new grain is "bread from the earth" (Ps. 104:14).
- The manna was, according to Rabbi Akiva, "bread that the angels eat" (*Yoma* 75b); the Omer, brought from barley, was coarse food, sometimes the feed of animals.

The manna was special. The Israelites did not have to work for it. There was no plowing and planting and tending and reaping. It was God's gift; it fell from the sky. New manna appeared every day and all they had to do was collect it. Entering the land must have seemed in one sense a disappointment, an entry into the prosaic quotidian world of labor in the fields and waiting anxiously to see whether the harvest would be a good one or whether it would be ruined by drought as often happened in the land of Israel.

Judaism, though, has historically and from the outset taken a different view of the world of work. It contains a deep polemic against the idea of a leisured class, and a strong sense of the dignity of labor. God Himself, in Genesis 2, plants a garden and fashions the first human from the earth. The first man is charged with serving and protecting the garden. "Sweet is the sleep of a laboring man," says Kohelet (5:11). "When you eat the fruit of your labor, happy and fortunate are you," says the psalm (128:2). The vision of happiness in the prophets is "each man under his vine and his fig tree" (Mic. 4:4).

Flay carcasses rather than be dependent on others, said the third-century *Amora* Rav (*Pesaḥim* 113a). Someone who does not engage in *yishuv ha'olam*, constructive work, is invalid as a witness in Jewish law

---

26. To be sure, the grain the Israelites ate at Gilgal in the days of Joshua was not the result of the Israelites' work but that of the Canaanites. Nonetheless it represented the fruit of human labor, which in the future would be that of the Israelites themselves.

(*Sanhedrin* 24b). Rabbi Yehoshua said of the *nasi* Rabban Gamliel, "Woe to the generation that has you as a leader," since you do not understand people's struggle to earn a livelihood (*Berakhot* 28a). Work is a source of dignity and self-respect. Dependence is the opposite. As we say in the Grace after Meals, "Do not make us dependent on the gifts or loans of other people ... so that we may suffer neither shame nor humiliation." Jewish mysticism coined the phrase *nahama dekisufa*, "the bread of shame," for food you receive from others without having to work for it.

Work is dignity. Work without cease, however, is slavery. *Parekh*, the term used to characterize the labor the Egyptians imposed on the Israelites, probably means work without rest and without an end in sight.[27] That is why Shabbat is central to the project of constructing a world that is not Egypt. Keep Shabbat, said Moses in the second iteration of the Ten Commandments, in Deuteronomy, so that "your male and female slaves may rest as you do. Remember that you were slaves in Egypt.... It is for this reason that the Lord your God has commanded you to observe the Sabbath day" (Deut. 5:13–14). Freedom does not mean not working. It means the ability to stop working. Shabbat is the first taste of freedom. That is why the first day of Pesaḥ is described in the Torah as Shabbat.

What is the larger significance of the phrase *maharat haShabbat*, "the day following the rest day"? To understand this we have to go back to the story of creation itself. In six days God created the world, and on the seventh He rested. As the sages read the text, dovetailing the two accounts in Genesis 1 and 2–3, God created the first humans on the sixth day. That same day they sinned and were sentenced to exile from the garden. God granted them one complete day in paradise, Shabbat itself. Immediately after Shabbat they left Eden for the darkness of the world. God however made them "garments of skin" (read in the school of Rabbi Meir of the Mishna as "garments of light")[28] and, according to rabbinic tradition, taught them how to make fire, which is why we make a blessing over light in *Havdala*, the service to mark the end of Shabbat (Yerushalmi, *Berakhot* 8:5). Again, this has far-reaching implications.

---

27. Ex. 1:13, 14; normally translated as "with rigor"; *Sifra, Behar* 6:6.
28. Gen. 3:21; Genesis Raba 20:12.

On Shabbat we celebrate the world God creates. The day after Shabbat is when we celebrate the world we create. The phrase *maḥarat haShabbat* is a metaphor for human endeavor and achievement – the space God makes for us.

The argument between the Boethusians and the Pharisees now takes on a completely new dimension. It is generally argued by scholars that the Sadducees and Boethusians were an elite. They were either priests in the Temple or officials or landowners, as close as Judaism came to a leisured class. The sectarians at Qumran were an elite community who had turned their backs on society as a whole. The Pharisees were, as far as we can tell, largely made up of the working class. Certainly the image we have of figures like Hillel, Rabbi Akiva, Rabbi Yehoshua and others is that they were poor but refused to live on charity. It is to them that we owe many of the key rabbinic statements about the importance of independence and of working for a living.

We can now hypothesize that for the Boethusians, Sadducees and sectarians, the event we would wish to memorialize is the first falling of the manna. This was holy, miraculous, spiritual, the gift of God, bread from heaven that fell through no earthly labor. This, the bread that first fell on Sunday, is what we recall when we offer the Omer, whose dimensions (one tenth of an ephah) are precisely those of the manna itself.

For the Pharisees the complete opposite was the case. As long as the Israelites were completely dependent on God they were querulous, ungrateful, rebellious and immature. That is what dependence does. It arrests the growth of character. The one time the Israelites achieved their real dignity was when they labored together to build the Tabernacle. They worked; they gave of their time and skills and possessions. There was harmony. They gave so much that Moses had to say "Stop." That was their true apprenticeship in liberty.

The supreme moment of religious achievement came when, no longer homeless nomads, they entered the land God had promised Abraham. The first moment they ate of its produce was the first taste of that long-delayed fulfillment. Each year that moment was recaptured in a single symbolic moment: the first produce of the grain harvest. This was the dream finally made real: a holy people working the land God had called holy – at last, His partners in the work of creation. The land was His, the labor was theirs; the rain was His, the grain was theirs. They had sown in tears; now they were reaping in joy. And though the grain was coarse – barley – and though it was entirely non-miraculous, coming from earth not heaven, it was precious in their eyes because it was precious in God's eyes. It was the humble symbol of the-day-after-Shabbat, the first day of human creation after the seven days of God's creation. They had received so much from God. Now God had given them the greatest gift of all – the ability to give Him a gift. What mattered was not that it was refined like the finest wheat flour (that came later, in the two loaves of Shavuot) but that it was the work of their hands.

Now, too, we can understand the significance of counting the days. Genesis 1 describes divine creation. God said, "Let there be light," and there was light. For God there is no delay between conception and execution, the idea and the fact. For humans, however, there is a delay. It is the ability to endure the delay that makes all human creative achievement possible. It takes time to become a farmer, to learn how to plow and plant and tend. It takes time to become anything worth becoming.

A slave never learns this. He or she lives in the moment. The master commands, the slave carries out the task. The slave does not have to worry about long-term risks and consequences. In this sense, the manna the Israelites ate in the wilderness was not yet the bread of freedom, for it involved no time consciousness. It fell each day; it had to be eaten each day; with the exception of Friday, it could not be kept for the morrow. The Israelites ate it the way slaves eat their daily subsistence diet. It had the taste of holiness but not yet the taste of freedom. A free human being has to learn the art of time that goes with risk-taking and creation. He or she has to acquire skill and wisdom, patience and the ability to persist through many failures without giving way to despair. The fundamental lesson of the wilderness years, as Maimonides emphasizes in *The Guide for the Perplexed* (III:32), is the time it takes for erstwhile slaves to acquire the mental and emotional habits of free and responsible human beings. In the case of the Israelites it took a generation.

The mark of a free human being is the ability to count time, to endure a lengthy delay between the start of a journey and its completion.

"Teach us rightly to number our days," says the psalm, "that we may gain a heart of wisdom" (Ps. 90:12). Counting the days, without impatience or attempting shortcuts, is the precondition of all creative endeavors – and at the heart of the Pharisees' and rabbis' creed is the belief that the God of creation wants us to be creative rather than be dependent on the creativity of others. There were some who believed otherwise: the wealthy Sadducees, the apocalyptic desert dwellers of Qumran, mystics like Rabbi Shimon bar Yoḥai who at one stage apparently believed that the words, "you shall gather in your grain, wine and oil," were not a blessing but a curse and who viewed with contempt those who plowed fields (*Berakhot* 35b; *Shabbat* 33b). But these were voices at the margins. The mainstream held otherwise.

The Omer is the immensely powerful symbol of an offering from the first fruits of the humanly planted and reaped grain, brought on the anniversary of the day the "bread from heaven" ceased and "bread from the land" of Israel began. Coarse and unsophisticated, yet the combined work of land and rain from God and labor from man – partners in the work of creation. The journey to freedom begins on Pesaḥ with the Shabbat, "the rest day," the first taste of freedom, which is knowing that you do not have to work without cease. But immediately, on the second day, it passes to "the day following the rest day," the world of human work, the day on which Adam and Eve left paradise to make their way in the world, a task full of difficulties and threats, yet one in which they were robed, in Rabbi Meir's lovely phrase, in "garments of light." You do not have to live in Eden to be bathed in divine light. Work that is creative is not the work of slaves. But it requires one discipline: the art of counting time or as Freud put it, the ability to defer the gratification of instinct. Indeed most of Jewish law is a form of training in the art of disciplining and deferring the gratification of instinct.

So the argument about the Omer and its significance was a deep one and not just about the authority of the Oral Law. It was about the nature of the religious life. Does God want us to be involved with society, contributing to it and being creative within it, or is that for others, not for us? It is fair to say that the argument has not yet ceased. This side of the End of Days, perhaps it never will.

II. Two Concepts of Time

More minor, but in its way no less interesting, is the disagreement that arose between two of the great sages of the period of the *Geonim* (sixth to tenth century) on a seemingly minor detail of the command to count the Omer. The Torah states the law in the following terms:

> And you shall count seven complete weeks from the day following the [Pesah] rest day, when you brought the Omer as a wave-offering. To the day after the seventh week you shall count fifty days. Then you shall present a meal-offering of new grain to the Lord. (Lev. 23:15–16)

The following question arose: What is the law for someone who forgets to count one of the forty-nine days? May he continue to count the remainder, or has he forfeited the entire commandment for that year? There were two sharply contrasting views. According to the *Halakhot Gedolot* (a work usually attributed to Rabbi Shimon Kayyara, first half of the ninth century) the person has indeed forfeited the chance to fulfill the command. According to Rav Hai Gaon he has not. He continues to count the remaining days, unaffected by his failure to count one of the forty-nine (see *Tur, OH* 489).

How are we to understand this disagreement? According to the *Halakhot Gedolot*, the key phrase is "seven full [*temimot*, i.e. complete] weeks." One who forgets a day cannot satisfy the requirement of completeness. On this view, the forty-nine days constitute a single religious act, and if one of the parts is missing, the whole is defective. It is like a Torah scroll: if a single letter is missing, the entire scroll is invalid. So, too, in the case of counting days.

According to Rav Hai Gaon however, each day is a separate command – "You shall count fifty days." Therefore, if one fails to keep one of the commands, that is no impediment to keeping the others. If, for example, one fails to pray on a given day, that neither excuses nor prevents one from praying on subsequent days. Each day is a temporal entity in itself, unaffected by what happened before or after. The same applies to the Omer. Forgetting one day does not invalidate the others.

The final law mediates between these two opinions. Out of respect for Rav Hai, we count the subsequent days, but out of respect for the *Halakhot Gedolot* we do so without a blessing – an elegant compromise (*Terumat HaDeshen*, 37).

We might, before moving on, note one salient fact. Usually in the case of a dispute about Jewish law, the doubt lies in us, not in the biblical text. God has spoken, but we are not sure what the words mean. In the case of counting the Omer, however, the doubt lies *within the biblical text itself*. Unusually, the command is specified in two quite different ways:

- "Count seven complete weeks."
- "Count fifty days."

There is a view that this dual characterization signals two distinct commands, to count the days, and to count the weeks (Abaye in *Menaḥot* 66a). However, as we have seen, it also suggests two quite different ways of understanding the counting itself – as a single extended process (*Halakhot Gedolot*) or as fifty distinct acts (Hai Gaon). This duality was not born in the minds of two halakhic authorities. It is there in the biblical text itself.

Within Judaism there are two kinds of time. One way of seeing this is in a talmudic story about two of the great sages of the Second Temple period, Hillel and Shammai:

> They used to say about Shammai the elder that all his life he ate in honor of the Sabbath. So, if he found a well-favored animal he would say, "Let this be for the Sabbath." If he later found a better one, he would put aside the second for the Sabbath and eat the first. But Hillel the elder had a different approach, for all his deeds were for the sake of heaven, as it is said, "Blessed is my Lord for day after day" [Ps. 68:20]. It was likewise taught: The school of Shammai says, "From the first day of the week, prepare for the Sabbath," but the school of Hillel says, "Blessed is my Lord for day after day." (*Beitza* 16a)

Shammai lived in teleological time, time as *a journey toward a destination*. Already from the beginning of a week, he was conscious of its end. We speak, in the *Lekha Dodi* prayer, of the Sabbath as "last in deed, first in thought." Time, in this view, is not a mere sequence of moments. It has a purpose, a direction, a destination.

Hillel, by contrast, lived each day in and for itself, without regard to what came before or what would come after. We speak in our prayers of God who "in His goodness, continually renews the work of creation, day after day." From this perspective, each unit of time is a separate entity. The universe is continually being renewed. Each day is a universe; each has its own challenge, its task, its response. Faith, for Hillel, is a matter of taking each day as it comes, trusting in God to give the totality of time its shape and direction.

The dispute is strikingly similar to the more recent disagreement about the nature of light. Is it a continuous wave or a series of discrete particles? Paradoxically, it is both, and this can be experimentally demonstrated.

The argument, however, goes deeper. Much has been written by historians and anthropologists about two distinctive forms of time consciousness. Ancient civilizations tended to see time as a circle – *cyclical time*. That is how we experience time in nature. Each day is marked by the same succession of events: dawn, sunrise, the gradual trajectory of the sun across the sky to its setting and to nightfall. The year is a succession of seasons: spring, summer, autumn and winter. Life itself is a repeated sequence of birth, growth, maturity, decline and death. Many of these moments, especially the transition from one to another, are marked by religious ritual.

Cyclical time is time as a series of eternal recurrences. Beneath the apparent changes, the world remains the same. The book of Kohelet contains a classic statement of cyclical time:

> Generations come and generations go, but the earth remains forever. The sun rises and the sun sets, and hurries back to where it rises.... All streams flow into the sea, yet the sea is never full. To the place the streams come from, there they return again.... What has been will be again, what has been done will be done again; there is nothing new under the sun. (Eccl. 1:4–9)

In Judaism, priestly time is cyclical time. Each part of the day, week and year has its specific sacrifice, unaffected by what is happening in the world of historical events. Halakha – Jewish law – is priestly in this sense. Though all else may change, the law does not change. It represents eternity in the midst of time.

In this respect, Judaism did not innovate. However, according to many scholars, a quite new and different form of time was born in ancient Israel. Often, this is called linear time. I prefer to call it *covenantal time*. The Hebrew Bible is the first document to see time as an arena of change. Tomorrow need not be the same as yesterday. There is nothing given, eternal and immutable about the way we construct societies and live our lives together.

Time is not a series of moments traced on the face of a watch, always moving yet always the same. Instead it is a journey with a starting point and a destination, or a story with a beginning, middle and end. Each moment has a meaning, which can only be grasped if we understand where we have come from and where we are going to. This is time not as it is in nature but as it is in history. The Hebrew prophets were the first to see God in history.

A prophet is one who sees the future in the present, the end already implicit in the beginning. While others are at ease, he foresees the catastrophe. While others are mourning the catastrophe, he can already see the eventual consolation. There is a famous example of this in the Talmud. Rabbi Akiva is walking with his colleagues on Mount Scopus when they see the ruins of the Temple. They weep. He smiles. When they ask him why he is smiling, he replies: "Now that I have seen the realization of the prophecies of destruction, shall I not believe in the prophecies of restoration?" (*Makkot* 24b). Rabbi Akiva's companions see the present; he sees the future-in-the-present. Knowing the previous chapters of the story, he understands not only the current chapter, but also where it leads. That is prophetic consciousness – time as a narrative, time not as it is in nature but in history, more specifically in covenant history, whose events are determined by free human choices but whose themes have been set long in advance.

If we look at the festivals of Judaism – Pesaḥ, Shavuot and Sukkot – we see that each has a dual logic. On the one hand, they belong to cyclical time. They celebrate seasons of the year – Pesaḥ is the festival of spring, Shavuot of first fruits and Sukkot of the autumn harvest.

However, they also belong to covenantal/linear/historical time. They commemorate historic events. Pesaḥ celebrates the Exodus from Egypt, Shavuot the Giving of the Torah and Sukkot the forty years of wandering in the wilderness. It follows that the counting of the Omer also has two temporal dimensions.

It belongs to cyclical time. The forty-nine days represent the period of the grain harvest, the time during which farmers had the most to thank God for – for "bringing forth bread from the earth." Thus understood, each day of the counting is a separate religious act: "Blessed is my Lord for day after day." Each day brought forth its own blessing in the form of new grain, and each therefore called for its own act of thanksgiving. This is time as Hillel and Rav Hai Gaon understood it. "Count fifty days" – each of which is a command in itself, unaffected by the days that came before or those that will come after.

But the Omer is also part of historical time. It represents the journey from Egypt to Sinai, from exodus to revelation. This, in the biblical worldview, is an absolutely crucial transition. The late Sir Isaiah Berlin spoke of two kinds of freedom, negative liberty (the freedom to do what you like) and positive liberty (the freedom to do what you ought). Hebrew has two different words for these different forms of freedom: *ḥofesh* and *ḥerut*. *Ḥofesh* is the freedom a slave acquires when he no longer has a master. It means that there is no one to tell you what to do. You are master of your own time.

This kind of freedom alone, however, cannot be the basis of a free society. If everyone is free to do what they like, the result will be freedom for the strong but not the weak, the rich but not the poor, the powerful but not the powerless. A free society requires restraint and the rule of law. There is such a thing as a constitution of liberty. That is what the Israelites acquired at Mount Sinai in the form of the covenant.

In this sense, the forty-nine days represent an unbroken historical sequence. There is no way of going directly from escape-from-tyranny to a free society. The attempt to do so only results in a new form of tyranny (sometimes the "tyranny of the majority" as Alexis de Tocqueville called it). In human history prophetically understood, time is an ordered sequence of events, a journey, a narrative. Miss one stage, and one is in danger of losing everything. This is time as *Halakhot Gedolot* understood it: "Count seven complete weeks," with the emphasis on "complete, full, unbroken."

Thus, both forms of time are present in a single mitzva – the counting of the Omer – as they are in the festivals themselves.

We have traced, in the argument between the two authorities of the period of the *Geonim*, a deeper duality, going back to Hillel and Shammai, and further still to the biblical era and the difference, in their respective forms of time-consciousness, between priests and prophets. There is the voice of God in nature, and the call of God in history. There is the word of God for all time, and the word of God for *this* time. The former is heard by the priest, the latter by the prophet. The former is found in halakha, Jewish law; the latter in Aggada, Jewish reflection on history and destiny. God is not to be found exclusively in one or the other, but in their conversation and complex interplay.

There are aspects of the human condition that do not change, but there are others that do. It was the greatness of the biblical prophets to hear the music of covenant beneath the noise of events, giving history its shape and meaning as the long, slow journey to redemption. The journey *has* been slow. The abolition of slavery, the recognition of human rights, the construction of a society of equal dignity – these have taken centuries, millennia. But they happened only because people learned to see inequalities and injustices as something other than inevitable. Time is not a series of eternal recurrences in which nothing ever ultimately changes. Cyclical time is deeply conservative; covenantal time is profoundly revolutionary. Both find their expression in the counting of the Omer.

Thus an apparently minor detail in Jewish law turns out, under the microscope of analysis, to tell us much about the philosophy and politics of Judaism – about the journey from liberation to a free society, and about time as the arena of social change. The Torah begins with creation as the free act of the free God, who bestows the gift of freedom on the one life-form that bears His image. But that is not enough. We must create structures that honor that freedom and make it equally available to all. That is what was given at Sinai. Each year we retrace that journey, for if we are not conscious of freedom and what it demands of us, we will lose it. To see God not only in nature but also in history – that is the distinctive contribution of Judaism to Western civilization, and we find it in one of the most apparently minor commands: to count the days between negative and positive liberty, from liberation to revelation.

III. Surviving Grief

Beginning in the period of the *Geonim*, from the eighth century onward, we find the period of the Omer given a character it had not had before, as a time of mourning. The customs developed not to celebrate a wedding during this period, or have a haircut.[29] The earliest sources speak of this applying to the whole of the Omer period with the exception of Lag BaOmer, the thirty-third day. Later sources speak of thirty-three days of mourning only, but here customs start to diverge. Sephardim – the Jews of Spain and Portugal, as well as the majority of those in Israel – observe the period from Pesah to Lag BaOmer (*Shulhan Arukh, OH* 493:2), while Ashkenazi communities begin the ban on weddings and haircuts after Rosh Hodesh Iyar (Rema ad loc. 493:3).

The custom of mourning during the Omer is not mentioned in the Talmud. Surprisingly, since he knew the literature of the *Geonim* in which it is mentioned, Maimonides makes no reference to it in his halakhic code, the *Mishneh Torah*. Unraveling the complex story behind the custom and its later variants yields a fascinating insight into how Jews responded to tragedy and may even guide us in understanding the response of religious Jewry to the Holocaust.

The sources all cite, as the basis of the custom, a passage in the Babylonian Talmud:

> Rabbi Akiva had twelve thousand pairs of disciples from Gabbatha to Antipatris, and all of them died at the same time because they did not treat each other with respect. The world remained desolate until Rabbi Akiva came to our masters in the South and taught the Torah to them. These were Rabbi Meir,

---

29. Rabbi Yitzhak ibn Ghayyat (Spain, 1038–1089), *Me'a She'arim*, 109; *Tur, OH* 493.

Rabbi Yehuda, Rabbi Yose, Rabbi Shimon and Rabbi Elazar ben Shammua; and it was they who revived the Torah at that time. A *Tanna* taught: "All of them died between Pesaḥ and Shavuot." Rabbi Ḥama ben Abba, and some say Rabbi Ḥiyya ben Abin, said: "All of them died a cruel death." What was it? Rabbi Naḥman replied: "Croup." (*Yevamot* 62b)

This is a tantalizing passage. We have no other evidence of a plague that mysteriously claimed the lives of twenty-four thousand students, nor is it clear in what way they "did not treat each other with respect." It is hard to believe that this was true of the disciples of the man who taught that "You shall love your neighbor as yourself" was the great principle on which the Torah was based (Yerushalmi, *Nedarim* 9:5), and who said that reverence for your teacher should be as great as your reverence for Heaven itself (*Kiddushin* 57a). Equally, as a number of commentators point out, it is puzzling as to why this event should be marked through the ages as an extended period of mourning, when there is no special day of mourning for other and more innocent deaths. Nor does the Talmud itself suggest that this incident be memorialized.

There is, however, a significantly different version of events given in the famous letter of Rabbi Sherira Gaon (906–1006). The letter, a reply to a series of queries about historical events, is our main source for many otherwise obscure events in rabbinic history up to the geonic era and is highly regarded for its accuracy. Rabbi Sherira writes:

After the death of Rabbi Yose ben Kisma [killed by the Romans for teaching Torah in public], Rabbi Akiva handed himself over [to the Romans] to be killed. Rabbi Ḥanina ben Teradyon was also killed, and after these deaths, wisdom decreased. Rabbi Akiva had raised many disciples, but a decree of persecution [shemada] was issued against them. Authority then rested on the secondary disciples of Rabbi Akiva, as the rabbis said: Rabbi Akiva had twelve thousand pairs of disciples from Gabbatha to Antipatris, and all of them died between Pesaḥ and Shavuot. The world remained desolate until they came to our masters in the South and taught the Torah to them.

Note the differences between Rabbi Sherira's account of events and that given in our text of the Talmud. First, the disciples did not die because of an epidemic, but as a result of religious persecution by the Romans. Secondly, the deaths occurred after Rabbi Akiva had been killed, not beforehand. This places a completely different construction on events.

Twice before, Jews in Israel had risen against the Romans. First came the great rebellion of 66 CE, which led to the destruction of the Second Temple under Vespasian and Titus. Second was the rebellion – not confined to Jews or Israel – that spread through the Roman Empire under Trajan between 115 and 117. Third was the revolt of Bar Kokhba that began in 132. The Roman emperor of the time, Hadrian, had initially been tolerant in his approach to the various nations under Roman rule, but he became less so over time, undertaking a program of enforced Hellenization that included a ban on circumcision and the transformation of Jerusalem into a pagan Roman city.

For as long as Hadrian was in the region, there was no large-scale open revolt, but as soon as he left, Jews rose against their rulers in defense of their religious freedom. Bar Kokhba was a charismatic leader. Rabbi Akiva supported him, believing that he would liberate Israel and prove to be the Messiah. It is not clear that Bar Kokhba himself had any messianic pretensions. In contemporary documents he is referred to as a *nasi*, a leader or prince, rather than as a king. Other sages strongly dissented from Rabbi Akiva's position. The Talmud Yerushalmi (*Ta'anit* 4:5) states that Rabbi Yoḥanan ben Torta said, "Akiva, grass will grow from your cheeks and still the son of David will not come" (i.e. the Messiah will not come in your lifetime).

Initially the rebellion succeeded. The Roman forces in Israel were defeated. The nation briefly regained its independence. Coins were struck, carrying the date of the relevant year "after the redemption of Israel." The Romans sent additional troops from Syria and Egypt. These too were defeated. Realizing that nothing short of all-out war would save Rome from humiliation, Hadrian summoned Julius Severus, the governor of Britain, together with his troops and others from the Danube region. Slowly the war turned against the Jewish forces, until only a refuge at Beitar, southwest of Jerusalem, remained. Beitar fell in the summer of 135 CE. Tradition dates its defeat to the Ninth of Av (Tisha B'Av).

The result was devastating. The contemporary Roman historian Dio estimated that 580,000 Jews died in the fighting, plus countless others through starvation. Fifty of the country's strongest forts were destroyed, together with 985 towns and settlements. "Nearly the entire land of Judea lay waste." Jerusalem was leveled to the ground and rebuilt as a Roman polis named Aelia Capitolina. Jews were forbidden entry except on Tisha B'Av. Hadrian even changed the name of the land from Judea to Syria-Palestina, the origin of the name Palestine by which it was known until 1948.

Even more acute than the physical destruction was the spiritual catastrophe. Countless rabbis were put to death, giving rise to the famous account of "the Ten Martyrs," recited in different versions on Tisha B'Av and Yom Kippur. One sage, Rabbi Natan, has left us this account of what became almost commonplace at this time:

> "Those who love Me and keep My commandments" – those are the Jews who live in the land of Israel and give their lives for the sake of the commandments. Why are you to be killed? For having circumcised my son. Why are you to be burned? For having studied the Torah. Why are you crucified? For having eaten matza. Why are you flagellated? For having blessed the lulav. (*Mekhilta, Baḥodesh 6*)

Jews were prevented from meeting in synagogues, engaging in communal prayer, studying the Torah or maintaining communal institutions. It was a devastating period. There were Jews who lost their faith; the story of Elisha ben Abuya, the rabbi who became a heretic, dates from this period. Others de-Judaized and became Hellenistic in their way of life. Yet others despaired of the Jewish future. In human terms it was the worst disaster of Jewish history before the Holocaust.

We can now revisit the talmudic passage that speaks of the death of Rabbi Akiva's students. If Rabbi Sherira Gaon's account is accurate, we have in the Babylonian Talmud a highly veiled reference to the persecutions that occurred shortly before, and then after, the Bar Kokhba revolt. It is not unknown for the Babylonian Talmud in particular to speak indirectly and allusively about historic events that were almost too painful to bear. It records a statement dating from this period, that "by rights we should issue a decree that no Jew should marry and have children, so that the seed of Abraham might come to an end of its own accord" (*Bava Batra* 60b). It seemed like the end of Judaism and the Jewish people.

This is what we mourn between Pesaḥ and Shavuot: the massacres and devastation that accompanied the failure of the Bar Kokhba rebellion, the loss of hundreds of thousands of Jewish lives, the de-Judaization of Israel and Jerusalem, and the loss of an entire generation of rabbis, among them almost all of the disciples of Rabbi Akiva. We can only guess at what is meant by the phrase "because they did not treat each other with respect," but the simplest explanation is that it refers to the deep division within the ranks of the sages as to whether the revolt was justified or not, whether it was likely to succeed or bring disaster, and whether or not Bar Kokhba himself warranted the messianic expectations Rabbi Akiva had of him. Divided, the Jewish people could not stand.

Another traumatic tragedy, almost a thousand years later, explains the differences of custom between Ashkenazim and Sephardim as to whether the thirty-three days of mourning are at the beginning or end of the Omer period. In 1095 Pope Urban II proclaimed the First Crusade, to take back Jerusalem and the Holy Land from Muslim to Christian hands. On their way toward the East, the Crusaders interrupted their journey in order to massacre Jewish communities in northern Europe. As Rabbi Solomon ben Samson, a Jewish chronicler of those times, puts it, the Crusaders argued, "Here are the Jews dwelling in our midst.... First let us take vengeance on them and destroy them as a people, so that the name of Israel shall no longer be remembered."[30]

Jews in Cologne, Metz, Mainz, Speyer and Worms called on the emperor, lords and local bishops to defend them, often offering large sums of money to do so, but to little avail. Some bishops did act

---

30. Rabbi Solomon ben Samson, *The Massacres of 1096*, quoted in H.H. Ben Sasson (ed.), *A History of the Jewish People* (Cambridge, MA: Harvard University Press, 1976), 413.

heroically. Others found themselves powerless before the mob. Eight hundred Jews were murdered in Worms, eleven hundred in Mainz. Many families of Jews committed collective suicide rather than fall into the hands of the Christians, who they knew would torture and kill them if they refused to convert. Three years later when the Crusaders reached Jerusalem, they gathered together all the Jews and burned them alive.

The massacres of 1096 traumatized Ashkenazi Jewry, as the Hadrianic persecutions had done in their time and as the expulsions of 1492 and 1497 would later do for the Jews of Spain and Portugal. Jews in Europe now knew that they were unsafe, whatever protection had nominally been offered to them. Rulers could turn against them whenever it was in their interest to do so. So could the Church, so could the mob. Here and there, there might be exceptions. Bishop Johann of Speyer, for example, was praised in Jewish sources for resisting and punishing the Crusaders and preventing a massacre. But even well-intentioned Christians could no longer be relied on. From then on, for at least seven centuries, the situation of Jews in Europe was fraught with risk and fear.

The Rhineland massacres took place during the latter weeks of the Omer. An Ashkenazi custom developed to say special lament-type prayers from early Iyar onward. Later, the mourning customs of the Omer were associated with the same period. The Sephardi communities of Spain and Portugal were unaffected by the Crusades, so they continued the earlier custom of mourning for the victims of the Bar Kokhba revolt.

This, then, is the explanation of the custom of mourning during the Omer period, and why Ashkenazim and Sephardim do so in different ways. The Omer was Jewry's Holocaust memorial before there was a Holocaust. What is remarkable, though, is the rabbis' obliquity. There is not a word said during the Omer about the victims of the Romans: that is left to the story of the Ten Martyrs on Tisha B'Av and Yom Kippur. As for the victims of the Crusaders, they are recalled in the prayer *Av HaRaḥamim*, said before Musaf on Shabbat, as well as in a number of *Kinot* on Tisha B'Av.

In general, Jewish communities set limits to their grief, knowing that if they looked back too directly on the destruction, they might, like Lot's wife, be turned into a pillar of salt by their tears. Despite the many Jewish martyrs in history, it remains the Jewish way to look forward, to affirm life, to survive.

The same has proved true since the Holocaust. With some exceptions, the great religious leaders of Jewry, especially those who were Holocaust survivors themselves, spoke relatively little about the *Sho'a* for several decades. Instead they focused on rebuilding their shattered world in new lands. They encouraged their disciples to marry and have children. They built schools and yeshivot. Today they are the fastest growing group in the Jewish world.

The custom of mourning during the Omer without saying exactly why testifies to the extraordinary Jewish capacity to suffer tragedy without despair, surviving and enduring through faith in the future and in life itself. Jews never forgot the victims of the past, but they contained their sorrow, saving their tears and confining their grief, for the most part, to Tisha B'Av, so as not to be overwhelmed by the accumulated weight of unredeemed affliction. They carried the past with them, but even while doing so they looked forward, not back.

Perhaps it is no coincidence that, having had no new days added to the calendar in more than two thousand years, four have been added in living memory: *Yom HaSho'a* (Holocaust Memorial Day), *Yom HaZikaron* (Memorial Day for Israel's fallen), *Yom HaAtzma'ut* (Israel Independence Day) and *Yom Yerushalayim* (Jerusalem Day), all of them within the seven-week period of the Omer. It is as if the journey from Egypt to Mount Sinai continues to be fraught with history, beginning in tears yet ending in the joy of the Jewish return to the holy land and the holy city at its heart.

The Song of Songs: Faith as Love

The biblical "love of one's neighbor" is a very special form of love, a unique development of the Judaic religion and unlike any to be encountered outside it. (Harry Redner, *Ethical Life*)

If love in the Western world has a founding text, that text is Hebrew. (Simon May, *Love: A History*)

My soul thirsts for you, my body longs for you, as in a dry, parched land where there is no water. (Ps. 63:2)

Shir HaShirim, the Song of Songs, is the strangest book in the Hebrew Bible, one of the strangest ever to be included in a canon of sacred texts. It is written as a series of songs between two human lovers, candid, passionate, even erotic. It is one of only two books in Tanakh that does not explicitly contain the name of God (Esther is the other) and it has no obvious religious content. Yet Rabbi Akiva famously said: "The whole world is not as worthy as the day on which the Song of Songs was given to Israel, for all the [sacred] Writings are holy but the Song of Songs is the Holy of Holies" (*Yadayim* 3:5).

Rabbi Akiva's insight is essential. The Song of Songs, a duet scored for two young lovers, each delighting in the other, longing for one another's presence, is one of the central books of Tanakh and the key that unlocks the rest. It is about love as the holy of holies of human life. It is about the love of Israel for God and God for Israel, and the fact that it is written as the story of two young and human lovers is also fundamental, for it tells us that to separate human and divine love and to allocate one to the body, the other to the soul, is a false distinction. Love is the energy God has planted in the human heart, redeeming us from narcissism and solipsism, making the human or divine Other no less real to me than I am to myself, thus grounding our being in that-which-is-not-me. One cannot love God without loving all that is good in the human situation.

Love creates. Love reveals. Love redeems. Love is the connection between God and us. That is the faith of Judaism, and if we do not understand this we will not understand it at all. We will, for example, fail to realize that the demands God makes of His people through the prophets are expressions of love, that what Einstein called Judaism's "almost fanatical love of justice" is about love no less than justice, that the Torah is God's marriage contract with the Jewish people, and the mitzvot are all invitations to love: "I seek You with all my heart; do not let me stray from Your commands" (Ps. 119:10).[31]

Sadly, one must emphasize this point because it has long been said by the enemies of Judaism that it is a religion of law not love, justice not forgiveness, retribution not compassion. Simon May in his *Love:*

---

31. Psalm 119, which is entirely about Torah and mitzvot, contains the word "love" twelve times.

A History rightly calls this "one of the most extraordinary misunderstandings in all of Western history."[32]

If we seek to understand the nature of biblical love, the place to begin is the Exodus itself. One feature of the narrative from the beginning of Exodus to the end of the book of Numbers is unmistakable. The Israelites are portrayed as ungrateful recipients of divine redemption. At almost every stage of the way they complain: when Moses' first intervention makes their situation momentarily worse, when they come up against the barrier of the Sea of Reeds, when they have no water, when they lack food, when Moses delays his return from the mountain and when the spies return with a demoralizing report about the Promised Land and its inhabitants.

They sin. They rebel. They make a golden calf. They engage in false nostalgia about Egypt. More than once they express the desire to return whence they came. God gets angry with them. At times Moses comes close to despair. So unlovely is the portrait painted of them in the Torah that it almost seems to invite the thought, "How odd / of God / to choose / the Jews."

Yet as we proceed through Tanakh another picture emerges. We hear it in the eighth century BCE from one of the first literary prophets, Hosea. The story Hosea has to tell is extraordinary. God appears to him and tells him to marry a prostitute, a woman who will bear him children but will be unfaithful to him. God wants the prophet to know what it feels like to love and to be betrayed. The prophet, uncertain perhaps about whether the children are in fact his, is to call them "Unloved" and "Not my people."

He will then discover the power and persistence of love. He will wait until his wife is abandoned by all her lovers, and he will take her back, despite her betrayal. He will love her children, whatever his doubts about their parentage. He will change their names to "My people" and "Beloved." He will, in other words, know from his own experience what God feels about the Israelites. It is an astonishing and daring narrative, suggesting as it does that God cannot, will not, cease to love His people. He has been hurt by them, wounded by their faithlessness, but His love is inextinguishable. Hosea then hears God say this:

---

32. Simon May, *Love: A History* (New Haven, CT: Yale University Press, 2011), 20.

I will lead her into the desert and speak tenderly to her. There
I will give her back her vineyards, and will make the Valley of
Trouble a door of hope. There she will sing as in the days of her
youth, as in the day she came up out of Egypt. (Hos. 2:16–17)

This is a *retelling of the Exodus as a love story*. In Hosea's vision, it
has become something other and more than the liberation of a people
from slavery. Israel left Egypt like a bride leaving the place where she
has lived to accompany her new husband, God, on a journey to the
new home they will build together. That is how it was "in the days of
her youth" and how it will be again. The desert is now no longer simply
the space between Egypt and Israel, but the setting of a honeymoon in
which the people and God were alone together, celebrating their company, their intimacy.

Two centuries after Hosea, the people are now in exile in Babylon. There the prophet Ezekiel retells the past in a different but related
way. God had first seen Israel as a young girl, a child. He watched over
her as she grew to adulthood:

You grew and matured and came forth in all your glory, your
breasts full and your hair grown, and you were naked and exposed.
Later I passed by, and when I looked at you and saw that you were
old enough for love, I spread the corner of My garment over you
and covered your nakedness. I gave you My solemn oath and
entered into a covenant with you, declares the Sovereign Lord,
and you became Mine. (Ezek. 16:7–8)

Again, a daring love story. God sees Israel as a young woman and
cares for her. He "spreads the corner of His garment" over her, which as
we recall from the book of Ruth (3:9) constitutes a promise to marry. The
marriage itself takes the form of a solemn oath, a covenant. The Giving
of the Torah at Mount Sinai has been transformed by the prophet into
a marriage ceremony. Hosea and Ezekiel both envisage the Exodus as
a kind of elopement between a groom – God – and His bride – Israel.
However, in both cases it is God who loves and God who acts. It was
left to Jeremiah, Ezekiel's somewhat older contemporary, to deliver

the decisive transformation in our picture of the Exodus, saying in the name of God:

> I remember of you the kindness of your youth, your love when you were a bride; how you walked after Me in the desert, through a land not sown. (Jer. 2:2)

Now it is not just God who calls, but Israel who responds – Israel who follows her husband faithfully into the no-man's-land of the desert as a trusting bride, willing in the name of love to take the risk of traveling to an unknown destination. The message of Hosea, Ezekiel and Jeremiah is that the Exodus was more than a theological drama about the defeat of false gods by the true One, or a political narrative about slavery and freedom. It is a love story – troubled and tense, to be sure – yet an elopement by bride and groom to the desert where they can be alone together, far out of sight of prying eyes and the distractions of civilization.

That is the theme of the Song of Songs. Like God summoning His people out of Egypt, the lover in the song calls on his beloved, "Come... let us leave" (2:10). The beloved herself says, "Come, draw me after you, let us run!" (1:4). Then in an image of extraordinary poignancy we see the two of them emerging together from the wilderness. Who is this, rising from the desert, leaning on her beloved? (8:5).

Israel, leaning on God, emerging, flushed with love, from the wilderness: that is the Exodus as seen by the great prophets. Nor were they the first to develop this idea. It appears, fully fledged, in the book of Deuteronomy, where the word "love" appears twenty-three times as a description of the relationship between God and the people. When we read the Song of Songs on Pesaḥ as a commentary to the Exodus, it spells out Jeremiah's message. God chose Israel because Israel was willing to follow Him into the desert, leaving Egypt and all its glory behind for the insecurity of freedom, relying instead on the security of faith.

I. God Loves

The depth and pathos of this idea goes much deeper, however. Monotheism as it appears for the first time in the Hebrew Bible raises a fundamental question. Why would an infinite God create a finite universe? The idea of creation did not arise in the world of myth. Matter was eternal. The gods themselves were part of nature. They argued, fought, established hierarchies of dominance, and that is why the world is as it is. But in Judaism, God transcends nature. Why then would He create nature? Why make a creature as troublesome as Homo sapiens, the one being capable of defying His will?

The Torah does not give an explicit answer, but one is implicit. God loves. Love seeks otherness. Love is emotion turned outward. Love seeks to give, to share, to create. Rabbi Yaakov Tzvi Mecklenburg translated the repeated phrase in Genesis 1 not as "God saw *that* it was good" but as "God saw *because* He is good."[33] Goodness creates goodness. Love creates life. God sought to bestow the gift of being on beings other than Himself. We exist and the universe exists because God loves.

This is one of the most radical ideas ever to have transformed the human mind. The very fact that we can say the words "God loves" is itself a measure of the influence Judaism has had on the West. It is an idea that would have sounded strange, counterintuitive, even incomprehensible to the ancient world.

In the world of myth, the gods did not love human beings. When one of the immortals, Prometheus, steals for humans the secret of fire from the gods, he is punished by Zeus by being chained to a rock and having his liver pecked out by an eagle every day. At best the gods were indifferent to human beings; at worst they were actively hostile.

Equally, the idea that God loves would have been unintelligible to the Greek philosophers who rejected myth. Plato thought that we love what we lack. Since God lacks nothing, by definition He cannot love. Aristotle thought similarly, though for a different reason. To love as husband and wife or parent and child love, we must focus on the particular: this person, not that. But for Aristotle, God did not have knowledge of particulars, only universals. So the idea of a loving God in the biblical sense would have been unintelligible to him also. The God of Aristotle might love humanity but not individual humans. Plato and Aristotle

---

33. Rabbi Yaakov Tzvi Mecklenburg, *HaKetav VeHaKabbala* to Gen. 1:4.

wrote insightfully about interpersonal love. But that the relationship between God and humanity might be one of love – that to them would have seemed like a categorical mistake, an intellectual absurdity.

What made Israel different was its belief that "in the beginning, God created...." In love God brought energy, matter, stars and planets into being. In love He created the biological forms of self-organizing complexity that constitute life. In love He created the one being capable of asking the question "Why?" – setting His own image on each of us. In love He fashioned the first human from the dust of the earth, breathing into him His own breath. In love, so that man should not be loveless, He created woman, bone of his bone, flesh of his flesh.

Even for God, however, love involves risk. Again the idea sounds paradoxical in the extreme. God is God, with or without the universe, with or without the worship of man. Yet whether one is finite or infinite, to love is to make oneself vulnerable. That is the story the Torah tells in its opening chapters. Having made humanity in love, bestowing on it His own image, God finds that His love is not reciprocated. Adam and Eve disobey His command. Cain murders. Within a few chapters we find ourselves in an earth "filled with violence" (Gen. 6:13). God "regretted that He had made man on earth and He was grieved to His very core" (6:6).

God brings a flood and begins again, making a covenant, through Noah, with all humanity. Still, divine love is not reciprocated. Humans build Babel, a cosmopolis, a man-made civilization in which humans do not serve God but seek to make God serve them by turning religion into an endorsement of a hierarchical society in which kings are priests, even demigods. Religion becomes a force for injustice. Where is there a human being willing to abandon this entire civilization of self-aggrandizement and follow God out of self-sacrificing love? God calls. Abraham hears. That is the act of love with which Judaism begins. It is also, as we have seen, the first of several prefigurations of the Exodus.

When Rabbi Akiva called the Song of Songs the holy of holies of religious poetry, he was reading it in the context of the entire story of Israel. For it was Israel's willingness, first in the days of Abraham, then later in the time of Moses, to leave behind the great civilizations of their time and live in a land where they could never found an empire, never grow rich like the Mesopotamians and Egyptians, where they would be vulnerable to famine, drought, invading armies and surrounding powers, but where their love for God vindicated God's love for humanity. It was an imaginative leap but not a blind or irrational one to conclude that the lovers of the Song of Songs are God and His people, seeking one another in the wilderness of space and time.

II. Eros

That is the first level of meaning in the Song of Songs. But there is a second. For the Song of Songs is unmistakably a book about *eros*, love as sexual passion. An old Western tradition, the result of a synthesis of Christianity and the culture of ancient Greece, has contrasted *eros*, love as physical desire, with *agape*, love as selfless devotion. *Eros* is physical, *agape* spiritual. *Eros* is about the body, *agape* about the soul. *Eros* seeks personal pleasure, *agape* bestows impersonal, generalized care. This may make sense in terms of a Platonic bifurcation of body and soul, but it makes little sense in terms of the union of body and soul characteristic of the Hebrew Bible. What then is the place of *eros* in Judaism?

To understand this we have first to turn to one of the great theological puzzles of Judaism. It concerns the book of Genesis. The central theme of the Hebrew Bible is the battle against idolatry. Abraham, if not the first monotheist, is at least the first to rediscover monotheism. In Jewish legend he breaks his father's idols. According to Joshua (24:2), "Teraḥ, father of Abraham … served other gods." Maimonides believed that the rationale of most of the *ḥukkim*, the laws of the Torah for which there is no apparent reason, is that they are barriers against idolatrous practices.

Yet, with the possible exception of the subplot of Rachel stealing her father Laban's "images" (Gen. 31:19), there is very little mention of this theme. In Genesis we see Abraham, Isaac, Jacob and their families, evidently living among idolaters – Canaanites, Hittites, Egyptians and the rest – but we find a lack of reference to idolatry, no polemic against it. If Genesis is about monotheism as against idolatry, should it not be more present?

One theme however *is* significantly present. It figures so regularly that it cannot be dismissed as mere happenstance – namely, sexual anomie: the power of *eros* to disturb law and justice, threatening life itself. Leaving aside the question of whether *eros* was involved in the first sin – Adam, Eve, the serpent and the forbidden fruit – it is certainly the key element in at least six other stories in Genesis.

Three are variations of the same basic situation. Famine forces the patriarchal family to leave home in search of food. Abraham is forced first to Egypt, then to Gerar and the land of the Philistines. Isaac similarly has to travel to Gerar (Gen. 12, 20, 26). In all three cases the patriarch fears that he will be killed so that his wife – Sarah, Rebecca – can be taken into the local harem. They have to pretend that they are brother and sister.

The fourth scene is Sodom, city of the plain. There, seeing Lot's two visitors, the members of the town – "all the men from every part of the city of Sodom, both young and old" (Gen. 19:4) – demand that they be brought out for an act of homosexual rape. In an attempt to placate them, Lot offers the mob his two daughters, "who have never known a man," giving the townsmen permission to "do what you like with them" (ibid. 8). Lot has become corrupted, as have his two daughters, who after the destruction of Sodom both engage in an act of incest with their father.

The fifth episode is the story of Dina who goes out "to visit the women of the land" (Gen. 34:1) in Shekhem, where she is abducted, raped and held hostage by the son of the local king. This prompts an act of bloody vengeance on the part of her brothers Simeon and Levi, for which Jacob never forgives them.

Sixth is the story of Joseph and Potiphar's wife. Seeing that the Hebrew servant is handsome, she attempts to seduce him. He replies, "My master has withheld nothing from me except you, because you are his wife. How then could I do such a wicked thing and sin against God?" (Gen. 39:9). It would be an act of disloyalty as well as adultery, and a sin as well as an immoral deed. Potiphar's wife takes her revenge by successfully accusing him of rape.[34]

---

34. There is a seventh story about Judah and Tamar (Gen. 38) which has many sexual under- and overtones. However, it is more complex than the other six. Here it is Judah and his sons who, having become separated from the rest of the family and married into a Canaanite environment, have become morally lax, while Tamar acts with propriety throughout.

These six episodes tell a story. When a member of the covenantal family leaves his or her domestic space and enters local territory they enter a world of sexual free-for-all, with all its potential for violence, murder, rape, false accusations and unjust imprisonment.

The setting of the scenes is also significant. For the most part they take place in cities; cities are not good places in Genesis. The first city is built by Cain the first murderer (Gen. 4:17). The great city, Babel, becomes a symbol of hubris. Sodom represents the lawlessness that exists in ancient cities toward foreign visitors. There may even be a linguistic connection between the Hebrew word *ir*, city, and the verb *ur*, a keyword of the Song of Songs which means (sexual) arousal. Cities are places where sexual fidelity is compromised.

We cannot be sure precisely what we are meant to infer from these stories, but this seems possible: *eros* allied to power is a threat to justice, the rule of law and human dignity. When a ruler sees an attractive woman it is taken for granted that, if she is married, the life of her husband is in danger. A mob will not stop at homosexual rape and those like Lot who try to stop them are themselves in danger. A prince protected by his father can get away with abduction and rape. The combination of sexual desire and lawless power results in people being used as means to ends, with no respect for persons. So it was; so it will be. So it is among the primates: the alpha male dominates access to females. It was this that led Freud to believe that sexual envy is at the heart of the Oedipus complex.

The argument against idolatry in Genesis is conducted almost entirely in terms of sexual ethics, or more precisely, the conspicuous absence of a sexual ethic. The gods in myth cohabited promiscuously, often incestuously, sometimes bestially. Pagan temples often had sacred prostitutes. Herodotus documents this in the case of Mesopotamia, from which Abraham came. Strabo says the same about Egyptian priestesses in the Temple of Amun in Thebes. Rameses II, often believed to be the Pharaoh of the Exodus, married his own daughter. Baal, the Canaanite god, having defeated the goddess of the sea is then conquered by the god of death but is resurrected each year to impregnate the earth. And so on. Outlandish sexuality by the gods and their devotees was regarded as essential to the fertility of the land and the life it sustained.

All of this, Genesis testifies, is profoundly shocking to the monotheistic mind. Faithfulness in marriage is not merely a biblical norm: it is the closest human equivalent to the relationship between God and His people. There is one God and there is one people, Israel, who have chosen to bind themselves to one another in a covenant of faith. That is why the prophets consistently describe idolatry as a form of adultery: it is an act of infidelity, the betrayal of a marriage vow. The covenant is love-as-loyalty and loyalty-as-love. *Eros* plus power leads to violence and death. *Eros* plus faithfulness leads to caring and life. The difference between love and lust is that lust is the service of self, love is the service of the Other. The love that is faith is *eros* moralized. As Hosea beautifully put it in the name of God:

> I will betroth you to Me forever; I will betroth you to Me in righteousness and justice, loving-kindness and compassion: I will betroth you to Me in faithfulness, and you will know the Lord. (Hos. 2:21–22)

In Judaism there is no renunciation of the physical: no monasteries, convents, celibacy or other asceticisms of the flesh.[35] In this context, the Song of Songs is a restatement of the case for *eros*. It is not passion that corrupts, but power. The two lovers sing of a love that is faith, not faithlessness. Their songs evoke the innocence of Eden before the sin. They seek to escape from the city to the garden, the hills, the countryside. This is love as it might have been without the serpent, love that is as strong as death, love like purifying fire. The Song of Songs is about the power of love purged of the love of power.

III. Three Biblical Books About Love
But the Song of Songs is not the only biblical book about love. It is a complex emotion that cannot be defined from a single perspective, nor

---

35. The major exception was the voluntary adoption of Naziriteship, about which some of the sages were critical. The sages even interpreted Miriam and Aaron's criticism of Moses (Num. 12:1) as condemnation of his refusal to have relations with his wife (*Sifri*, 99).

do all its dimensions become apparent at the same time. In a way that is subtle and richly complex, the three pilgrimage festivals all have their special book, each about love but about different phases of it. The Song of Songs on Pesaḥ is about love as passion. The lovers are young. There is no mention of marriage, a home, children, responsibility. They have no thought for the morrow nor for others. They are obsessed with one another. They live conscious of the other's absence, longing for the other's presence. That is how love should be some of the time if it is to be deep and transforming all the time.

The book of Ruth, the scroll we read on Shavuot, is about love as loyalty: Ruth's loyalty to her mother-in-law Naomi, and Boaz's to Naomi, Ruth and the family heritage. It is about "loving-kindness," the word coined by Myles Coverdale in his Bible translation of 1535 because he could find no English word that meant *ḥesed*. Beginning as it does with death, bereavement and childlessness, and ending with marriage and the birth of a child, it is about the power of love to redeem grief and loneliness and "make gentle the life of this world." It is about what the Song of Songs is not: about marriage, continuity and keeping faith with "the living and the dead" (Ruth 2:20). That too, in Judaism, is a significant part of love, for we are not just selves. We are part of the living chain of generations.

On Sukkot we have a third story about love: love grown old and wise. Kohelet is a book easy to misread as a study in disillusionment, but that is because of sustained series of mistranslations of its key word, *hevel*. This is variously rendered as "vanity," "vapor," "meaningless," "futile," "useless," leading readers to think that its author finds life without purpose or point. *Hevel* does not mean that; it means "a fleeting breath." It is about the brevity of life on earth. It begins with the author seeking happiness in philosophy (*ḥokhma*), pleasure, laughter, the accumulation of wealth, fine houses and pleasure gardens, the perennial secular temptations. He discovers that none of them can defeat death. Objects last but those who own them do not. Wisdom may be eternal, but the wise still die.

We defeat death not by seeking a this-worldly immortality but by *simḥa*, the spiritually and morally textured exhilaration about which William Blake wrote, "He who binds to himself a joy / Does the winged life destroy. / He who kisses the joy as it flies / Lives in eternity's sun rise." Kohelet learns that happiness is to be found not in what you own (bind to yourself) but in what you share. It exists not where you invest your money but where you give of yourself. It lives in work and love: "Enjoy life with the woman you love all the days of this fleeting life you have been given under the sun, all the fleeting days, for that is your portion in life and in all your labor under the sun" (Eccl. 9:9). This is love that has grown from passion to responsibility to existential joy: the joy of being with one you love.

The essential message of Judaism is contained in no one of these books but in the combination of all three. *Eros* is the fire that gives love its redemptive, transforming, other-directed quality. Marriage is the covenantal bond that turns love into a pledge of loyalty and brings new life into the world. Companionship, experience and a life well lived bring *simha*, a word that appears only twice in the Song of Songs, not at all in Ruth but seventeen times in Kohelet.

Love as passion; love as marriage and childbirth and continuity; love as abiding happiness – three stages of love, traced out in the course of a life and the course of a year and its seasons: the Song of Songs in spring, Ruth in harvest time, Kohelet in autumn as the days grow colder and the nights longer. With a wonderful touch of serendipity, Kohelet ends with the advice, "Remember your Creator in the days of your youth, before the days of trouble come and the years approach when you will say, 'I find no pleasure in them'" (12:1), thus leading us back to youthfulness, spring and the Song of Songs where we began.

IV. Love and Justice

Judaism is about love. But it does not make the mistake of thinking with Virgil that *omnia vincit amor*, "Love conquers all." Much of Genesis, surprisingly, is about the problems love creates.

With Abraham, loves enters the world. But it is not an easy love. The first time in the Torah that we encounter the verb *a-h-v*, "love," is at the start of the greatest trial of them all: the binding of Isaac. "Take your son, your only son, whom you love – Isaac" (Gen. 22:2). What the trial is about is not simple, but it is certainly about love. The conventional reading is that God is testing Abraham by asking him to sacrifice what he loves most, to show that he loves God more than he loves his son. The reading I prefer is that the trial is a definitive rejection of the principle, common in the ancient world and known in Roman law as *patria potestas*, which held that a child is the property of its parent. What God sought from Abraham at the trial was not his willingness to kill his son – in Judaism, child sacrifice is not the highest virtue but the lowest vice – but rather his willingness to renounce ownership of his son. That, though, is a subject for elsewhere. Here we merely note how precisely the note is struck in the Torah. Love is not simple. It leads to conflict and to the question: whom do you love more?

The verb "to love" occurs fifteen times in Genesis, always between humans and almost always as the prelude to strife. Isaac loves Esau while Rebecca loves Jacob, thus setting in motion one of the great sibling rivalries of the Bible. Jacob loves Rachel but is induced unwittingly to marry Leah. Leah feels unloved ("And God saw that Leah was hated" – 29:31), and this leads not only to a palpable tension between the two sisters, but also between their respective children. Jacob's love for Joseph ("more than his other sons" – 37:3) leads to envy on the part of the other brothers, talk of murder, and eventually the sale of Joseph into slavery in Egypt, the act that begins the long sequence of events that leads to exile.

This is an important and unexpected insight. Love – real, passionate, the very love that humanizes us, leading us to great acts of self-sacrifice – unites and divides, divides as it unites. It creates rivalries for attention and affection. Without such love, an essential element of our humanity is missing. But it creates problems that can split families apart and lead to estrangement and violence.

Something else must enter the scene: *love as justice*. Something larger than the family must be its vehicle. Love must be transformed from a form of kinship into a societal bond. It is this that makes exile necessary. That is why Genesis must be followed by Exodus. The way to the Promised Land lies through the formative experiences of persecution and the wilderness.

Three things must happen before love can become the basis of a nation. First, people must feel bound to one another by the common experience of suffering. They must be more than an extended biological family. Families argue and split apart. In Genesis, Abraham's children are a family. It is only in the first chapter of Exodus that we hear a word used to describe them that has not been used before: *am*, a people. The word *am* is related to *im*, "with." A people is a group who are, in a strong sense, *with* one another. They suffer the same fate, recall the same history; they have been through a journey together. That is the first thing that happens to them.

The second is that they become not just an *am* but also an *eda*, a congregation, a community, from the word *ed*, "witness," and *y-a-d*, "to designate, specify, arrange." There must be more than fellow-feeling and kinship. There must be an act of shared testimony and commitment to work together for the sake of the common good.

Third, the Sovereign of the nation thus formed must be someone beyond the human situation, God Himself, otherwise the nation will fall like all others into a competition for status and power, in which the strong prevail, the weak suffer and the people are divided into rulers and ruled. It must be a society in which the only legitimate form of power is delegated power, held conditionally on honoring a moral code, and always subject to moral limits. It must be "one nation under God." Otherwise justice will become what Thrasymachus tells Socrates it is: the interests of the stronger party. That is not justice but its abuse.

This is the essential journey traced out in *Sefirat HaOmer*, the counting of days between Pesaḥ and Shavuot. In Egypt the Israelites become an *am*. They suffer together. They develop a sense of shared fate. Two weeks prior to their departure, they receive their first collective command (to fix the calendar, to structure time) and become, in that act, an *eda* (Ex. 12:1–3). At Sinai, on Shavuot, they enter into a covenant with God making Him their sole Sovereign, and making each responsible for the fate of the nation as a whole. Covenant – a political form of treaty in the ancient Near East – here becomes a kind of marriage-writ-large, a bond of love between God who loves this people, descendants as they are of those who first heard and heeded His call, and the people who owe their liberty to God. At that moment, covenant – a bond of love as loyalty – received its highest expression as the code and destiny of a nation.

V. *The Politics of Love*

So we arrive at one of the most remarkable projects ever undertaken by a nation: a society held together by love – three loves. You shall love the Lord your God with all your heart, all your soul and all your might. You shall love your neighbor as yourself. And you shall love the stranger, for you were once strangers in the land of Egypt. There is no other morality quite like it.

A society is thus formed on the basis of love of neighbor and of stranger. This is not an abstract kind of love. It is translated into practical imperatives. Provide the poor with food from the corners of the field and the leavings of the harvest. Let them eat freely of the produce of the field in the seventh year and provide them with a tithe on the third and sixth. One year in seven, release debts and Hebrew slaves. One year in fifty, return all ancestral land to its original owners. Make sure there are courts throughout the land and that everyone has access to justice. Ensure that no one is left out of the festival celebrations, and no one denied access to dignity. Treat employees and debtors ethically and give slaves rest one day in seven. Here in a magnificent passage is how Moses describes this ethic of love:

> And now, O Israel, what does the Lord your God ask of you but to fear the Lord your God, to walk in all His ways, to love Him, to serve the Lord your God with all your heart and with all your soul.... To the Lord your God belong the heavens, even the highest heavens, the earth and everything in it. Yet the Lord set His affection on your ancestors and loved them, and He chose you, their descendants, above all the nations, as it is today. Circumcise your hearts, therefore, and do not be stiff-necked any longer. For the Lord your God is God of gods and Lord of lords, the great God, mighty and awesome, who shows no partiality and accepts no bribes. He defends the cause of the fatherless and the widow, and loves the stranger, giving him food and clothing. And you shall love the stranger, for you yourselves were strangers in the land of Egypt. (Deut. 10:12–19)

This is a unique vision that shaped the moral horizons of the West (there are Eastern religions, notably Buddhism, that are also based on love, but of a more cosmic, less personal form). The moral life as Judaism conceives it is a combination of love – *ḥesed* and *raḥamim* – and justice – *tzedek* and *mishpat*. Love is particular; justice is universal. Love is interpersonal; justice is impersonal. Love generates ethics: the duties we owe those to whom we are bound by kinship or consent. Justice generates morality: the duties we owe everyone because they are human. Both are ultimately based on our love for God and His for us. It is the fusion of the moral and spiritual that is the unmistakable mark of Israel's prophets.

Simon May's comment is very much to the point:

> What we must note here, for it is fundamental to the history of Western love, is the remarkable and radical justice that underlies the love command of Leviticus. Not a cold justice in which due deserts are mechanically handed out, but a justice that brings the other, as an individual with needs and interests, into a relationship of respect.[36]

This is the kind of love that exists within the family transposed to society as a whole, built on *tzedaka* as loving justice and *ḥesed* as loving charity. Out of it emerges the first great attempt in history to build a society (as opposed to a state) on the basis of a radically extended love.

This too is part of the relationship between the Song of Songs and Pesaḥ. It highlights the radical contrast between a society based on fear and one based on love. The persecution of the Israelites in Egypt began with the words of Pharaoh: "The Israelites have become far too numerous for us. Come, let us deal shrewdly with them or they will become even more numerous and, if war breaks out, will join our enemies, fight against us and leave the country." Oppression is the result of the politics of fear. Its opposite is the politics of justice and love, of covenant and collective responsibility, a principled respect for the humanity of each under the sovereignty of God.

VI. To Love and Be Loved
Judaism is incomprehensible without love. How else would God have stayed faithful to a people that so often abandoned Him? How often

---

36. May, *Love: A History*, 17.

would a people have stayed loyal to a God who seemed sometimes to have abandoned them? There is a passion, an intensity, a fervor to the books of the Bible explicable in no other terms. There is daring language throughout. Speaking to Hosea, God compares Israel to a prostitute. Speaking to his fellow mourners in the ruined Jerusalem, the author of Lamentations says that God has become "like an enemy" (2:5). Each accuses the other of desertion. There are fierce arguments on either side. God calls to humanity, "Where are you?" There are times when humanity makes the same cry to God. There is not the slightest suggestion anywhere in Tanakh that love is easy, calm, idyllic. Yet it is never less than passionate. The epicenter of that passion is contained in the Song of Songs, and it is this that makes it, as Rabbi Akiva said, the holy of holies of Scripture.

That love has been the text and texture of Jewish life ever since. It was there in the second century when Rabbi Akiva prepared to die as a martyr, saying, "All my life I have been wondering when I will have the opportunity to fulfill the command, 'Love the Lord your God…with all your soul' [Deut. 6:5], meaning, 'even if He takes your soul.' Now that I have the opportunity, shall I not seize it?" (*Berakhot* 61b). It was there when the Jews of northern Europe died at their own hands during the Crusades rather than be forcibly converted to Christianity. It was there in the twelfth century when Maimonides defined what it is to serve God with love:

> What is the love of God that is befitting? It is to love God with a great and exceeding love, so strong that one's soul shall be knit up with the love of God such that it is continually enraptured by it, like lovesick individuals whose minds are at no time free from passion for a particular woman and are enraptured by her at all times…. Even more intense should be the love of God in the hearts of those who love Him; they should be enraptured by this love at all times. (*Laws of Repentance* 10:3)

It was there in the sixteenth century in Tzefat when Rabbi Eliezer Azikri wrote the passionate song to God we sing every Shabbat, "Beloved of the Soul":

Like a deer will Your servant run and fall prostrate before Your
beauty. To him Your love is sweeter than honey from the comb,
than any taste.

It is there every weekday when Jewish men put on the tefillin,
"like a seal on your arm," saying, as they wrap its strap around the finger
like a wedding ring, the words of Hosea: "I will betroth you to Me forever.... I will betroth you to Me in faithfulness, and you will know the
Lord" (2:21–22).

Jews were and often still are the God-intoxicated people. For the
knowledge of God in Judaism is not a form of theology; it is a form
of love. That is what the Hebrew verb "to know" means. It is inescap-
ably an *eros* word: "And Adam knew Eve his wife; and she conceived"
(Gen. 4:1). It is the knowledge of intimacy: deep, emotive, physical and
spiritual at once. Through love, and only through love, divine blessing
flows into the world. Kohanim, as they prepare to bless the congregation, recite the blessing, "who has commanded us to bless His people
Israel with love," because only when we love do we become vehicles
for God's love.

Plato held that we love what is beautiful. Judaism believes something subtly but fundamentally different: what we love *becomes* beautiful.
Beauty does not create love. Love creates beauty. That is why the Jewish
people, derided by others for centuries as pariahs, never internalized
that image. "I am dark yet fair, daughters of Jerusalem" (Song. 1:5). If
they were beautiful in God's eyes, that was sufficient. That seems to me
to be the right source of self-respect and the right sort of love. For to
love God is to love the world He made and the humanity He fashioned
in His image. To love God is to love His people, despite its many faults.
To be loved by God is the greatest gift, the only one we can never lose.

Renewing the Covenant:
On the Haftara of the Second Day

How do you defeat the decline and fall of civilizations, the fate of almost
every world power since the dawn of history itself? That is the question
posed and implicitly answered in the Haftara for the second day.

It records a momentous event in Jewish history. The year was 622 BCE and the young King Josiah had been engaged in a massive program of reform to remove the idolatrous shrines and pagan practices of his grandfather, King Manasseh. During the course of the cleansing of the Temple a copy of the Torah was found, evidently hidden during Manasseh's reign for fear it would be destroyed.

Reading it, the king and his advisers were forcibly reminded of Moses' teachings in the book of Deuteronomy, which identified the nation's fate with its faithfulness to its covenant with God. Deuteronomy records a terrifying series of curses spelling out what would happen to the people if they strayed from the covenant. This struck fear into the king. These were not abstract theological reflections. They were a clear and present warning of what might happen to the nation now if they did not collectively return and repent. A century earlier, a not dissimilar fate had happened to the northern kingdom, Israel, at the hands of the Assyrians, and now only the smaller kingdom of Judah was left.

The king assembled the people and together with them renewed the covenant:

> He read to them all that was written in the Book of the Covenant that had been found in the Temple. The king stood on his platform and made a covenant before the Lord, [pledging] to walk after Him and to observe His commandments and statutes and laws with all his heart and all his soul, to observe the words of that covenant written in the scroll of the Torah – and all the people committed themselves to the covenant. (II Kings 23:2–3)

The king redoubled his efforts to purify the kingdom. That year, as part of the national renewal, there was a massive celebration of Pesaḥ in Jerusalem: "For the Pesaḥ had not been observed [with such ceremony] in the times of the judges who judged Israel, nor throughout the times of all of the kings of Israel or the kings of Judea" (II Kings 23:22).[37]

This was not the only historic occasion on which Pesaḥ marked a covenant renewal. A similar event took place earlier in the days of King

37. See also the parallel account in II Chr. 35:1–18.

Hezekiah. The king had messengers go throughout the land, including those sections of the northern kingdom (the text mentions members of the tribes of Ephraim, Manasseh, Issachar and Zebulun) who remained, inviting them to come not just to celebrate the festival but also to renew their commitment to God and the covenant: "People of Israel, return to the Lord, the God of Abraham, Isaac and Israel, that He may return to you who are left, who have escaped from the hand of the kings of Assyria" (II Chr. 30:6).

Many came. The text reports, "There was great joy in Jerusalem, for since the days of Solomon, son of David, king of Israel, there had been nothing like this in Jerusalem" (II Chr. 30:26). Evidently Josiah's later celebration eclipsed even this, because in the days of Hezekiah not all the members of the northern tribes responded favorably to his invitation.

These two great celebrations of Pesaḥ represent something fundamental about biblical politics. They are rooted in the idea of a covenant. Covenants were widely known and used in the ancient Middle East as treaties between nations. Uniquely in the case of Israel, the covenant was between God and a people, through which the people recognized God as their Sovereign and committed themselves to keeping His law. The entire book of Deuteronomy is structured as such a covenant.

The idea of covenant reentered the West in the sixteenth and seventeenth centuries, notably in Switzerland, Holland, Scotland, England and the first colonies in America. Only in America does it continue to exist, if not as an active principle, then at least as part of its rhetoric of self-understanding.

Covenant is a distinctive form of politics, different from three others. One is *hierarchical* society, of which the greatest in the past were the ancient civilizations of Egypt and Mesopotamia. Another is the *civic republican* society, inspired by the city-states, especially Athens and Sparta, of ancient Greece. Most recently, a further type emerged in the liberal democracies of the West in the second half of the twentieth century: the *contract* society, a new phenomenon in which the state is seen as an enterprise restricted to keeping the peace and providing services in return for taxation.

Covenant societies tend to be politically, though not economically, egalitarian. They are fundamentally opposed to hierarchy. They aim to create a nation, in Abraham Lincoln's phrase, "conceived in liberty, and dedicated to the proposition that all men are created equal." Although all societies contain some hierarchical, non-egalitarian elements, covenant societies insist that all are equal in dignity and must be treated as such.

They are also opposed to one feature of civic republican societies, namely the belief that there is no higher good than the state. Civic republican societies came into vogue in the modern era with the French Revolution and they tend to turn politics into a form of religion, which is as dangerous as turning religion into a form of politics. So in the European nation-states of the nineteenth century, politics became replete with the trappings of the ceremonial: flags, symbols, emblems, anthems, parades, oaths, coins, national gatherings and institutions. The state became an object of worship with an exclusive claim on loyalty. This, in biblical terms, is idolatry.

As for the politics of contract, it is too new to know what its future will be. The phrase "social contract" is associated with Hobbes, Locke and Rousseau, but they did not mean by it what Western liberal democracies have taken it to be since the 1960s: societies with no shared morality, where the supreme values are autonomy and rights, and the primary political calculations are those of advantage. Almost certainly such societies are too shallow to survive in this form, especially since they fail to make sense of the one value on which all politics depends, namely loyalty.[38]

One important feature of the politics of covenant, though, is illustrated by the Pesaḥ celebrations of Hezekiah and Josiah. Covenantal societies are conscious of their origin at a specific time and place. They emerge out of history: usually a history of persecution, followed by the experience of liberation, often involving a struggle, a journey and a conscious new beginning driven by certain principles of a moral nature. In the case of Israel it was to honor God, keep His commandments and serve Him alone, thus becoming "a kingdom of priests and a holy nation" (Ex. 19:6).

---

38. See Michael Sandel, *Liberalism and the Limits of Justice* (Cambridge: Cambridge University Press, 1982); Paul Kahn, *Putting Liberalism in Its Place* (Princeton, NJ: Princeton University Press, 2005).

Covenants can be renewed. That is what happened in the last month of Moses' life (Deut. 29), at the end of Joshua's life (Josh. 24), in the time of Jehoiada, High Priest during the reign of Joash (II Chr. 23:16) and in the days of Ezra and Nehemiah (Neh. 8–10), as well as during the reigns of Hezekiah and Josiah. The renewal – a national ceremony freighted with religious gravitas – always takes the form of a retelling of the history of the people, emphasizing the kindness of God and the waywardness of the nation. When it obeyed God it prospered; when it disobeyed, it suffered defeat. Therefore the people pledge themselves to remain true to the covenant and loyal to God. Covenant renewal is part historical recollection, part mission statement, part rededication, and there is nothing quite like it in other political systems.

This had real historical repercussions. As Shelley made unforgettably clear in his poem "Ozymandias" (see above), even the greatest empires have declined, fallen and been consigned to archeological relics and museums. Except in the case of Israel and the Jewish people, it has become a law of history. The fourteenth-century Islamic thinker Ibn Khaldun (1332–1406) said that when a civilization becomes great, its elites get used to luxury and comfort, and the people as a whole lose what he called their *asabiyah*, their social solidarity. The people then become prey to a conquering enemy, less civilized than they are but more cohesive and driven.

Italian political philosopher Giambattista Vico (1668–1744) described a similar cycle: "People first sense what is necessary, then consider what is useful, next attend to comfort, later delight in pleasures, soon grow dissolute in luxury, and finally go mad squandering their estates." We might call this the law of entropy – the principle that all systems lose energy over time – applied to nations.

Covenant renewal defeats national entropy. A people that never forgets its purpose and its past, that reenacts its story in every family every year, a nation that attributes its successes to God and its failures to itself, cannot die. It may go into exile but it will return. It may suffer eclipse but it will be reborn. That is no small exception to the otherwise universal law of the decline and fall of nations – no small gift of Pesah to the eternity of Israel.

The Division of the Reed Sea:
On the Torah Reading for the Seventh Day

One thing makes God laugh: human beings who think they are gods. This is a divine response we often do not recognize because we were neither looking for it nor expecting it. The use of humor is one of the Torah's most subtle devices, and its intent is deadly serious. God mocks those who mock Him. Not because He is jealous of His honor. To the contrary, as Rabbi Yoḥanan said in the Talmud: God's greatness is His humility (*Megilla* 31a).

God mocks those who set themselves up above others, who have divine or semi-divine pretensions, because He cares for their victims. His use of humor is precisely judged and measure-for-measure. Those who are high He brings low. Those who are low He lifts high. Those who take themselves seriously, He turns into jokes. Those the world laughs at, He takes as His own. Unless we understand this, we will miss an essential dimension of the division of the Reed Sea. We will see it as a mere miracle – the sea divided, water turned into dry land, the order of nature overturned – which it is, but only secondarily. Its real point is more serious. It is about the will to power, the ethics of militarism and faith in arms and armies. Its message is deep, precise, ominous and very much still relevant.

The best way of understanding the Torah's approach to human self-pretension is through examples. The obvious case is Balaam. Balaam is the archetype of the shaman, the wonder-worker who uses religion in a way the Torah regards as blasphemous, as a means of enlisting super-natural powers to human ends. As Balak, King of Moab, says to him:

> Now come and put a curse on these people, because they are too powerful for me. Perhaps then I will be able to defeat them and drive them out of the land. For I know that whoever you bless is blessed, and whoever you curse is cursed. (Num. 22:6)

Balaam goes through the usual formalities. He cannot, he says, do anything against God's will. He must first find out whether the mission is acceptable. This turns out however to be mere show because when he

first asks God, God says no. But when a second attempt is made to persuade him, promising him more honor and reward, he asks God again,
proving that he believes that God, like man, can change His mind. God is
angry, though the text does not tell us this yet. The form His anger takes
is that He gives permission to Balaam to go. Since Balaam has shown
he only half-accepts the answer "No," God gives him the answer "Yes."
The sages described this as the rule that "where you want to go, that is
where you will be led" (*Makkot* 10b). The next morning Balaam sets out,
and the famous scene with the ass takes place.

A joke is being played on Balaam. His ass sees an angel that
Balaam, the greatest seer of his age, cannot see. The ass speaks, proving
what God told Moses at the burning bush: "Who gave human beings
their mouths? Who makes them deaf or mute? Who gives them sight
or makes them blind? Is it not I, the Lord?" (Ex. 4:11). Balaam has the
hubris to think he is the master of God's word, that he can decide who
will be blessed and cursed. God shows him that even an ass can see and
speak if God wills it. Balaam cannot see an angel with a drawn sword
even when it is directly in front of him, and far from cursing the Israelites
finds himself losing a moral argument with a talking donkey.

Satire descends into farce as the man to whom Balak has offered
a fortune to curse the Israelites proceeds to bestow on them some of the
most unforgettable blessings in the entire Torah. This happens because
Balak and Balaam believe that blessings and curses are for sale and that
divine powers can be exploited for human ends.

The second scene occurs in the story of the Tower of Babel. The
people on the plain of Shinar propose to build a city with "a tower that
reaches heaven" (Gen. 11:4). This is one of the biblical narratives for which
the realia are well known through archeology. More than thirty Mesopotamian ziggurats or towers have been unearthed, the most famous of which,
and one of the largest, was that of Babylon which rose to a height of some
three hundred feet from a square base, with a sanctuary at the summit.

At the beginning of the second millennium BCE, the Sumerian
ruler of Lagash, Gudea, says of the temple of Eninnu that "it rose to the
sky." Later Esarhaddon says of the temple of Ashur that he made "its
top high as heaven." The same language is used of the temple of Marduk in Babylon. So the ambition was real. The towers of the first great

civilization on earth, the place Abraham and his family left, were man-made structures, artificial holy mountains, on which it was believed people – kings especially – could ascend to heaven to meet the gods.

The biblical text, having described this briefly and with precision, then says: "God said ... 'Come, *let us descend*'" (11:6–7). So miniscule is the tower that God has to "descend" to be able to see it at all: a joke we can only fully appreciate now that we are able to fly over skyscrapers from a height of thirty thousand feet and see how small the highest building looks from even a modest elevation in the sky. The builders had been led to this hubris by a simple technological advance: the use of kilns to make bricks harder and more durable than their sun-dried equivalents.

No sooner had they achieved this than they began to believe that humans can make mountains, reach the sky and be like gods. In response God uses no high technology, no miracle. He merely confuses the language of the builders. Immediately the serious project of human self-aggrandizement is reduced to farce as orders are shouted out by the supervisors and no one understands what they are saying. Not only can the builders not converse with the gods, they cannot even converse with one another. It is a *coup de theatre* designed to make fun of those who take themselves seriously as masters of the universe.

The result is precisely judged. The builders sought to make the city so that they "would not be scattered over the face of the earth" (v. 4). The result is that they were "scattered over the face of the earth" (vv. 8–9). They sought to "make a name for ourselves" (v. 4) and they succeeded, but not as they intended. Babel became the eternal name, not for order but for confusion.

The logic of these and similar narratives is given in Psalm 2, the text that speaks about God's laughter:

> Why do the nations clamor, why are the peoples speaking futilities? The kings of this earth have assembled; the leaders have banded together against the Lord and His anointed. "Let us cut their bonds," they have said, "and cast from us their cords." The One who presides in heaven shall laugh; the Lord will jeer at them. (Ps. 2:1–4)

Turning to the division of the Reed Sea, we begin by noting a pointed ambiguity in the Torah's description of what happened and how:

> Moses raised his hand over the sea, and the Lord *moved the sea with a strong easterly wind* all that night; it turned the sea into dry land, and the waters were divided. So the children of Israel walked into the midst of the sea on dry land, and the water was *like a wall for them on their right and on their left*. (Ex. 14:21–22)

Of the two phrases emphasized above, the second phrase, "the water was like a wall," suggests a supernatural event. God suspended the laws of nature. The Israelites walked on dry land between walls of water held in place by the divine will alone. This is the first reading, with all its drama. The Egyptians, with their horse-drawn chariots, see themselves as an invincible military power about to crush a group of powerless, fugitive slaves. God unleashes against them the forces of nature itself, using the sea (in ancient times a symbol of primal chaos, the Ugaritic god Yam, or in Egyptian mythology Apep, enemy of the sun god Ra), wielding it as a weapon to defend His otherwise defenseless people to overthrow the army of the man who thought himself a god.

But the first phrase, *moved the sea with a strong easterly wind*, suggests a different reading. No suspension of the laws of nature is needed for a strong east wind, in the right place at the right time, to uncover dry land where, at other times, there was sea. To mention just one of many recent scientific accounts, in September 2010, researchers at the US National Center for Atmospheric Research and the University of Colorado showed by computer simulation how a sixty-three-miles-per-hour east wind, blowing overnight, would have pushed back water at a point in the Nile Delta where an ancient river merged with a coastal lagoon. The water would have been driven back into the two waterways and a land bridge opened at the bend, allowing people to walk across the exposed mud flats. As soon as the wind died down, the waters would have rushed back. The leader of the project said when the report was published: "The simulations match fairly closely with the account in

Exodus."³⁹ This is one of several explanations offered by scientists to show how the division of the sea might have happened naturally.

This does not mean that it was not a miracle. Rather, it suggests a different way of understanding the nature of a miracle: not an event that suspends the laws of nature but rather one that, by happening when, how and to whom it did, constituted a deliverance that was a signal of transcendence, written unmistakably in God's handwriting, a divine intervention but not a scientific impossibility.⁴⁰

The second reading suggests a quite different way of understanding the events that took place at the sea. The military dominance of the Egyptians was based on the horse-drawn chariot, introduced into Egypt by the Hyksos in the sixteenth century BCE. This made the Egyptian army invincible. It was the symbol of their strength. There is however one form of terrain in which the horse-drawn chariot is a source not of strength but of weakness, namely an uncovered, saturated seabed. The Israelites, traveling on foot, were able to walk across, but the Egyptians, pursuing after them in their chariots, found that "the wheels of their chariots were unfastened and drove with difficulty" (Ex. 14:25). They became stuck in the mire, unable to move forward or back. Their very obsession with catching up with the Israelites had driven them heedless into danger. By the time they found themselves trapped, they were helpless. As the wind dropped and the waters returned, they were caught, defeated not by an army but by their own desire to exercise power over the vulnerable and by their own reliance on military technology.

39. A report can be found at https://www2.ucar.edu/atmosnews/news/2663/ parting-waters-computer-modeling-applies-physics-red-sea-escape-route. For another account by a professor of materials science at Cambridge University, see Colin Humphreys, *The Miracles of Exodus* (London: Continuum, 2003).

40. The sages offered a third, mediating possibility. By a play on the word *le'eitano*, "the sea returned *to its original strength*," the sages said, this means *letano*, "to its condition," suggesting that "the Holy One, blessed be He, made a condition with the elements of the universe during the six days of creation." One of these was that the sea should split before the Israelites (Genesis Raba 5:5). On this reading the division of the sea was programmed into the script of nature from the beginning of time. Thus did the sages seek to reconcile the supernatural with the natural: miracles happen but the universe retains its law-like character.

On this reading the significance of the event is not its supernatural quality but something more consequential, an irony that echoes through the centuries: those who trust in weapons of war, perish by weapons of war. Those who worship military technology eventually become its victims. We become, says Psalm 115 (part of Hallel), what we worship. If we worship instruments of death, we die. If we worship the God of life, we live. Or, as Psalm 147 puts it:

> He does not take delight in the strength of horses, nor pleasure in the fleetness of man. The Lord takes pleasure in those who fear Him, who put their hope in His loving care. (Ps. 147:10–11)

The scene of the Israelite refugees, on foot, crossing the sea to safety while the Egyptian army floundered, rendered helpless by the very vehicles that had made them believe they were invulnerable, is unforgettable. The powerful have been rendered powerless while the powerless make their way to freedom. The truth conveyed by that image does not require for its proof a suspension of the laws of nature. It is one of the laws of human nature, forgotten in every generation by those who worship power. Those who see themselves as more than human become less than human. Those who laugh at God become the laughingstock of history.

Empathizing with Your Enemies: On Some Laws and Customs of Pesaḥ

There are two aspects of Pesaḥ that make it different from the other pilgrimage festivals, Shavuot and Sukkot. First, in the Torah, the word *simḥa*, "rejoicing," does not appear at all in connection with it. In Leviticus the word appears specifically in connection with Sukkot. In Deuteronomy it figures twice in connection with Sukkot, once with Shavuot. But there is no explicit command to rejoice on Pesaḥ.

The second is that a Full Hallel is said only on the first day (outside Israel, the first two days). The Talmud (*Arakhin* 10a–b) gives a reason for this. The sacrifices offered in the Temple did not vary on the seven days of Pesaḥ, (Num. 28:24), whereas they did on Sukkot. This gives each day of Sukkot something of the status of a festival in its own right whereas on Pesaḥ, the subsequent days are a mere repetition of the first. However, the answer of the Talmud is not sufficient to explain one phenomenon: the fact that we do not say a Full Hallel on the seventh day. According to tradition, the division of the Reed Sea took place on the seventh day. Moses had initially asked Pharaoh for permission to travel with the people three days into the wilderness to worship God. When it became clear that they were not about to return, Pharaoh was notified on the fourth day. He and his chariots traveled on days five and six. On the seventh the Israelites crossed the Sea and sang the Song (Rashi to Ex. 14:5). That is why the crossing of the Sea is the Torah Reading for the seventh day. The Talmud, in its discussion of the origin of Hallel (*Pesaḥim* 117a), lists a number of historic occasions on which it was sung. The first of these is *at the Reed Sea!* In other words, according to the Talmud, Hallel originated on the seventh day of Pesaḥ. Therefore, regardless of the sacrifices, it should at least be said on that day.

A midrash (*Yalkut Shimoni, Emor* 654) gives a similar answer to both questions. Rejoicing is not mentioned in connection with Pesaḥ because it was a period "during which the Egyptians died." We do not say a Full Hallel other than on the first day because of the principle (Prov. 24:17), "Do not rejoice when your enemy falls; when they stumble, do not let your heart be glad" – a prohibition against Schadenfreude. This recalls another passage in the Talmud (*Sanhedrin* 39b), which says that during the division of the Reed Sea, the angels above wanted to sing a song of triumph like the Israelites below. God silenced them with the words, "The works of My hands are drowning in the sea and you wish to sing a song?"

There is an obvious question: If God stopped the angels singing, why did He not stop the Israelites? The technical answer is that there is a halakhic difference between Hallel said at the time of the event and Hallel said subsequently on the anniversary of the event. The first is a direct expression of emotion; the second is an act of memory. The first does not require a blessing, the second does. That is why we do not make a blessing on the Hallel said at the Seder table whereas we do in the synagogue. At the Seder table there is a halakhic requirement that "each person must see himself as if he himself had come out of Egypt"

(*Pesaḥim* 10:5). Therefore Hallel for us is as it was for the Israelites at the time: an immediate personal experience. At the time of a miraculous escape we are overwhelmed with gratitude and a sense of relief and release. It is not a time for balanced emotion and detachment. However, for the angels (and for the Israelites themselves on subsequent years), Hallel was not the result of an immediate experience. Hence it was overridden by the prohibition against taking pleasure at seeing your enemy fall, and only an abridged version ("Half Hallel") is said.

The same reasoning – "Do not rejoice when your enemy falls" – appears in the famous explanation offered by Abudraham (Abu Dirham, Seville, fourteenth century) as to why we spill drops of wine while reciting the Ten Plagues at the Seder table: to remind ourselves of the suffering of the Egyptians. The implication may be that we should feel sorry for the Egyptians who suffered for the recalcitrance of a single individual, Pharaoh (Moses once said to God, "Shall one man sin and will You be angry with the whole congregation?" [Num. 16:22]). Or perhaps the point is that even the execution of justice should occasion mixed feelings. The Talmud rules that the command, "You shall love your neighbor as yourself," applies even to a criminal who has committed a capital crime (*Sanhedrin* 52a). Death must be as painless as possible, because though a person has forfeited his life, he has not forfeited his status as a human.

Are these sentiments merely the products of post-biblical Judaism? Or do they have some basis in Tanakh itself?

There are two puzzling passages which may shed light on the question. The first is the strange insistence by God that, before they leave, the Israelites should ask their Egyptian neighbors for "articles of silver and gold" (Ex. 11:2). Did they need silver and gold for the journey? Besides which, as the sages pointed out, if they had not taken gold from Egypt they would not have been able to make a golden calf (*Berakhot* 32a). Yet there is nothing minor or accidental about this detail. God mentioned it to Moses before he had even started his mission (Ex. 3:22). Centuries earlier He alluded to it to Abraham: "Afterward they will come out with great possessions" (Gen. 15:14). Even before then it had been a feature of Abraham's own exile to Egypt: "Abram had become very wealthy in livestock and in silver and gold" (Gen. 13:2).

It cannot be that the years of exile and suffering were for the sake of wealth. Divine blessings are to be found in Israel, not exile. Nor is there anything to be said for taking money from the wicked. As Abraham said to the king of Sodom, "I will accept nothing belonging to you, not even a thread or the strap of a sandal, so that you will never be able to say, 'I made Abram rich'" (Gen. 14:23).

Instead, the explanation is to be found in the later law of Deuteronomy about releasing a slave:

> When you set him free from your service you must not send him away empty-handed. You must give generously to him of your flock, your granary and your wine vat with which the Lord your God has blessed you; so you shall give him. And you shall remember that you were once a slave in the land of Egypt and the Lord your God redeemed you; this is why, today, I command you thus. (Deut. 15:13–15)

There are two elements at stake here. The first is that when you release a slave you must give him initial support to start a new life in freedom. The other and more significant is emotional closure. Slavery is humiliating. The parting gift from the master does not compensate for the years of freedom lost, but it does mean that there is a final act of goodwill. It is there precisely to mitigate the resentment that otherwise exists between a former slave and his or her master. It is there to prevent some form of revenge (see Lev. 19:18).

The law in Deuteronomy refers to an Israelite releasing a slave. But there is no reason to doubt that the same logic applies to God's insistence that the Israelites receive gifts from the Egyptians. The Torah is calibrated to human nature. It was, as the sages say, "not given to angels" (Berakhot 25b). Humiliation, resentment and the desire for revenge have destroyed civilizations in the past.[41] They are no basis for a nation about to create a free society under the sovereignty of God. The Israelites were to leave Egypt without a legacy of hate.

---

41. See Rene Girard, *Violence and the Sacred* (Baltimore: Johns Hopkins University Press, 1977).

The same logic applies to the arresting statement of Moses: "You shall not despise an Egyptian, for you were strangers in his land" (Deut. 23:8). This is one of the great apparent non-sequiturs in the Torah. The Egyptians enslaved our ancestors. They tried to carry out a program of genocide. It is not as if Moses wanted the people to forget their suffering in Egypt. To the contrary, God had commanded the Israelites never to forget it, never to cease reenacting it once a year.

Rather, the explanation is this: If the Israelites continued to resent the Egyptians for the way they had been treated, then Moses would have taken the Israelites out of Egypt, but would not have taken Egypt out of the Israelites. In a psychological sense they would still be slaves to the past. They would see themselves as victims, and victimhood is incompatible with freedom. Victimhood defines you as an object, not a subject, as someone others act upon, not someone who takes destiny into his own hands. Victims destroy; they do not build. Victims look back, not forward. *To be free, you have to let go of hate.* That is the burden of Moses' command.

Egypt never became, in the Jewish imagination, a symbol of evil. That was reserved for the Amalekites. The humanizing of the Egyptians led Isaiah to one of the most remarkable prophecies in all religious literature. The day will come, he says, when the Egyptians will themselves suffer from a tyrannical leader. On that day they will cry out to God, who will respond by performing the same kind of miracle for them as once before He had performed for the Israelites:

> When they cry out to the Lord because of their oppressors, He will send them a savior and defender, and He will rescue them. So the Lord will make Himself known to the Egyptians, and on that day they will acknowledge the Lord. (Is. 19:20–21)

There will come a day when God Himself will bless the Egyptians, saying, "Blessed be Egypt, My people" (ibid. 25).

This same biblical concern that one should not dehumanize one's enemies is a key theme of the book of Jonah. It is the lesson God seeks to teach the prophet by sending him a leafy plant to give him shade during the day. When the plant dies, Jonah curses his fate. God then says:

"You cared about that plant, which you did not toil for and did not grow, which appeared overnight and was lost overnight. And am I not to care for the great city of Nineveh, which has more than 120,000 people in it – who do not know their right hands from their left – and many animals?" (Jonah 4:10–11)

The fact that the Assyrians were Israel's once and future enemies does not justify depriving them of the chance to repent and be forgiven.

This entire cluster of attitudes is extraordinary, yet it is central to our understanding of the Exodus. The sin of the Egyptians was that they dehumanized the Israelites. Therefore if Israel is to be the antitype, the opposite, of Egypt, it must not dehumanize the Egyptians. We must not hate them. We must not say a Full Hallel on the day they drowned in the Sea. Because Egyptians died, our entire "joy" on the festival is muted, not even mentioned in the Torah at all.

Retribution is not revenge. Punishment is not hate. Justice is not vindictiveness. The moral system of the Torah depends on making a fundamental distinction between interpersonal emotion and impersonal law. Revenge, hate and vindictiveness are all I-Thou relationships. Justice is the opposite: the principled refusal to let I-Thou relationships determine the fate of individuals within society. Justice means that all must submit to the impartial process of law. Retribution is an act of restoring moral order to society. It has nothing to do with revenge which is, strictly speaking, lawless. When law and justice prevail, there can be punishment without animosity. The law-based society envisaged by the Torah is one where people hate not the sinner but the sin.

One of the recurring dangers of religion, indeed of civilizations generally, is that they divide humanity into the saved and the damned, the redeemed and the accursed, the believer and the infidel, the civilized and the barbarian, the children of light and the children of darkness. There is no limit to the evils that can be visited on those not of our faith, since one is doing so in the name of God, truth and right, and since one's victims are less than fully human. That is an abomination, an offense against God and His image – humankind.

Spilling wine during the recitation of the plagues, refraining from Full Hallel on the seventh day, not hating an Egyptian: all these and more are fundamental to the Torah's insistence that *our humanity precedes our religious identity.* Man was made in God's image long before the covenant with Abraham or the Israelites. To be a Jew is the Jewish way of being human. It is not a justification for seeing others as less than human.

If Rabbi Yaakov Emden is right, then there is a statement to this effect at the very beginning of the Seder. The first words we say at the opening of *Maggid* are: "This is the bread of oppression our fathers ate in the land of Egypt. Let all who are hungry come in and eat; let all who are in need come and join us for the Pesaḥ." The difference between the first invocation and the second, says Rabbi Emden, is that the first, "Let all who are hungry come in and eat," is addressed to non-Jews, on the basis of the principle that "We must support non-Jews as well as Jews because of the ways of peace" (*Gittin* 61a).[42]

This is no small principle. We are commanded not to forget the victims of our victories, not to lose empathy with our enemies, nor to dehumanize the human other. That does not mean abandoning the search for justice – quite the reverse. But law is one thing, interpersonal emotion another. There is a haunting line in the account of the plagues, when Pharaoh's own advisers tell him: "Let the people go…. Do you not yet realize that Egypt is ruined?" (Ex. 10:7). Hate destroys the hater, not just the hated.

To be free, you have to let go of hate.

---

42. Rabbi Yaakov Emden, *Siddur Amudei VeShaʿarei Shamayim.*

Shavuot

The Greatest Gift

The Enigma of Shavuot

Shavuot is a riddle wrapped in a mystery inside an enigma.

It is the only festival in the Torah without a specific date in the Jewish calendar. We know exactly when Pesaḥ and Sukkot occur. The same is true for Rosh HaShana and Yom Kippur. Each has its given day or days in the cycle of the year. Not so Shavuot. Nowhere does the Torah say that we should celebrate it on such-and-such a day in a specific month. Instead it says: "And you shall count seven complete weeks from the day following the first day of the festival, when you brought the Omer as a wave-offering.... And you shall proclaim on that day – it shall be a sacred assembly for you: you may not perform any laborious work" (Lev. 23:15–21). The text in Deuteronomy is even less specific: "Count for yourselves seven weeks; when the sickle begins to cut the standing grain" (Deut. 16:9).

Not only does the Torah not specify a date, for a prolonged period, until the calendar was fixed by calculation in the fourth century, it could fall on three *different* days, depending on whether in any given year Nisan and Iyar were both short months of twenty-nine days, or both long, of thirty days, or one was long, the other short. If both were long, Shavuot fell on the fifth of Sivan. If one was long and one short, it was celebrated on the sixth, and if both were short, it occurred on the seventh. This makes it difficult to understand how it could be a commemoration of any historical event, since events happen on particular days of the year, while Shavuot did not.

These, though, are minor problems when it comes to dating Shavuot. The larger problem lies in the phrase the Torah uses to describe the day on which the seven-week count begins. Above, we translated it as "the day following the first day of the festival." However, the text actually says *mimaḥarat haShabbat*, literally "the day after the Sabbath." Reading the phrase literally, this means Sunday, from which it follows that Shavuot, the fiftieth day, also falls on a Sunday. This gave rise to an extraordinary range of interpretations, reflecting the deep schisms between rabbinic Judaism and other sects. The latter adopted the literal reading, celebrating the Omer on a Sunday, and Shavuot on the Sunday seven weeks after that. The former, holding by the Oral tradition, interpreted "the day after the Sabbath" as "the day after the first day of the festival."[1]

The result was chaos, at least one mark of which is still evident today in the institution known as *Yom Tov sheni shel galuyot*, the second day of the festival observed outside Israel. Often this is thought of as the result of the ancient system by which the new moon was determined, month by month, on the basis of eye-witness testimony. No one could tell in advance of the court's decision when the new month would begin. Immediately after the month had been fixed, messengers were sent out to notify communities, and since it took them a long time to make the journey, Diaspora communities had to keep festivals for two days because of the doubt as to whether the previous month was long or short.

In fact, the real reason is significantly different. During the Second Temple period there was no need for a second day even in Babylonia because the decision of the court was conveyed that night by the lighting of a series of bonfires that stretched from Israel to Babylonia. However,

---

1. For a detailed discussion of the different customs of the various sects, see "The Omer: Three Studies" in the previous chapter.

as a result of controversies about the calendar, one of which was about the determination of the date of Shavuot, the bonfires were sabotaged. Thereafter, the news had to be conveyed by messengers instead (*Rosh HaShana* 2:2). So the second day owes its existence not to the absence of a system of rapid communication, but rather to a lack of unity and mutual respect within the Jewish people itself. Ironically, serving one God did not always create one nation.

The second strange fact about Shavuot is that nowhere does the Torah link it to a specific historical event. Pesaḥ recalls the Exodus from Egypt. Sukkot is a reminder of the forty years in the desert when the Israelites lived in temporary dwellings. Shavuot is given, explicitly in the Torah, no such historical dimension. We know it as *zeman matan Torateinu*, "the time of the giving of our Torah," the anniversary of the revelation at Mount Sinai. But this identification appears nowhere in the Torah or elsewhere in Tanakh. Only in the Talmud (see, for example, *Pesaḥim* 68b, among others) do we begin to find this connection.

What is more, until the fourth century, as we have seen, Shavuot could occur on the fifth, sixth or seventh of Sivan. So whichever date the Torah was given, Shavuot did not necessarily fall on that day. Nor was there agreement as to which day the Torah was in fact given. The Talmud records a dispute between the other sages and Rabbi Yose. The sages held that it was given on the sixth of Sivan. Rabbi Yose disagreed and argued that it was given on the seventh (*Shabbat* 86b). His view could not be lightly dismissed, since Rabbi Yose had a reputation for clarity and precision that often gave his rulings authority (*Eiruvin* 46b; *Gittin* 67a). It follows that, at least in Israel where Shavuot is observed for only one day, the sixth of Sivan, in Rabbi Yose's view Shavuot falls *not* on the day the Torah was given, but the day before.

So, according to the written sources, biblical and post-biblical, there was intense debate as to when Shavuot is celebrated and why. That is what makes the study of this particular festival so fascinating, for the conflict of interpretations has to do not just with the wording of the Torah and its connection with historical events. It has to do with one of the most fundamental questions of all: what it is to be a Jew and why. Shavuot will turn out to be, among other things, the festival of Jewish identity.

I. Celebrating the Land

One fact emerges with great clarity from the biblical sources. Shavuot is an agricultural celebration. Exodus calls it the "time of the first wheat harvest" (Ex. 23:16). Numbers calls it "the day of the first fruits" (Num. 28:26). Deuteronomy defines the start of the seven-week count as "when the sickle begins to cut the standing grain" (Deut. 16:9). Leviticus 23 interrupts its account of holy days to add, immediately after giving the details of Shavuot, a command that has nothing to do with festivals: "And when you reap the grain of your land, do not finish reaping the corner of your field, and do not collect the fallen remnants of your harvest; you must leave them for the poor and for the stranger." This is the practice vividly described in the book of Ruth. Whenever Shavuot is mentioned in the Torah, we can almost smell the fragrance of fields, feel the open air and see the harvested grain. It is supremely the farmers' festival.

According to one talmudic passage (*Menaḥot* 65a), this was the logic behind the sectarians' practice of always celebrating Shavuot on a Sunday. Challenged by Rabban Yoḥanan ben Zakkai as to why, unlike all the other festivals, Shavuot should have a fixed day in the week rather than in the month, an elderly Boethusian gave the following explanation: Moses was "a lover of Israel" and, in his compassion for the farmers who would be exhausted after seven weeks' hard labor, he (or rather, God) decided to give them a long weekend. Since Shavuot, unlike Pesaḥ and Sukkot, lasts for only one day, ensuring that it always fell on Sunday gave weary farmers two consecutive days of rest.

However, the problem remains. Pesaḥ and Sukkot are also agricultural and seasonal. Pesaḥ is the festival of spring. Sukkot is the festival of ingathering, the autumn harvest. But each also had a historical dimension. That is what made these festivals unique in the ancient world. Every society had agricultural festivals. There was nothing odd in seeing God in nature. None before Israel, though, had seen God in history or regarded collective memory as a religious obligation. It may therefore have been that Shavuot also had a historical dimension from the outset, but one that had to do with the land. It was the day that celebrated the gift of the Promised Land.

This is purely speculative, but it is supported by several considerations. First is the seven-week countdown that we find in no other festival. The obvious analogy is with the seven-year cycle of *shemitta*, the year of release, culminating in the fiftieth or Jubilee year. These had primarily (though not exclusively) to do with fields, produce, agricultural labor and the ownership of land. The count was set in motion by the offering of the Omer from the first of the barley harvest, while on Shavuot itself the key offering was two loaves of bread from the wheat harvest. So the seven weeks were the time when the people were most conscious of God's blessing in "bringing forth bread from the earth." Rabbi Yehuda HeHasid (Germany, twelfth–thirteenth century) suggested that the fifty-day count was instituted because people were so busy and preoccupied in the fields that they might otherwise forget to celebrate the festival on time. It was the obvious time to celebrate the land promised, and blessed, by God.

Second, there is a clear lacuna in the pilgrimage festivals themselves. Pesah is about the start of the journey from Egypt. Sukkot recalls the forty years of the journey itself. What is missing is a festival celebrating journey's end, the arrival at the destination. Logic would suggest that this was Shavuot. Interestingly, this is what it became again in the kibbutzim during the early years of the modern state. Secular Israelis re-appropriated Shavuot precisely as a celebration of the land.

Third, the theme of the Mosaic books as a whole is *the promise of the land*. In Genesis, God makes the promise seven times to Abraham, once to Isaac and three times to Jacob. Jewish history begins with Abraham leaving his family and traveling to "the land that I will show you" (Gen. 12:1). The rest of the Torah from Exodus to Deuteronomy is about the Israelites' journey from Egypt toward it. If the gift of the land is the supreme divine promise, it would be extraordinary *not* to have a festival marking its fulfillment.

Fourth, the book of Joshua tells us that it was *the act of eating the grain of the land* that made the Israelites vividly aware that the wilderness era had ended. We read, "They ate of the produce of the land on the day after the Pesah, matzot and roasted grain, on that very day. And the manna ceased [to come down] the next day, when they ate of the produce of the land, and the children of Israel no longer had manna;

they ate of the crops of the land of Canaan that year" (Josh. 5:11–12). The manna stopped, in other words, on the day that became fixed as the offering of the Omer that began the seven-week count to Shavuot. Historically, therefore, the new grain each year was a reminder of how the Israelites first tasted the produce of what Moses described as "a land of wheat and barley" (Deut. 8:8).

We know precisely how this history was celebrated. The Torah defines Shavuot as "the festival of the first fruits," and tells us that on bringing first fruits to the central Sanctuary, each farmer was to make a declaration:

> My father was a wandering Aramean, and he went down into Egypt.... And the Egyptians dealt cruelly with us and oppressed us, and imposed hard labor on us.... And the Lord brought us out of Egypt with a strong hand and an outstretched arm.... He brought us to this place and gave us this land, a land flowing with milk and honey; and now I bring the first fruits of the soil that You, Lord, have given me. (Deut. 26:5–10)

We are familiar with this passage because, for at least the last two thousand years, it has occupied a central place in the Haggada on Pesaḥ, but its original context was the bringing of first fruits to the Temple on Shavuot. *The first regular historical declaration made by the people as a whole had to do with the gift of the land.* This then is the most likely historical dimension of the festival during some periods of the biblical age. It was the day when once a year, coupled with an act of thanksgiving for the grain harvest, the Israelites came to the Temple and told the story of their arrival at the land itself. It was when the nation gave expression to the sense of gratitude Moses believed they ought to have:

> For the Lord your God is bringing you into a good land – a land with brooks, streams and deep springs gushing out into the valleys and hills; a land of wheat and barley, vines and fig trees, pomegranates, olive oil and honey; a land where bread will not be scarce and you will lack nothing.... You will eat and be satisfied, then you shall bless the Lord your God for the good land He has given you. (Deut. 8:7–10)

This was traditionally understood as the biblical source of the command to say Grace after Meals, but it is not impossible that it was also the basis for an annual celebration on Shavuot. This, to repeat, is pure conjecture. What gives it force, however, is that were it not so, there would have been no annual celebration of the single most important fact about Israel's existence as a nation, namely that it lived in the land given by God in fulfillment of the promise He had made to their ancestors at the dawn of their history. Neither Pesaḥ nor Sukkot are about this. They are festivals of exodus and exile. Shavuot completes the cycle by being the festival of homecoming. That was its historical dimension, made explicit in the *Viduy bikkurim*, the declaration accompanying the first fruits, and symbolized in the two loaves of wheat that were the special offering of Shavuot.

If so, we can understand two longstanding customs of Shavuot: eating dairy food and decorating the synagogue with flowers and foliage. The milk recalls the phrase most associated with Israel – "a land flowing with milk and honey" – that appears no fewer than fifteen times in the Torah. The flowers and foliage recall God's blessing if the people follow Him: "I will give grass in your field for your cattle, and you shall eat and be satisfied" (Deut. 11:15).

It would also follow that the three pilgrimage festivals correspond to three different kinds of bread. Pesaḥ is about the "bread of oppression" our ancestors ate in Egypt. Sukkot is about the manna, the "bread from heaven" they ate for forty years in the wilderness, the sukka itself symbolizing the clouds of glory that appeared just before the manna fell for the first time (Ex. 13:21; 16:10). Shavuot, with its offering of "two loaves" (Lev. 23:17), is about the bread of freedom made with the grain of the land itself. So it might once have been. But something happened that decisively changed people's understanding of the day itself.

II. Exile and Identity

What changed was that Israel lost the land. In 722 BCE Assyria conquered the northern kingdom and transported its population, known to history as the Lost Ten Tribes. In 597 BCE Babylonia defeated Judah, the kingdom of the south, taking its king and other leaders captive. In 588–586 BCE it attacked again, this time, after a prolonged siege, destroying the Temple. In the book of Lamentations we can still sense the trauma, undiminished by time.

You cannot celebrate the land when you have lost it. You cannot rejoice over the produce of the fields if the fields are no longer yours. You cannot thank God for the gift of home when you are in exile. "How can we sing the Lord's song on foreign soil?" asked the people, weeping by the waters of Babylon (Ps. 137:4). All the hopes that had accompanied Abraham's descendants since he and Sarah began their journey to the Promised Land lay in ruins. It was the worst crisis of the biblical age.

It was then that a curious feature of Israelite history played a decisive role. In the normal experience of nations, first comes the land and only then, the law. People settle a region. They evolve from group to clan to tribe. They take up agriculture. They build villages, then towns and cities, then nations and sometimes empires. Only relatively late in this process do structures of governance emerge and with them, laws governing relationships in society. The "where" precedes the "how." When it comes to the history of nations, connections with the land are primal, visceral. Legislation is secondary and contingent.

In Israel's case, uniquely, it was the other way around. First came the law, and only then the land. At Mount Sinai, a mere seven weeks after leaving Egypt, the Israelites underwent a unique experience that transformed their identity. They made a covenant with God. They accepted Him as their sovereign. They pledged themselves to live by His laws. This was their foundational moment as a body politic.

The consequence could not have been more far-reaching. *If the law preceded the land, then even when they lost the land, they still had the law. If the covenant came before they had achieved political independence as a territorial state, it might still be in force even when they had lost their independence and state.* That is what God had promised even before they entered the land. The terrifying curses at the end of Leviticus contain a remarkable promise:

> Yet in spite of this, when they are in the land of their enemies, I will not reject them or abhor them so as to destroy them completely, breaking My covenant with them. I am the Lord their God. (Lev. 26:44)

That became the message of all the prophets who lived through or foresaw conquest and exile. "Where is your mother's certificate of divorce with which I sent her away?" asked God through Isaiah (Is. 50:1). Only if the sun, moon and stars cease to shine, said Jeremiah in God's name, will Israel cease to be a nation (Jer. 31:34–35). "I shall open your graves and lift you out of your graves, My people; I shall bring you to the land of Israel," said God through Ezekiel in his chilling vision of the nation as a valley of dry bones (Ezek. 37:12).

In Babylonia, through individuals like the prophet Ezekiel, the exiles began to understand that they had lost their country but they still had the covenant. They were still God's people. He was still their King. That was when the Torah became, in Heinrich Heine's famous words, "the portable homeland of the Jew." It was their country of the mind, their extraterritorial landscape, their metaphysical refuge. The Torah was the record of their past and their assurance of a future. Never have a people owed more to a book.

What happened in the Babylonian exile we do not know but we can reasonably infer. It was there that they rediscovered Torah as the key to Jewish identity. We know this because of what happened when two major Jewish figures, Ezra the scribe and Nehemiah the politician-administrator, left Babylon to return to Israel in the mid-fifth century BCE. Dismayed at the low ebb of Jewish life, they undertook an initiative with far-reaching consequences. They assembled a national gathering at the Water Gate in Jerusalem and conducted the first-recorded adult education seminar in history.

The book of Nehemiah describes how Ezra stood on a wooden platform in the Temple courtyard and read Torah to the people:

> Ezra opened the book. All the people could see him because he was standing above them; and as he opened it, the people all stood up. Ezra praised the Lord, the great God; and all the people lifted their hands and responded, "Amen! Amen!" Then they bowed down and worshiped the Lord with their faces to the ground. The Levites…instructed the people in the Law while the people were standing there. They read from the Book of the Law of God, making it clear and giving the meaning so that the people understood what was being read. (Neh. 8:5–8)

Shortly thereafter, the people formally rededicated themselves to the covenant. It was the start of a movement that gathered pace over the next five hundred years, turning Jewry into the people of Torah for whom, when the Temple was destroyed a second time, scholars took the place of priests and prophets, and study became a substitute for sacrifice.

What Ezra and Nehemiah understood was that the spiritual battle was ultimately more consequential than the military one. This became clear in the second century BCE, when the Seleucid Greeks under Antiochus IV attempted to force the pace of Hellenization, banning the public practice of Judaism and introducing pagan practices into the Temple. The Maccabees, a pietistic group led by the sons of an elderly priest, Mattityahu, fought back and won, rededicating the Temple in the ceremony we still commemorate on Ḥanukka.

However, their successors, the Hasmonean kings, rapidly became Hellenized themselves, choosing Greek names and combining kingship with priesthood in a way incompatible with the separation of powers implicit in the Bible. It was probably at this time that a group of priests disgusted by what they saw as the corruption of the Temple decided to leave Jerusalem and live in seclusion in Qumran, the sect we have come to know through the Dead Sea Scrolls.

The religious fragmentation of Jewry in the last days of the Second Temple was extreme and tragic. The people were religiously divided, says Josephus, into Sadducees, Pharisees and Essenes. The Pharisees themselves were fragmented to the point at which the sages said that the split between the schools of Hillel and Shammai threatened to divide the Torah into two (*Sota* 47b; *Sanhedrin* 88b). A political rift grew among the population as to whether to live with or rebel against the increasingly repressive Roman rule. There were moderates, zealots, and terrorists known as the Sicarii. Josephus, an eye-witness of those events, paints a terrifying picture of Jews inside the besieged Jerusalem more intent on fighting one another than the enemy outside. A house divided against itself cannot stand, and so Jerusalem fell again, as it was to do a third time sixty-five years later with the failure of the Bar Kokhba revolt.

These were devastating blows, and unlike the Babylonian exile, this time there were no prophets to offer a compelling vision of imminent hope. It was the end of Israel as an actor on the historical stage for almost two thousand years. Tradition has left us a famous story about how Rabban Yoḥanan ben Zakkai arranged to have himself smuggled outside the besieged city and taken to Vespasian, the Roman general leading the campaign. Correctly predicting that the general would soon be made Caesar, he extracted a promise in return: "Give me the academy of Yavneh and its sages" (*Gittin* 56b). This became the best-known memory of Jewish survival after catastrophe. From here onward Judaism would become a religion of teachers, schools and houses of study, the faith of a people dedicated to the book, not the sword.

The years following the destruction of the Second Temple proved to be the definitive test as to which form of Judaism would survive the loss of the land and its institutions. Within a remarkably short time, the Sadducees had disappeared along with the Qumran sectarians. We hear no more of the Essenes. The Samaritans persisted but in small numbers. The survivors were the rabbis, heirs to the Pharisees, who saw Torah study as a higher religious experience than even prayer and who created in the form of the Mishna, the Jerusalem and Babylonian Talmud and the halakhic and aggadic midrashim a heavenly city of the mind. Celebrating scholarship, "dispute for the sake of Heaven" (*Ethics of the Fathers* 5:21) and intense focus on the divine will as translated into halakha, they became co-architects with the Torah itself of the rich, variegated and intensely detailed universe of Jewish law. Thus Jewry survived, despite persecutions, expulsions and occasional sectarian schisms, until the late eighteenth century.

It was an astonishing achievement. The rabbis achieved what no other leadership group has done in all of religious history. They had shaped a way of life capable of surviving in the most adverse environments, turning every setback into a catalyst for new creativity. It was they who spoke of Shavuot as *zeman matan Torateinu*, the "time of the giving of our Law [Torah]," the anniversary of the revelation and covenant at Mount Sinai.

Life is lived forward but understood only backward, in retrospect. It was in the aftermath of the two great historical catastrophes, the Babylonian conquest and the failed rebellion against Rome, that the nature of Jewish history became clear. *The law did not exist for the sake of the land.* It was the other way round: *the land existed for the sake of the law.* It was in order that the Israelites should create a sacred society of justice and compassion that God gave Israel the land. You do not need a territorial base to encounter God in the private recesses of the soul, but you do need a land to create a society in which the Divine Presence is real in the public square.

It was only when they lost the land but knew they still had the Torah that Jews fully realized that this is what Shavuot had been about from the very beginning.

III. The Day of Covenant

There is evidence that Shavuot was, from the outset, the anniversary of the Giving of the Torah.

First, according to all of the views as to the date of Shavuot, it took place in the third month, and there is only one significant event in the Torah that happened then. The Israelites arrived at the Sinai desert "on the third new moon" after they had left Egypt (Ex. 19:1). There then follows a series of exchanges between Moses and God, and Moses and the people, each of which involved ascending and descending the mountain. God then told Moses to tell the people to prepare for a revelation that would take place on the third day. Then we read, "On the third day, in the early morning – thunder and lightning; heavy cloud covered the mountain, there was a very loud sound of the shofar, and all of the people in the camp quaked" (Ex. 19:16). There are different ways of calculating the chronology of these events, but the revelation at Sinai clearly took place in the third month, and there is only one festival in the third month: Shavuot.

Nor can we doubt the centrality of the Sinai event. We can see this by the sheer space the Torah dedicates to it. The Israelites arrived at Sinai at the beginning of Exodus 19, and not until Numbers 10:11, "On the twentieth day of the second month of the second year," did they leave. *They spent less than a year at Sinai, but the Torah devotes approximately one third of its entire text to it,* while passing over thirty-eight of the forty wilderness years in silence other than to record the places where the Israelites stopped. It would be astonishing if this event were not commemorated in the Jewish calendar while a relatively minor feature of the wilderness years, the fact that the Israelites lived in sukkot, booths, has a seven-day festival dedicated to it.

There is other evidence. We read in the second book of Chronicles about how King Asa, after cleansing the land of idols, convened a national covenant renewal ceremony:

> They assembled at Jerusalem *in the third month* of the fifteenth year of Asa's reign…. They entered into a covenant to seek the Lord, the God of their ancestors, with all their heart and soul…. They *took an oath* to the Lord with loud acclamation, with shouting and with trumpets and horns. All Judah rejoiced about the oath because they had sworn it wholeheartedly. They sought God eagerly, and He was found by them. So the Lord gave them rest on every side. (II Chr. 15:10–15)

The fact that the ceremony was held in the third month suggests that it coincided with Shavuot, and that the festival itself was associated with the covenant at Mount Sinai. There is even a hint in the text of an early association between the word *Shavuot,* "weeks," and *shevua,* "oath," used here to mean commitment to the covenant.

Then there is the fascinating evidence of the Book of Jubilees. This is a text written in the middle of the second century BCE, author unknown but almost certainly a priest, which retells the whole of biblical history in terms of fifty-year, jubilee cycles. It was not accepted as part of Tanakh, but it occasionally records traditions unknown elsewhere, and that is the case here. According to Jubilees (6:15–19), Shavuot was first celebrated *by Noah* to celebrate the covenant God made with him, and through him with all humanity, after the Flood. "For this reason it has been ordained and written on the heavenly tablets that they should celebrate the Festival of Weeks during this month, once a year, to renew the covenant each and every year" (6:17). Jubilees goes on to say that God made His covenant *with Abraham* on the same date in the third month (14.20). Thus there was an early tradition that held that Shavuot was supremely the covenant-making and renewal day for all three biblical covenants between God and human beings: with Noah, Abraham and the Israelites in the days of Moses.

Rabbi David Zvi Hoffman (*Commentary to Leviticus,* vol. 2, 158–168) adds that the rabbinic name for the festival – *Atzeret,* or in Aramaic,

Atzarta – meaning "assembly" or "gathering," may be related to Moses' own description of the day the Torah was given as *Yom HaKahal*, "the day of the assembly" (Deut. 9:10, 10:4, 18:16). He also suggests that the reason the Torah relates the festivals to historical events is simply to explain why we perform certain acts, such as sitting in a booth on Sukkot. Since Shavuot has no distinctive mitzva, it needed no historical explanation. As to why there is no distinctive mitzva on Shavuot, he argues that it is to emphasize that at Sinai the Israelites "saw no image; there was only a voice" (Deut. 4:12). There is no symbolic action that could capture the experience of hearing the voice of the invisible God.

Why then, if Shavuot is the anniversary of the covenant at Sinai, does it not have a fixed date in the calendar? The answer was set out by Nahmanides in his Commentary to the Torah (Lev. 23:36). The relationship between Shavuot and Pesaḥ, he says, is like that between Shemini Atzeret and Sukkot. In both cases there is a count of seven – seven days in the case of Sukkot, seven weeks in the case of Pesaḥ and the counting of the Omer – followed by a concluding festival. That is how he understands *Atzeret*, the name the Torah gives to the eighth day of Sukkot, and that the rabbis called Shavuot, deriving it from the verb *a-tz-r* meaning "stop," "close," "cease," "conclude." Though both are festivals in their own right, both celebrate the end of something; they are not stand-alone celebrations. They are defined in terms of what went before.

Thus the days of counting the Omer between Pesaḥ and Shavuot are like Ḥol HaMo'ed, the intermediate days of a festival. *Pesaḥ and Shavuot are the beginning and end of a single extended festival.* That is why Shavuot is not given a date in the Jewish calendar – because what matters is not what day of the week or month it falls but the fact that it marks the conclusion of the seven weeks initiated by the Omer. That, in fact, is why the Oral tradition held that the Omer begins not on a Sunday (the literal meaning of "the day following the rest day") but after the first day of Pesaḥ, because the Omer is not a free-standing institution but the start of a seven-week count linking Pesaḥ to Shavuot.

The nature of that link was stated at the very beginning of the Exodus narrative, when Moses met God at the burning bush. God told Moses his mission and then said, "*And this will be the sign to you that it is I who have sent you: when you have brought the people out of Egypt, you will worship God on this mountain*" (Ex. 3:12). The Exodus from Egypt, in other words, was only the beginning of a process that would reach its culmination when the people worshiped God at Mount Sinai.

Pesaḥ and Shavuot are inseparable. Revelation without the Exodus was impossible. But Exodus without revelation was meaningless. God did not bring the people out of Egypt only to leave them to the hazards of fate. They were His people, "My child, My firstborn, Israel," as He told Moses to say to Pharaoh (Ex. 4:22).

Why then the forty-nine days? Maimonides and the *Zohar* give subtly different explanations. The *Zohar* (*Emor*, 97a) sees the Giving of the Torah at Sinai as a marriage between God and the people. Just as a bride must purify herself by keeping seven "clean" days and then going to the *mikveh*, so the Israelites, defiled by the impurities of Egypt, had to keep seven "clean" weeks, each day purifying one of the forty-nine combinations of *sefirot*, the sacred emanations linking creation with God.

Maimonides says that since the Giving of the Torah was anticipated by the Israelites as the supreme culmination of the Exodus, they counted the days "just as one who expects his most intimate friend on a certain day counts the days and even the hours" (*Guide for the Perplexed*, III:43).

The most significant hint, though, lies in the name tradition gave to Pesaḥ: *zeman ḥeruteinu*, "the time of our freedom." Freedom in Judaism means more than release from slavery: individual freedom. It means law-governed liberty, "the rule of laws, not men": collective freedom. Thus the Israelites did not achieve freedom on Pesaḥ when they left Egypt. They acquired it on Shavuot when, standing at the foot of the mountain, they accepted the covenant and became a holy nation under the sovereignty of God. That is why Pesaḥ and Shavuot are not two separate festivals but the beginning and end of a single stretch of time – the time it took for them to cease to be slaves to Pharaoh and to become instead the servants of God.

IV. Forgetting and Remembering

The real question is not when or why Shavuot became *zeman matan Torateinu*, "the time of the giving of our Torah." It is, rather, why it ever ceased to be.

At the core of Israel's collective memory, at the heart of its self-definition, is the idea that faithfulness to the covenant at Sinai is its raison d'être and the key to its survival and flourishing. That is the moral of almost every book in Tanakh and the burden of all the prophets. They, especially Amos, Hosea, Isaiah and Jeremiah, told the people candidly and with great passion that faithlessness to God would lead to military defeat and political disaster. The closer this came, the more the prophets were ignored, culminating with Jeremiah who was ridiculed, mocked, insulted, abused, sentenced to death and thrown into a pit for telling the people what they did not want to hear.

The story we read in Tanakh of the centuries in which the Israelites were in possession of the land, from the time of Joshua to the Babylonian conquest, is not a happy one. Time and again the people find themselves drawn to the local gods and to pagan practices, and this goes hand in hand with political corruption, the abuse of power, sharp practices in business and mistreatment of the poor. Amos speaks of those who "have sold for silver those whose cause was just, and the needy for a pair of sandals, trampling the heads of the poor into the dust of the ground" (Amos 2:6–7). Isaiah declares, "Your rulers are rogues and cronies of thieves, every one avid for presents and greedy for gifts; they do not judge the cause of the orphan and the widow's cause never reaches them" (Is. 1:23).

To be sure, there were reforming kings – among them Asa, Jehoshaphat, Hezekiah and Josiah – but the impression we receive is that their efforts, however well intentioned, were too little, too late. Repeatedly in the narratives of Israel's and Judah's kings, we read the verdict that "he did evil in the eyes of the Lord." The overriding question that comes to mind when reading the Hebrew Bible is: Why did the people so often ignore the warnings of the prophets, the teachings of Moses and the lessons of their own history? Isaiah well expresses this sense of amazement when he says, "An ox knows its owner, an ass its master's crib; Israel does not know, My people take no thought" (Is. 1:3). Animals know to whom they belong; Israel sometimes forgets.

It should be obvious from every syllable of Jewish history, the prophets say, that faith and fate, loyalty and liberty, go hand in hand. Yet the people continue to ignore the message. Ironically, one of the few instances in Tanakh where an entire people heeds the words of a prophet occurs in the book of Jonah, where the people concerned are Israel's enemies, the Assyrians in the military city of Nineveh.

Why was it so hard to persuade people that idolatry was their weakness and faith in the God of Abraham and the covenant of Sinai their strength? Because we are seeing history with hindsight. We have read the book. We know how it ends. At the time it did not seem that way at all.

One passage sheds light on the whole era of Israel's kings. It occurs in the book of Jeremiah. The prophet had been warning the people that they faced disaster. If they continued on their present course they would be conquered by the Babylonians and the result would be national catastrophe. So it happened. Jerusalem and Judah lay in ruins. Now, once again, he addresses the people, begging them finally to acknowledge their error and return to God. Defiantly, the people refuse:

> "We will not listen to the message you have spoken to us in the name of the Lord. We will certainly do everything we said we would: we will burn incense to the Queen of Heaven and will pour out libations to her just as we and our ancestors, our kings and our officials, did in the towns of Judah and in the streets of Jerusalem. *At that time we had plenty of food and were well off and suffered no harm. But ever since we stopped burning incense to the Queen of Heaven and pouring out libations to her, we have had nothing and have been perishing by sword and famine.*" (Jer. 44:16–18)

As far as the people were concerned, as long as they served idols (the Queen of Heaven was probably Ishtar, the Mesopotamian goddess of fertility, love and war), they prospered. When they stopped doing so (the reference is probably to the reforms of Josiah) they began to suffer. We need to let these words sink in.

There is no immediate short-term correlation between faithfulness to God and national success in the arena of history. That is the problem. Jeroboam II was one of the northern kingdom's most successful kings. He reigned for forty-one years and "restored the boundaries of Israel from Lebo Hamath to the Dead Sea" (II Kings 14:25). Yet he "did evil in the eyes of the Lord" (ibid. 24), perpetuating the sins of his namesake,

Jeroboam son of Nebat. Manasseh, Hezekiah's son, reversed the religious reforms of his father and reintroduced idolatry into the kingdom, leading the people astray "so that they did more evil than the nations the Lord had destroyed before the Israelites" (II Kings 21:2). He is also said to have "shed so much innocent blood that he filled Jerusalem from end to end" (ibid. 16). Yet he ruled, apparently, successfully, for fifty-five years, while his grandson, Josiah, one of Tanakh's most righteous kings, died prematurely in battle.

A contemporary observer would have understood why Jeremiah was unheeded, and why people resented the bad news he brought. The Talmud (*Sanhedrin* 102b) tells us that King Manasseh appeared to Rav Ashi in a dream. The rabbi had been about to deliver a lecture on how evil a king he had been. In the dream, the king said to the rabbi, "Had you been there at that time, in that place, you would have caught hold of my coattails and followed me." Only in retrospect does the truth of a prophet's words become apparent.

There is a technical name for this phenomenon: the J-curve effect. This says that the result of any necessary correction to a trend – from devaluing a currency to revolution against a repressive regime – will initially be negative and only subsequently positive. Things get worse before they get better. Psalm 92, the Psalm of the Sabbath Day, tells us that the wicked grow like grass, the righteous like a tree. In the short term, evil flourishes, but not in the long. The essence of prophecy is that it is long term. While others are at ease, the prophet sees the coming cataclysm. While others are traumatized and grief-stricken, the prophet sees the distant consolation.

The prophet will always be at a disadvantage vis-à-vis the large cast of false prophets and flattering courtiers who tell rulers what they want, not what they need, to hear. The reply of the people to Jeremiah was, within its own terms, devastating. If you are looking for an immediate correlation between sanctity and success, repentance and reward, you will look in vain. That is the fact with which Israel's prophets wrestled for much of their lives. Bad things happen to good people, while evildoers flourish. That troubled Jeremiah and Job and all who sought to discern God's justice through the mists of history and circumstance.

For most of the biblical era, land seemed primary and law secondary. It was far easier, on Shavuot, to thank God for the fields and the food than for the Torah and its obligations and restraints. That is what makes the history of Shavuot so telling an insight into the state of the collective Jewish soul. It is one of the ironies of Jewish history that its most creative periods of spirituality occurred before they possessed the land, in the days from Abraham to Moses, or when they were exiled from it, after the Babylonian conquest, and then again after defeat at the hand of Rome.

By contrast, when they had both land and independence they tended to lapse into idolatry and civil strife. The era of the judges ended in chaos and civil war. In the age of monarchy, after the reign of a mere three kings, the kingdom split in two. The Hasmoneans, who had started as religious purists, soon became Hellenized and corrupt. Moses was right in his visionary speeches in Deuteronomy. The real challenge, he said, would not be slavery but freedom; not the privations of the wilderness but the affluence of home. As Paul Johnson put it in his *A History of the Jews*, "In self-government and prosperity, the Jews always seemed drawn to neighboring religions, whether Canaanite, Philistine-Phoenician or Greek. Only in adversity did they cling resolutely to their principles and develop their extraordinary powers of religious imagination, their originality, their clarity and their zeal."

It took the Babylonian exile to produce Ezra and Nehemiah, and the Roman conquest to yield Yoḥanan ben Zakkai and the academy at Yavneh. Only after a sequence of tragedies culminating in the defeat of the Bar Kokhba revolt and the ensuing Hadrianic persecutions, did the people hear again the original message of Shavuot, that it was not just about grain and first fruits, but about the way of life by which they had covenanted to live more than a thousand years before.

We who were born after the Holocaust know that divine providence is not always waiting in the wings, ready to intervene in history and save us from our enemies and ourselves. The connection between faith and fate is deeper and more demanding than that. What the prophets knew and the people sometimes forgot was that Israel is a small country in a region of large empires and brutal politics. Only if its people believe in something greater than themselves will they become stronger than themselves, which they will need to be to survive. Jews became the eternal people because of their faith in the eternal God. Without this, they would almost certainly have gone the way of their neighbors, the Canaanites, Jebusites and Perizzites, the Moabites and Edomites, and even great empires like Assyria and Babylon.

For this reason Shavuot was, for a long time, the hardest of festivals to appreciate. It was easy to celebrate the land, difficult to rejoice in the demanding covenant they had made with God when they had nothing but water from a rock, manna from heaven and the desert as a home. Yet this always was the source of their strength: that unforgettable moment at an otherwise unmemorable mountain, when God gave the people His word, and they gave Him theirs: "All that the Lord has spoken, we shall perform."

V. People of the Book

There are moments when you can see an entire civilization reimagining itself. That is what happens in a talmudic vignette about the life of King David (*Shabbat* 30b). Once, says the Talmud, David asked God to tell him when he would die. God refused to answer, saying that no one is granted this knowledge. "Then at least tell me," said David, "on which day of the week I will die." "You will die," said God, "on Shabbat." Thenceforth, every Shabbat, David spent the whole day in study.

When the scheduled moment came for him to die, the Angel of Death found him engaged in uninterrupted learning: "His mouth did not cease from study." As long as this continued, the angel discovered he had no power over him, so he devised a stratagem. He made a rustling sound in a nearby tree. Climbing a ladder to see what was making the noise, David slipped and fell. For a moment, as he was falling, no Torah came from his lips. At that moment, the angel took his soul and he died.

Simple though it is, this story tells us what had changed in Jewish life. For the rabbis, David was no longer primarily the military hero, victor of Israel's greatest battles, or the astute politician, or even the man who initiated the plan to build the Temple. He had become a sage. The battles he fights are in the mind. His home has become a house of study.

David had become a new kind of symbol for an old-new people that no longer predicated itself on a land, a king, an army, a Temple, sacrifices and a priesthood, but lived instead in synagogues, schools and academies. So long as the Jewish people never stops studying, the story intimated, the Angel of Death has no power over it. Jews had become, in the most profound sense, people of the book, of Shavuot, of Sinai. Theophrastus, a pupil of Aristotle, called them "a nation of philosophers." In the first century, Josephus could write, "Should any one of our nation be asked about our laws, he will repeat them as readily as his own name. The result of our thorough education in our laws from the very dawn of intelligence is that they are, as it were, engraved on our souls."

Ezra and Nehemiah's public reading of the Torah had set in motion a profound change in Jewish life, one whose early details are hard to come by because of the shortage of literary materials from Jewish sources between the fourth and second centuries BCE. But we can take up the story with Shimon ben Shetah in the first century BCE. Until then, education had largely taken place within the family. Shimon ben Shetah established the first national educational system in Israel, creating schools throughout the country for sixteen- and seventeen-year-olds. This was not entirely successful, and around 63–65 CE, Joshua ben Gamla established a more comprehensive structure, later described by the Talmud in these words:

> May the name of that man, Joshua ben Gamla, be blessed, because, were it not for him, the Torah would have been forgotten from Israel. For at first, if a child had a father, his father taught him, and if he had no father, he did not learn at all…. They then made an ordinance that teachers of children should be appointed in Jerusalem…. Even so, however, if a child had a father, the father would take him up to Jerusalem and have him taught there, and if not, he would not go up to learn there. They therefore ordained that teachers should be appointed in each prefecture, and that boys should enter school at the age of sixteen or seventeen. However, if the teacher punished them they used to rebel and leave the school. Eventually Joshua ben Gamla came and ordained that teachers of young children should be appointed in each district and each town, and that children should enter the school at the age of six or seven. (*Bava Batra* 21a)

This was the first system of its kind in the world. The Talmud also contains the world's first regulations about teacher provision and class size. As H.G. Wells noted in his *Outline of History,* "The Jewish religion, because it was a literature-sustained religion, led to the first efforts to provide elementary education for all children in the community." By contrast, universal compulsory education did not exist in England until 1870. There was nothing remotely similar in the ancient world. Even the great academies of ancient Greece were confined to an elite. Rabbinic Judaism set itself to achieve a society of universal literacy. Paul Johnson calls it an "ancient and highly efficient social machine for the production of intellectuals."

Quite how deeply the passion for education went can be seen in the following law. The Torah rules that someone found guilty of manslaughter was to be exiled to one of the Cities of Refuge. The rabbis ruled that *if a student is exiled, his teacher must go with him* – not because he shares in the blame, but because the Bible says that the exiled person shall live, "and *life without a teacher is not life."*[2] When the fourth-century teacher Rava found one of his students late for class because he was praying slowly he said, "You are forsaking eternal life for the sake of life in the here-and-now" (*Shabbat* 10a). Study was a religious experience higher than prayer, because in prayer we speak to God, but in study we learn to hear God speaking to us.

To a degree unrivaled by any other culture, Jews became a people whose very survival was predicated on the school, the house of study, and life as a never-ending process of learning. A community that had made no provision for the Jewish education of its children, ruled the rabbis, was to be excommunicated until teachers had been appointed, because "the world only exists in virtue of the sound of children at their studies" (*Shabbat* 119b). When does the obligation to study begin? asks Maimonides, and answers, "As soon as a child can talk." When does it end? "On the day of death" (*Laws of Torah Study* 1:6, 10).

So, throughout the ages, Jewish communities made education their first priority. The fees of poorer children, and sometimes the salaries of teachers, were paid for by the community. The funds were raised

2. Maimonides, *Laws of the Murderer* 7:1 following *Makkot* 10a.

by taxes, or obligatory contributions on being called to the Torah, or house-to-house collections. In twelfth-century France, Rabbeinu Tam ruled that where there was a shortage of funds for education, money designated for other purposes could be diverted to schools and teachers. At a time when their neighbors were often illiterate, Jews lived a life devoted to study, and gave the seats of honor in the synagogue to scholars. A twelfth-century monk, one of Abelard's disciples, wrote that "a Jew, however poor, if he had ten sons, would put them all to letters, and not for gain as the Christians do, but for the understanding of God's law; and not only his sons but his daughters."

The quality of education varied from country to country and from century to century, but until the modern era there was virtually no Jewish community, however small, without its own school and teachers. Benjamin of Tudela, traveling in Provence in 1165, could report that in Posquieres, a town of a mere forty Jews, there was a great yeshiva. Marseilles, whose Jewish population numbered three hundred, was "a city of *geonim* [outstanding scholars] and sages."

In fifteenth-century Spain, where Jews were facing constant persecution, the 1432 Valladolid Synod established taxes on meat and wine, circumcisions, weddings and funerals, to create a fund to establish schools in every community where there were fifteen householders.

In the *shtetl* (small township) in Eastern Europe, learning conferred prestige, status, authority and respect. Men of wealth were honored, but scholars were honored more. In their study of the *shtetl*, *Life Is with People*, Zborowski and Herzog describe the impact this made on the Jewish family:

> The most important item in the family budget is the tuition fee that must be paid each term to the teacher of the younger boys' school. "Parents will bend the sky to educate their son." The mother, who has charge of household accounts, will cut the family food costs to the limit if necessary, in order to pay for her son's schooling. If the worst comes to the worst, she will pawn her cherished pearls in order to pay for the school term. The boy must study, the boy must become a good Jew – for her the two are synonymous.

These values had been part of Judaism from the beginning. In Genesis, God says of Abraham, "For I have chosen him, *so that he will instruct his children* and his household after him to keep the way of the Lord..." (Gen. 18:19). Abraham was chosen to be a father and a teacher. In two of the key passages of Jewish faith, the first and second paragraphs of the Shema, Moses placed education at the heart of Jewish life: "Teach them [these words] repeatedly to your children, speaking of them when you sit at home and when you travel on the way, when you lie down and when you rise" (Deut. 6:7). But it took crisis – defeat and exile – to bring this value back to the fore.

Few have put more eloquently than Jacob Neusner what Jews remembered and Shavuot taught:

> Civilization hangs suspended, from generation to generation, by the gossamer strand of memory. If only one cohort of mothers and fathers fails to convey to its children what it has learned from its parents, then the great chain of learning and wisdom snaps. If the guardians of human knowledge stumble only one time, in their fall collapses the whole edifice of knowledge and understanding.[3]

In their darkest moments Jews rediscovered this ancient truth. It was the Giving of the Torah at Sinai on the first Shavuot that proved to be the gift of eternity.

What Happened at Sinai?

The scene was terrifying. There was a storm: thunder and lightning. Thick cloud covered the mountain. Fire blazed. A shofar sounded. The mountain shook and the earth trembled. Something immense was about to happen. It seemed as if the world were shaking to its foundations. The event that day at Sinai when God revealed Himself to an entire people was a singularity – less an event in time than an event that transformed time. As Maimonides

---

3. Jacob Neusner, *Conservative, American and Jewish* (Lafayette, La.: Huntington House, 1993), 35.

wrote, "We struggle to understand it and fail because there was nothing to compare it to, before or since" (*Guide for the Perplexed*, II:33).

Einstein taught that light – even time itself – is distorted, curved, as it travels in close proximity to the sun. Something like that can be observed in the Torah as it approaches the moment when a group of escaping slaves met God at a mountain in the desert, and there their destiny was born. Time slows almost to a standstill.

By contrast, the book of Genesis covers the whole of time past from the birth of the universe to the descent of Jacob's children to Egypt. Deuteronomy, the book of Moses' visions at the end of his life, charts time future from the Israelites' entry into the Promised Land to the furthermost horizon of their not-yet-written history. The first half of Exodus and the second half of Numbers track the Israelites' forty-year, forty-two-stage journey from Egypt to the bank of the Jordan. But their stay at Sinai takes up fifty-nine chapters, from Exodus 19 to Numbers 10, including the whole of Leviticus, despite the fact that they were there for less than a year. As an object accelerates toward the speed of light, time decelerates. So, judging by the metronome of biblical prose, it was at Sinai.

The descriptions of the Giving of the Torah in Tanakh focus largely on externalities. "You came near and stood at the foot of the mountain while it blazed with fire to the very heavens, with black clouds and deep darkness," said Moses (Deut. 4:11). "The earth shook, the heavens poured, the clouds poured down water. The mountains quaked before the Lord," sang Deborah (Judges 5:4–5, see also Ps. 68:8–9). Yet, when something similar happened to Elijah centuries later, standing on the same mountain (I Kings 19), the Bible makes it clear that God was not in the whirlwind or the earthquake or the fire but in a "still, small voice," a sound on the edge of silence (v. 12). As Moses himself emphasized, at Sinai, "You saw no image; there was only a voice" (Deut. 4:12).

What was unique, transfiguring and still hard to understand was that the nation, as a nation, heard the voice of God. God spoke – not just to a prophet, not in a vision or a trance, not as a sound within the soul but as an event in public space and time. As a brilliantly ambiguous phrase in Deuteronomy (5:19) puts it, it was a *kol gadol velo yasaf*, a great voice that was *never* heard again, and that was *ever* heard again (Rashi, ad loc.). It happened once but it reverberated for all time.

The rabbis debated as to exactly what the Israelites heard (Song of Songs Raba 1:2:2; *Pesikta Rabati* 22). Some said they heard all ten commands, others that they heard only the first two, yet others that they heard all ten but as a single burst of sound that Moses had to decode, word by word. Some said that they heard not only what was eventually written on the tablets of stone and set out in the Written Torah but also what the Oral tradition would eventually infer from each word and phrase on the basis of its interpretive principles.

One thing, though, is clear from both the Exodus and Deuteronomy accounts. The sound was of almost unbearable intensity. The Israelites clamored around Moses begging him to ask God to stop: "You speak to us and we shall listen, but let God not speak to us, lest we die" (Ex. 20:16). When a voice from beyond the universe enters the universe the result is both terrifying and transformative. Yet though we cannot say what happened or how, we can at least hypothesize as to why. *The voice of revelation was intimately related to the voice of creation.* The God who said, "I am the Lord your God, who brought you out of the land of Egypt, from the slave-house," was the God who said, "Let there be light," and there was light. To understand this, we have to go back to the beginning of the biblical account of humankind and ask why Judaism is a religion of holy words and God-given law.

The pagan cultures of ancient times and today's science-based atheism have one thing in common. They hold that all that exists is bounded by the physical, essentially material world of nature. The ancients spoke of the gods of the sun, the moon, the sea, the storm, the famine, the flood, the wind and the rain. Today scientists speak of the strong and weak nuclear force, cosmic antigravity, quantum fluctuations and the six mathematical constants that make the universe the size and shape it is. Where the ancients saw random, capricious fate, science sees the opposite: the ordered regularity of nature charted by cosmology, physics, chemistry and biology. But for neither is there a concept of *revelation*. What we know is, in the broadest sense, what we see. Reality is bounded by what we, given the current state of technology, can detect and measure.

Judaism, however, is about meaning, and meaning is something we hear, not see. It is about what makes us human, and why we behave the way we do, and why we so often destroy what is most precious. These are things that cannot be reduced to atoms, particles and forces. Judaism speaks, above all, of a monumental series of encounters between human beings and a reality beyond the quantifiable and predictable, a reality that is to the universe what the soul is to the body. The question of questions is therefore: How can we relate to something so utterly beyond us?

The biblical answer, astonishing in its beauty and simplicity, is that the meeting between us and God is like the meeting between two persons, myself and another. I can see your body but I cannot feel your pain. How then can I enter your world? Through words. You speak, I listen. I ask, you answer. We communicate. Language is the narrow bridge across the abyss between soul and human soul. So it is between us and the Soul of the universe. Revelation takes place through speech. That is what happened at Sinai. Infinity spoke and the world trembled. In the silence of the desert the Israelites heard the voice of God.

Why, if God spoke at the beginning of time, did He need to speak in the midst of time? The answer lies in what the Bible sees as the most fateful event in the history of the world. God, having created a being in His image, gave it freedom. But the being He created was physical, and thus subject to desires that conflict with those of others. So began the long, bitter, brutal story of humankind.

God created order and gave humans freedom. Humans then proceeded to create chaos. That is the story of Adam and Eve, Cain and Abel and humanity before the Flood – a world of *freedom without order*. After the Flood, humans created empires that had social stability, but they did so by depriving others of their liberty. That is the biblical story from the Tower of Babel to the Egypt of the Pharaohs. The result was *order without freedom*. How then can order and freedom coexist? The whole of Judaism is an answer to that question, and all of Jewish history is a commentary to it.

The biblical answer is *law*: not physical, scientific law, the law of cause and effect that applies to mindless particles on a micro- or macro-scale, but moral, ethical and spiritual law: the law that speaks to human beings in full acknowledgment of their freedom. That is why God spoke at Sinai. Creating a mindless universe, implies the Torah, is easy. In Genesis, it takes a mere thirty-four verses. Creating a social order in which free human beings act justly and compassionately is difficult. That is why the story of Sinai takes fifty-nine chapters. At the beginning of time God spoke the laws that frame the natural universe. At Sinai He spoke the laws that shape the moral universe, inviting the Israelites to construct a society that would serve as a pilot project for humanity as a whole.

The humans God addressed in the desert were liberated slaves. They knew what it was to be treated as less than fully human. That was now behind them. God spoke – and it was essential that He did so not to an elite, but to everyone, men, women and children. He told them that though He was the God of all humanity ("the whole earth is Mine," Ex. 19:5), He was willing to risk His own profile in history by linking His name with theirs. He was offering them a covenant that if followed would – in priestly terminology – turn them into "a kingdom of priests and a holy nation" (Ex. 19:6). In prophetic language, He would "betroth them in righteousness and justice, loving-kindness and compassion" (Hos. 2:21). In the vocabulary of wisdom, He would give them statutes that would be their "wisdom and understanding in the eyes of the nations" (Deut. 4:6).

For it is law, voluntarily accepted, conscientiously practiced, studied, meditated on, internalized, taught by parents to children across the generations, spoken of "when you sit at home and when you travel on the way, when you lie down and when you rise," a law transcending all earthly principalities and powers, that alone reconciles freedom and order. It is only by voluntary self-restraint, born of learned habits of law-abidingness, that we preserve our own freedom while at the same time extending it to others. That is what God spoke at Sinai.

What proof do we have that this really happened, that what the Israelites heard that day was indeed the voice of God? Religion is not science. The revelation of the One *beyond* space and time *within* space and time is not an empirical event demonstrable by experiment or describable within the normal parameters of history. Yet we are not without evidence. Among the unpublished papers found in his desk after he died in 1778, Jean-Jacques Rousseau left the following fragment:

> But an astonishing and truly unique spectacle is to see an expatriated people, who have had neither place nor land for nearly two thousand years, a people mingled with foreigners, no longer perhaps having

a single descendant of the early races, a scattered people, dispersed over the world, enslaved, persecuted, scorned by all nations, nonetheless preserving its characteristics, its laws, its customs, its patriotic love of the early social union, when all ties with it seem broken. The Jews provide us with an astonishing spectacle: the laws of Numa, Lycurgus, Solon are dead; the very much older laws of Moses are still alive. Athens, Sparta, Rome have perished and no longer have children left on earth; Zion, destroyed, has not lost its children.

They mingle with all the nations and never merge with them; they no longer have leaders, and are still a nation; they no longer have a homeland, and are always citizens of it …. Any man whosoever he is, must acknowledge this as a unique marvel, the causes of which, divine or human, certainly deserve the study and admiration of the sages, in preference to all that Greece and Rome offer of what is admirable in the way of political institutions and human settlements.[4]

The laws the Israelites received from God that day at Sinai did indeed become their "wisdom and understanding in the eyes of the nations." They transformed a small, fractious and otherwise undistinguished nation into a people who outlived empires and permanently enlarged the moral landscape of humankind.

I. *Torah from Heaven*

The revelation at Mount Sinai was not just a religious event. It was a *political* event of a unique kind. It was the birth of a nation. Throughout Genesis, the heirs of Abraham had been an extended family. At the beginning of Exodus we hear them for the first time described as an *am*, a "people." Pharaoh says, "Look, *the people of the children of Israel* are too many and powerful for us" (Ex. 1:9).

What made them a people were many things. There was kinship: they were all descendants of Jacob. There was culture: they were shepherds which made them suspect to the Egyptians. There was history: they were newcomers to the land; their origins lay elsewhere. Above

---

4. Rousseau, *Cahiers de brouillons, notes et extraits*, no. 7843 (Neuchâtel).

all, there was shared suffering. Isaiah Berlin noted that it is usually a sense of an injustice done to one's people that is the crucible in which nations are formed. Israel became a people in Egypt, bound by *brit goral*, a covenant of shared fate.

At Sinai, however, they became an *eda*, a body politic. God invited them to become a "kingdom of priests…a holy nation" (Ex. 19:6) – the first mission statement of the Jewish people, perhaps the first of any nation anywhere. The covenant they agreed to then became their written constitution as citizens in the republic of faith under the sovereignty of God.

It is the last phrase that is crucial here: "under the sovereignty of God." It is sometimes thought that the Ten Commandments were a moral revolution in humankind. This is not so in the sense usually understood. It did not take divine revelation to tell humans that they must not murder, or rob, or give false testimony in court. Humans have always known this. Cain was punished by God for killing his brother Abel, but God had not yet commanded, "Do not murder." Every rational moral rule has been binding on humans since they first appeared on earth, said Rabbeinu Nissim (*Derashot HaRan* 1). It is not here that the originality of Sinai lies.

It lies in something deeper. *The Torah is a sustained critique of the abuse of power.* It is a response to and a reaction against the world's first empires, those of Akkad under Sargon (c.2334 to 2279 BCE, see Gen. 10:8–10) and Egypt under the pharaohs, where whole populations could be enslaved to further the self-aggrandizing projects ordered by rulers to ensure their earthly and heavenly immortality.

In the ancient world, politics and religion were inseparably intertwined. The head of state was also head of the religion and regarded as semi-divine. Power was projected in the form of monumental buildings, ziggurats, pyramids, palaces, temples and royal tombs. Akkadian kings were identified with the god of their city-state. The pharaohs were regarded as deities in their lifetime and worshiped after their death. In Babylon, the king was the earthly equivalent of the god Marduk who had established order by his victory over Tiamat, the goddess of chaos. Among the Hittites, the king was High Priest and on his death joined the gods. Isaiah speaks caustically about an Assyrian ruler who imagines that "I will ascend to the heavens; I will raise my throne above the stars of God…. I will make myself like the Most High" (Is. 14:13–14).

What underwrote such cultures was cosmological myth. There was hierarchy in the heavens – the sun ruled the sky. There was hierarchy in the forest – the lion ruled the beasts. So there was hierarchy in society. Some were born to rule, others to be ruled. That alone is how order is sustained. The Torah is a protest against this entire view of the human condition, on two grounds: first, it turns some people into gods; second, it turns others, the majority, into slaves. The Torah's first and most decisive statement on the subject appears in its opening chapter when it says that God created human beings in His image and likeness (Gen. 1:26–27). All humans, not just rulers, carry within them the image of God, but no human is a god. At best, we – and everyone else – are in His image. There is and must be an absolute boundary between heaven and earth, God and humankind. That, above all, applies to power.

The idea that one human being should exercise power over others is a profound insult to the human condition. This was the sin of Nimrod, instigator of the Tower of Babel according to the Midrash. This is how John Milton describes him in *Paradise Lost*:

> O execrable son! so to aspire Above his brethren; to himself assuming Authority usurped, from God not given: He gave us only over beast, fish, fowl, Dominion absolute; that right we hold By his donation; but man over men He made not lord; such title to himself Reserving, human left from human free. (Book XII, lines 64–71)

No human has the right to rule over others against their will. That is what the judge and military hero Gideon meant when the people asked him to become their king. He replied, "I will not rule over you nor will my son rule over you. God will rule over you" (Judges 8:23).

That is what Sinai was about. What the people agreed to was that God alone would be their king, legislator, law-giver. This is the principle known in the rabbinic literature as *kabbalat ol malkhut shamayim*, "acceptance of the yoke of the kingship of heaven." According to the sages, it is what we are doing when we say the first paragraph of the Shema. It is an oath of allegiance to God: "Listen, Israel, the Lord is our God, the Lord alone." Or as we say in the prayer *Avinu Malkeinu*, "We have no king but You." The Israelites became "one nation under God."

This is the core meaning of the idea of *Torah min hashamayim*, "Torah from heaven." Later, under the impact of Second Temple sectarianism, then of Christianity and Islam, all of which challenged the Jewish understanding of Scripture, it came to mean much else besides, but its basic meaning is simply this: all law – Torah – comes from God. He is Israel's sole law-giver.

This is what Moses meant when he said: "See: I have taught you rules and laws as the Lord my God has commanded me.... What great nation has decrees and laws as perfect as all this Torah that I am setting before you today?" (Deut. 4:5–8). It is what the psalmist means when he says: "He has declared His word to Jacob, His statutes and laws to Israel. He has done this for no other nation; such laws they do not know" (Ps. 147:19–20). Other nations had their gods to whom they prayed, but only Israel had God, not a human being, as their head of state and sole legislative authority. Only when kingship is in heaven can there be equality of dignity on earth.

To be sure, in practical terms, this principle came under strain. For several centuries after their entry into the land, Israel was led, temporarily at times of war, by charismatic leaders known as judges, but the book of Judges ends on a negative note. The nation was sliding into social and moral decline. The people came to Samuel, asking him to appoint a king. Reluctantly and at God's bidding, he did so.

Monarchy gave rise to two radically different schools of thought within Judaism. Some saw it as an ideal, especially in the person of David, and later after the experience of exile, in the idea of the Messiah, a Davidic king who would restore Israel's glory and usher in an era of peace (Maimonides, *Laws of Kings* ch. 11). Others were deeply critical of it, precisely because in principle Israel should have no other king but God. In the midrashic work Deuteronomy Raba (5:8–11), as well as the medieval commentaries of Ibn Ezra, Rabbeinu Baḥya and Abrabanel, monarchy was seen as a concession to human weakness and the people's wish to be "like all the nations around" (Deut. 17:14). The book of

Samuel records God as saying, when the people first asked for a king, "It is Me they have rejected as their King" (I Sam. 8:7).

On either view, however, monarchy as portrayed in Tanakh was unique in the ancient world. First, *the king had no legislative power*. He could institute temporary measures in response to the needs of the time, but not make permanently binding law. Second, *the king had no special status in the religious sphere*. He was not even a priest, let alone chief intermediary with God. Henri Frankfort, in *Kingship and the Gods*, noted that "the relationship between the Hebrew monarch and his people was as nearly secular as possible in a society wherein religion is a living force." Michael Walzer noted that even in the biblical account of David, the almost-ideal king, "there is no hint of the conventional magnifications of monarchy: no mysteries of state, no divine descent, no royal magic, no healing touch." Third, *kings could be criticized*, by the prophets and by the biblical text itself. There is no parallel for any of this in the ancient world.

Israel was not the only ancient nation to have laws. They all did. Some became famous, for instance the Sumerian Code of Ur-Nammu and the Babylonian Code of Hammurabi. But these were edicts of the king. Justice was a common value in the ancient Near East, but the idea that this was the domain of the gods would have struck people as absurd. The gods were capricious, quarrelsome, and did not like human beings at all. As Shakespeare put it in *King Lear*, "Like flies to the wanton boys are we to the gods; they kill us for their sport."

In Judaism, law comes from God alone. *Torah min hashamayim*: law is made in heaven. Kings, priests, prophets and sages were empowered to interpret the law and in some cases make enactments to safeguard it, but not to make it or annul it. All earthly authority is subject to the law: this is the basic principle of human equality and the foundation of a free society.

That is what happened at Sinai. Accepting the covenant, the Jewish people became a nation under the direct sovereignty of God, with no other legislative authority. All law, to be valid, must be traceable back to Sinai and the voice of God. There was nothing like this before and – as we saw in the quotation from Rousseau – it survived all vicissitudes of Jewish history. At Sinai God gave the people the gift of law, and it became their constitution of liberty.

II. Social Covenant, Social Contract

At Sinai, a new kind of politics was born.

From Plato's *Republic* to modern times, political philosophy has focused on power and the state. Judaism has its own theory of the state, but it also has a *political theory of society*, something rare in the history of thought, and to this day a vision unsurpassed in its simplicity and humanity.

The theory of the state and the role of power is signaled in Deuteronomy and described in detail in the book of Samuel. It is about the appointment of a king. We saw in the previous section why Judaism is ambivalent about this. Ideally the Israelites should have no other king but God. Nonetheless, God tells Samuel not to refuse to appoint a king but rather to warn the people of the high price they will have to pay. Samuel does so. The king, he warns, will take their sons and daughters for his service, appropriate their property for his own use and much else besides. "When that day comes you will cry out for relief from the king you have chosen, and the Lord will not answer you in that day" (I Sam. 8:18). The people nonetheless insist: they still want a king. God grants permission, and Samuel duly anoints Saul. Israel becomes a monarchy. For the first time it has a unified, central government.

Commentators have long been puzzled by the biblical approach to monarchy. If it is disapproved of, why is there a command in the Torah to appoint a king (Deut. 17:14–15)? If it is approved of, why did God say that, in asking for a king, the people were rejecting Him (I Sam. 8:7)? And why does He tell Samuel to warn the people? A brilliantly simple answer, given by Rabbi Zvi Hirsch Chajes (1805–1855) in his *Torat Nevi'im*, is that Samuel was proposing what Hobbes and Rousseau called a *social contract*.

The idea behind it is this: Without a central power capable of enforcing the rule of law and the defense of the realm, a nation is at risk, internally of anarchy, externally of defeat by a foreign power. Under these circumstances, the people may seek a central power vested with the authority to achieve these ends. But this power can only be brought into being if the people are prepared to hand over certain of their rights of property and liberty so that the king can levy taxes and recruit an army. There is a transfer of rights and powers from the individual to the state. This carries with it the risk that the power thus created will become tyrannical and corrupt. That is the equation Samuel sets out. God gives the people the right to be governed this way, so long as they do so freely and in full knowledge of the price and risk. The Israelites agreed, as Hobbes thought rational individuals always would. Without a central government, which in those days meant a king, life and liberty would be difficult to defend.

It is no accident that this theory, the foundation of modern politics, made its first appearance in the Hebrew Bible – because it was there that the key ideas emerged of the sanctity of life, the dignity of the individual, the integrity of private property and the insistence on freedom as the basis of society. For the first time, no power of one person over another – even a king over his subjects – could be taken as part of the natural order. The biblical revolution was that *no* human hierarchies are self-justifying. Ideally a society should be comprised of free citizens, all equally under the sovereignty of God. All earthly power structures, therefore, are necessary evils. None is written into the fabric of the universe, and none is good in itself.

Yet what made the politics of the Hebrew Bible unique was not its theory of the *state* in the days of Samuel, but rather its conception of *society*, which came into existence centuries before, at Mount Sinai. The difference was fundamental. The state was created by a *social contract* among the people. The *eda*, the society, was created by a *social covenant* between the people and God. That is what God proposed and the people accepted at Sinai on the first Shavuot. It was an event unique in the religious history of humankind.

The *outward form* of the agreement was nothing new. Covenants or treaties were a familiar feature of the ancient Near East. Genesis records several such treaties. Abraham made one with Avimelekh, king of Gerar, at Be'er Sheva (Gen. 21:27–32). So did Isaac (Gen. 26:28–31). Jacob did so with Laban (Gen. 31:44–54). Besides, God had already made covenants with Noah (Gen. 9) and Abraham (Gen. 17).

What was new at Sinai has become clearer in the light of the discovery in the mid-twentieth century of engraved records of ancient Mesopotamian treaties, among them the "Stele of the Vultures" commemorating the victory of Eannatum, ruler of Lagash in southern

Mesopotamia, over the people of Umma, and that of Naram-Sin, king of Kish and Akkad, with the ruler of Elam. Both date from the third millennium BCE, that is to say, before the time of Abraham.

These treaties are of two kinds: between parties of roughly equal power ("parity treaties") and those between a strong one – what today we would call a superpower – and a weak one. These latter are known as "suzerainty treaties," *suzerain* meaning the dominant power in a particular region. The Sinai covenant between God and the Israelites was a suzerainty treaty. Three features, though, made it unique.

First is the fact that *one of the parties was God Himself.* This would have been unintelligible to Israel's neighbors, and remains extraordinary even today. The idea that God might bind Himself to human beings, linking their destiny to His, making them His ambassadors – His "witnesses" – to the world, is still radical and challenging.

Second, the other party to the covenant was not, as it invariably was in the ancient world, a king or ruler, but *the people as a whole.* Their collective participation was essential. It is a point the Torah repeatedly emphasizes: "*All the people* responded as one" (Ex. 19:8); "*All the people* responded with one voice" (24:3). In the Hebrew text, the phrase "the people" appears seventeen times in Exodus 19 (the covenant proposed), and five times in Exodus 24 (the covenant accepted). This is not democracy in the modern sense, but it is the basis of what Michael Walzer calls "Israel's almost-democracy," and it had lasting implications.

It meant that every Israelite, as party to the covenant, was co-responsible with the people as a whole for its being kept. From this flowed the rabbinic idea of *Kol Yisrael arevin zeh lazeh,* "All Jews are responsible for one another" (Rashi, Lev. 26:37 following *Shevuot* 39a), as well as the much later American idea of "We, the people." *It meant that the basis of social order in Judaism is not power but collective responsibility.* Power belongs to God. Responsibility belongs to us.

This meant that every Jew had to know the law and teach it to his or her children. Each had to know the story of his or her people, reciting it at key religious moments in the year. This is covenant politics, based not on hierarchical power but on a shared sense of history and destiny. It is a moral politics, dedicated to creating a just and gracious society honoring the dignity of all, especially the downtrodden, the poor, the powerless and the marginal: the widow, the orphan and the stranger.

The third key feature was God's insistence that Moses had first to secure the people's assent before the revelation could take place. This was essential, for the Bible portrays God not as an overwhelming force but as a constitutional monarch. The supreme power makes space for human freedom. *There is no justified government without the consent of the governed, even if the Governor is Creator of heaven and earth.* The people agree three times (Ex. 19:8; 24:3, 7). Thus the Judaic basis of a free society is not democracy as such. The rule of the majority can lead, as it has many times, to tyranny and the persecution of minorities. Freedom, in Judaism, is based on the consent of the governed and the overarching authority of God-given rules of justice. These establish the moral limits of power.

What happened at Sinai was a covenant, not a contract. Contracts are made between individuals on the basis of self-interest. A contract creates a limited partnership for mutual gain. A covenant creates a more enduring bond of mutual commitment and loyalty. Partners to a covenant have more than self-interest at stake. They have *shared* interests. A covenant relationship is one in which the parties come together, each respecting the freedom and dignity of the other, to create together something that neither could achieve alone – love, friendship, loyalty, communication, trust. Covenants create not personal gain but *the common good*, meaning things that only exist in virtue of being shared.

For the Bible, the key example of a covenant is marriage, understood as a *bond of identity* between husband and wife. A marriage is held together not by power or mutual advantage but by a moral bond of love and fidelity. Virtually all the prophets compare the bond between God and Israel to a marriage. The significance of Sinai is that, long before the Israelites had a state, they had a society, and they did so because they had a social covenant before they had a social contract. That is why, uniquely, Jews remained a nation even in exile and dispersion. Though they had lost their state, they still had their *eda*, their community of faith. Though they had lost the land, they still had the law.

III. The Ten Utterances

What the Israelites heard at Sinai has become known as the "Ten Commandments." But this description raises obvious problems. First, neither the Torah nor Jewish tradition calls them the Ten Commandments. The Torah calls them *aseret hadevarim* (Ex. 34:28), and tradition terms them *aseret hadibrot*, meaning "the ten utterances." Second, there was much debate, especially between Maimonides and Nahmanides, as to whether the first verse, "I am the Lord your God...," is a command or a preface to the commands. Third, there are not ten commandments in Judaism but 613. Why, then, these but not those?

Light has been shed on all these issues by the discovery, already mentioned, of ancient Near-Eastern suzerainty treaties, most of which share certain features and forms. They begin with a preamble stating who is initiating the covenant. That is why the revelation opened with the words, "I am the Lord your God." Then comes a historical review stating the background and context of the covenant, in this case, "who brought you out of the land of Egypt, from the slave-house."

Next come the stipulations, first in general outline, then in specific detail. That is precisely the relationship between the "ten utterances" and the detailed commands set out in later chapters and books of the Torah. The former are the general outline; the latter, the details. So the "ten utterances" are not commandments as such but an articulation of basic principles. What makes them special is that they are simple and easy to memorize. That is because in Judaism, law is not intended for judges alone. The covenant at Sinai was made by God with an entire people. Hence the need for a brief statement of basic principles that everyone could remember and recite.

Usually they are portrayed as two sets of five, the first dealing with relationships between us and God (including honoring our parents since they, like God, brought us into being), the second with the relations between us and our fellow humans. However, it also makes sense to see them as three groups of three.

The first three – no other gods besides Me, no sculptured images and no taking of God's name in vain – are about God, the Author and Authority of the laws. The first states that divine sovereignty transcends all other loyalties (No other gods besides Me). The second tells us that

God is a living force, not an abstract power (No sculptured images). The third states that sovereignty presupposes reverence (Do not take My name in vain).

The second three – the Sabbath, honoring parents and the prohibition of murder – are all about the principle of *the createdness of life*. Shabbat is the day dedicated to seeing God as Creator, and the universe as His creation. Honoring parents acknowledges our human createdness. "Do not murder" restates the central principle of the Noahide covenant that murder is not just a crime against man but a sin against God in whose image we are created. So the fourth, fifth and sixth commands form the basic jurisprudential principles of Jewish life. They tell us to remember where we came from if we seek to know how to live.

The third three – against adultery, theft and bearing false witness – establish the basic institutions on which society depends. Marriage is sacred because it is the human bond closest in approximation to the covenant between us and God. The prohibition against theft establishes the integrity of property, which John Locke saw as one of the bases of a free society. Tyrants abuse property rights. The prohibition of false testimony is the precondition of justice. A just society needs more than a structure of laws, courts and enforcement agencies. It also needs basic honesty on the part of us all. There is no freedom without justice, and no justice without each of us accepting individual and collective responsibility for truth-telling.

Finally comes the stand-alone prohibition against envying your neighbor's house, wife, slave, maid, ox, donkey or anything else belonging to him or her. This seems odd if we think of the "ten words" as commands, but not if we think of them as the basic principles of a free society.

The greatest challenge of any society is how to contain the universal phenomenon of envy: the desire to have what belongs to someone else. Rene Girard, in *Violence and the Sacred*, argued that the primary driver of human violence is mimetic desire, that is, the desire to have what someone else has, which is ultimately the desire to be what someone else is. Envy can lead to breaking many of the other commands: it can move people to adultery, theft, false testimony and even murder. It led Cain to murder Abel, made Abraham and Isaac fear for their lives because they were married to beautiful women, and led Joseph's brothers to hate him and sell him into slavery. It was envy of their neighbors that led the Israelites often to imitate their religious practices and worship their gods.

So the prohibition of envy is not odd at all. It is the most basic force undermining the social harmony and order that are the aim of the Ten Commandments as a whole. Not only though do they forbid it; they also help us rise above it. It is precisely the first three commands, reminding us of God's presence in history and our lives, and the second three, reminding us of our createdness, that help us rise above envy.

We are here because God wanted us to be. We have what God wanted us to have. Why then should we seek what others have? If what matters most in our lives is how we appear in the eyes of God, why should we seek anything else merely because someone else has it? It is when we *stop* defining ourselves in relation to God and start defining ourselves in relation to other people that competition, strife, covetousness and envy enter our minds, and they lead only to unhappiness.

Thirty-three centuries after they were first given, the Ten Commandments remain the simplest, shortest guide to the creation of a good society.

Ruth: The Book of Loyalty and Love

The story of Ruth is one of the most beautiful in the Bible. It begins in dislocation and grief. Famine leads Elimelekh, together with his wife Naomi and their two sons, to leave their home in Bethlehem, Judah, to go to Moab to find food. There, the sons marry Moabite women, but all three men die, leaving Naomi and her two daughters-in-law childless widows. Naomi decides to return home, and Ruth, who had married her son Mahlon, insists on going with her. There, in Bethlehem, in a field at harvest time, Ruth meets a relative of Naomi's, Boaz, who acts kindly toward her. Later at Naomi's suggestion, Ruth asks him to act the part of a kinsman-redeemer. Boaz does so, and he and Ruth marry and have a child. The book that begins with death ends in new life. It is a story about the power of human kindness to redeem life from tragedy, and its message is that out of suffering, if transformed by love, can come new life and hope.

The book itself is a literary masterpiece. It owes much of its vividness to the fact that of all books of the Hebrew Bible, it has the highest proportion of direct speech to descriptive narrative: fifty-five of its eighty-five verses are in dialogue form. Its four chapters are structured as a chiasmus, a mirror-image symmetry, so that, for example, the end with its account of births and genealogies mirrors the beginning with its recitation of deaths and childlessness. It is held together by a series of key words and recurring themes, among them "return," "redemption" and "blessing." Seven times people bless one another in the book, sustaining the sense that divine providence is at work beneath the surface of events. Not always but often, good things happen to good people, even if they take time.

The practice of reading a megilla on a festival began with the book of Esther on Purim, despite the fact that the book itself was one of the last to be canonized. The reason is that without it, there would be no festival. The book records the events the festival commemorates as well as explaining its basic practices. The talmudic tractate dealing with the day is called not *Purim* but *Megilla*. During the mishnaic and talmudic period, if you used the word "megilla," you meant the book of Esther. Also early was the custom of reading Lamentations on Tisha B'Av: the book of grief on the day of grief.

The custom of reading the Song of Songs on Pesaḥ, Ruth on Shavuot and Kohelet on Sukkot came later – first mentioned in the tractate of *Soferim* (14:16), dating to the seventh or eighth century. The commentators make two primary connections between Ruth and Shavuot. The first is seasonal. The key events in the book are set during the barley and wheat harvests, the time of the counting of the Omer and Shavuot itself. The second is substantive. Ruth became the paradigm case of a convert to Judaism, and to become a convert you have to enter the covenant of Sinai with its life of the commands: what the Israelites did when they accepted the Torah on the first Shavuot.

There is, though, a deeper dimension. Reading a megilla on the three pilgrimage festivals sets up a field of tensions and associations that function as a profound commentary on the festival itself. They add depth and drama to the day.

All three megillot read on the pilgrimage festivals are about love: the stages of love as we experience it in our growth from youth to maturity to old age. The Song of Songs, read on Pesaḥ, the festival of spring, is about love in the spring: the passion between two lovers that has nothing in it of yesterday or tomorrow but lives in the overwhelming intensity of today. The book is structured as a series of duets between beloved and lover, their voices freighted with desire. There is nothing in it about courtship, marriage, home-building and having children: the world of adult responsibilities. The lovers long simply to be together, to elope.

Kohelet read on Sukkot, the festival of autumn, is about love in the autumn of life, as the heat cools, light fades, the leaves fall, and clouds begin to hide the sun. "Live well, with the woman you love," says Kohelet (9:9). This is love as companionship, and it is rich in irony. Kohelet is written as the autobiography of King Solomon, the man who married seven hundred wives and three hundred concubines (I Kings 11:3), and in the end concluded, "And this is what I found: woman is more bitter than death, for she is all traps, with nets laid in her heart; her arms are a prison" (Eccl. 7:26). A thousand wives will not bring you happiness. Faithfulness to one will.

Ruth is about the love at the heart of Judaism, the love of summer, when the passion of youth has been tamed and the clouds of age do not yet cover the sky. Ruth is about love as loyalty, faithfulness, committing yourself to another in a bond of responsibility and grace. It is about caring for the other more than you care about yourself. It is about Ruth setting her own aspirations aside to care for her mother-in-law Naomi, bereaved as she is of her husband and two sons. It is what Boaz does for Ruth. The root *a-h-v,* "love," which appears eighteen times in the Song of Songs, appears in Ruth only once. By contrast, the words *ḥesed,* loving-kindness, and the verb *g-a-l,* "to redeem," do not appear at all in the Song of Songs, but figure in Ruth respectively three and twenty-four times.

The megillot are framing devices that force us into seeing the festivals themselves in a new light. When we read the Song of Songs on Pesaḥ it transforms our understanding of the Exodus from a political event, the liberation of slaves, into an elopement and honeymoon, which is precisely how the prophets portray it. The book reminds us of the Exodus as Jeremiah saw it when he said, "I remember of you the kindness of your youth, your love when you were a bride; how you walked after Me in the desert, through a land not sown" (Jer. 2:2).

Kohelet turns Sukkot into a philosophical reflection on the sukka as a symbol of mortality, the body as a temporary dwelling. It is the sobering story of how Solomon, wisest of men, sought to deny death by taking refuge in possessions, wives, servants and worldly wisdom, yet at every step he found himself face to face with the brevity and vulnerability of life: "the shallowest breath, it is all but breath" (1:2). Only at the end did he discover that joy is to be found in simple things: life itself, dignified by work and beautified by love.

Ruth likewise invites us to reframe Shavuot, seeing the making of the covenant at Sinai not simply as a religious or political act, but as an act of love – a mutual pledge between two parties, committing themselves to one another in a bond of responsibility, dedication and loyalty. The covenant at Sinai was a marriage between God and the children of Israel. That is how the prophets saw it.

Ezekiel does so using an image drawn from the book of Ruth itself. Ruth, at night, lying at Boaz's feet, asks him to spread his mantle over her (Ruth 3:9). That, says Ezekiel, is what God did for Israel: "Later I passed by, and when I looked at you and saw that you were old enough for love, I spread the corner of My garment over you and covered your nakedness. I gave you My solemn oath and entered into a covenant with you, declares the Sovereign Lord, and you became Mine" (Ezek. 16:8).

It fell to the prophet Hosea to retell the story of the covenant as an act of love and marriage in wondrous words that Jewish men say each weekday morning as they put on the strap of the tefillin:

> I will betroth you to Me forever; I will betroth you to Me in righteousness and justice, loving-kindness and compassion; I will betroth you to Me in faithfulness; and you shall know the Lord. (Hos. 2:21–22)

The covenant at Sinai was a bond of love whose closest analogue in Tanakh is the relationship between Boaz and Ruth.

One of the most sustained libels in religious history was Christianity's claim that Judaism was a religion not of love but of law; not of compassion but of justice; not of forgiveness but of retribution. The book of Ruth, read on Shavuot, is the refutation. Judaism is a religion of love, three loves: loving God with all our heart, our soul and our might (Deut. 6:5); loving our neighbor as ourselves (Lev. 19:18); and loving the stranger because we know what it feels like to be a stranger (Deut. 10:19).

Judaism is, from beginning to end, the story of a love: God's love for a small, powerless and much afflicted people, and a people's love – tempestuous at times to be sure – for God. That is the story of Ruth: love as faithfulness, loyalty and responsibility, and as a marriage that brings new life into the world. That is the love that was consecrated at Sinai on the first Shavuot of all.

I. The Personal and the Political

About two biblical books, the sages asked, why were they written? One is Ruth, about which Rabbi Zeira said: "This scroll contains no laws about impurity or purity, forbidden or permitted. Why then was it written? To show how great is the reward of those who perform acts of kindness" (Ruth Raba 2:14). The other is Genesis. Rashi begins his Commentary to the Torah with almost the same question. Why, if the Torah is a book of law, does it begin with creation and the early history of humankind? It should begin with the first law given to the Israelites, which does not appear until the twelfth chapter of Exodus.

Ruth and Genesis have much else in common. In both, "there was a famine in the land." What happened to Elimelekh in the beginning of Ruth, a famine that forced him to leave home, happens four times in Genesis: twice to Abraham, once to Isaac and once to Jacob. In both books, future marriage partners meet as strangers, apparently by chance, in a public place. What happened to Ruth and Boaz happens twice in Genesis, when Abraham's servant encounters Rebecca, and when Jacob meets Rachel.

One passage in particular drives the connection home. In their first encounter amid the alien corn, Boaz says to Ruth: "I have heard what you have done for your mother-in-law, since your husband died; *of how you left your father, your mother, the land of your birth* and came to a people you knew not the day before" (Ruth 2:11). The echo is unmistakable. We are immediately reminded of God's call to Abraham, the first recorded syllables of Jewish time: *"Leave your land, your birthplace and*

your father's house, and go to the land that I will show you" (Gen. 12:1).
Ruth is portrayed as a female equivalent of Abraham.

To be sure, there are differences. Abraham is responding to a call
from God, Ruth to a moral imperative. Yet both are leaving behind all
they know: their family, their friends, their country and culture, and
both have the courage to journey to a place where they will be seen as
strangers, outsiders, aliens. Both, too, are among the Bible's supreme
exemplars of *ḥesed,* love as kindness and as deed.

More substantively, both Genesis and Ruth are preludes, introduc-
tions to a new chapter in the history of Israel. The book of Ruth, in its opening and closing words, positions itself precisely within the biblical story. It
begins, "Once, in the days when the judges judged." It ends with the birth
of Oved, father of Yishai, father of David, Israel's second and greatest king.
The book is a connecting link between two distinct periods of Jewish history, the era of the judges and that of kings. It functions as a preface to the
first book of Samuel, which tells of how Israel's monarchy was born. There
is even a subtle verbal connection between the two. In the last chapter of
Ruth, the townspeople say to Naomi that her daughter-in-law "is better to
you than seven sons could be" (Ruth 4:15). In the first chapter of the book
of Samuel, Elkanah says to his wife Hannah, "Am I not better to you than
ten sons?" (I Sam. 1:8). The echo connects the two books.

Genesis, too, is a prelude, in this case to the story of Israel as a
people, its exile and enslavement and its liberation by the hand of God.
We can now state the connection between the two books. Genesis is a
prelude to the birth of Israel as a *nation.* Ruth is a prelude to the birth
of Israel as a *kingdom.* Together the two books make an immensely
consequential statement of *the primacy of the personal over the political.*

The Hebrew Bible is largely about politics: kings and their battles,
society and its tensions and the relationship between Israel and neighboring powers. However, Tanakh does not see politics as an end in itself.
In this it differs fundamentally from the civic culture of ancient Greece
and Rome. There, the polis was the embodiment of all that is best in
the people. Service to it was the highest calling.

Judaism, by contrast, is skeptical about politics. It knows all too
well the force of Lord Acton's dictum that power tends to corrupt, and
absolute power corrupts absolutely. It knows, too, the truth stated by

Oliver Goldsmith: "How small, of all that human hearts endure, / That part which laws or kings can cause or cure." Politics in Judaism is a concession to necessity, not an end in itself. In Judaism, people do not exist to serve the state. The state exists to serve the people, and the people exist to serve God.

What Genesis and Ruth tell us is: do not think you can change the world or the human condition by politics and power alone. What matters is about how human beings – ordinary human beings, not just kings, courtiers and commanders – behave toward one another. An empire can have the world's strongest army, yet if it lacks justice and compassion it will eventually crumble.

More important than politics is the way we treat our fellow humans in our day-to-day interactions – and the quality of those relationships will itself be the surest indicator of our relationship with God. *You cannot serve God while exploiting or oppressing your fellow humans.* That is the message of all the prophets, and it is the story of Abraham and Sarah, Ruth, Naomi and Boaz. Love of God and loving-kindness toward our fellows go hand in hand.

The book of Judges ends with the terrible story of a concubine assaulted, raped and killed in the town of Gibeah, a crime that shocks the nation and leads to civil war (Judges 19–21). The episode resembles nothing so much as the story of Sodom (Gen. 19), where the people of the town attempt sexually to assault Lot's two guests. The message could not be more clear: everything that had happened to the Israelites – the Exodus, the wilderness years, the conquest of the land, the miracles and deliverances – did not stop the people of the covenant from lapsing into the worst conduct of their neighbors.

There is no shortcut to freedom. Neither military victories nor divine deliverance can achieve it. Without virtue, politics fails. Without habits of law-abidingness on the part of the people, even God cannot or will not save a nation. A free society depends on the character and virtues of its citizens, their willingness to sacrifice for the sake of others and to take responsibility for the weak and vulnerable, the orphan, the widow and the stranger within the gates. Abraham takes responsibility for Lot. Ruth takes responsibility for Naomi. Boaz takes responsibility for Ruth. They are their brother's and sister's keepers. Society is prior to the state, the family is prior to both, and what sustains them all is *ḥesed*, the kindness that is the mark of human greatness and the sign of those who truly understand what God wants from us.

The simplicity and tenderness of the book of Ruth should not deceive us. Its message is blunt and basic. What would matter in the end about David, whose name is the last word of the book, would not be his military genius or his political vision but the quality of his personal morality. That is a complex story in its own right, but what reverberates across the centuries is the simple fact that Abraham, great-grandfather of the children of Israel, and Ruth, great-grandmother of their greatest king, ruled no nation, performed no miracles and held no formal office. It was their *ḥesed*, their loving-kindness, that ultimately transformed the world.

II. A Tale of Two Women

As the book of Ruth hastens to its conclusion, there is a surprise in store. Their child, Oved, turns out to be the grandfather of King David. However, to those with an attentive ear, there is a far greater surprise. When the townspeople congratulate Boaz and Ruth on their marriage, they say *"May your house be like that of Peretz, whom Tamar bore to Judah growing from the seed that the Lord will give you from this young woman"* (4:12).

What have Peretz and Tamar to do with Ruth? They have played no part in the narrative. Yet when David's genealogy is set out at the end of the book it begins with Peretz, Boaz's distant ancestor. It is then that the attentive reader goes back to reread the story of Tamar and makes a remarkable discovery. It has so many parallels to that of Ruth that the similarity cannot be accidental.

The story of Tamar is told in Genesis 38. In the previous chapter, Judah had persuaded his brothers to sell Joseph as a slave. He then leaves his brothers and marries a Canaanite woman with whom he has three sons, Er, Onan and Shelah. When Er grows up, Judah finds him a wife, Tamar. Tragedy strikes. Er dies. Judah – practicing a pre-Mosaic form of levirate marriage – tells his second son Onan that he must marry his brother's widow so that she can bear a child in memory of her dead husband. Onan resents the fact that the child would be regarded as his brother's, and he "spills his seed." For this he is punished, and he too dies.

Judah tells Tamar that she must "live like a widow" until Shelah is old enough to marry her. But he delays, fearing that his third son too may die. This places Tamar in a situation of living widowhood, unable to marry anyone else because she is bound to her remaining brother-in-law, unable to marry him because of Judah's fear.

Taking destiny into her own hands, she seizes the opportunity when she hears Judah is on his way to Timnah to shear his sheep. Covering her face with a veil, she dresses as a prostitute and positions herself on the route she knows her father-in-law will take. Judah approaches her and sleeps with her. She returns home and removes the disguise. She becomes pregnant. Three months later, her condition is apparent. People tell Judah, who is indignant. She must, he reasons, be guilty of adultery since she is bound to Shelah, whom Judah has kept from her. He orders: "Bring her out and have her burned."

Tamar, however, had prepared for this eventuality. During her deception, she had insisted on a pledge against payment: Judah's seal, cord and staff. By the time Judah sent a messenger to pay her and reclaim the pledge, she had disappeared. Now she produces the items and sends them to Judah with the words, "I am pregnant by the man who owns these." It is a masterly stroke. She has established her innocence without shaming Judah. Judah admits his error. He says, "She is more righteous than me." Eventually she gives birth to twins whom she names Peretz and Zeraḥ.

The stories of Tamar and Ruth are very different. But they have a number of striking similarities.

In both cases the story begins with a "going down," the separation of a key character – Judah in Genesis, Elimelekh in Ruth – from the rest of his family or people.

In both cases the journey is a questionable one. Judah lives among the Canaanites and marries a local woman, despite the fact that Abraham had told his servant to ensure that Isaac, Judah's grandfather, did not do so: "I want you to swear by the Lord, the God of heaven and the God of earth, that you will not get a wife for my son from the daughters of the Canaanites, among whom I am living" (Gen. 24:3). Elimelekh goes to Moab, where his children marry local women despite the apparent biblical prohibition: "No Ammonite or Moabite or any of their descendants may enter the assembly of the Lord, not even in the tenth generation.... Do not seek a treaty of friendship with them as long as you live" (Deut. 23:3, 6).

In both stories two sons die: Er and Onan in the case of Judah; Maḥlon and Kilyon in that of Elimelekh. In each case their names prefigure their fate. Er means "childless," Onan signifies "mourning," Maḥlon means "sickness" and Kilyon "destruction."

Tamar and Ruth are both childless widows. Both are concerned to have a child out of a sense of duty to "to raise the name of the dead."

In both cases there are clear obstacles to their doing so. Judah refuses to allow Tamar to marry his third son, Shelah, the natural candidate for levirate marriage (the marriage of a childless widow to her brother-in-law). Naomi tells Ruth there is no chance she will have another child; therefore, she has no chance of marrying within the family.

In both cases, it is the women themselves who take the initiative in ensuring that nonetheless a child will be born, and that the father will be someone from their husband's family.

In both cases they do so by a daring act open to misinterpretation. Tamar dresses as a prostitute and positions herself to be seen by Judah. Ruth goes at night to Boaz, uncovers his cloak and sleeps at his feet. In both cases, care is taken so that the men concerned will not be exposed to shame. Tamar, by taking a pledge from Judah, is able to convince him he is the father of her child without anyone else becoming aware of the fact. Ruth takes care not to be seen going to or from Boaz at night.

In both cases, a non-normative form of levirate marriage is involved. Neither Judah nor Boaz is a brother-in-law. In both cases there is a closer relative to whom the duty applies: Shelah and the anonymous "Such-and-such." Both times, it is the woman who shows the deepest loyalty to her late husband's family and name – more so than Judah or Naomi's anonymous relative.

The family tree lists ten generations from Peretz to the birth of David. A ten-generation genealogy is a highly charged phenomenon in the Bible. There are ten generations from Adam to Noah, and ten from Noah to Abraham. The ten generations from Peretz to David carry the same sense of preordained destiny. The beginning of such a family tree is significant. So too is the seventh, the number associated with holiness. *David's family tree begins with Peretz, the son born to Judah and Tamar. The seventh generation is Oved, the son born to Ruth and Boaz.* The key progenitors of Israel's great and future king are Tamar and Ruth. Theirs are in fact the only stories told in any detail about David's female forebears.

This is astonishing. The heroes in David's background are two women who stand at the very edge of Israelite society. In the biblical era there were no more vulnerable individuals than childless widows. But Tamar and Ruth were in a far worse situation still. They came from groups traditionally despised by the Israelites: the Canaanites and the Moabites. They had no natural place in the society in which they found themselves. *It was these two women, Tamar and Ruth, whose loyalty and steadfastness were the key factors in giving birth eventually to King David,* the man who became king of Israel, united the nation, initiated the plans for building the Temple and wrote some of the finest poetry in the religious history of humankind.

This is worthy of serious reflection. Otto Rank, in his classic *The Myth of the Birth of the Hero*, points out that there are common elements in the stories told about the heroes of myth. Though raised by lowly adoptive parents, they are of noble birth. They have royal blood or are descended from the gods. The story of David turns this convention on its head. David has the kind of family background most people would seek to hide.

It is exceptionally moving that the Bible should cast in these heroic roles two figures at the extreme margins of Israelite society: women, childless widows, outsiders, aliens. Tamar and Ruth, powerless except for their moral courage, wrote their names into Jewish history as role models who gave birth to royalty – to remind us, in case we ever forget, that true royalty lies in love and faithfulness, and that greatness often exists where we expect it least.

III. Healing an Ancient Wound

The word *tikkun*, as in *tikkun olam*, "mending the world," and *tikkun leil Shavuot*, the custom of staying up and studying Torah all night on the first night of the festival, has a curious history. In mishnaic Hebrew, that is, until the third century, it meant no more than social order, the rules that made society a safe and predictable place (see *Gittin*, ch. 4 and 5). In Jewish mysticism it came to mean something more metaphysical: mending the fractures in the universe that made life on earth so full of suffering and injustice, chief symbol of which was the Jewish condition in exile.

According to Rabbi Isaac Luria, the great mystic of the sixteenth century, this had to do with the fact that something had gone wrong with creation itself. The divine light of the first day of creation had proved too intense for the physical vehicles meant to contain it. The vessels had shattered, leaving debris and fragments of light scattered everywhere. Ours, said the mystics, is a broken world, and the fractures are so deep that they affect the Divine Being Itself. Exile is not just a human phenomenon. It represents a rift between God as He is in Himself – the Infinite, the *Ein Sof*, the Without-End – and the *Shekhina*, the Divine Presence, God as He is among us. When Jews went into exile, the *Shekhina* went with them. So we, by our mystical endeavors, have to help heal the fractures in the Divine. Every religious act, if done with sufficient intensity of mind and soul, does something to reunite *Kudsha Berikh Hu*, the Holy One, blessed be He, and *Shekhintei*, His immanent Presence.

There is, though, a third sense of *tikkun* that is not mystical at all but makes powerful sense in terms of the Jewish vision of the world. Bad things happen between people. The innocent are harmed. There is envy, jealousy, anger, resentment. There is injustice, oppression, exploitation. The human world is full of tears. If you believe, as polytheists did in the ancient world and some atheists do today, that life is essentially conflict, a Darwinian struggle to survive, then there is nothing odd about a world full of pain. That is how it is. There is no right; only might. Justice is whatever serves the interests of the strong. History is written by the victors. The victims are mere collateral damage of the fight to impose our will on the world or, in the language of the neo-Darwinians, to hand on our genes to the next generation.

That, though, is not how Jews understand it. The natural condition of the world is harmony, like a well-ordered garden or a loving family or a gracious society. That is how it was in the beginning when God made the universe and saw that it was good. God, though, gave humans freedom, and humans often use that freedom to disobey Him. God created order. We create chaos. That is, or would be, the human tragedy if Jews believed in tragedy. But we do not. We believe in hope, and hope has the power to defeat tragedy – as we have the power to mend what we or others have broken.

That is the philosophy that lies behind the central Jewish idea of *teshuva*, meaning "repentance" or "return." Through *teshuva*, we can heal some of the pain we or others have created. Though the concept of *teshuva* does not figure explicitly in the stories of Genesis, it is there nonetheless beneath the surface. Broken relationships are mended. Ishmael, Abraham's child by the slave-woman Hagar, was sent away when he was young, yet we see him standing together with his half-brother Isaac at Abraham's grave. Jacob and Esau, divided by Jacob's act of taking Esau's blessing, meet twenty-two years later and embrace with no evident trace of lingering resentment. Joseph forgives his brothers who sold him into slavery. Genesis ends on a note of reconciliation. There are wounds that can be healed.

Neither Tanakh nor the rabbis, nor even the mystics, called this *tikkun*, but that is what it is: the intensely human ability to repair damaged relationships and restore order to the social world. But what if the moment passes? What if those who did the damage and those who suffered it are no longer alive? Can what we do in the present mend something broken long ago, before our time? That is one of the subtexts of the book of Ruth, and it applies to two people: Ruth herself, and Boaz.

First, Ruth. She was, we are told no fewer than five times, a Moabite. This raises a powerful question not touched on in the book itself. The Torah explicitly states that "a Moabite shall not come into the congregation of the Lord even to the tenth generation" (Deut. 23:4). The rabbis solved this problem simply and ingeniously. The Hebrew for Moabite, *Moavi*, is masculine, not feminine. So the prohibition applies to men but not women (*Yevamot* 76b–77a). This, they said, was one of the rulings given "in the days when the judges judged."

There was a reason for this. The Torah explains the original prohibition by saying, "They did not come to meet you with bread and water on your way when you came out of Egypt, and they hired Balaam son of Beor from Pethor in Aram Naharaim to pronounce a curse on you" (Deut. 23:45). The Moabites, the Torah implies, had a natural hostility to the Israelites. They were mean-spirited and worse: they had paid the pagan prophet Balaam to put a curse on them.

Why so? The Torah itself tells a story about this, early in the history of Abraham's family. Leaving his land, birthplace and father's house, Abraham took his nephew Lot with him. In Genesis 13, the first recorded argument within the family, we see the shepherds of Abraham and Lot arguing. They had returned from Egypt rich in sheep and cattle, and there were too many to be grazed in the same area. Abraham suggested to Lot that, rather than quarrel, they should separate, and he offers Lot the choice of where to go.

Lot, seeing the affluence of the Jordan valley, "like the garden of the Lord" (v. 10), chooses to settle there in the town of Sodom. Immediately, though, the Torah adds a warning note. The people of Sodom are "wicked and sinning greatly against the Lord" (v. 13). Soon, Lot's life was in danger. Four neighboring kings attacked Sodom, taking many captives, including Lot. Abraham gathered a force, pursued the invading army, rescued the hostages and returned Lot to his home (Gen. 14).

Five chapters later, two strangers come to visit Lot. They are in fact angels sent to warn him that the town was about to be destroyed. That night all the inhabitants of the town crowd round Lot's house, demanding that he bring out the visitors so that they can be assaulted. Lot refuses but does something even worse: offers them his daughters. The angels intervene. Smiting the townspeople with temporary blindness, they urge Lot to leave. Lot reports this to his sons-in-law, who treat his remarks like a joke. The angels then force Lot, his wife and daughters to leave and the area is almost immediately destroyed. Against the angels' instructions, Lot's wife looks back and is turned into a pillar of salt, leaving Lot and his two daughters as the sole survivors.

Sheltering in a cave among the mountains, Lot's daughters, suspecting there is no one in the region left alive, decide to get their father drunk and sleep with him. They do so, they become pregnant, and eventually give birth. The elder calls her son Moab ("from father"). That is the Torah's account of the origin of the Moabites. They are the outcome of an incestuous relationship, and they have acquired the characteristics of the people of Sodom. They are hostile to strangers, sexually amoral and the result of a division within the Abrahamic family – Lot's decision to live among the people of the cities of the plain.

Turning now to the story of Ruth, we see certain similarities between it and that of Lot. In both cases there is a man and two women. There is anxiety as to whether there will be a next generation. In both cases it is the women rather than the man who take the initiative, and in both, the man has been drinking. In both, there is an encounter in the dark, at night, and in both a child is born.

The differences, though, are immense. Sodom is a place of hostility to strangers. Ruth's is a story of kindness to strangers. Lot separated from Abraham; Ruth refused to be separated from Naomi. Lot's daughters are licentious. Ruth, alone with Boaz, is chaste. Sodom is a symbol of the absence of *ḥesed*; Ruth is a symbol of its presence.

Ruth, in her life and by her example, performs a *tikkun*. Though there is no element of *teshuva* involved, the verb *shuv*, in the sense of "return," appears thirteen times in the book. Something has been healed. By her conduct and character, she shows that not all Moabites lack kindness. They, too, ultimately come from the same family, that of Teraḥ, as Abraham himself. Ruth has redeemed something of the past. Reuniting two long-separated branches of the family, her great-grandson became the person who united the nation. That is *tikkun*. By our acts in the present we can heal some of the wounds in the past.

IV. Boaz and Judah
There is another *tikkun* in the book of Ruth.

There can be no doubt as to why the book was written and included in Tanakh. It ends with the birth of David and a genealogy tracing his descent. Heavily emphasized throughout is its setting in Bethlehem, Judah. Despite the prominence of Joseph in the book of

Genesis, and the tribe of Levi – in the form of Moses, Aaron and Miriam – in the rest of the Pentateuch, the kings of Israel descended not from them but from Jacob's fourth son, Judah.

Yet Genesis raises real doubts about Judah's character. Like Elimelekh at the beginning of Ruth, Judah left his brothers, in his case to live among the Canaanites. He married a Canaanite woman. He later used the services of what he took to be a prostitute. He was willing to have his daughter-in-law sentenced to death for a sin she had not committed. Most fundamentally, however, it was Judah who was responsible for selling Joseph into slavery in Egypt. The brothers initially proposed killing him. Reuben, planning later to rescue Joseph, suggested that they threw him in a pit and left him to die. But it was Judah who said the chilling words:

> "*What will we gain* if we kill our brother and cover up his blood? Come, let's sell him to the Ishmaelites and not lay our hands on him; *after all, he is our brother, our own flesh and blood.*" (Gen. 37:26–27)

Note, first, that he did not say, "It is wrong to kill our brother." He said, "What will we gain?" if we kill him. This is the language not of principle but pragmatism. Second, he proposed selling Joseph as a slave at the very moment he recognized that "he is our brother, our own flesh and blood." It is as if Judah were echoing Cain when he said, "Am I my brother's keeper?"

To be sure, after his encounter with a righteous woman, Tamar, Judah appears as a changed character. He became, de facto, the leader of the remaining brothers. He was their spokesman in their last great dialogue with the viceroy of Egypt. Faced with the opportunity to repeat the earlier sin, by leaving his brother Benjamin as a slave, he showed that he had changed. He offered himself as a slave, so that Benjamin could go free.

He had repented, but in highly unusual circumstances. Unbeknown to the brothers, the viceroy was in fact Joseph himself, who had been putting them through a series of trials to see if they acknowledged their guilt and had changed. Was this sufficient to establish that the descendants of Judah would not also share his moral weaknesses, above all his failure to act as his brother's guardian, surely the first requirement of a leader?

One of the powerful techniques of biblical literature is its inter-textuality, its use of literary devices to connect one passage with another. This prompts the listener or reader to ask, "Now where have I heard those words before?" We make connections between one text and another, and slowly begin to realize that they are part of a single story, that the later passage is a commentary on the earlier one. There is a dramatic instance in the book of Ruth.

It happens at the first encounter between Ruth and Boaz. Ruth has gone to gather grain in a field belonging to one of Naomi's relatives. We know this because the text tells us so, but Ruth, at this point, does not. He is simply a local landowner, clearly a man of substance but not someone she knows. Boaz, seeing her, asks the overseer of the field who she is, and he tells him that she is a Moabite who came with Naomi. Boaz then goes to speak to her, showing her great kindness and sensitivity. She is profoundly moved, prostrates herself "low, to the ground," and says: "Why is it that I have found favor in your eyes, that you give me recognition [*hakireini*] such as this, when I am a stranger [*nokhriya*]?" (2:10).

What makes this a most unusual sentence is a detail lost in transla-tion. There is a very rare linguistic phenomenon known as a contro-nym, a word with two meanings that are diametrically opposed. One example in English is "cleave," which means both to split apart and to cling together. Another is "sanction," which means to permit, and the opposite, to forbid and punish. The Hebrew verb *n-kh-r* in some forms means "to recognize," and in others, the opposite, "to be, or act as, a stranger," that is, someone *not* recognized. The appearance in a single sentence of the word in both meanings is arresting and very rare.

There is only one other place in Tanakh where it occurs: when Jacob's sons go to Egypt to buy food during a famine. They come before the viceroy, who is, unknown to them, their brother Joseph:

> When Joseph saw his brothers, he recognized them [*vaya-kirem*], but he pretended to be a stranger [*vayitnaker*] and spoke harshly to them. "Where do you come from?" he asked.

"From the land of Canaan," they replied, "to buy food." Joseph recognized [*vayaker*] his brothers; they did not recognize him [*hikiruhu*]. (Gen. 42:7–8)

To "recognize," in biblical Hebrew, is a complex idea. It is cognitive: "I recognize you" means "I know who you are." But it means something legal and moral also. It says there is kinship between us. We are part, literally or metaphorically, of the same family. I have special duties toward you that I do not have toward everyone. The Torah states, "Do not recognize faces in judgment" (Deut. 1:17). This means, do not let kinship distort the course of justice. From the negative we can infer the positive, that when it comes not to justice but compassion, then to "recognize a face" means to show the kind of care that family members should have to one another. That is why Ruth asks, "Why have I found favor in your eyes that you recognize me?" meaning, why have you shown me such special treatment?

When she goes on to say, "I am a foreigner," the word she uses, *nokhriya*, is far stronger than the usual biblical word for stranger, *ger*. A *ger* in biblical times was a temporary resident without citizenship rights. *Nokhri*, by contrast, means "an alien, an outsider," someone who does not belong here and would normally be viewed with suspicion and hostility. When Ruth calls herself a *nokhriya*, she is referring to the fact that she is a Moabite, fully aware of the historic tensions between her people and Naomi's.

Returning to Joseph, we see that in its description of the brothers' first encounter in Egypt, the Torah is hinting at something larger than the meeting itself. When Judah said, years earlier, "Let's sell him... after all, he is our brother, our own flesh and blood," he was committing a kind of contronym of the mind. He knew Joseph was his brother, but he treated him like an alien, someone with no claim to his care. What Joseph proceeds to do over the next few chapters is to force the brothers to experience what he himself suffered, to see if this role reversal will get them to understand what they had done wrong. He acts as if they are strangers, for that is how they – specifically Judah – acted toward him.

What we see in Ruth's first encounter with Boaz – the seventh-generation descendant of Judah – is a precise reversal of that earlier scene. She really is an alien, a foreigner, a Moabite, a *nokhriya*. Yet he extends to her the kindness he would show to a member of his own family: he "recognizes" her. He also immediately explains why. He has heard of what she has done for his relative, Naomi. It would be perfectly understandable if he refused to treat her as a member of the family. She came, after all, from a nation distrusted by Israelites as immoral, cruel and hostile. But he immediately treats her as a full and respected member of the family.

The intertextual resonance of the verb *n-kh-r* in its two opposite senses tells us that a larger drama is being played out here. Boaz is repairing, redeeming, performing a *tikkun* toward Judah's past. Judah treated his brother as a stranger. Boaz treats a stranger like a member of the family. That is the *tikkun* that had to take place before a descendant of Judah, David, could become a king of Israel.

V. Ruth and the De-Ethnicization of Judaism

Something happened at Sinai that fundamentally changed the terms of Jewish existence. Until then, God's covenant with Abraham had been with his biological descendants. The Abrahamic family was a kinship group, a clan, a tribe. You were born into it. You could not enter it from the outside. To be sure, not every descendant of Abraham was part of it. Isaac was chosen but not Ishmael, Jacob but not Esau. But with Jacob, this ended. All of his children became tribes within the larger family of Israel. The covenant was closed to outsiders.

Hence the concern Abraham and Isaac showed that their children marry within the family. Abraham, sending his servant to find a wife for his son, made him swear that he would not take anyone from among the Canaanites but would go instead "to my country and my own family" (Gen. 24:3–4). When Esau married two Hittite women, it was "a source of grief" to Isaac and Rebecca (Gen. 26:34–35).

Yet as the story unfolds, this principle comes under ever-greater strain. Judah married a Canaanite woman. Joseph married the daughter of an Egyptian priest. Moses married the daughter of a priest of Midian. Each of these women, on marriage, surely adopted the religion of her husband, but there was as yet no formal conversion procedure, nor could there be. The covenant was a family heritage you were born into, not a set of commitments you could choose to adopt.

That changed with the Giving of the Torah. Judaism now had a set of commands that defined it as a way of life. In principle, conversion became possible. In some sense, what the Israelites themselves underwent at the time was a kind of conversion (*Yevamot* 46b; *Keritot* 9a). The men were circumcised in Egypt (Josh. 5:5). The people purified themselves before the revelation (Ex. 19:10). At the revelation itself, the people said, "All that the Lord has spoken, we shall perform" (ibid. 8) – essentially the same act that constitutes conversion itself: *kabbalat hamitzvot*, "acceptance of the commandments." Israelite identity became a matter of *assent*, not just *descent*.

There are several instances in Tanakh of outsiders aligning themselves with the fate of Israel, Rahab in the book of Joshua (ch. 2) for example, or Yael in the book of Judges (ch. 4). There is, though, only one episode that resembles a conversion: Ruth's declaration to Naomi, "Wherever you walk, I shall walk; wherever you lie down, there shall I lie. Your people is my people; your God is my God." This subsequently became the model on which conversion was based (*Yevamot* 47a–b). Note that it has two elements: joining both a covenant of fate ("your people is my people") and a covenant of faith ("your God is my God").

This possibility of joining the Jewish people through an act of choice, the voluntary acceptance of religious responsibilities, turned Judaism from an ethnicity into something broader and more open, all the more so in light of the fact that the person who became the role model for conversion came from Moab, the group whose ethnicity was among the most problematic to the Israelites.

The story of Ruth de-ethnicizes Judaism, as did the covenant at Sinai. Being Jewish ceased to be a race and became a responsibility. This has a bearing on one of the great questions of Judaism: Did God choose the Jewish people because they were special, or did they become special because God chose them? Is Jewish distinctiveness a cause or consequence of election? Are Jews intrinsically, ethnically, spiritually different, or is it living the life of the commandments that makes them so? Is Jewishness a genetic endowment, as it were, or an acquired characteristic?

There is a line of thought in Judaism that suggests that Jews are indeed different: that something special has been passed on to them by the patriarchs and matriarchs and more than a hundred generations of ancestors who kept the faith through all the hardships. We find this in some passages of the Talmud and Midrash, the *Zohar* and the writings of Judah HaLevi and Maharal (Rabbi Judah Loewe) of Prague. The difficulty in this view is how to understand the act of conversion itself. How can someone not ethnically Jewish become so?

Against this stands the view of Maimonides, for whom there is no ontological difference between Jews and gentiles. All humans are in the image of God. All are capable of moral and intellectual greatness. If Jews are close to God it is because of their performance of the commands and the study of Torah. The one refines our character, the other elevates our mind.

Nowhere does Maimonides make the point more emphatically than at the end of his *Laws of the Sabbatical Year and the Jubilee*. There he explains that the tribe of Levi had no share in the land because they were set apart to serve God and minister to Him. He then adds:

> Not only the tribe of Levi but *every single individual from among the inhabitants of the world* whose spirit moves him and whose intelligence gives him the understanding to withdraw from the world in order to stand before God to serve and minister to Him ... such an individual is consecrated to the Holy of Holies and his portion and inheritance shall be in the Lord forever and ever more. The Lord will grant him in this world whatever is sufficient for him, the same as He had granted to the priests and the Levites. (*Laws of the Sabbatical Year and the Jubilee* 13:13)

This is an extraordinary passage, set right at the center of Maimonides' law code, the *Mishneh Torah* (it is the last law of the seventh of fourteen books), which also begins and ends on a universalistic note.

Maimonides' attitude is made even more clear in his letter to Ovadia, a convert to Judaism who had written to him in some distress, apparently having been told by a rabbi that he could not say words in prayer such as "Our God *and the God of our fathers*," since in his case his father was a gentile. Maimonides had no hesitation in telling him that he may say these words and all others, exactly like a born Jew. Abraham, he writes, is not only the biological "father" of the Jewish people, but also and equally the spiritual father of all who convert to Judaism. There is, says Maimonides, no difference between you and us. What is more, he says, in Egypt, "our fathers were mostly idolaters; they had mingled with the pagans in Egypt and imitated their way of life." Therefore, "you should not consider your origin as inferior" to ours. We are both, born Jew and convert alike, descended from those who did not worship the true God. We have all been brought under the wings of the Divine Presence.

He ends the letter on a beautiful note. He quotes a line from Isaiah in which the prophet says that a day will come when "I will pour out My spirit on your offspring, and My blessing on your descendants." At that time:

> Some will say, "I belong to the Lord"; others will call themselves by the name of Jacob; still others will write on their hand, "The Lord's," and will take the name Israel. (Is. 44:5)

The phrase, "Some will say, 'I belong to the Lord,'" says Maimonides, refers to converts, while "others will call themselves by the name of Jacob" refers to born Jews.[5] "Do not let your ancestry be a small thing in your eyes," he concludes, "for we are descendants of Abraham, Isaac and Jacob while you derive from Him by whose word the world was created."

Ruth stands as the eternal model of one who made the journey to join the people of the covenant. In her merit, Israel was blessed by King David and the book of Psalms, as it will be, one day, by the Messiah and a world at peace.

Shavuot Today

On the face of it, Shavuot is a brief festival with few distinctive practices and, at least as far as the Torah is concerned, no specific historical content. This chapter has argued otherwise. Shavuot is the festival of

---

5. *Letters of Maimonides*, ed. Yitzhak Sheilat [Hebrew and Arabic], vol. 1 (Maale Adumim: Maaliyot, 1988), 231–35.

Jewish identity, and the controversies to which it gave rise through the ages are evidence of how variously at different times that identity was conceived. The sociologist Peter Berger once defined modernity as a condition of permanent identity crisis. For Jews that is not the mark of modernity: it is our recurring, perennial fate.

For Judaism is not just a set of beliefs and practices. It is also a field of tensions: between the universal and particular, exile and home, priest and prophet, halakha and Aggada, rationalism and mysticism, tradition and revolution, acceptance and protest, the walls of the house of study and the stalls of the marketplace. Its greatness is that, by and large, it has kept these tensions in play. That is what has given it gifts of survival and creativity unmatched by any other religious tradition in the West.

Shavuot is defined by those tensions. One, as we saw, was that between law and land. Judaism is supremely a religion of the land – the whole of Torah from Abraham to the death of Moses is a journey toward it – and Shavuot was the supreme festival of the land. There were agricultural elements on Pesaḥ and Sukkot also, but Shavuot was the time of the grain harvest and of bringing first fruits to the Temple and declaring: "My father was a wandering Aramean.... And the Lord brought us out of Egypt.... He brought us to this place and gave us this land, a land flowing with milk and honey."

If Pesaḥ commemorated the beginning of the journey from Egypt, and Sukkot the forty years of the journey, then – so this chapter has argued – Shavuot celebrated its culmination: the entry into the land itself. On it people recalled not "the bread of oppression our ancestors ate in Egypt," nor the miraculous "bread from heaven" they ate in the desert, but bread made from the grain of the Holy Land itself.

To be sure, it had also from the outset been the festival of the Giving of the Law, seen as the culmination of the seven-week journey that began with Pesaḥ. But every nation had laws, and for much of the biblical era, other issues, political, military and cultural, held center stage. The prophets tirelessly argued that without faithfulness to God and justice and compassion to their fellow humans, Israel would eventually suffer a momentous defeat, but all too few were listening, and the reforms of kings like Hezekiah and Josiah proved too little too late.

Only with the experience of the Babylonian exile did people come to see that the law of Israel was unlike that of any other nation – not just because of its content but because of who gave it, when and where. It was given not at Mount Zion in Jerusalem but at Mount Sinai in the desert. The law came before the land. Therefore, though they had lost the land, they still had the law. Though they had lost the country, they still had the covenant. The law of Israel was *not* like the law of every other nation – the decree of kings or the edict of a legislative assembly. It came from God Himself, the Infinite Eternal. Therefore it could never be lost or nullified.

That was when the full significance of Shavuot began to come clear. The real miracle was not the land but the law that preceded the land. Ezra and Nehemiah understood this after the Babylonian exile, as did Rabban Yoḥanan ben Zakkai in the midst of the rebellion against Rome. Without them it is highly doubtful whether Jews or Judaism would have survived.

As we have seen, Shavuot embodies other tensions as well: between covenant and contract, society and state, and the question of whether Judaism is primarily about politics and power or about morality, civil society and the ties that bind us to one another in a community of fate and faith. It is about Ruth and Boaz and the power of *ḥesed* to defeat tragedy and create hope. Not accidentally also, the book of Ruth ends with the birth of David, who made Jerusalem the capital of Israel. Shavuot thus brings together the two mountains that frame Jewish destiny: Mount Sinai in the desert where the Israelites made their covenant with God and Mount Zion in Jerusalem where they worshiped Him in sacrifice and song.

For the better part of two thousand years Jews lost their land, and once again – as it was for the exiles in Babylon – it was Torah that sustained the people as a people, giving them the assurance that one day they would return. So Shavuot has been reborn in our time – first among the early kibbutzim as a festival of the land, and more recently as the festival of the *tikkun*, the all-night study session that today embraces Jews of all shades of belief and practice, constituting them again as the people of the Book in the land of the Book, hearing again the *kol gadol velo yasaf*, the great sound of Sinai that pierced the desert silence once and continues to reverberate for all time.

To see the crowds converging on the Kotel from all parts of Jerusalem just before dawn, having studied all night and ready now to say *Shema Yisrael* together, as the first rays of the rising sun light the sky with red and gold, is to see one of the miracles of human faith and endurance, and to know how deeply we owe thanks to God who "gave us the Torah of truth, planting everlasting life in our midst."

For in truth this always was our greatest gift: the Torah, our constitution of liberty under the sovereignty of God, our marriage contract with Heaven itself, written in letters of black fire on white fire, joining the infinity of God and the finitude of humankind in an unbreakable bond of law and love, the scroll Jews carried wherever they went, and that carried them. This is the Torah: the voice of heaven as it is heard on earth, the word that lights the world.

About the Author

An international religious leader, philosopher, award-winning author, and respected moral voice, Rabbi Lord Jonathan Sacks (1948–2020) was the laureate of the 2016 Templeton Prize in recognition of his "exceptional contributions to affirming life's spiritual dimension." Described by HRH The Prince of Wales as "a light unto this nation" and by former British Prime Minister Tony Blair as "an intellectual giant," Rabbi Sacks was a frequent and sought-after contributor to radio, television, and the press, both in Britain and around the world.

He served as chief rabbi of the United Hebrew Congregations of the Commonwealth for twenty-two years, between 1991 and 2013. He held seventeen honorary degrees, including a Doctor of Divinity conferred to mark his first ten years in office as chief rabbi, by the then-archbishop of Canterbury, Lord Carey.

In recognition of his work, Rabbi Sacks won several international awards, including the Jerusalem Prize in 1995 for his contribution to Diaspora Jewish life, the Ladislaus Laszt Ecumenical and Social Concern Award from Ben-Gurion University in Israel in 2011, the Guardian of Zion Award from the Ingeborg Rennert Center for Jerusalem Studies at Bar-Ilan University, and the Katz Award in recognition of his contribution to the practical analysis and application of halakha in modern life in Israel in 2014. He was knighted by Her Majesty the Queen in 2005 and made a Life Peer, taking his seat in the House of Lords in October 2009.

The author of more than thirty books, Rabbi Sacks published a new English translation and commentary for the *Koren Sacks Siddur*, the first new Orthodox siddur in a generation, as well as powerful commentaries for the *Rosh HaShana, Yom Kippur, Pesaḥ, Shavuot*, and *Sukkot Maḥzorim*. A number of his books have won literary awards. *Not in God's Name*, was awarded a 2015 National Jewish Book Award in America and was a top ten Sunday Times bestseller in the UK. Others include *The Dignity of Difference*, winner of the Grawemeyer Award in Religion in 2004 for its success in defining a framework for interfaith dialogue between people of all faiths and of none, and National Jewish Book Awards for *A Letter in the Scroll* in 2000, *Covenant & Conversation: Genesis* in 2009, and the *Koren Sacks Pesaḥ Maḥzor* in 2013. His Covenant & Conversation commentaries on the weekly Torah portion, which are translated into Hebrew, Spanish, Portuguese, and Turkish, are read in Jewish communities around the world.

After achieving first-class honours in philosophy at Gonville and Caius College, Cambridge, he pursued post-graduate studies in Oxford and London, gaining his doctorate in 1981 and receiving rabbinic ordination from Jews' College and Yeshivat Etz Chaim. He served as the rabbi for Golders Green Synagogue and Marble Arch Synagogue in London before becoming principal of Jews' College.

Rabbi Lord Sacks was married to Elaine for fifty years. They have three children and several grandchildren.

www.rabbisacks.org / @RabbiSacks

The fonts used in this book are from the Arno family

The Covenant & Conversation Series:

Genesis: The Book of Beginnings
Exodus: The Book of Redemption
Leviticus: The Book of Holiness
Numbers: The Wilderness Years
Deuteronomy: Renewal of the Sinai Covenant

Ceremony and Celebration
Essays on Ethics
Judaism's Life-Changing Ideas
Lessons in Leadership
Studies in Spirituality

Maggid Books
The best of contemporary Jewish thought from
Koren Publishers Jerusalem Ltd.